THE PHILOSOPHY
OF SCHLEIERMACHER

The

PHILOSOPHY
OF SCHLEIERMACHER

The Development of His Theory of Scientific and Religious Knowledge

BY

RICHARD B. BRANDT

GREENWOOD PRESS, PUBLISHERS
NEW YORK   1968

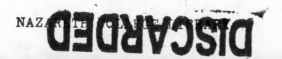

CONTENTS

PREFACE

Something should perhaps be said in explanation of the appearance of a book on Schleiermacher at this time. Several years ago I became convinced that many of the things philosophers of religion are most interested in knowing are beyond the limits of possible human knowledge and even meanings unless there is some form of immediate knowledge in religious experience, probably some kind of emotional intuition similar to that which value theorists had argued is present in the experience of values. A first reading of Schleiermacher suggested that he had such a conception. It was clear that such an idea required a more elaborate defense than I had been able to find anywhere. The fact of Schleiermacher's great influence on the empirical movement in theology attracted me to a further study of his work in the belief that he must have attempted such a defense. The hope of finding somewhere in his work an able, systematic, logical, and phenomenological support for a doctrine of immediate intuition was fostered by the knowledge that he was an able philosopher as well as a theologian, well read in the work of Kant and the German idealists.

An analysis of the achievement of Schleiermacher's thought on this subject is the center of the present study. But happily the attempt to excavate his theory on this point led to the discovery of other unexpected and useful aspects of his thought, such as his concept of "intuition" in his earlier years (which is altogether different from usual ideas of intuition) or his analyses in subjects like the theory of knowledge. These seemed at least as interesting and important as his conception of religious experience. This discovery led me to undertake a broader treatment of this spot in philosophical history, which seemed to me for various reasons to have been unduly neglected in English literature.

The book as it now stands is an abbreviated and in some parts revised form of a dissertation submitted to the faculty of Yale Uni-

vii

versity in 1936 in partial fulfillment of the requirements for the Ph.D. degree.

The reader will note that the references and less important footnotes are printed at the end of the book. In quoting, I have used square brackets to mark off my own comments or interpolations.

I wish to thank Messrs. T. and T. Clarke of Edinburgh, publishers of The Christian Faith, the English translation of the second edition of Schleiermacher's book of the same name, edited by H. R. Mackintosh and J. S. Stewart, for their courtesy in granting permission to make use of this translation. Some of the quotations from this book, however, and so far as I know all those from his other books, are my translations.

It is a privilege to acknowledge my indebtedness and gratitude to Doctor F. R. Tennant and Doctor John Oman of Cambridge University for their advice and encouragement; to the electors for the Burney Studentship in Cambridge University and for the Stanton Studentship in Trinity College, Cambridge, for the financial assistance made available by these studentships; to Professor Theodor Haering, Professor Karl Heim, and Professor Georg Wehrung of the university at Tuebingen for their assistance and cordial hospitality; to Professor W. M. Urban, Professor W. H. Sheldon, and Professor R. L. Calhoun of Yale University who read parts (Professor Urban practically the whole) of the original manuscript and offered valuable advice; to my colleagues, Professor J. W. Nason and Professor M. H. Mandelbaum, both of whom have read the entire manuscript and have offered important criticism and assistance; and to my wife for her aid in correcting the proofs and her suggestions for the improvement of the idiom of the manuscript.

In addition, I must pay tribute to the great achievements of Wilhelm Dilthey, Hermann Süskind, and Professor Wehrung for the invaluable contributions their tireless and brilliant scholarship has made to the literature on Schleiermacher to which every student of Schleiermacher must feel greatly obligated at every step.

Some readers may find it preferable to pass from Chapter I at once to Chapter VI, the analysis of his mature system of philosophy, reading the earlier parts later in the light of it.

R. B. B.

August, 1940

THE PHILOSOPHY
OF SCHLEIERMACHER

CHAPTER I

INTRODUCTION: SCHLEIERMACHER'S LIFE AND WORKS

Schleiermacher's significance in the history of modern philosophical thought lies along two main lines: theology and the theory of knowledge (although he did influential work in other branches of philosophy such as ethics and aesthetics). In the theory of knowledge his achievement was the development of a kind of empirical realism, sophisticated by an appreciation of the psychological and logical contributions of Kant. His work in this field brought him considerable recognition in Germany during his lifetime so that he rivaled Hegel in popularity among the students at Berlin,[1] and after his death it had considerable influence on the Continent and is studied in Germany today. In theology, on the other hand, his importance lies in his original development and derivation of theology from subjective religious experience, in contrast to traditional formulations based upon metaphysical arguments and supernatural revelations. His theological achievement has been more extensively and profoundly influential. Albrecht Ritschl ranked his work with that of Aquinas as an indispensable prerequisite to the understanding of theology. Other writers have compared his theological significance with the contribution in other fields of Bacon and Kant because of his novel use of experience and the self-consciousness in theology.

Whether he did possess the originality and success as a thinker to justify the claim that he has made a contribution of permanent value to thought, this is not the place to say. A later chapter will outline the most important points of his impact on religious and philosophical thought, and his various contributions will be weighed in their place. Nevertheless it may be of use to enumerate further which of Schleiermacher's main ideas seem to me to comprise his claim to having made a substantial contribution to European thought.

1

We may begin with his more specifically theological work. I except such detailed matters as his reinterpretation of traditional Christian doctrines, important as they are. First, there is his idea of religious knowledge and his account of its relation to ordinary scientific or philosophical thought. Needless to say, it is this idea which is the crux of his system and which must be made to bear the burden of supporting a nonmetaphysical "experiential" theology. Second, there is his account of the origin and nature of the statements of dogmatic theology. This theory is dependent on his theory of religious knowledge, and is the background and presupposition of his account of the specific doctrines of Christianity. Third, there is his methodology for the investigation of religious phenomena (to which he called attention as a special group of facts) and his view of the nature and purpose of the philosophy of religion as the source of a deduction of the naturalness and necessity of certain forms of religion. Finally, there is his unusual emphasis on the moment of feeling in religion, or rather, his view that religion is a kind of feeling, emotion, or sentiment.

Of his work in the other branches of philosophy two main lines are most deserving of mention. First, there is his theory of knowledge, including a dualistic-realistic account of perception and a corresponding analysis of the nature and validity of scientific thought. Second, founded upon his theory of knowledge, there is a metaphysical doctrine of God as the "Absolute Identity of the Real and the Ideal," along with a theory of the relation of God to the world and of the limitations of knowledge of God. (His idea of God stands closer to Spinoza, Schelling, and Hegel than to traditional Christian theism.) There are many aspects of these main ideas which might be mentioned, but the ideas I have suggested are the central ones. There are also many parts of his philosophy (such as his work in ethics and aesthetics) which I have not mentioned and which I do not intend to discuss because they do not belong to the themes which are the most significant part of his work.

It is a mistake to regard his theological work as separable from his philosophy; in fact they are so closely knit that even if his philosophical contribution were slight on its own account it would have to be known by anyone who hoped to understand fully his philosophy of religion. There are two reasons for this, the first of which is an accident. The first one is that his theological books are often badly written, obscure, and misleading because of their fragmentariness. His ideas about religion have to be read in connection with his whole system of thought before the cloudy becomes relatively clear, the misleading seen in its true light. The second reason is independent of Schleiermacher's habits as a theological writer and lies in the nature of the subject matter. Like every theory of religion or system of theology, the fundamental principles of his system are logical and epistemological. His views on religion are as a whole not intelligible by themselves, and he has, I think, often been misunderstood because his statements about religion were read outside their general context. Schleiermacher professed to make theology an independent science in some sense, but he did not intend to be an exception to the rule that no great system of religious thought can be set up except on a basis of philosophical ideas. In fact, he thought it necessary to set up a partially independent "science" of theology partly because of his logical and epistemological conclusions, certainly not in spite of them. His view of the nature and extent of theological knowledge, his consequent view of the limited task of dogmatic theology, his view of the existence and nature of God, of man's relation to God, of the significance of man's ethical aspirations, of his prospects for survival after death, of the nature and value of religion—his view of all this is determined by his general philosophical system.*

There are several causes for the relative neglect of his purely philo-

---

* Wilhelm Dilthey put it in the following way in a well-known article on Schleiermacher: "Schleiermacher's system of theology has been epoch-making because of its ingenious relating of the standpoint of the Critical Philosophy with the conceptions of the historical school. In his system, the place of objectively valid statements about God and the supersensible world is taken by the religious event which occurs in the human consciousness, and the historical knowledge of its forms. The criteria of this consciousness of God are formulated in the ideal for religious knowledge developed in his Dialectic, and his Ethics defines more exactly the nature of religion and the religious community, and shows the basis of the historical forms of religion in its essence. Schleiermacher's philosophy is thus the basis of his theology, both in respect of its achievement and of its defects." While reserving judgment on the details of his comment, we must accept his dictum on the interrelation of the two studies. Quoted from an article in the Allgemeine Deutsche Biographie (1890), vol. 31, pp. 422-457 (reprinted in his Gesammelte Schriften, vol. 4, 1921); this article is the source of much of my biographical material on the later years of his life.

sophical work, particularly in England and America. First, he was outshone by Hegel and his work lost sight of because of the vast influence of Hegel's speculative idealism. Second, he was a somewhat cloudy writer, although in this he was at least equaled by the more influential Hegel. Third, and probably most important, the amount of purely philosophical material which he himself prepared for the press was small. The vast bulk of his work was published only after his death, on the basis of his lecture notes. These notes were so brief and even enigmatic that supplementation from students' records of his lectures was indispensable, and despite careful work of editors the result not only lacks the clarification it would doubtless have received had he prepared the material for the press himself, but also the completeness of detail and essential illustration which he could have furnished it. His ideas on theology and the philosophy of religion are not intelligible apart from his purely philosophical theories, but the latter are difficult of access for this reason.

A word must be said of the fact that the exposition is chronological instead of systematic. This approach which would be absurd in the case of a philosopher like McTaggart is difficult to avoid in the case of Schleiermacher, whose books represent stages in a development which are not understandable in isolation from the process which led to them. It is desirable to avoid the appearance of having sprung out of the air, which is possessed by some of the ideas of his better known books when their relation to earlier opinions or to criticism of his contemporaries is not understood. Moreover, important differences in his views at different periods cannot be passed over without introducing confusion. Finally, a chronological account not only makes possible what amounts to a commentary on some of his major books, but is the only feasible way of clearing up otherwise obscure but apparently fundamental remarks in his major works, for example, in the second edition of the *Discourses on Religion*.

1. BIOGRAPHICAL COMMENTS

A knowledge of Schleiermacher's personal history, beyond its usefulness for general orientation, is of some value to the philosopher because his personality and experience (especially in early life) had more to do with his speculation than has been the case with most philosophers. H. R. Mackintosh wrote: "The philosophy of Kant . . . can be made fairly intelligible to a reader who knows little or nothing of the philosopher's personal career, but the thought of Schleiermacher is luminous only when read in the light of his biography."* This judgment is perhaps exaggerated; Kant's moral experience, for example, was very significant for his philosophy as it has been for others of the great systematizers. But certainly Schleiermacher's philosophy depended less than that of many philosophers on sheer analysis of problems of logic, epistemology, or ontology; while it was strongly moved by his appreciation of realms of experience such as emotion and faith, moral aspiration, and aesthetic enjoyment, and by a desire to do justice to them and accord them some status and reality in the economy of the universe. This motivating force of his thinking depended on his nature and experiences and not on sheer analytical acuteness. Thus, although knowing the causes of a man's accepting certain theories is not essential to an understanding of the logical structure of his system, it may be—and it is the case in this instance— that his system becomes more intelligible in the broad sense in the light of some insight into his character and experience.

The following biographical comments can be amplified from the brilliant accounts of Dilthey, on which part of what I have to say is based. I shall later deal in more detail with special periods of his early life.

Friedrich Daniel Ernst Schleiermacher was born in Breslau on November 21, 1768, thirteen years before the publication of Kant's *Critique of Pure Reason*. He was the son of an army chaplain of the Reformed Church. His family had representatives in the clergy on both sides, as a result of which fact Schleiermacher was later able to form friendships with some of the leading figures in German ecclesiastical life.

In 1783 his parents sent him to a boarding school of the Mora-

* *Types of Modern Theology*, pp. 31-32. There is a little material for the psychologist. Schleiermacher had a slight physical deformity (causing lameness), and suffered recurrent attacks of stomach trouble throughout much of his life. He was not at all robust. He had emotional difficulties in his early life, particularly in connection with religion. He seems to have been an introvert. This suggests the possibility of repressions and attempts at compensation (e.g., in his association with the romanticists). He himself suggested that the nature of his thought was grounded in his character (*Briefe*, vol. I, p. 82; vol. III, p. 285).

vians, a pietistic sect where, as we shall see, he was subject to a religious atmosphere which influenced his view of religion and its value during the remainder of his life. First he was at the school at Niesky, in upper Lusatia, and then at the seminary at Barby. Here Schleiermacher read avidly both in philosophy and general literature. But he soon found himself in conflict with the theological outlook and confined intellectual horizons of these institutions, and in 1787, after some painful correspondence with his father, departed to study at the University of Halle.

Schleiermacher studied at Halle from the summer semester of 1787 until the spring of 1789. Since I shall refer again to his work during that period in more detail, I shall remark only that he there became acquainted with the debate among philosophers concerning the philosophy of Kant, with the Leibniz-Wolffian school through its eminent representative, J. A. Eberhard, and with the general history of philosophy, especially Plato and Aristotle. At this time he translated parts of the Nicomachean Ethics and composed a number of philosophical essays, including papers on ethics, largely critical of Kant. Probably his interest in Plato which culminated in his important studies and translations originated in the classical atmosphere of Halle.

For a year following his departure from Halle he lived with his uncle, Stubenrauch, at Drossen (near Frankfurt an der Oder), continuing his philosophical study and writing. He sketched some plans for an extensive defense of determinism in connection with his other studies in ethics. During the summer of 1790 he passed the church examination in theology.

In October of 1790 he accepted a position as tutor in the household of Count Dohna of Schlobitten, with whom he remained until 1793. The years with the family of Count Dohna seem to have been a time of skepticism. (There is a reference to such a period in the Discourses.) In 1792 Stubenrauch wrote that he was not worried by Schleiermacher's "doubting," although he did not believe Schleiermacher really was a doubter because his understanding always "disapproved of the demands of the imagination."[2] Two essays on ethics and value were brought to paper at this time. These essays, and in fact his work in general during the period, are important landmarks

in the molding of his philosophical thought. According to Schleiermacher's own account, the years with the family of the Count were
significant in the forming of his *Weltanschauung* because they afforded him a vision of human life at its best. The family was cultured, art-loving, and deeply pious. Schleiermacher later declared that
it was there that he learned the true nature of humanity and "freedom," his view of which was one of the important factors in the
development of his ideas of morality and religion.

Certain disagreements brought about Schleiermacher's decision
to give up his position with Count Dohna, but they parted on the
friendliest of terms in 1793. For a time thereafter Schleiermacher
worked as a teacher in a boys' school, but in 1794 he received a
church appointment in Landsberg an der Warthe where he served
for about two years. His duties involved a certain amount of preaching
and he composed a number of sermons later published in his collected
works. He collaborated with Sack, an important figure in the Reformed Church, in the translation of a volume of sermons by the
Edinburgh professor, Blair. (He translated another volume of Blair's
sermons later and also a volume by Fawcett.) More important for the
development of his philosophical thought was the formation of an
interest in the work of Spinoza through reading Jacobi's *Briefe über
die Lehre des Spinoza*, published in 1785. This interest resulted in
the composition of some essays on Spinoza. Spinoza's ideas left their
mark upon his thinking in later life, so much so that Spinoza is to
be ranked along with Kant, Friedrich Schlegel, Plato, and Schelling
as one of the sources of his philosophical system.

In 1796 Schleiermacher moved to Berlin as a chaplain of the Reformed Church. He remained in this position for six years. During
this period there appeared in print his earliest and philosophically
most influential works, the *Discourses on Religion* and the *Soliloquies*
(a book somewhat like Fichte's *Destiny of Man*, which, whatever its
comparative worth, has attained a more conspicuous place in German
literature than Fichte's book). Probably the most important factor
in the maturing of his thought was his friendship with members of
the romantic circle, especially with Friedrich Schlegel (with whom he
shared rooms for a period beginning in 1797) and Henriette Herz, a

Jewish woman whose connection with Schleiermacher was much talked about in Berlin at the time.

This period of his life was one of great intellectual activity, and it was during this time that the most interesting if not the most mature of his work was written. Schleiermacher's philosophical diary, the relevant parts of which are published in an appendix to the first edition of Dilthey's *Leben Schleiermachers*, contains evidence that he was thinking about a variety of subjects. He contributed to the "Fragments" of the *Athenaeum*. From midsummer of 1798 he was occupied for a year almost exclusively with the *Discourses on Religion*. Contemporaneously with the *Discourses* (1799) he published the *Briefe bei Gelegenheit des Sendschreibens jüdischer Hausväter*. In 1800 he wrote off the *Soliloquies* in a few weeks and shortly thereafter he printed a volume of sermons. In the same year he published his widely read *Confidential Letters on Fr. Schlegel's Lucinde*, a pamphlet in which he defended Schlegel's unfortunate work which had been condemned as both inartistic and indecent. This last work marked the high point of a tension between him and the authorities of the church, coming as it did as the result of a friendship with the romanticists which had been expressly disapproved by church leaders. Needless to say, Schleiermacher's close personal relationship to Schlegel and Henriette Herz had not helped his reputation and standing in the church. Even his *Discourses* had been widely condemned as Spinozist and pantheistic.

At this point Schleiermacher became entangled in an unfortunate love for a married woman, Eleonore Grunow, who was unhappily bound to a husband quite unsuitable to her. Schleiermacher was anxious for a divorce and later marriage to him, not, strange as it may seem, for primarily selfish reasons but because he saw the hopelessness of her situation and believed that any other course would involve lifelong unhappiness. Schleiermacher was in his day accounted liberal in his view of marriage and the marriage tie, although his ideas do not appear unusual when compared with many modern attitudes on the subject. Haym has suggested that there is some reason to believe that he shared or even originated Schlegel's suggestion that marriages should be a quatre, since he remarked in one of his letters that "often, if one took three or four couples together, really good marriages could arise, if they dared exchange."[3] However that may be, there is nothing known about his personal affairs to suggest that the highest motives did not dominate his conduct. Perhaps the most unfortunate part of the affair was that the woman in question first made him unhappy by vacillating for a period of years and then plunged him into despair by deciding that she ought to remain with her husband.

All these circumstances resulted in pressure being brought upon Schleiermacher to depart from Berlin, and he accepted a charge in Stolpe in Pommerania in 1802. He regarded this removal as a kind of exile.

Schleiermacher remained at Stolpe until the fall of 1804, when he went to Halle as extraordinary professor in theology and university preacher. The two years spent at Stolpe were extremely unhappy ones because of his personal affairs, but he consoled himself by burying himself in work. His thinking from 1800 to 1804, as I shall show later, resulted in the outline of the general scheme of his mature philosophical system. During the latter part of his residence at Stolpe he seems to have studied the works of Schelling carefully, but his system seems to have been worked out largely independently.

In addition, he had brought with him to Stolpe two large projects conceived at an earlier date. One of these was a plan to translate the works of Plato into German, with a commentary. The plan had been suggested originally by Friedrich Schlegel as a work to be done by the two of them jointly but was given up, partly because Schlegel could not be counted upon to do the actual work of translation which he promised and partly because Schlegel's temperament was not equal to the detailed linguistic and structural analysis of Plato's works which was necessary for the project. After Schlegel's withdrawal Schleiermacher decided to complete the work alone and the first volume was published in 1804. Schleiermacher's work on Plato, which was of great importance in the history of German Plato scholarship, left its mark on his own original thinking. In particular, Plato's ethical views and his theory of ideas influenced Schleiermacher's ethics, his theory of knowledge, and his idea of God.

The second project was a general historical and critical study in ethics. Schleiermacher seems to have planned this as early as 1798; it was published in 1803 and entitled *Outlines of a Critique of Previ-*

ous *Theories of Ethics.* This book is a ponderous criticism of ethical systems devised in a very unattractive, formal way. Schleiermacher's own views are scarcely visible in it although he undoubtedly had in mind their general outlines, at least by the time he finished writing the book. Dilthey has very appropriately compared his view to that of Herbert Spencer.

During this time Schleiermacher also published some papers concerning church affairs, one advocating the union of the Lutheran and Reformed Churches, another proposing alterations in the form of religious services.

With his entrance into the faculty of the university at Halle in 1804, Schleiermacher's pen became more active than ever. Two more volumes of his translation of Plato appeared in 1805. He wrote several reviews and published a critical work on the New Testament, to which he applied the methods of research developed in his work on Plato. He prepared lectures on the theory of the interpretation of the Scriptures, on the writings of St. Paul, on dogmatic theology, Christian ethics, church history, and an "encyclopedia" of theology. Of much greater importance for the philosopher, however, are three other achievements: the revised edition of his *Discourses on Religion,* his popular essay entitled *The Celebration of Christmas* (*Weihnachtsfeier*), and two sets of lectures on philosophical ethics. These last three pieces of work are of importance to the historian of philosophy, because by comparing them with the publications of 1800 and with items appearing in his scientific diary, it is possible to show that Schleiermacher's views had undergone considerable change during the period from 1800 to 1806.

Schleiermacher's work at the university at Halle was interrupted in the winter of 1806-1807 by the Napoleonic war, and was never again taken up. After the defeats at Jena and Auerstadt the area was thrown into general confusion and Halle itself was plundered by the French soldiery. Schleiermacher was relieved of his watch and other private possessions on this occasion. These events aroused his patriotism, and at considerable personal risk he became active in a movement for resistance and the recovery of German freedom. Even today Schleiermacher is known and honored in Germany for this work.

In the summer of 1807 Schleiermacher delivered lectures on the history of Greek philosophy in Berlin, and in the autumn of the same year he moved to Berlin where he resided for the rest of his life. At about the same time he became engaged to the widow of a young minister who had been a friend and who had died of a fever while serving in the war in 1807. Schleiermacher became engaged to the young woman (many years his junior) in 1807 and married her in 1808. Her name was Henriette von Willich (maiden name, von Mühlenfels). This marriage can hardly have been based upon a romantic attachment such as Schleiermacher had felt for Eleonore Grunow, but Schleiermacher professed great happiness in his domestic life and apparently attained emotional stability in it. There were several children by the union, among them a brilliant son who died in his youth.

Schleiermacher continued both private teaching and public lecturing in Berlin. In 1808 he was appointed Reformed preacher at the Trinity Church in Berlin, and its pulpit gave him a great opportunity for ecclesiastical and political influence. In 1810 the University of Berlin was constituted and Schleiermacher (along with De Wette and Marheineke) was appointed professor on the theological faculty.

From 1808 to 1810 Schleiermacher was deeply concerned with political affairs. He worked both through the pulpit and with his pen to instill a greater sense of unity in the German people, and to emphasize the importance of the good of the national community as compared with the private well-being of a few individuals. He was one of the leaders of an organization for the securing of German freedom, and in connection with this work he came in contact with the political and military leaders of Germany.

Schleiermacher's position in the church also made him a leader in the organization of ecclesiastical affairs. He worked tirelessly for a union of the Protestant churches in Germany, for the freedom of the church from the authority of the state in matters concerning itself, for a decentralizing of church authority which would allow more freedom to the individual church bodies, and for the inclusion of theological seminaries in the universities as one department with absolute freedom of thought and teaching.

Doubtless Schleiermacher's preoccupation with church and state affairs (which was much more extensive than I have been able to describe) was one of the factors which prevented him from formulating more exactly and publishing his philosophical system. His time was also taken up with extensive historical and philological studies. There were further volumes of his translation of Plato (which was never completed) and numerous papers read before the Berlin Academy, of which he became the secretary.

His lectures at the University of Berlin during the last twenty years of his life covered an immense range of subjects. He gave historical lectures on Greek, medieval, and modern philosophy. He gave a course on Christian ethics. He expanded his interests to include courses on the theory of the state, the theory of education, and aesthetics. More important for theology were his lectures on dogmatic theology, of which his *Brief Exposition of the Theological Study* and *The Christian Faith* were the most important published results. He lectured and wrote on the critical understanding of certain parts of the New Testament and devised a reconstruction of the life of Christ. He even gave courses of lectures on psychology in which, as we shall see, some useful hints for an understanding of his theology and philosophy are to be found. His most important philosophical work was the composition of lectures on philosophical ethics and on what he called *Dialectic*, a course which covered the theory of knowledge in the broad sense and what he took to be its metaphysical implications. Schleiermacher had begun writing his *Dialectic* for publication, but it was interrupted by his death after the completion of only a few sheets of the introduction. His ethical views have a more satisfactory but very brief expression in a series of papers read to the Berlin Academy. Such are the subjects to which Schleiermacher's comprehensive learning and critical analysis were devoted during the closing years of his life.

Schleiermacher died in 1834. He had never been robust. His friends were surprised that his very active life was able to continue as long as it did. Among the last words recorded by his friends was a sentence which is expressive of his attitude toward theology, religion, and philosophy, and is therefore worth preserving: "I must think the deepest speculative thoughts, and they are fully one with the inmost religious feelings."[4]

2. SCHLEIERMACHER'S PHILOSOPHICAL WORKS

The edition of Schleiermacher's collected works consists of thirty-one volumes and is divided into three parts. The first consists of theological material; the second is a collection of sermons; and the third comprises his philosophical studies. I have referred to this edition throughout as *Werke*. Newer editions of specific parts of Schleiermacher's work have shown a great improvement over the work of the first editors on many points. Particularly noteworthy are G. C. B. Pünjer's critical edition of the *Discourses on Religion* (Jena, 1879), in which the texts of the several editions are compared; Schiele's and Mulert's critical edition of the *Soliloquies* (Leipzig, 1911), also containing a useful comparison of the texts; the new edition of his *Ethics* in the four-volume edition of his major works edited by Otto Braun (Leipzig, 1927), which includes all the manuscript material in full; the new edition of his *Aesthetics*, a much clearer and more reliable version done by R. Odebrecht (Berlin, 1931); and a new edition of the *Dialectic* by Isidor Halpern (Berlin, 1903). Where I have mentioned the *Dialectic* in the text, however, I have always referred to the older edition which has the advantage of containing each entire manuscript in its original order. In addition to these new editions, the collected works must be supplemented by material not included in them at all. The two chief sources of such material are his letters (*Aus Schleiermachers Leben in Briefen*, in four volumes, edited by Jonas and Wilhelm Dilthey), which includes reviews and a brief autobiography not conveniently available elsewhere, and the appendix to the first edition of Dilthey's *Leben Schleiermachers* (Berlin, 1870, first volume only) which supplies condensations of and citations from the most important passages of his early manuscripts (which were never published during his lifetime), and also the interesting parts of a philosophical diary which he kept from about 1797 to 1803. The major portion of his manuscript remains, part still unpublished, is deposited with the *Preussische Akademie der Wissenshaften* in Berlin and is the property of the *Literatur-Archiv-Gesellschaft*. Occasional publications in the *Mitteilungen aus dem Literaturarchiv in Berlin* and elsewhere have made more and more of the unpublished material available.[5]

Of the entire amount of material written by Schleiermacher now available, only a comparatively small amount, less than half, is related to his philosophy, and several volumes of these are of little importance for our purpose, such as his books on education, the theory of the state, and aesthetics. The work related to philosophy is to be divided into four periods, each one incorporating a more or less distinct viewpoint, although of course lines cannot be sharply drawn. I list below these groups of works.

(1) To 1797

Letters in the collection of *Briefe*. Included among them is a brief autobiography of Schleiermacher.

Two essays on ethics, one of them largely a criticism of Kant, the other an examination of the nature of value and the worth of life. These appear in the Appendix to Dilthey's *Leben Schleiermachers*.

An essay on the freedom of the will, also in Dilthey's Appendix.

Two essays on Spinoza, one of them in Dilthey's Appendix, the other in the volume devoted to his *History of Philosophy*, *Werke*, pt. III, vol. IV, pt. I.

(2) 1797 to 1802.

Contributions to the "Fragments" of the *Athenaeum*, 1799, collected in Dilthey's Appendix.

A scientific diary with entries throughout the whole of this period, in Dilthey. Also the letters in *Briefe*.

On Religion: Discourses Addressed to its Cultured Despisers, 1799. This was published anonymously, although the name of its author was soon widely known.

Soliloquies: A New Year's Gift, 1800.

Confidential Letters on Fr. Schlegel's Lucinde, 1800. Reprinted in *Werke*, pt. III, vol. I.

Sermons, 1801. These are thought by some to be an important addition to his other works. For a discussion of this view, see pp. 104 f.

Reviews: Kant's *Anthropology*, Fichte's *Destiny of Man*, Garve's last published writings, and Engel's *Philosoph für die Welt*. All of these appeared either in 1799 or 1800, in the *Athenaeum*. With the exception of the review of Kant, which is reprinted in the fourth volume of the *Briefe*, these reviews are available in *Werke*, pt. III, vol. I.

(Scholars were for some time misled by another book which was published anonymously, like most of his other early writings, and for some years ascribed it to Schleiermacher. This book, which is entitled *Mythologie und Offenbarung*, appeared in 1799 and was thought to be the oldest of his published works. Schleiermacher formally denied authorship of it in the *Jen. Lit. Zeitung*, number 54. It is now attributed to J. A. Grohmann. See H. Mulert, *Die angeblich älteste Schrift Schleiermachers*, in *Theologische Studien und Kritiken*, 1919, second number.)

(3) 1803 to 1808.

There is a bridge between the most important productive years of this period and the earlier one in the form of the diary in Dilthey's Appendix and the letters.

Outlines of a Critique of Previous Ethical Theory, 1803. This contains little original material and Schleiermacher regarded it rather as the end of his earlier period than as the beginning of something new. *Werke*, pt. III, vol. I.

A review of Schelling's *Lectures on the Method of Academic Studies*, reprinted in *Briefe*, vol. IV.

Notes for his lectures on ethics, 1804-1805, in the Braun edition of his ethics, volume 2 of the Meiner collection. These last two items are discussed in Appendix I. They seem to represent a transitional period.

The first volume of his translation of Plato, 1804. Four further volumes up to 1810.

Notes for his lectures on ethics, 1805-1806. An important document for the philosopher; it represents a new point of view. Printed in the Braun edition.

Second edition of the *Discourses on Religion*, 1806. To be compared with the first edition. An important document for the understanding of his new point of view.

A *Christmas Celebration* (*Die Weihnachtsfeier: Ein Gesprach*), 1806. Of some interest to the philosopher.

Manuscript for his lectures on church history, 1806. *Werke*, pt. I, vol. XI. Of interest for its comments on historical method.

Review of Fichte's *Characteristics of the Present Age*, 1807, reprinted in *Briefe*, vol. IV.

Occasional Thoughts on Universities in the German Sense, 1808. An essay drawing out the implications of his view of philosophy and science for the organization of a university faculty. Reprinted in *Werke*, pt. III, vol. I.

These works dating between 1805 and 1808 can be grouped together for they represent a fairly consistent point of view. There are several books which appeared slightly later, and it is not clear whether they should be classified with those just mentioned or with his most mature work described below. In my opinion Schleiermacher's thought after

1806 underwent a process of maturing rather than of sharp alteration, on most points, and in conformity with this view it does not seem to me to make a great deal of difference whether one classifies these books with his earlier or later work. They are:

Manuscript for his lectures on *Christian Ethics*, 1809.
The second edition of the *Soliloquies*, 1810. To be compared with the first edition. See Schiele's and Mulert's edition.
A *Brief Outline of Theological Study*, 1811.
The first series of lectures on *Dialectic*, 1811.
Lectures on the *History of Philosophy*, 1812. *Werke*, pt. III, vol. IV, pt. I.

Incidentally, Schleiermacher's work on Plato had considerable influence on Plato scholarship in Germany. Schleiermacher undertook to discover the development of Plato's thought and classify the *Dialogues* on the basis of a study of the logical relations between them. He felt that the *Phaedrus* was the key to the whole. Today his work has been superseded but to him must be attributed the merit of having given great impetus to this department of scholarship in Germany. His translation is incomplete.

(4) 1812 to 1834. Most of this material, it will be noted, was published posthumously and was never prepared for the press by Schleiermacher himself. It consists of manuscript notes amplified from the lecture notes of his better students.
The *Christian Faith*, first edition 1821-1822; second edition, 1830. Two volumes. There is considerable and interesting variation, especially in the first part. The first edition shows more clearly the relation to the rest of his philosophical system and uses more terminology with which the reader has become familiar through these other works.
"Letters to Dr. Lücke concerning *The Christian Faith*," 1829, reprinted in *Werke*, pt. I, vol. II. A valuable discussion of the nature and purpose of his theological book.
Third edition of the *Discourses on Religion*, 1821 (fourth edition, little changed, in 1831). There are only a few changes in the text of the later editions, but in 1821 Schleiermacher added lengthy and interesting explanations in which he tried to harmonize his earlier and later work.
Manuscript notes on logic and epistemology, entitled *Dialectic*. This work ranks first of all his works in interest for the philosopher. There are six strata of notes which originated in 1811, 1814, 1818,

1822, 1828, and 1831, and in addition a few sheets which he had written out more fully just before his death with the intention of eventually publishing the whole. There are some significant differences. Professor Wehrung has recently examined the relationship of these manuscripts in his book, *Die Dialektik Schleiermachers*. Printed in *Werke*, pt. III, vol. IV, pt. II, and in a newer edition by Halpern in which the various manuscripts have been integrated into one.

Manuscript notes on ethics, the most complete being dated 1812 and 1816. Published separately in Braun's edition.

Manuscript notes on psychology, originating in 1818, 1830, and 1833-1834. Of particular value for his discussion of religious feeling. *Werke*, pt. III, vol. VI.

Manuscript notes on aesthetics, one edition (covering his lectures of 1818) edited by Odebrecht, the older edition (covering his lectures of 1833-1834), edited by Lommatzsch, in *Werke*, pt. III, vol. VII.

Manuscript notes for his lectures on the theory of the state (*Werke*, pt. III, vol. VIII) and on the theory of education (*Werke*, pt. III, vol. IX). These are of little value for our purposes.

I have not yet mentioned a large number of short papers read before the Berlin Academy of Sciences, some of which are published in his collected works (pt. III, vols. II and III), and some in the *Jahrbuch* of the Berlin Academy. Some have been lost. Most of them deal with historical subjects, but they contain an excellent brief account of his ethical theory and reflections on aesthetics and the theory of the state. Almost all the historical essays relate to Greek philosophy, but there are two on Leibniz and one on the relation of Descartes to Spinoza. I mention some of the titles.

"On the Significance of the Concept of Virtue," 1819.

"On the Scientific Treatment of the Concept of Duty," 1824.

"On the Difference between the Law of Nature and the Moral Law," 1825. This is perhaps the most important of the essays on ethics.

"On the Concept of the Highest Good," two essays, 1827 and 1830. All the foregoing appear in *Werke*, pt. III, vol. II.

"On the Scope of the Concept of Art in relation to the Theory of Art." Two essays, dated 1831 and 1832. *Werke*, pt. III, vol. III.

The titles of some of his essays on Greek philosophy are: "On Diogenes of Apollonia," 1811; "On Anaximander of Miletus," 1812; "On the Fragments of Democritus," 1814; "On the Significance of Socrates as a Philosopher," 1815; "On Diogenes Laertius' Catalog of the Works of Democritus," 1815; "On the Ethical Works of Aristotle," 1817; "On the Fragments of Empedocles in Relation to his Pythagoreanism," 1820; "On the Commentaries to Aristotle's *Categories and Analytics*," 1821.

There is a vast amount of material on other subjects—many volumes of sermons, notes for lectures on the New Testament, on internal and external criticism of documents, on the life of Christ, on church history, on practical theology, and on the doctrines of the Trinity and predestination. This work has had considerable influence in Germany on the special subjects in question but adds nothing of interest to the philosopher.

My treatment of Schleiermacher falls into four parts corresponding to the groups of writings I have mentioned. Chapter two deals with the first and earliest period. The fourth chapter examines the writings published around 1800. The fifth chapter deals with material originating around 1806. The sixth chapter contains a statement of the system expressed in his most mature works. The third chapter breaks the continuity by taking up the background of philosophical thought in which his first published works were written.

CHAPTER II

EARLY PHILOSOPHICAL REFLECTIONS

wwwwwwwwwwwwwwwwwwwwwwwwwwwwwwwwwwwwwwwwwwwwwwwwwwwwwwwwwwwwwwwwwwwwwwwwww

1. SCHLEIERMACHER'S MORAVIAN BACKGROUND

Schleiermacher's boyhood environment was conservative religiously. His sensitive mind was much impressed by the doctrines of orthodox theology. These matters, and in particular the doctrine of eternal punishment, actually caused him sleepless nights as early as his eleventh year. In 1783 he was sent to a Moravian school at Niesky, in upper Lusatia, a school chosen for its moral atmosphere and spirit of "innocent piety." This connection with Moravian theology accentuated his religious conflicts, which troubled him almost continuously during the time of his association with the Moravians. The natural corruption of man and the nature and necessity of the supernatural work of grace were emphasized, he tells us, in almost every class hour. He had the misfortune, he complains, of being deprived of his conviction of the moral adequacy of man without, however, becoming assured of his own salvation through supernatural means.

I struggled in vain for the right supernatural feelings [he writes]. Of their necessity I was convinced by every inspection of myself with reference to the doctrine of the future condition of requiting punishment. Of their reality outside me I was persuaded by every lecture and every song, yea, by every glimpse of the people whom such a disposition made so charming. But me alone they seemed to elude.[1]

His parents, however, viewed with satisfaction the life of young Schleiermacher and his sister at Niesky, and the father wrote of it:

What has given us the greatest satisfaction is that here [in Niesky] as in all the congregations of the Brethren, the process of becoming one with God is founded on the only true basis, the reconciling sacrifice of Christ's blood. . . . We consider it an act of God on the children's hearts that their eyes have been opened in the matter of human damnation.[2]

19

The instruction at Niesky sems to have been competent, however, and he received a good foundation for his further study. He was interested in Greek literature and read Homer, Hesiod, Sophocles, Euripides, and Pindar, and after his advancement to the seminary at Barby in 1785, his intellectual life rapidly broadened. He acquired access to books not normally allowed to students, like Wieland's poems and Goethe's *Werther*. Despite the rather confined theological atmosphere of the institution, he read Kant's *Prolegomena*[3] and became acquainted with the work of Jacobi and Wolff.

This reading of the philosophers and his becoming acquainted with rationalism in religion eventually proved to be incompatible with remaining with the Moravians. Whether on account of purely theological differences or because he yearned to get into a wider world, Schleiermacher began to complain that he did not feel at home and that the students were not being schooled in modern theological knowledge. "The fact that our teachers fear to lay them before us," he wrote, "awakens in many minds a suspicion that the objections of the innovators must have proved acceptable to the intellect, and be difficult to refute."[4]

The matter came to a climax in January, 1787, when Schleiermacher wrote to his father, recounting the events of a losing struggle to keep his "faith." It is notable that his "unbelief" at this time concerned only Christological doctrines, not the existence of God or immortality. He wrote:

I cannot believe that he, who called himself the Son of Man, was the true eternal God; I cannot believe that his death was a vicarious atonement, because he never said so himself; and I cannot believe it to have been necessary, because God, who obviously did not create men to attain perfection, but to pursue it, cannot possibly intend to punish them eternally because they have not attained it.[5] [He replied to his father's unsympathetic condemnation:] You say the glorification of God is the end of our being, and I say the glorification of the creature. Is not this in the end the same thing? Is not the Creator more and more glorified, the happier and more perfect his creatures are? . . . I entertain doubts about the doctrine of the atonement and the divinity of Christ, and you speak as if I were denying God.[6]

Schleiermacher went to the university at Halle to study philosophy and theology, but the influence of his association with the Moravians and their "religion of feeling" lingered, so much so that it must be seriously taken into account in any attempt to understand his later work. He remarked after the publication of the *Discourses* that one need not be very sharp-witted to see traces of his Moravian background there. The atmosphere and religion (as distinct from the theology) were so congenial to him that on more than one occasion he confessed that if it were not for differences of theology and for certain external circumstances he would gladly return and spend his life with them. "I am convinced," he wrote in retrospect, "that the Moravians have a really good cause in religion; only, their theology and Christology are certainly unfortunate. But those are the externals."[7]

Three points at which Moravian religion very probably influenced his later work may be mentioned. First, there was the emphasis on the emotional side of religion; this sect was part of a reaction to rationalistic intellectualism. Second, they gave religion a remarkably central position in their life, both personal and social. It was the center of their educational program. Taste for music was developed as a channel to religious emotion; contemplation of the ubiquitous benevolence of God was recommended to them; the students were urged to bring religion into their friendships, to share each other's experiences, to learn to appreciate each other's various talents for religion. When Schleiermacher later advocated doing everything "with religion" (albeit a religion of a rather different kind), this sort of permeation of all relationships with religious significance was doubtless what he had at the back of his mind. Third, the Moravians distinguished abstract philosophy from religion. Schleiermacher's father wrote to him: "You will doubtless learn to see that even the most triumphant refutation of infidelity does not suffice to establish a tranquillizing and living faith in Jesus, as the author and finisher of our faith." In later years, Schleiermacher would not have distinguished philosophy from religion in just the way in which they did, but he did think them different. He wrote that by his philosophy he wished only to clear away the obstacles to his own living faith which he called "mysticism." This appreciation for the distinctively religious experience came from his association with the Moravians, who have been called "the Romantic branch of the religion of that age."

Schleiermacher summed up the debt he owed to the Moravians rather eloquently in the following words:

It was here that I awoke for the first time to the consciousness of the relation of man to a higher world. . . . Here it was that that mystic tendency developed itself, which has been of so much importance to me, and has supported and carried me through all the storms of scepticism. Then it was only germinating; now it has attained its full development, and I may say that after all I have passed through, I have become a Moravian again, only of a higher order.[8]

2. AT THE UNIVERSITY OF HALLE

The faculty at Halle included a number of eminent men, including J. A. Eberhard, a critic of Kant, and F. A. Wolf, the classical scholar. Schleiermacher did not make much use of the lectures, however, and argued that quantity of information is less important than one's firsthand understanding of the material. So he audited one course on history and another on philosophy (Eberhard), "in order to have data to which I could connect my own reflections."

Eberhard, a representative of the Wolffian tradition in philosophy, was at the time lecturing on Aristotle's ethics, Plato, and Wolff. Perhaps as a result of the influence of this teacher, Schleiermacher acquired a lifelong interest in the first two of these philosophers.

Schleiermacher's interests at this time were quite extensive. He read widely both in classical literature and in modern philosophy. He began a study of the philosophy of Kant to which he devoted a large portion of several years and which became clearly one of the major influences in his philosophical development.

Before discussing his philosophical biography further, it is necessary to take note of some evidence defining his attitude toward religion and morality at this time. It was natural for him to react against Moravian conservatism in theology, when he recognized the intellectual problems which a religious believer is forced to face. That is what happened. We find him commending his uncle for giving up a belief in the substitutionary death of Christ and for believing that religion is simply an effective means of promoting morality. He interpreted the historical origin of Christianity in a way consistent with this attitude. But he did not lose interest in religion altogether. He

devoted much time to the study of historical Christianity, and defended the discipline of philosophical theology against the charge that
it is out of place in theology because the pious Christian does not
need it and out of place in philosophy because it is not purely philosophical. Between the philosopher and the unphilosophical believer,
he says, "is the pious intellect, or the philosophical Christian, who
needs such a discipline, who requires some means of unifying the intuitions of the heart with the understanding of the head. This discipline is the study of dogmatic theology."[9]

Schleiermacher's later views on ethics are foreshadowed in a letter
of this period. Writing in vigorous criticism of the hedonistic spirit
of his society, he says:

> The religion and philosophy of our present cultivated world have made
> ineffective all really serious and high motives. . . . Still less is it possible
> to produce respect and a reception for virtue and morality through their
> own inner beauty and loveliness, since no one outside the philosophers
> believes in an essentially spiritual beauty or indeed in any beauty at all,
> for this word has long since become an empty sound.[10]

In contrast to much of the opinion of his day even among theologians, where emphasis was placed upon the religious sanctions and
rewards for altruistic conduct, he seems to be advocating virtue because of the beauty and value of virtue itself—a fact which makes
Nicolai Hartmann say of his later position that he anticipated the
modern idea of moral value.*

The major influence upon his metaphysical views at this time,
however, was his growing acquaintance with Kant. Although he never
found himself entirely in accord with Kant's views, the Königsberg
philosopher's writings seem to have been the starting point of his
youthful speculation. We shall find that although the *Critiques* seem
far removed in spirit from Schleiermacher's *Discourses on Religion*,
there is a most important relationship between them. Dilthey has
remarked on this fact:

> If Schleiermacher's theology did not rest, from the very bottom, on the
> foundation of Kant, on the proof of that great thinker that there is no

---

* Die Philosophie des deutschen Idealismus, vol. I, p. 266. There is similarity
here to the ideas of Shaftesbury and Hutcheson. I do not know how early he read
their works. He had read them later and I suspect they influenced him to some
extent.

universally valid scientific knowledge beyond the realm of possible experience, which is independent of the moral constitution of man, I should not be able to understand it. It would seem to me, because of its thoroughly subjective character, only a romantic "inspiration."

Whatever may be the validity of Dilthey's judgment, Schleiermacher himself praised Kant because "he brings back Reason from the desert wastes of metaphysics to its truly appointed sphere."[11] In 1789 he advised a friend that if he were having philosophic doubts he could do no better than shelter under Kantianism. A year later he wrote: "I can sincerely assure you that from day to day I increase in my belief in this philosophy, and the more so, the more I compare it with Leibniz."[12] He defended Kant against the attacks of his own teacher, Eberhard, and claimed that Eberhard had misunderstood the Critical Philosophy.[13] The essays which he composed in his university and early post-university years were largely concerned with criticizing or improving Kant's results. It appears that Schleiermacher, like the post-Kantian idealists, felt that a philosophical position was to be won only by struggling with the conclusions of the Critical Philosophy.

Schleiermacher fully realized, I think, the weight of the skeptical implications of Kant's work. The Kantian criticism of the traditional proofs for God, for example, was so effective that to Schleiermacher it very probably seemed that the only alternative was either Kant's new moral proof or else some radically revised concept of God and his relation to the world. This may be the reason why his first essays considered the validity of the moral proof such a critical issue.

3. CRITICISM OF KANT'S ETHICS

During the latter part of his stay at the University of Halle, or immediately thereafter, Schleiermacher worked on a criticism of the ethical part of Kant's philosophy, particularly the moral arguments used to establish the existence of God and human immortality. His discussion of Kant's moral proof for God will be considered first.

Kant had argued for the existence of God by claiming that the educated moral consciousness is dissatisfied unless virtue ultimately is conjoined with happiness; the virtuous deserve to be made happy. But this relation which would occur of itself in a perfect world does not naturally take place in our world. Therefore, unless there is a being powerful enough to make it possible and who can accomplish it in the future, the universe is morally unintelligible.

In this first critical essay, Schleiermacher tried to take the sting out of Kant's reasoning by showing that it is not true that the moral consciousness demands a conjoining of proportionate happiness with virtue. It is clear that if he could make good this contention, Kant's argument would collapse. (I am of course ignoring other fallacies in the argument with which Schleiermacher does not deal.)

Kant's belief about the demands of the moral consciousness is in accord with the moral feeling of many people. Most people do believe that it would be better for all virtuous people to be happy and the vicious unhappy than for the opposite arrangement to hold. Most people believe that there is some sense in which the good man who has willed what is right steadfastly in the face of temptation deserves to be happy in a way in which his morally weaker fellow men do not. This common-sense moral belief is the foundation of Kant's argument and it is this that Schleiermacher attacks. He adduces three different lines of argument.

The first attack is a direct frontal movement against this position held by Kant and common-sense. Kant had written:

For the complete good to be present, happiness is required, and indeed, not simply in the eyes of the interested party, but also in the judgment of impartial reason. For, both to need and to be worthy of happiness, without actually participating in it, cannot be consistent with the perfect will of a rational being. . . .[14]

To this argument, Schleiermacher objects flatly that it involves a 'misunderstanding of the moral insight involved.) There is no rational apprehension of the necessity of such an apportionment of happiness; moral feeling will not be outraged without it and it is not essential for the realization of the highest ideal. What we mean when we say that a man is "worthy" of something, he says, is not that what he is worthy of is appropriate or merited in the ordinary sense of these words. What we really mean is only that "he is capable of using it well, i.e., of getting from it the greatest possible contribution to the advancement of the general well-being."[15]

Obviously, Schleiermacher's analysis is not sufficient to refute the claim of Kant, although of course what he says may well be true.

Nevertheless, Schleiermacher assumed that this position had been established, not only in this work but apparently throughout the rest of his life—with all the far-reaching consequences of such a point of view.

As a second line of attack on Kant's contention, Schleiermacher disparages the idea that happiness is a part of the true good, in a manner similar to some of the later writings of Green and Mackenzie. He argues that happiness cannot consistently be made an ideal or goal, first, because the whole of pleasurable experience which is desired can be realized only in time as a set of temporally successive parts, and second, because the pleasurable satisfaction of one desire weakens the capacity to enjoy the satisfaction of some other desire.

These arguments again are fallacious. One may believe that happiness is a good or even the only good, without having to believe that one can enjoy every possible pleasure at once; nor need even the hedonist be specially disturbed by the fact that the enjoyment of one pleasure sometimes materially decreases the capacity for another pleasure through the satisfaction of some other desire.

Schleiermacher's final objection to Kant's argument depends upon his peculiar view of the relationship between "the good" and "duty" or the moral law. He urges that Kant's argument consists first in a judgment that something is good and second in an analysis of the conditions which are necessary for its attainment. This procedure, Schleiermacher claims, is erroneous because the highest good cannot be isolated and evaluated in this manner, which is applicable only to the "goods" which are valued because they are the objects of some desire. The highest good, in contrast, is not an "end in the ordinary sense, i.e., an object of desire, for the sake of which we will something else which is really not contained in the end itself."[16] Analysis of moral judgments exposes the fact that the highest good is rather "the complete essence of everything which it is possible to attain according to certain rules, and by a certain manner of procedure, viz., the purely rational." By definition, the highest good is what is realized through doing one's duty. It is related to what is known to be one's duty just as a curve is related to the mathematical function which defines it.[17] In contrast to the utilitarians, Schleiermacher (like Kant) takes the notion of duty to be primary in ethics and defines the good as "that which occurs as a result of doing one's duty." This procedure is possible, he thinks, because it is not necessary to know antecedently what is the highest good before one can know what is right; what is right can be determined by pure reason alone. It is what a purely rational being would do. An act is morally obligatory, then, if and when it can be willed as a law universally governing the conduct of men; and whatever is the outcome of such action constitutes the highest good.

The validity of these criticisms is of course not important for an historical understanding of Schleiermacher. The essential point is that he apparently thought they were valid, and that if acceptable they do destroy Kant's argument for God, just as Schleiermacher says.

His criticism of Kant's proof of immortality is more effective. Kant had argued that the moral consciousness recognizes a duty to be morally perfect. But because men are creatures whose motives are bound to sense desire, moral perfection cannot be acquired in a finite length of time. It is, however, morally obligatory to become perfect and what is morally obligatory cannot be impossible. Therefore the conditions of actualization of perfection must be given and man must have at his disposal an infinite length of time in which to become perfect. That is, he is immortal. Immortality must be a fact, because it is a "ground of the possibility of realizing the necessary object of pure practical reason";[18] and a "necessary object of pure practical reason" is "a purpose . . . which is represented as practically necessary by a categorical imperative directly determining the will."[19] There is a moral obligation to be perfect—a demand of reason itself. It must therefore be possible and immortality must be a fact.

Schleiermacher's replies to this line of reasoning are largely sound. He begins by arguing that it is a curious fact that, whereas Kant in the consideration of the ideals of reason in his *Critique of Pure Reason* adjudged them to be of only regulative value, here he seems to regard them as not only possible but necessary for noumenal objects. Perfection may perfectly well demand recognition as the moral ideal even if we know that its realization will never be possible. And as a matter of fact, in beings like ourselves whose desire to do right is a motive power which must contend with other motives in the determination of behavior, perfection *is* not possible.[20] Moreover, Kant's analysis of moral feeling is simply mistaken. For surely the ideal of moral perfection is regarded as obligatory in quite a different sense from that in which some particular act is thought to be obligatory. If this be admitted, Kant's belief in immortality loses its logical support.

Finally, Schleiermacher points out that Kant's two arguments (for God and immortality, respectively) contradict each other. The argument for God assumes that the highest good is the conjunction of virtue and pleasure (through satisfaction of desire). But the argument for immortality assumes that the moral ideal involves the extinction of desire. So that if the moral ideal is to be achieved, the "complete good" is impossible; and if virtue is to be conjoined with the pleasant satisfaction of desire, the moral ideal of perfection becomes unattainable.[21]

In addition to its main contentions this essay gives first expression to Schleiermacher's lifelong conviction of the truth of determinism. To his mind there is not "freedom" of choice in the sense that the outcome of moral deliberation can ever be anything different from what it actually is. This theory of motivation which was important for the development of his philosophy and theology was the subject of Schleiermacher's second critical essay and will be discussed in a moment.

Perhaps the most striking characteristic of his first work is its sharp separation of "the highest good" from what is desired, liked, or enjoyed. This feature is again characteristic of his later work. Schleiermacher almost always rejected anything that savored of hedonism. "Happiness," he said in a later essay, "is alien to my moral feeling,"[22]— an expression which was perhaps the crystallization of that reaction to the society of his day which we have already noted.

The manner in which this first piece of thinking contains the germs of his later philosophy will become clearer as we proceed. There is continuity between it and his affirmation that duty must be done not because anyone likes the consequences, but because it is a task set by Reason, or the Infinite, of which man himself is a "part." It is related to his disagreement with Fichte's moralistic interpretation of the world, because Schleiermacher, as a determinist, could not believe that the sole meaning of the world is its providing an arena for moral struggles. It is ultimately tied up with his rejection of traditional theism and immortality, so that he had to seek a "meaning" for the world within it and not outside it—a "meaning" which is elaborated in the Discourses on Religion. Apparently Schleiermacher's reaction to the life and philosophy of his day had already predisposed him for the "mystical" romanticism of 1800.

4. Ethical Determinism

The problem of the freedom of the will was the occasional object of Schleiermacher's reflection for about four years after 1789. He first planned and partially completed a dialogue in three parts. The first section, he wrote, showed "that one must treat the force of volition like any other force," a contention he elaborated at some length in order to avoid "any untenable half-way positions." The second part dealt with the problem of "whether remorse would be a delusion, in his system . . . and whether this kind of necessity would lead to ethical quietism." The third part (unfinished) was to have considered Kant's theory of freedom.

The second of these sections was then elaborated into a longer treatise (probably composed in 1791), which is included, in the form of selections and summary, in Dilthey's collection. It is a thoroughgoing confession of determinism.

Schleiermacher believes that determinism as he defines it is perfectly compatible with certain senses of "freedom." To his mind human beings are free in the sense that their behavior is not merely a matter of reflex response to stimuli or of instinctive actions. Human behavior obviously involves reflective deliberation on the results of alternative modes of action and of their relative worth. Furthermore, men sometimes adopt rules of conduct into which they attempt to introduce logical coherence, and conduct consistent with this system of rules may itself become the object of desire. And this desire can sometimes dominate conduct.

If freedom in this sense were not the case there would be no meaning to moral obligation, according to him. Obligation, he says, requires several conditions: First, the system of rules mentioned above must be capable of recognition as an ideal which ought to be realized in human conduct. Second, action in accord with such an ideal must not be incompatible with the character of human nature as such; that is, human nature in itself must not essentially involve conduct out of conformity with this system of precepts. Finally, the ideal must be capable of being the object of some desire, so that there is some possibility of its actually determining human conduct. This desire and the emotion connected with it are called "reverence for the moral law."[23]

So much Schleiermacher believed to be the case. But indeterminists usually go further and insist upon raising an additional question: In the case of any given act, is it possible that what the person does "could" have been different? If I betray a friend, "could" I have done otherwise? Indeterminists believe this question to be fundamental because there is no moral obligation where there are no real alternatives for conduct. "Ought implies can." If, then, the state of the universe before any act was such that that act—whether right or wrong—followed inevitably from that state of affairs, so that the event "could not have been otherwise," then it would seem to indeterminists that talk of moral obligation is nonsense.

Schleiermacher affirms freedom of choice in *his* (above) sense; he denies it in the indeterminist's sense. Human conduct at any moment, according to him, is determined by the state of affairs at the preceding moment—by external stimuli, by the state of one's desires, by the associations of ideas, and by habits and established modes of behavior.[24]

Schleiermacher apparently adopted this view, both because he felt that *indeterminism* is incompatible with moral obligation and because he thought that, when scrutinized, morality does not require freedom other than that which he believed in.

Schleiermacher argues that if indeterminism means that there is no necessary connection between the self and its acts, viz., if the acts of human individuals are a matter of chance or occur at random, then talk of obligation, guilt, etc., is clearly absurd. The establishing of a "good habit" would be impossible because the present acts of the self could not determine its future nature and conduct. Moral reform would be impossible. There would be no point in punishing a person in order to reform him because future acts are not dependent upon the nature of the self. Neither could an individual be held responsible for his acts in the past, for he could argue that his acts were not necessarily connected with the state of his present self and he should therefore not be punished for his past conduct.[25]

Thus Schleiermacher seemed to be faced with a dilemma: If indeterminism is the case, then moral obligation is impossible; but if determinism is true, if an act could not have been other than it was, moral obligation is still not possible.

The essence of his solution of the dilemma is contained in a passage dealing with the conditions of imputation or blame. How, he asks, can a person be blamed if we know that he could not have done otherwise than he actually did? He answers by saying that this question is confused. All that we have a right to ask is: Was the doing of the right act consistent with human nature in general? The answer to this question, he says, is in the affirmative; there is no property essential to human nature which makes impossible the doing of any moral act. Thus "the event which reason [conscience] demanded is possible not only in itself but in the constitution of the subject, and is *impossible only at this time and in this sequence* . . . , but this particular determination of time was not at all what reason was asking about." In other words, Schleiermacher admits that this particular act at this particular time and place could not have been other than it was; but in general it would not have been incompatible with human nature that something else should have occurred.

He further claims that if a person denies that imputation of guilt is compatible with his kind of "freedom," he must also deny that any kind of moral obligation is compatible with it—whereas we are all perfectly sure that moral ideals are binding, whatever be the feebleness of the desire to do right.[26]

Other ethical problems Schleiermacher solves or interprets along the same lines. Moral blame, he says, is simply the transfer of feelings aroused by the moral judgment of an act to the person who is its cause—a procedure analogous to one's attitude toward a great artist when one's imagination depicts vividly the kind of person who could be the cause of an inspiring work of art.[27] The importance of good character and moral growth, he argues, is also best appreciated by the determinist, whose view can make intelligible the possibility of the cultivation of a reliable moral personality. Again, determinism explains how punishment can be justified by its reformatory effect upon the character of the criminal.[28] Schleiermacher is not unaware of the problem of how the state can have a moral right to inflict punishment, if the wrongdoing is itself due only to an unfortunate disposition. His answer is that there is no reason why there cannot be a universal agreement to inflict a lesser evil in order to reduce or prevent the effect of crime.[29]

Whatever one may think of the satisfactoriness of such a position, Schleiermacher seems to have been quite convinced by it and I believe did not depart from it in any important respect during the rest of his life. The remarkable thing is that along with this determinism he believed in the absolute obligation to realize the highest good for its own sake. The moral ideal is to remain obligatory even though in any given instance moral conduct may be impossible.

The conclusions which Schleiermacher reached in this matter encourage speculation about his opinion of Kant's theory of the noumenal self. The essay itself contains the beginning of a discussion of Kant which breaks off suddenly. Apparently Schleiermacher was dissatisfied with Kant's suggestion that the self is phenomenally determined but noumenally free; the outcome of the argument just outlined, at any rate, implies that Kant was mistaken in believing that moral obligation presupposes the noumenal freedom of the self. This suggests some possibilities about Schleiermacher's attitude toward Kant. What was his view of Kant's theory of the relation of the noumenal and the phenomenal world? Did he think there is any sense in which the noumenal world contains free moral agents? Were these conclusions in moral philosophy in any way connected with his later emphasis on man's complete ignorance of the noumenal world, his insistence that it cannot be known even whether there are different entities in it? This would harmonize with his later expressed objection to the whole idea of permanent substantial selves which can accrue merit for which they are to be paid off by God in happiness—a view which he thought reduced morality to selfishness. The pages which come closest to an explicit discussion of his whole appreciation of Kant are contained in a comparison of Kant and Spinoza to be discussed in a moment.

The most interesting outcome of this essay, from the point of view of understanding the relation between his youthful speculations and his later view of religion, is the lead it gives in the matter of speculation on the meaning or purpose of existence in this world. As a determinist Schleiermacher must understand the world in such a way that free moral choice and the rewards or punishments consequent to it (according to the accepted religious doctrine of the day) do not exclusively constitute its purpose. Therefore the conclusion of this essay dallies with several possible ways in which the accepted beliefs of religion might be remodeled in order to make them compatible with the moral views of the determinist.

Schleiermacher first throws out, simply as a suggestion I think, the idea that inequalities of moral character might be accounted for if we held that they are not dependent on God's will but are the expressions of the characters of different substances which have been eternally what they are.[30]

A second idea which he works out more fully is that the present life, in which moral differences suggest arbitrariness and chance, is really intended as a period of education. Moreover, he suggests that it may not be true that some have naturally stronger characters than others; it may be that all persons have approximately equal moral aptitudes, except that some excel at one thing, others at another. Acceptance of the idea of eternal punishment for wrongdoing is of course incompatible with this view. So he says:

> The external conditions after death probably effect a complete change [redistribution] in the sum total of feelings of pleasure and pain, in which this inner determination [i.e., of moral status] is only a moment: in an infinite period of time, they lead all souls to the same goal, only by different paths.[31]

A third suggestion, which is much more closely related to the ideas he entertained in his mature published works, is to the effect that moral differences between individuals are themselves of intrinsic worth.[32] Finding an analogy with the unequal distribution of other goods, contemplation of which only reminds him of a future common approximation to a common goal, Schleiermacher discovers in moral differences only a sign of the wisdom and love of God which have secured to man the edifying vision of the great panorama of moral development.

The variety of imperfection, compared with the most universal perfection to which it leads, must fill everyone with all the delight of which feeling is capable. Why do we not recognize with joy the love and wisdom of the being who wished to secure to every rational member of his kingdom, who is capable of such contemplation—and without real harm to a single individual—the immense and instructive view of how our own nature extends from the bestial crudeness of the cannibal and the horrible depravity of the most despicable villain to the amazing perfection of the wisest mortal, and to the divine virtue of a Christ or a Socrates.*

These speculations which are a part of the theological implications of his deterministic inclination are not necessarily incompatible with each other, but those of them which assume the permanent existence of human individuals in some way are not easy to reconcile with his attitude toward Kant's moral proofs for God and immortality. In view of his later work, there can be no doubt of the direction in which his thought was gradually moving—and it was away from the theistic concepts of God and personal immortality.† He wrote at this time of Christianity: "I have taken my stand irrevocably, and even if Wizenmann‡ and Socrates should rise to the defence of Christianity, they would not bring me back." He went on to say that while he felt there is undeniably something to be said for immortality, he could not convince himself of it.[33] It must be recalled that from this time on Schleiermacher apparently never accepted any of the classical proofs for God; he later defined God as an impersonal being which is the source of the unity of the ideal and the real; his belief in immortality was never orthodox. All these facts and in addition the eagerness with which he shortly laid hold on Spinoza, and his later ready embrace of romanticism which led to the Discourses on Reli-

* Dilthey, Leben Schleiermachers, Appendix, p. 35. This idea, made more definite by the romantic idea of individuality, appears in the Discourses on Religion, where he says religion sees the value of immorality as an expression of the caprice of the universe. Dilthey, op. cit., p. 326, says the first statements about individuality occur in some notebooks on Leibniz. Professor A. O. Lovejoy has made much of this relation to traditional ideas in Leibniz in his discussion of Schleiermacher in The Great Chain of Being.

† In his Critique of Ethics, published in 1803, he remarked that the concepts of freedom, God, and immortality are superfluous both in ethics and metaphysics. Werke, pt. III, vol. I, p. 22.

‡ Thomas W. Wizenmann (1759-1787), a student of theology and philosophy who, deeply troubled about the truth of Christianity, had written a famous letter in which he said he could not decide whether to be a Christian or an atheist. Admired and befriended by Jacobi and Schiller, his early death was widely lamented. Kant paid a tribute to him in the Critique of Practical Reason.

gion, suggest that these early essays mark his rejection of the deistic view of God, religion, and immortality, and all that went with it.*

Having come to doubt the validity of the orthodox picture of the world, Schleiermacher was seeking other concepts which might make reality intelligible. The third of the suggestions offered above is a step in this direction—toward a "this-worldly" solution to his problems which he later worked out in the *Discourses*, through the idea of a universe perfect in its harmony and individuality.

In concluding our account of his work during this period it is necessary to mention briefly an essay on the nature of value and the worth of human existence which he wrote at this time as an expansion of a New Year's sermon of 1792. I omit a detailed consideration of it because it is very confusing and because it does not seem to have any important implications for his further development. The main points in it are (1) that he thinks that happiness is in some way related to value, probably as a "sign" of the presence of value or the harmonious working of the self (and in so far this essay constitutes a departure from Kant's moral dualism although Schleiermacher himself was radically opposed to hedonism); and (2) that the distribution of happiness in the world is not unjust, because a person's deficiencies in one respect are usually made up for by an unusual capacity for it in some other direction. (This attitude toward the distribution of evil is consistent with his lifelong tendency to take an optimistic view of the world, to be impressed little by the amount of pain or its unequal distribution.) Both these affirmations are perfectly consistent with our belief that at this time Schleiermacher was already attempting to understand the world in terms of immanent organization and perfection, not in terms of the transcendent purposes of God and a future life.

5. The Influence of Spinoza

The conclusions on theological and metaphysical issues to which Schleiermacher had been brought by his work in moral philosophy and his attention to Kant's theoretical and moral discussions of the

---

* These views must have placed him in an awkward position, since he preached every Sunday. In 1790 he said the theological examinations required answering questions on subtleties at which he really smiled. He consoled himself with the thought that Eberhard, "with all his heresy, once had himself examined by a consistory." *Briefe*, vol. IV, p. 47.

theological ideal were confirmed and extended by a study of Spinoza
which took place probably between 1793 and 1796. It was apparently
between these dates that he composed two essays on Spinoza, *Kurze
Darstellung des spinozistischen Systems*[34] and *Spinozismus*,[35] both
based upon quotations from Spinoza's works (unavailable at that time
to Schleiermacher) contained in Jacobi's *Briefe über die Lehre des
Spinoza* (1785).

These essays were intended to present a fairer picture of Spinoza
than Jacobi had painted, although Schleiermacher's only material
was what Jacobi's work included. There are a few inaccuracies in interpretation, probably because he had to work with scrappy quotations,
but the essays do make clear that Schleiermacher had seriously considered and thought through the main ideas of Spinoza. Moreover,
they evince a careful and critical study of the doctrines of both Leibniz and Kant, with whom Schleiermacher compares Spinoza on certain points. If the essays cannot be called a complete success as an
exposition of Spinoza, they do exhibit penetration, care, and skill
which mark Schleiermacher at this early age as an able thinker.

Fortunately for us, Schleiermacher's papers are not merely ex-
pository; they are devoted mostly to a critical comparison of the three
philosophers mentioned, between the systems of whom Schleiermacher carefully picks what he believes the surest way. Consequently
we have here a record of his own metaphysics at this time, which incidentally is a close approximation to the identity theory of Schelling
and has often been called the first expression of this type of meta-
physic.

As might be expected, Schleiermacher is most sympathetic with
Spinoza's opposition to the theistic idea of a transcendent God. After
citing some of the reasons which had as he thinks led Spinoza to
take the line he did, Schleiermacher remarks that on this matter
Spinoza "is in every respect superior"[36] to Leibniz. Although he does
not expressly agree with Spinoza, it is clear that he had been deeply
impressed by Spinoza's criticism of the doctrines of creation and the
personality or spirituality of God. It is further evident that he believes that Kant, the moral argument excepted, had not really suggested a theological ideal fundamentally different from Spinoza's God.
For the "unconditioned being" which Kant suggests might be re-

garded as the ground of the series of contingent beings is not to be
in the series of phenomenal objects as the first in time or the cause
of the beginning of the phenomenal series; and if it is not, Kant ought
then to recall that the category of causality is inapplicable to the
noumenal world and that it is not clear that there is any reason for
believing that they require a condition outside themselves. In other
words, it may be that the system of noumenal objects is itself the unconditioned reality, and Kant has certainly offered no reason to
believe the contrary. Kant considers a transcendent God only "because
of an inconsistent remnant of the old dogmatism."[37]

Schleiermacher therefore believes that there is a rough parallel between Spinoza's infinite substance and the Kantian things-in-themselves. The fact that he is interested in this parallel at this time is
important for an appreciation of the development of his thought, for
in 1799, in the *Discourses on Religion* his central concept of the
universe or the Infinite is strongly suggestive of Spinoza; and after
1805 he held a form of identity philosophy very like that of Schelling.

To follow out the nature of this parallel somewhat further, it must
be observed, first, that Schleiermacher contends that in both cases the
unconditioned object is introduced because in some respect the
common-sense world is not self-contained and self-explanatory, but
requires the reality of a condition not itself directly known in the
same way as are common-sense objects. Schleiermacher of course notes
that the relation between the phenomenal objects and the noumenal
world in Kant is different from the relation between objects and God
in Spinoza; otherwise, as he says, Spinoza would have discovered the
Critical Philosophy himself.[38] And the specific manner in which the
common-sense world is thought to require an unconditioned object is
different in the two systems. Spinoza argues to the one, simple, eternal
object, the one true individual, from the requirements of the flux
and contingency of ordinary objects,[39] whereas Kant's argument (although Schleiermacher does not explicitly discuss it) moves from the
incapacity of the world of sense to meet certain demands of thought
without contradiction, and from his assumption that there cannot be
appearances unless there is something to appear.

In the second place, Schleiermacher thinks that both Kant and
Spinoza agree that ordinary objects are in both space and time, but

that there is some sense in which their ground is out of space-time. With Spinoza, he says, as with Kant,

space and time are not only the form but the source of all change and of everything variable. What is determined by space-time is also, according to him, not in the [unconditioned] thing itself, but is only a modification of a thing; space-time is the modifying medium. Only, [he differs from Kant in that] he does not place it [this form] in us, but in an unknown infinite stuff.[40]

In the third place, both Spinoza and Kant hold that there is some sense in which the unconditioned object cannot be characterized. In the case of Kant, the fundamental categories of thought are derived from the concept of an object in a temporal order, known by intuition; there is no reason to believe that they apply to the noumenal realm, and Kant even says that they have no definite meaning except in relation to some content of sense intuition. In the case of Spinoza, "the Infinite Being cannot be defined essentially in terms of the predicates which determine the nature of particular objects," for otherwise the peculiar nature of God which escapes the limitations essential to finite objects will have been missed.[41] Schleiermacher apparently very much approved of this agnostic attitude toward God, and went on to indicate that Spinoza and Kant had both overlooked some inconsistencies on this point. Spinoza, for example, had no real right to assert the simplicity, unity, and infinity of the unconditioned. Kant made the opposite error and assumed without the shadow of a justification that there is a plurality of entities in the noumenal world.[42] Schleiermacher remarks that Leibniz, too, had never given any justification for asserting a plurality of metaphysical substances.[43] "That which is certainly most closely connected with that in us which most really exists, viz., Reason, individuates us the least, and the contemplation of it rather brings us back from the delusion of individuality."[44] It is presumptuous, he concludes, to make any statement about the noumenal world; we should speak, more properly, only of "the world as noumenon."

Schleiermacher is also pretty plainly out of sympathy with Leibniz' attempt to give thought the primacy in God, although he criticizes Spinoza because he thinks Spinoza has gone too far in

the other direction and has really made extended matter fundamental.[45]

How much can safely be said about Schleiermacher's own views,
on the basis of the foregoing summary? We can venture, I think, to
make the following statements. First, Schleiermacher does not accept
the orthodox theistic view that there is a reality outside the world
which is required by the contingent existence of finite objects and
which in any sense has created them. Second, he believes that the
world does require a "ground" which is in some way immanent in
it, but which is not itself spatial and temporal. Space and time are the
forms of human sensibility and not the forms of ultimate reality.
Third, the unconditioned ground is unknown and unknowable; it is
impossible to assert even that it is a unity or that it consists of a plurality of entities. Fourth, it is not legitimate to say that the principal
attribute of God is thought.

There is one further point on which Schleiermacher's views as
stated here have an important relation to his previous essays. This
concerns the significance for ultimate reality of human individuals,
moral persons. Does moral experience furnish any clue to the nature
(e.g., the plurality) of the foundational reality any more than other
parts of experience? Schleiermacher obviously thought this an important question, and devoted the second half of Spinozismus to a
consideration of it. In the other essay he points out that an outstanding question to be solved is the origin and basis of the idea of individuality.

Schleiermacher's general contention is that the recognition of an
individual self in the phenomenal world, just as that of the individual
physical object, is an independent problem which is in no way affected
by any beliefs one may have about noumenal "individuality." The
concepts of moral personality and responsibility are again independent
of metaphysical beliefs about the transempirical. The upshot of his
discussion is that there can be no inference from phenomenal individuality to noumenal individual substance. As I have remarked, he
says that the universality of thought which is man's most intimate
contact with the real tends to "bring us back from the delusion of
individuality."[46]

This result seems to conform perfectly with what he had previously said about these matters. Recall, for example, his determinism. He objected to the indeterminist's refusal to regard the human person as a member of a causal series, and to the contention that the self through free choice can somehow accumulate a degree of merit or guilt which ought to be rewarded or punished in the future. The whole idea of reward of virtue through an appropriate distribution of happiness, again, was the very one which Schleiermacher objected to in his first essay on ethics. Happiness and rewards are not properly parts of the moral ideal; what is good should be sought on account of its goodness alone. Now these main contentions of the indeterminist to which he so clearly objected would apparently be lost if it could be denied that the moral person is an ultimately real individual, at least partly independent of other individuals. Perhaps Schleiermacher thought that a sweeping denial of the noumenal individuality of the self would clear away many positions which he believed mistaken without bringing with it any new difficulties.

I have already suggested that Schleiermacher's determinism, his belief that moral experience, far from requiring, is actually irreconcilable with "free will," implied some break with Kant's belief about the noumenal self. This is the direction which he took: the complete severance of moral personality from metaphysical individuality, the utter unknowableness of the ultimately real.

We shall see that in 1799 Schleiermacher believed that the individual self is not an ultimate metaphysical unit and that its significance lies in the fact that, though only an evanescent ripple on the surface of the Infinite, it represents the Infinite from an individual point of view. For an instant the Infinite is individually conscious in it. The reason why personal existence occurs at all is its revelation of the universe.

Two important questions ought to be kept in mind as we approach the period of Schleiermacher's first publications, in 1799 and 1800. The first and less significant is: does he continue in 1799 to regard space and time as phenomenal, a character of appearances exclusively conditioned by the nature of human sensibility? The second one is: what becomes of his distinction between the unknowable noumenal ground of experience and the phenomenal world of common sense? How far, if at all, does he give up Kant's subjectivist view of phenomena, his agnostic attitude toward things-in-themselves? This second question is particularly important, for the interpretation of two of his best known ideas, his concept of the universe and his theory of religious "intuition" (which have often been connected with Spinoza's idea of God and his highest kind of knowledge, respectively) depends to a great extent on the answer to them.

It will naturally be expected that the philosophy of the *Discourses* is different from his philosophy of 1795. His thought was of course deepened and extended by study of Fichte and Schelling and by contact with Friedrich Schlegel and some of the romanticists. But it will be found that the conclusions reached so far are surprisingly similar to the "this-worldly" philosophy and theology of 1799 and 1800. We have only to see how they were reformulated by relation to romanticism and the idealism of Fichte and Schelling.

In the light of this evidence concerning the line of reasoning which led to his later philosophy, it would be a mistake to conclude that Schleiermacher's later views were only intuitive or devised with the aim of furnishing a prop for religion. Many of his objections to the Kantian philosophy are perfectly legitimate; and others of his contentions would be accepted by many philosophers at the present time. It is true that later he sometimes called himself a "mystic," but not because he disregarded the claims of thought. In fact, he disagreed with Jacobi on account of Jacobi's disparagement of philosophy and distrust of Kant. (Jacobi thought the Critical Philosophy ignored the claims of faith and mysticism.)

CHAPTER III

THE INTELLECTUAL CLIMATE IN 1799

A period of several years intervened between the composition of the essays we have been considering and the publication of Schleiermacher's first book. It was about the turn of the century that he produced the *Discourses on Religion*, the *Soliloquies*, the *Confidential Letters on Fr. Schlegel's Lucinde*, and two less well-known works,[1] along with a few contributions to the romantic journal, the *Athenaeum*.

Those intervening years, however, were eventful years, and an understanding of what happened to the course of German thought during them is useful for an appreciation of Schleiermacher. In fact, Schleiermacher himself believed that the *Discourses* would be hardly intelligible apart from knowledge of the intellectual climate in which they were written. Only seven years after the initial publication (1799), he prefaced a second edition with the words:

A work is certain to be evanescent, when it is so closely connected with the character of a definite period, and especially of one when not only the philosophy of professionals but the prevailing opinion and way of feeling have changed with the speed which we have just witnessed here in Germany; and the writer faces an entirely different type of reader and thinker, after the lapse of only a few years . . . This relation to the age . . . I could not change without reconstructing the whole so completely that the book would have been entirely different.[2] [Elsewhere he wrote in a somewhat similar vein:] This book bears throughout the marks of opposition [to other writers living at the time it was written].[3]

This period was one of the most productive in the history of Europe, not only in philosophy but in literature and art. One need mention only Goethe, Schiller, and the romanticists to establish its significance for the history of German literature. But philosophical circles, too, enjoyed a perhaps unprecedented period of activity, speculative daring, and system making. The various criticisms of Kant, the successive expositions of Fichte's philosophy, the series of Schelling's publications leading up eventually to his "identity theory," the thought of the as yet unknown Hegel, and the theories of Friedrich von Schlegel (the friend and roommate of Schleiermacher for several of these years): all these are characteristic of the philosophical ferment of the time.

Schleiermacher moved to Berlin in 1796 to become chaplain of an institution and remained there until the spring of 1802. During the earlier of these six years he roomed with Friedrich von Schlegel, who introduced him to Fichte when the latter came to Berlin after having been dismissed from a professorial chair at Jena on a charge of atheism. It may also have been Schlegel who interested Schleiermacher in the works of Schelling—as he certainly did interest him in romanticism and the literary and historical pursuits connected with that movement.

At any rate, the philosophy of the *Discourses* and *Soliloquies* is closely wed to the German thought of 1799, and it behooves anyone who wishes to understand even the independent and original features of Schleiermacher's thought to take account of the ideas of the time to which Schleiermacher's work is most relevant.

1. FICHTE'S ETHICAL IDEALISM

The critical philosophy of Kant was subjected to much criticism by various writers in the last years of the eighteenth century, partly because of the fact that the first *Critique* is not only obscure but does not present an altogether consistent argument. The apparent incompatibility of Kant's limitation of knowledge to the world of appearance with his theory of the thing-in-itself, or noumenal operations performed by the mind prior to consciousness, is only one of the more important difficulties of the *Critique of Pure Reason*. Moreover, Kant's different publications did not seem to depict clearly a systematic unity between his epistemology, his ethical views, his aesthetics and discussion of teleological judgments.

Reinhold, Schulze, Maimon, Beck, and Jacobi—philosophers who criticized and discussed the Critical Philosophy from various points of view and with various degrees of understanding—lay bare many of the lacunae and obscurities in Kant's work. They exposed the difficulty connected with the thing-in-itself, with the occasional suggestion that there is a transcendental mind as a set of faculties in a causal relation to their product (consciousness), and the need for a greater unity of system. But the writings of these men are of less importance for an understanding of the movement of thought at that time than those of Fichte, who, claiming only to complete and correct the Critical Philosophy, expanded it in the direction of an idealism emphasizing the moral consciousness.

The spirit of Kant's philosophy, at least in part, was faithfully reproduced in Fichte's idealism. Kant had said: "I had to deny knowledge to make room for faith"[4]—a statement expressing the priority of ethical considerations for his philosophy. This primacy of ethical convictions which was the basis of Kant's proofs for human freedom, God, and immortality was carried further in Fichte's philosophy.

In other respects Fichte departed far from the intent of the Critical Philosophy, his own belief to the contrary notwithstanding. We shall see what these differences were.

In one of Fichte's earliest publications, he asserted emphatically that a philosophical system which claims to give a firm foundation for knowledge must "deduce" everything (in a sense shortly to be explained) from a single first principle. In other words, philosophical procedure is essentially systematic and monistic. (The reasons he sets forth are insufficient to show that some type of dualistic philosophy is incapable of making experience intelligible; but unless his contention here is accepted, one will not understand his system.)

The works of Kant notoriously do not measure up to this dual ideal. First, he does not deduce everything from a single principle; his system is ineradicably dualistic. Second, his works do not contain a system. I mean by this that he often shows by analysis of experience that something is the case, but he often does not prove its necessity. For example, analysis of experience indicates, according to Kant, that there is a material element in experience which is absolutely given to the mind through its relation to the thing-in-itself of which it is the appearance; but he does not show the necessity of there being a given element in experience. Or again, with respect to Kant's forms of intuition (space and time), or forms of understanding (the categories), Fichte agreed that these are a result of the nature of human intelligence, so that the formal element in experience is due to the

"activity" of intelligence and not to any relation to things-in-themselves. But Fichte thought that Kant had not shown the necessity of
these forms of experience; he thought Kant had not proved how they
follow out of the very nature of intelligence. Kant came nearest to
this, according to Fichte, in the "metaphysical deduction" of the
categories in which he tried to relate the forms of understanding to
formal logic. But he never succeeded in showing how these various
aspects of experience are parts of a mutually implicative system. As a
result of these instances of "inadequacy" in the Critical Philosophy,
Fichte believed that Kant's work was desperately in need of sys-
tematization; he even said (with a great deal of justification, for Kant
never really harmonized the ideas of his most important books) that
each of Kant's Critiques had a different "absolute." At any rate, he
thought the salvation of the Critical Philosophy lay in the systematic
deduction which he, Fichte, could supply.

Fichte's next step (after affirming the necessity of some monistic
system derived from a single principle) was to narrow down the possible alternatives for the philosopher until only two were left. He
excluded any dualism because he thought that dualisms only provoke
intolerable muddles in philosophy.* So, either the philosopher will
make matter or the nonmental the highest principle and fundamental
idea in his system, or he will make mind or consciousness in some
way the one and only fundamental reality. In either case, he admitted,
there is an initial difficulty for experience seems to exhibit both the
activity of mind and the stubborn givenness of the nonmental; so that
any monistic system necessarily has a barrier to surmount, for it must
explain the possibility of experience's exhibiting a factor which seems
to be radically different from the assumed fundamental principle.
That is, the materialist must show the possibility of knowledge; the
critical idealist must show the possibility of the experience of the
nonmental.

The next move of the argument was to take sides with idealism.
He admits that, strictly speaking, it is not really possible to refute
materialistic "dogmatism." And in some passages he says that the

---

* Fichte believed that any theory allowing for nonmental objects existing independent of experience cannot avoid being a deterministic materialism incompatible
with moral experience.

choice of either materialism or idealism depends simply on one's character; that is, the person who lays great weight upon moral experience will be an idealist. Elsewhere, however, he argues that the advantage of idealism is that it is possible (as he will show in his system) to set up a first principle enunciating the fundamental character of mind and then to deduce the fundamental facts of experience from it; whereas the same cannot be said for the materialist. Conscious experience is the most fundamental and obvious fact; its reality is the presupposition of knowledge of any other reality; it absolutely must be accounted for but materialism cannot account for it. This denial that materialism can account for mind—which I suppose could be more successfully disputed by "emergent materialists" today than it could have been by materialists of his day—seemed to Fichte to eliminate materialism. Since he did not seriously consider any third alternative, he concluded that idealism must be right. Of course it must be remembered that he also had other reasons for believing that the idea of a nonpersonal thing-in-itself is a very difficult one to maintain, as he had learned from the fortunes of Kant.

The true philosophical system must be an idealistic one; it must take as its foundation stone the fundamental principle of conscious experience or the fact which makes consciousness possible. And it must deduce every assertion that it makes, or every fundamental fact about consciousness, from this first principle. Such was the task to which Fichte set himself. We come in a moment to a consideration of its execution.

The most striking distinction between Fichte's work and the philosophy of Kant, brought about by the above line of reasoning, was Fichte's elimination of the notion of the thing-in-itself (a notion which he believed inconsistent with the true spirit of the Critical Philosophy). Kant distinguished two elements within experience (which he did not believe, however, are ever given separately): on the one hand the stuff or given material (sounds, colors, tastes, etc.), and on the other hand the form imposed on the material by the mind's forms of intuition and categories of understanding (space and time and the categories). The stuff or matter of experience is to be accounted for by the relation to the things-in-themselves, in virtue of which the things-in-themselves are enabled to appear (albeit, according to Kant, in a form utterly unlike their independent natures). This given matter or stuff accounts for the *a posteriori* element in knowledge, according to Kant; the subjective contribution of the mind accounts for the *a priori* elements in knowledge. In other words, the roundness of a stool as against its possible squareness can be known only by experience, in contrast to its properties of being extended or in a causal order which are conditions of its being an object of experience and therefore can be anticipated prior to particular experience; and this roundness of the stool is due to some character of the thing-in-itself which would be different if the stool (as phenomenon) were square, although of course the stool's being extended in space at all is due to the mind's form of intuition. Kant's account here may be roughly compared with that of common-sense science, according to which the "seen" tree has certain of its important characteristics because of the nature of a "real" tree which is independent of experience, although in certain respects (e.g., the secondary qualities) the two trees are different.

Fichte denied the theory of the things-in-themselves. He denied that there are objects independent of experience which nevertheless get related to experience so that the phenomenal objects are "appearances" of them. He denied the necessity of assuming that there is something over against mind which makes intelligible the givenness of the matter of sense experience. For one reason, it is impossible to know that these things-in-themselves exist, for by hypothesis they cannot be directly known in experience (in which occur only the "appearances").[5] If their reality cannot be known directly, can it then be shown to be a necessary assumption? Fichte denied it. Such an assumption does not help to make the possibility of experience clear, and only leads back to the old dogmatic materialism which has already been eliminated. And there is another more successful hypothesis. This is the hypothesis that the principle of consciousness is fundamental. Fichte believed it is possible to deduce from this principle all the facts which formed the ground for the old assumption of things-in-themselves. He believed it possible to show that the experience of objects is fundamental to the nature of mind and follows out of that principle of consciousness; he believed that the facts to be deduced can be shown to be necessary for the very possibility of consciousness.

As he said: "The assumption of idealism is this: mind acts, but in virtue of its nature, it can act only in a definite way. . . . These ways of action . . . make up a system; i.e., that mind . . . acts just as it does can be explained further . . . from a single principle."[6]

There is also the positive side of his argument. In addition to his criticisms of dogmatism, materialism, and the doctrine of the things-in-themselves, he thinks there are positive grounds for accepting his idealistic hypothesis. His positive ground is simply the possibility of discovering the fundamental principle of consciousness, setting it up as a first principle, and showing the actual deduction from it of the facts which have to be deduced, viz., the spatio-temporal forms, the pervasive categorial aspects of experience, along with a character of experience which would naturally induce the hypothesis of things-in-themselves causing it, and so on.

According to Fichte, this "deduction" is to be accomplished in the following manner:[7] It is first shown that one fact is absolutely certain—in fact presupposed by any other knowledge and even by the laws of logic. This fact cannot be proved in the sense of being deduced from other more certain facts, for it is the ground of all certainty; but other assumed knowledge can be shown to presuppose it. Analysis of this fact shows that taken by itself it is incomplete, self-contradictory. A further fact must also be the case, if the first fact is to be the case; the first fact involves a second. And since the first fact is known to be the case, the second must be the case. But the first assertion and the second cannot both be true, he then shows, unless a third be true; and since the first and second are known to be true, therefore the third must also be true. And so on, until the system is completed. This type of procedure, by means of dialectical argument, foreshadowed the method of Hegel and was itself anticipated in large measure by Kant and Reinhold.

I shall not attempt to follow the sequence of Fichte's exposition, however, but shall merely state briefly what seems to me to be the essence of his positive argument.

Kant's arguments which were designed to prove that the mind makes, even if it does not create, the world, already lay behind Fichte's idealistic hypothesis. Fichte had argued furthermore that the hypothesis of the things-in-themselves is futile and that such an assumption solves no problems about the possibility of experience. To his mind the only feasible alternative is to assume that mind is responsible for the whole of experience. This does not mean that any particular instance of conscious experience can be accepted as a self-sustaining fact. Rather, what is to be explained is how that experience is possible. What must be discovered (and it must be discovered in consciousness) is the principle which makes consciousness possible. Fichte claims that if one introspects when asked to think of some object, one will immediately perceive what he means by a creative act of the ego (like Kant's transcendental unity of apperception). It is this activity which he believed to be the self-sustaining principle which makes consciousness and the world possible. At any rate he tries it as an hypothesis.

It must be pointed out that Fichte does not regard this activity as the activity of a substance. On the contrary, his argument is intended to prove that substance is a notion logically posterior to the notion of activity. Activity must be considered in itself as independent of any substance.

This activity, according to Fichte's hypothesis, must be the fundamental reality which determines everything else. But experience at once presents a problem to him, set by the fact that there seems to be an element in experience which is merely given and is what it is independent of the activity of the subject—the material to account for which Kant had invoked the affection of the mind by things-in-themselves. These two facts seem to be contradictory: on the one hand it is asserted that subjective activity must be the ground of all reality, but on the other hand the human subject is confronted with a given material which limits and resists it.

Fichte argues that there is only one way out of the difficulty. It is necessary to assume that the subjective activity is in some way the ground of the given and objective, its own opposite. The subjective activity is the fundamental fact, but for a reason (in order to make possible self-consciousness and the obstacles necessary for moral discipline) it must develop its own opposite, that is limit itself so that its own self-limitation may appear to be a relation to an object. This implies that in some sense the activity of the self known in introspection cannot be identical with the pure activity which is the ground of the existence of the nonego, or objective reality. For the activity directly intuited does not appear to be the ground of the nonego; it seems rather to be limited and confined by it. This means that in its finite manifestations intelligence is not identical with intelligence as absolute; for the one is limited by the nonego, the other absolutely free (absolutely free only as an ideal, however, for it cannot be itself, that is, self-conscious, without the limitation) and the ground of the nonego. A difficulty obviously arises from this conclusion, for the position suggests that Fichte has involved himself in a new dogmatism in assuming a fact which is not given in consciousness as such, but like the thing-in-itself must be simply assumed. However, this and other related difficulties cannot be discussed here.

The absolute self's limitation of its own activity results in the production of those given characters of experience which seem to be the opposite of thought or intelligence, and which are mistaken on the common-sense level of the plain man for an affection of the mind by things or nonmental objects. Actually, Fichte argues, there are no entities which exist independently of the mind. "There is no being in itself. . . . For the philosopher, it is action. . . . Being is only the negation of freedom."[8] "The immediate perception of this limitation of the self is feeling . . . the feeling of the sweet, the red, the cold."[9] These data, the self-limitation of the self's activity, are then subjected to the synthetic and reflective activities of the self, and by means of the categories of thought are raised to the status of objects with qualities so that self-consciousness and an objective world eventually become possible. In this manner intelligence is the creator of nature, the ground of the world of experience.

I have already stated that Fichte preserved the spirit of Kant's philosophy in that he, too, made moral experience central and exploited the results of his epistemology in a way suited to the establishing of the contentions of the moral consciousness.

In the first place, Fichte believed his system made clear the possibility of freedom of choice in the sense required for the legitimacy of moral imputation. For the categories and laws which intelligence applies on the level of nature are naturally not applicable to that which makes both nature and thought possible, i.e., that which is the ground of natural existence. The category of causality does not apply to the free activity of the absolute ego which is the ground of the nonego. So much is clear. But has Fichte established the freedom (in the required sense) not only of the absolute intelligence but of the finite intelligence, the self which acts morally? Here Fichte himself does not speak unambiguously. Sometimes he seems to say that the finite intelligence is not free; at other times he seems to say that the decision to actualize some ideal or purpose is absolutely undetermined. At any rate I think it is safe to say that Fichte thought he had opened the way to belief in freedom of the will.

In the second place, the practical, active nature of the self is more fundamental to it than its nature as thought. For the self as intelligence, as consciousness, presupposes the self as active. It is only by means of the infinite activity's limitation of itself that consciousness is possible at all. Intelligence and scientific thought are possible only on a derived and secondary level; they are logically derivative and presuppose the pure activity.

In the third place, the necessity of the moral experience is "explained" by this kind of transcendental idealism. Moral experience, according to Fichte, consists essentially in the accompaniment of certain ideals or purposes by a feeling of their necessity for conduct. The ideal of morality is that intelligence should be absolutely self-dependent, not determined by anything outside it and hence not subject to the promptings of sense desire. The ideal for intelligence is free action for the sake of action itself; the desires with which this ideal conflicts are desires for action for the sake of sense enjoyment. This ideal and the feeling of necessity which accompanies it are due to the fact that the absolute or infinite ego is implicit in the finite ego; the nature of the infinite ego, as absolutely free, is therefore recognized as the ideal for the finite ego—albeit an ideal which could not be realized without the destruction of consciousness, the possibility of which involves resistance to the activity of the self. Thus, for Fichte, obligation to act is not generated by the potential value of the object to be aimed at; rather, man must be moral simply for the value of being moral itself. Mind must vindicate its own nature; it must be absolutely active, absolutely free, by overcoming the barriers to activity and freedom which it has set up. Thus the truly free act is the act which excludes motivation by the objects of natural desire. Freedom from sense desire or egoism is the triumph of mind over its self-imposed limitation. "The independence of all Reason as such is our final goal."[10]

Consistently with these affirmations, Fichte holds that the very "significance" of the objective world is its relation to moral ideals. The moral striving of conscious persons (of which the external world is the condition, both in that it makes consciousness possible and in that it serves as an obstacle for the striving self) is the realization of the true nature of infinite activity; in this conscious striving the activity becomes conscious of itself for what it is, in that the infinite ego is envisaged as the ideal of moral conduct, and at the same time recognized as in some way the ground of all reality and thought. Thus the destiny of the objective world is to serve as a moral training ground, as a means to exercise the self and bring out its true nature. "Our world is the incarnated material for duty. This is the proper reality in things, the true reason for all appearance."[11]

In brief, although infinite activity is the essential nature of mind, this activity cannot be conscious (and consciousness is also the true nature of mind), nor really active (for activity requires obstacles to be overcome), unless the infinity is partially negated. The nonego, or limitation, is really essential to the active, conscious nature of intelligence. The experienced world must be, if mind is to actualize its true nature. This is the "explanation" of the ego's self-limitation which creates the objective world.

At least at one time, Fichte apparently identified the absolute ego with God. One of his contemporaries wrote that the "absolute or pure ego, and the unconditioned reality or immanent noumenon, are synonyms for the deity."[12] This statement expresses the way in which he was generally interpreted by his contemporaries. Fichte's earlier works are somewhat ambiguous on the point, probably because of the character of Fichte's interests at the time. In the essays which deal explicitly with his belief in God, he declares that God is identical with the moral order. This statement must not be taken to mean that there is a separate object to be called God; Fichte says explicitly that "I myself and my necessary destiny are the supersensible realm." But he apparently does believe that there is some sense in which moral acts achieve their ends even when they do not seem to accomplish any improvement in this world. The meaning of the world is such that moral action is effective and appropriate in it. I cite one of his most striking statements, which must perhaps be regarded as somewhat metaphorical:

It is a mistake to say that it is doubtful whether there is a God. It is not at all a matter of doubt, but the most certain thing in the world—yea, the foundation of every other certainty, the only absolutely valid objective fact—that there is a moral world order, that every rational individual is assigned his definite place in this order, and that his labor is counted on; that each one's fate, in so far as it is not determined by his own conduct, is a result of this plan; that, except in accordance with it, no hair falls from anyone's head, nor, in its own sphere of activity, any sparrow from a roof; that every truly good deed succeeds and every evil deed surely miscarries; and that all things work for the best of them who love the good.[13]

Such was the philosophical system which appeared at the time immediately succeeding Schleiermacher's attempt to systematize the results of Spinoza, Leibniz, and Kant. There is no doubt that this system—in conjunction with the work of Schelling, and its interpretation by the romanticists—exercised a considerable influence on Schleiermacher's thought; the real question concerns only the extent of that influence, a problem doubly hard because there is no paper extant in which Schleiermacher explicitly distinguishes his views from those of Fichte. And to the minds of some writers there is considerable doubt respecting Schleiermacher's understanding of the real purport of Fichte's argument. Medicus says generally of the romanticists that "one cannot really say of a single one of them that he had an accurate conception of Fichte's meaning," and of Schleiermacher in particular, that "the Wissenschaftslehre had made a great impression on him. He had not understood much of it—but he had the definite impression that there were very remarkable things in the book; even more remarkable than in the Critique of Pure Reason."[14]

At this stage of our discussion it will perhaps be most profitable simply to indicate briefly some points at which Schleiermacher's thought is related through agreement or disagreement to that of Fichte.

The most important problem for an understanding of his theory of knowledge is this: Did he accept Fichte's elaboration of Kant into idealism; did he give up the idea that there is any realm of objects, unknown as they are in themselves, which nevertheless *appear* in a way determined by the necessary nature of an object of experience? Or again, we have seen that he identified Kant's noumenal realm— the condition of experience—with Spinoza's infinite substance, and said nothing can be known of it except that it can "appear" in the form of our perception. Is it possible that Schleiermacher ever identified this concept of the Infinite with the Absolute of Fichte? Did he ever regard this infinite activity as the ground of the possibility of experience? Or if he did so, in what sense did he do so, and in how far was his understanding of Fichte modified by his study of the writings of Schelling? These problems which are perhaps the most interesting in the whole puzzle connected with Schleiermacher's thought, can be given, to my mind, only a partially satisfactory answer.

It is possible to speak with more assurance upon several of Schleiermacher's ultimate disagreements with Fichte. First, we must recall that Schleiermacher was a determinist—although it is true that it is possible that this fact forms no contrast to Fichte, who, so far at least as the willing self of experience is concerned, may also have been a determinist. At any rate, Schleiermacher was consciously a determinist; Fichte thought his system allowed room for freedom, in a sense requisite for according the greatest significance to moral experience. Second, although Schleiermacher agreed with respect to the importance of moral experience for an understanding of the world, he did not believe that freedom is the ideal which is the source of all moral obligation. We shall find that Schleiermacher's values or ideals included individuality and harmony, which as he understood them were of great worth, indeed *the* point of individuated existence. Third, although Schleiermacher went so far as to say that moral experience by itself is sufficient to establish idealism (in some sense), he apparently did not believe that the "meaning" or "purpose" of the world is its furnishing an arena for moral endeavor. For Fichte, life is primarily a succession of moral struggles, attempts by mind to overcome the limitation of its own free activity, to become once more the infinitely active self (free from all determination by sense desire) that in some sense it truly is. Religion, according to Fichte, is just the recognition of this moral order, faith in it, taking one's place in it. To

Schleiermacher's mind, however, (as indeed must be the case with a determinist), the world could not have an exclusively moral meaning. For him, the emphasis came to be not upon the striving but upon contemplation of the perfection, the harmony, the infinitely individuated form of God. So he said his views have "displaced modern philosophy from ethics into religion,"[15] a statement which is his own characterization of the relation of his philosophical work to that of Fichte.

Finally, Schleiermacher, along with other members of the romantic circle, probably felt that Fichte's treatment of nature was inadequate. Nature, according to the *Wissenschaftslehre*, is only mind's limitation of itself. "The world is nothing but an intuition . . . of our own internal action, as bare intelligence, inside of incomprehensible limits. . . . Its significance is thy place in the moral order of things."[16] This nature, moreover, is really only the nature of Newtonian physics. It is the concretion of the categories, of the laws of physics. Its "reality" (apart from its service as a sphere for duty) is the mathematical relations of the laws of physics. Medicus says of it:

Nature is no real being. Its life is no free, creative self-realization, but only a dead unrolling of an eternally self-identical law-abidingness. It may be that under the working of these laws the constellations of the phenomena are fully changed: the being of nature remains the same, bound in a similar way. There is no creative principle in it. The only creative principle is freedom.[17]

Schleiermacher objected to this belief that nature simply obeys the laws of physics. We shall see that he believed that nature is rather a self-organizing whole; its laws are not simply the laws of mechanics.* In fact, the criticism he made was much in the spirit of such modern movements as holism, emergent evolution, and the philosophy of organism.

Schleiermacher's attitude to the transcendental philosophy, however, cannot be understood until something has been said of Schelling and the romanticists.†

* A statement in his letters seems inconsistent with this: *Briefe*, vol. I, p. 239. The passage is quoted below, p. 131.

† Hegel made the following comment on the *Discourses on Religion*: "If productions like the *Discourses on Religion* do not immediately concern speculation, they and their reception, and especially the dignity which poetry and art . . .

2. SCHELLING'S PHILOSOPHY OF NATURE

The works of Schelling which first attracted general notice branded him as a disciple of Fichte. His ideas in these works are so closely similar, in fact, that they have been said to display little originality. But seven years (during which time Schelling published an enormous amount of material) changed this relation into its opposite. Fichte and Schelling drew steadily further apart, and around 1802 their friendship was terminated by bitter quarrels and recriminations.

The story of the gradual birth of Schelling's independent system is a long and complicated one which cannot be entered into here. Some writers think that Schelling and Fichte were mistaken in thinking that there was ever a really fundamental agreement between them, that the germs of Schelling's rebellion lay implanted in his very first publications and were possibly the result of differences in temperament and interest. Schelling had considerable interest in and detailed knowledge of the natural sciences (without possessing the critical reserve of the modern scientist), whereas he was in less congenial territory in dealing with the ethical questions so dear to Fichte. More and more, also, he came under the influence of the romanticists, from whom he caught the reverence for art displayed in what has sometimes been called his "aesthetic idealism." In 1795 he wrote to Hegel that he considered his version of transcendental idealism to be intimately related to the philosophy of Spinoza—a fact which is reminiscent of Schleiermacher's development.[18]

Schelling began with the belief that Fichte's philosophy was the consistent explication of the discoveries of Kant. Like Fichte, he thought that the Critical Philosophy really implied a repudiation of things-in-themselves as causes of sense experience. The givenness of sense experience which is the basis for belief in things-in-themselves is really a determinate state of consciousness and must be accounted for by appeal to the nature of consciousness itself and not to any alien

---

begin to get, nevertheless point to the need of a philosophy, by which nature is reconciled from the maltreatment she suffers from the Kantian and Fichtean systems, and Reason itself is put into agreement with nature—not in an agreement where she renounces herself or becomes an empty imitator of nature, but an agreement in that she forms herself into nature out of her inner strength." *Differenz usw.*, Lasson ed., pp. 6-7; *Werke*, vol. I, p. 165.

realm. The only reality is mind. It is infinite activity without substantial basis. It is pure act. This infinite "activity" must limit itself
if the empirical world of experience is to be possible, and it is as a
result of this limitation that experience is what it is.

The first really original work done by Schelling was in an extension
of Fichte's deductions into the realm of nature and science. Fichte's
work was intended to deal with and deduce primarily only the categories or a priori knowledge presupposed by scientific activity and the
logical basis of moral conduct. Neither he nor Schelling ever attempted to deduce the necessity of the particular nature or arrangement of events. But in between the deduction of the pure categories
and the deduction of the particular thusness of nature are the general
laws of science (such as Newton's laws, the inverse square laws of
gravitational attraction and others), the general processes, and the
"elements" of nature. These had not been touched by Fichte; they
presented an inviting field for activity to Schelling. He set about to
deduce their necessity.

The situation of science in the closing years of the eighteenth century was such as to encourage his undertaking. These years were a
time of great advances in research, the result of which was the suggestion of a much closer unity among the objects of scientific investigation than had previously been assumed. The idea of the reduction
of the phenomena of nature to a few fundamental principles was more
clearly envisaged. Galvani and Volta were opening up the field of elec-
trodynamics. In 1774 Priestley had discovered oxygen and there followed discovery of the fact that the atmosphere contains oxygen and
that the chemical combination of it with other substances is what
occurs in combustion, a phenomenon which had previously required
a special substance called phlogiston. It was found that water was composed of oxygen and hydrogen and could be synthesized from these
gases. New and suggestive geological theories were elaborated. Cuvier
founded the science of comparative anatomy. Kielmayer (a teacher
of Cuvier) attempted to demonstrate laws relating functions of sensi-
tivity and reproduction in organisms, and to connect contiguity in the
series of organic beings with successiveness of periods in the individual.[19] These discoveries encouraged hope for the realization of a more

unified system of the sciences than had previously been thought feasible.

In attempting to extend the system of transcendental idealism to the realm of natural science, Schelling was only following in the footsteps of Kant (in the *Metaphysische Anfangsgründe der Naturwissenschaft*, 1786). But he was more confident and less critical. It is possible, said he, for the philosopher to deduce the general laws of nature and thus to settle problems which inductive investigation leaves doubtful.[20] He wrote:

> After the blind and senseless kind of scientific procedure which has prevailed since the perversion of philosophy by Bacon and of physics by Boyle and Newton. . . . [his philosophy of nature] begins a higher knowledge of nature. Whoever has ascended to its level can scarcely avoid admitting that it opens the way to a solution, with certainty and necessity, of apparently insoluble problems of present day investigation.[21]

Schelling proposed to settle in this way, for example, the dispute concerning the particle and the undulatory theories of light.[22]

This extension of Fichte's idealistic deductions to the laws of nature (which Schelling called "only the carrying through of the attempt to exhibit the doctrine of ideas and of the identity of nature with the realm of ideas"[23]) shortly took a turn, however, which made it very difficult to reconcile with Fichte's idealism, and the development of which eventually led to the break between the two men. For Schelling's interpretation treated inorganic nature as the precondition of the occurrence of consciousness, as an "organic" teleological whole, of which consciousness is the "end." In the later works of this period, Schelling showed how there are several stages in nature, from matter through higher and higher forms of organization up to self-consciousness. These stages he regarded as stages of the self-development of the absolute ego—its unconscious acts prior to the rise of consciousness. Now clearly this manner of regarding the world of nature as something in some sense prior to human consciousness worked in a way opposite to the spirit of Fichte's reasoning in that it seemed to make nature more independent of experience, or unrelated to the subject of knowledge. Nevertheless, as late as 1800, Schelling declared that his philosophy of nature only *seemed* to be contrary to Fichte's idealism and to make nature in a sense independent of experience, because in his works nature was discussed from the level of common sense, from which it *is* something in itself. We shall have to return later to the nature of Schelling's break with Fichte.

Schelling's "solution" of the problems of physics and his discovery of the character of the unconscious acts of mind were accomplished by use of a dialectical procedure similar to Fichte's. Schelling began with the assumption of a duality of opposed forces (the infinite, and the reflective or self-limitative activities of Fichte), and showed that their existence requires a third fact, and so on, until he arrived at the highest stage of reflective self-consciousness.

Nature, then, according to Schelling, is a system of logically related stages of development in which the culminating event of self-consciousness is implicit. He believed that an atomism, for which the world is only a fortuitous combination of independent units, is incompatible with the facts. The systematic character of nature can be understood only if nature is really the self-development of mind. So Schelling's book of 1798 was entitled, *On the World Soul, an Hypothesis of the Higher Physics in Explanation of the Universal Organism*. He compared his view both with Leibniz' monad whose unconscious states eventually develop in accordance with its immanent laws into conscious perceptions; and also with Spinoza's *natura naturans*, the particular "products" of which form the *natura naturata*. Nature is the symbol of the unconscious dialectic taking place in Fichte's transcendental ego, the final "product" of which is conscious experience. Thus nature is the product of mind, but as for Fichte it is the product of mind unconscious and prior to consciousness, so that it is taken by common sense to be something independent of mind and over against it. In this "organic" treatment of nature, Schelling was probably influenced not only by Kant's work, including the *Critique of Judgment*, but by Goethe, with whom he came in contact while at Jena, and perhaps by Bruno.

Conscious volition, according to Schelling, is a continuation of the unconscious production of the ego. The difference is that in volition, the ideal end, what "ought to be," is consciously recognized and contrasted with the present fact. It occurs at a moment of time, whereas the original act of production falls outside time.[24] Like the original act of mind, he argued on behalf of the moral consciousness, moral volition is free, and might be otherwise, even if all previous events were unchanged. Nevertheless, he said (apparently inconsistently), the same teleological activity found in lower nature is working in free volition and accomplishes its end of realizing the moral order. This teleological activity is God, who reveals himself in history and in the free acts of human beings.

Presumably because of the influence of the romanticists, Schelling's *System of Transcendental Idealism* (1800) contained also a philosophy of art in which the artistic creation was appreciated to the extent of being made the very crown of creation. According to his account, the teleological spirit which is working in history is specially active in the artist. In the artistic creation, conscious and unconscious production, freedom and necessity, are to be found in combination. The fundamental nature of the universe is thus made manifest in the work of art, and intelligence whose goal is intuition of itself must find a feeling of satisfaction in contemplation of it. Thus the artistic genius, under the compulsion of his mission which is manifested in his consciousness as a feeling of "longing," is the special channel by which the transcendental ego comes to consciousness by intuiting itself; the artist brings the whole man to that level to which the intellectual intuition of the philosopher brings only a fragment of the mind.

The philosophy of Schelling up to 1800, in so far as it differed from that of Fichte, may be summarized as follows: First, it extended the dialectical procedure of Fichte to the realm of the general laws of nature. Second, there was a tendency—which came to maturity about 1802—to make nature independent of knowledge, and to think of nature as the symbol of the unconscious dialectic occurring in the absolute ego. In other words, Schelling gradually gave up the Fichtean idealism, which he regarded as subjective, for ontological idealism. For the former, he said, the ego is everything; while for the latter everything is ego. Thus, in later years Schelling did not say that only experience is real. He thought that everything which is real is pervaded with the logical system which must characterize whatever is an object of scientific knowledge. Third, he regarded nature as an organic system whose "end" is self-consciousness, and whose detailed nature can be investigated by dialectical thought, which reproduces in consciousness what the ego unconsciously produced as nature. Fourth, he thought that Fate or Destiny is working in moral conduct and in aesthetic creation, which last is the crowning stage of the universe, where the ego becomes conscious of the unity of conscious and unconscious production—sees itself everywhere in nature.

Friedrich Schlegel said of Schelling that his philosophy and that of Schleiermacher were as much alike as the characters of the two men were different. Although, curiously enough, Schleiermacher seldom spoke highly of Schelling, for a long period of time Schelling's work had a very considerable influence upon him. In almost all of the respects in which Schleiermacher differed from Fichte, Schelling was like Schleiermacher, at least in substance.

3. ROMANTICISM

Perhaps the most superficially striking aspect of the writings of the romanticist circle in Germany is their attitude toward life and the world—particularly the joyful at-one-ness which they felt with the universe. Man and the world are not opposed; man is not fallen but is the crown of the universe, the highest production of spirit in a world of which mind is the essence, a world which will yield its secrets to its own kind—the human mind—if they are searched for. Right conduct was not an ideal realizable only by the assistance of God, but was viewed as the free expression of the spiritual nature of man. The best in man, said Schleiermacher, comes naturally and without a struggle; it is the silent work of spirit. The finer spirits are "a more immediate image of the eternal."[25]

I believed I had deep insight into the secrets of nature [wrote Friedrich Schlegel]. I felt that everything lives eternally, and that even death is friendly, and only an illusion. . . . Love is not simply the quiet longing for the Infinite; it is also the holy enjoyment of a beautiful present.[26]

This reconciliation with the universe wrought a new enthusiasm which was the source of the romanticists' intellectual enterprise. "The root of Romanticism," writes Kircher, "is the idealism of humanity, belief in the power of soul whose breath is creative love, faith in the inward God, in the eternal goodness of the inward being."[27] "The infinity of the human soul," Schlegel wrote, "the divinity of all natural things, and the humanity of the gods, remain the great eternal theme of all these variations."[28]

This attitude toward the world, while it has affinities with Hamann, Herder, Jacobi, Goethe, and especially (on its philosophical side) with the philosopher Hemsterhuis,[29] seems to depend for its basic logical support upon the transcendental idealists whose work we have just outlined. The romanticists were not purely artists; as Walzel has pointed out, philosophical problems are always in the background, coloring their aesthetic ideas and creations.[30] In fact, Walzel has remarked that romanticism is "unthinkable without Kant, although the antithesis to Kant gives the movement its proper claim to existence."[31]

The romantic reconciliation of man with nature and God, and of reason with the sensuous, and their confidence in the "divinity" of human nature, seem to be the direct antithesis to the vigorous moralism of Kant and Fichte. And it is true that action, freedom from determination by sense desire, and conduct in accordance with moral law seem to have been ideas which awakened little response in these men. Nevertheless, so soon as it was thought that the whole universe is the creation of mind, that nature is an organism in whose essence is implicit its coming to consciousness in human beings (as the idealists believed), it was perhaps inevitable that the artistic temperament should discover perfect harmony in nature—since after all the idealists had brought a dualism into nature at the behest of only the moral consciousness, which did not speak to the romanticists in the same vigorous terms. In this sense, the romantic feeling of harmony between man, nature, and God, seems to be an outcome of the speculations of the transcendental idealists.

Although, as has been suggested, one may doubt whether any of the romanticists understood everything in the works of the transcendental philosophers, they were at least conscious of a great debt. So Friedrich Schlegel wrote that the poet's philosophy cannot be one

which changes reality into appearance, or refrains from all distinctions, or limits the flight into the supersensible, or pieces mankind together out of external objects. Thus it can be neither eudaemonism, nor fatalism, nor idealism, nor scepticism, nor materialism, nor empiricism. What does the poet have left? The creative philosophy, which begins with freedom and faith in it, and then shows how the human spirit stamps its law on everything, and how the world is its work of art.[82] [This philosophy, he thought, had been actualized by Fichte.] This [the Fichtean] philosophy [wrote Schlegel] is a philosophy on the material of the Kantian philosophy. Fichte does not talk much of form, because he is master of it. But if the essence of the critical method is that it unifies internally the theory of the determining faculty and the system of the determined results in mind, as fact and thought in preestablished harmony, then he may be a second power of Kant even in form . . . The new expositions of the *Wissenschaftslehre* are always both philosophy and philosophy of philosophy.[83] [He summarized the view of the romanticists in the following words:] The French Revolution, Fichte's *Wissenschaftslehre*, and Goethe's *Wilhelm Meister* are the great tendencies of our age. And whoever takes offence at this grouping . . . has not attained the lofty and far-seeing standpoint of the history of humanity.[84]

The belief that the universe is an organism has been called the key to an understanding of the romantic movement.[85] Wilhelm Schlegel wrote:

All of nature is organized . . . It is intelligence like ourselves—this we feel and understand clearly through speculative thought . . . [Nature is] not a mass of products, but something which actively produces . . . Hence there is no longer an objection to the principle that art should imitate nature. That is, it should, like nature, be independently creative, organized and organizing, and produce living works . . .[86]

Here the romanticists drew on their literary forebears for an idea for which they found substantiation in the speculations of the idealists and particularly of Schelling.

Many other details of the romantic *Weltanschauung* seem to be dependent on transcendental idealism and particularly upon Fichte's philosophy. Their joyful embrace of contradiction, their desire to be everything at once, their profession of longing for the Absolute, which longing they satisfied in their appreciation of human love, friendship, art, and religion, their concept of irony—all these ideas had a more or less close connection with some feature of transcendental idealism. The creative transcendental ego, infinite in its ultimate nature, was for Fichte the ideal of conduct, the object of human longing. This same longing for the Absolute the romanticists found in their mystical interpretation of the longing for love; in love, art, and religion (unlike Fichte) they thought this longing capable of satisfaction, the Infinite accessible in some sense. The free activity of this ego is reflected in the romanticist's glorying in contradictions, his distinction of the creative self from the finite and imperfect artistic creation, his esteem for the subjective element in art, its reflecting the mind of its author.

The members of the circle undoubtedly thought that in some respects they were actually extending and bringing to fruition tendencies implicit in transcendental philosophy. For example, they carried the uncritical scientific speculation of Schelling to a point where even he must have been astounded. Schelling had shown them that dialectical thought can probe into the recesses of nature and solve scientific problems; nature is an organism in which consciousness is implicit and to which thought (in "intellectual intuition") can attain. So Novalis and Friedrich Schlegel

not only carry over mental qualities to nature, but discern natural processes of chemical and electrical nature in mental processes . . . Novalis speaks not only of the tolerance and the cosmopolitanism of the flowers; but he calls thinking a movement of the muscles, wit is for him mental electricity; logic corresponds to meteorology . . . And just as he with particular fondness finds an analogy to the relation of the sexes, in nature, so conversely he affirms this thesis: "Woman is our oxygen."[37]

Encouraged by a wave of interest in hypnotism, Novalis related the hypnotic trance to the philosophers' "intellectual intuition," decided that philosophy could not get on without mystical ecstasy, in which the secrets of nature are laid bare for the poet's inspection. Plotinus and Jakob Boehme he found (like many of the other romanticists) to be spiritual companions, pioneers in the higher physics. Since the productive imagination of transcendental mind is the source of nature, so the dwelling place of imagination—the artist—is specially fitted to be a scientist. "Poetry is the absolutely real. This is the essence of my philosophy. The more poetic, the more true."[38] The empirical scientist is not the one who will understand nature; the secrets of the Absolute are opened first to the mystic and the artist.

As early as 1795, Friedrich Schlegel seems to have had in mind a scientific project which is of interest to us because of its possible connection with the later work of Schleiermacher. (It was by no means a new idea, having been considered, for example, in the writings of

Herder.) Schlegel was impressed with the desirability of a history of
literature, not merely in the sense of a catalogue of works, dates, and
sources, but in the sense of a systematic study of the interconnection
of literary production with the whole organism of civic life—the form
of government, the codes of morals, and so on.[39] The execution of
this project, he thought, presupposed the possession of the principles
of the philosophy of history and the philosophy of art and hence
would be a difficult one. But if such an account of the organic development of Greek literature were supplied, he believed, the way would
be open for an understanding of the development of literature in general—for he took the Greek to be the ideal of what is beautiful. In
fact, it would supply the key to a general history of culture. This historical task Schlegel connected with the philosophical ideas of the
transcendental idealists, once more showing his dependence on Fichte
(whose emphasis on the active ego as the ultimately real also brought
Schlegel to an appreciation of the "subjective" in art, and thus caused
him to reverse his standards of literary criticism). He wished to relate
his history of Greek literature to Fichte, because artistic creation, just
like knowing or acting, must be the product of a transcendental act of
mind. (This word "transcendental" he uses rather loosely, sometimes
meaning by it apparently no more than that the matter is related to
the relation of the ideal and the real.)[40] Mere psychology, he urged,
is not a science adequate for an understanding of literary production.

The chief error of sophistic aesthetics [he wrote] is to regard beauty
simply as a given object, a psychological phenomenon . . . [Actually] it
is one of the primary modes of action of the human mind—not merely a
necessary fiction, but also a fact, viz., an eternal transcendental one.[41]
[Thus] a philosophy of poetry in general would begin with the independence of beauty, with the proposition that beauty is and should be
separate from truth and morality, and that it has equal rights with them—
which, for anyone who can grasp it at all, is a direct consequence of the
proposition that the ego is identical with itself.[42]

In fact, Schlegel thought transcendental philosophy to be so important for his project that he ventured the hope that the various forms
of literary art might be *deduced* in a way analogous to the deduction
of the categories of objective thought.[43] (The transcendental philosophy, incidentally, is also according to him not to be too sharply sepa-

rated from history; it is not really complete until the *Wissenschafts-liebe* has been developed historically.) His conclusion seems to be that the products of mind in history are not purely contingent events; they are to be understood only in connection with their "*a priori*"—the acts of transcendental mind to which they are related. And since "the true being of human life consists in wholeness, completeness, the free activity of all powers,"[44] it would seem that the ideal of culture is realized only in the harmony of the various forms of transcendental activity.

It is perhaps incautious to attempt to discern Schlegel's exact meaning in this matter, but we may at least be sure that he thought a systematic study of the history of literature would reveal the norms of literary criticism, and that both history and these norms are to be related to and understood only in connection with the transcendental activity of mind, of Fichte's philosophy.

Another idea accented by the romanticists and important for our understanding of Schleiermacher came not from their philosophical contemporaries but from literary circles. This is the idea of individuality which had been increasingly emphasized by the artistic spirits of Germany. Schiller expounds it in his poems on *Schöne Individualität* and *Die Mannigfaltigkeit*. The most complete expression of it was, however, in the first part of *Wilhelm Meister*, where Goethe, according to the understanding of the romanticists, urged that the ideal of life is not to be and do everything but to cultivate one's individuality. This ideal was applied in the friendships of the romanticists, perhaps most enthusiastically by Schleiermacher. This did not mean that their friendships were sentimental and emotional, but rather the very opposite. The ideal of friendship became an appreciation of how the ideal of human nature is individuated in the personality of the friend, a perception of what the peculiar nature of everyone is in relation to all others, an understanding of how the individuality of a friend supplements one's own, to create a whole and rounded manifestation of the full nature of mind. This became also the ideal of love. Personal intercourse was to be the touching of all the chords of the other person's mind, the discovery of its hidden recesses. To do so without paining him is a sign of culture.[45]

The highest moment is when two friends see their own holiest nature . . . in the soul of the other, and feel their limitations only through the supplementation of the other. It is the intellectual intuition of friendship.[46] [So Schleiermacher spoke of the value of love for one] with whom, through exchange of thoughts and perceptions, he could form a union for the sake of reciprocal cultivation and an exalted consciousness.* His individual being and its relation to the Universe [wrote Schleiermacher] are what I seek; and to the degree to which I find and understand this, I can have love for him.[47]

Schleiermacher summarized his view in two letters to Henriette Herz:

I take human nature to be a necessary stage of life, and . . . considered thus, no one is insignificant, who has anything individual, which displays human nature from a peculiar angle.[48] [This individuality] is to progress in unbroken development . . . Are you not as much an individual as anyone? Have you not formed for yourself your own style of life? Are not many capacities fused in you in an individual way? Your loyalty to your calling, your love, your scientific mind, your sense for the world, . . . your practical talent . . .[49]

(We have already noticed that Schleiermacher had a similar notion in his suggestion that there is value in moral differences, for which he may have been indebted to Leibniz. The view he found among his romanticist friends was not new to him.[50])

Schleiermacher's nature was so receptive to the enthusiastic life of the friends in Berlin, their ideals of friendship and culture, of the discovery and development of individuality, that in the matter of this idea of individuality, he became the most inspired prophet of all. From his youth he had been gifted with extraordinary powers of self-analysis as well as a happy intuition of the nature of others. This peculiarly fitted him to apply the new ideas to friendship. His diary at this time was filled almost exclusively with remarks upon the art of living of which the paper, *Versuch einer Theorie des geselligen Betragens*[51] (published anonymously and only recently identified as Schleiermacher's) was the fruit. Schleiermacher became known among his friends as a virtuoso in friendship. Schlegel wrote to him: "What is so inexhaustibly fruitful in you, for me, is that you exist. To

* *Monologen*, edn. 1, p. 75. Cf. *Wilhelm Meister's Lehrjahre*, Bk. 8, ch. 5: "Only all men make up humanity, and only all forms, taken together, the world."

me, you are . . . for humanity what Fichte and Goethe are for philosophy and literature."[52]

This ideal of friendship and the practice of it in their little circle was doubly important for Schleiermacher. First, this evaluation of individuality enabled him to see some light on the problem of the meaning of individual finite existence, which problem had troubled him in the essay on Spinoza. Second, the practice of these ideals apparently filled his life with something for which it had been starving. To us it may seem artificial but there is little doubt that for Schleiermacher this outlook and its practice were embedded in emotional meaning supplied by his remarkably affectionate nature. He once wrote to Henriette Herz: "I cannot thrive in solitude. . . . I stretch all my roots and leaves in search of affection. It is necessary for me to feel myself in immediate contact with it, and when I am unable to drink in full draughts of it, I at once dry up and wither."[53]

Some writers have been inclined to disparage the amount of influence which romanticism in general and especially Friedrich Schlegel had upon Schleiermacher. It may seem superfluous to adduce evidence on this point in addition to the similarities in Schleiermacher's ideas and the evidence suggestive of their origin to be elaborated in later chapters. But it may be useful to the reader to bear several facts in mind. Although Schlegel's *Lucinde* was and is still thought by some writers to be an indecent book whose author cannot really have been close to a man with Schleiermacher's moral sensitiveness, one must note that Schleiermacher approved of the book on the whole, saying that it was the first attempt to give the sensual side its proper place in love.[54] He disagreed with the book on details, but, as Haym says, "These serve, on the whole, only to make the agreement on essential points more striking."[55] Moreover, Schleiermacher wrote of Schlegel:

> I love no one on account of his mind. Schelling and Goethe are two great minds. Yet I shall never be tempted to love them . . . But Schlegel is of a lofty moral nature, a man who carries the whole world lovingly in his heart . . . He is not at all unrighteous in spirit, even if he is, occasionally, according to the letter.[56]

Schleiermacher was not unaware of faults in Schlegel's character, but he wrote to his sister that he could reveal his philosophical views to Schlegel because he was convinced of his morality. Even if there was between them a "complete difference in ways of feeling,"[57] Schlegel's presence inspired him in his work.[58] In matters of philosophy, he said, they were in close agreement. What views he had in common with Novalis he also had in common with Schlegel.[59] His characterization of their friendship was: "Great similarity in the results of our thought, in view of science and history; both of us striving for the highest, thereby a brotherly union, participation in each other's work, no secret in life, relations, or actions."[60]

Schleiermacher was one of the most enthusiastic participants in the romanticists' literary campaign. One cannot say that the *Discourses* and *Soliloquies* are simply applications of romantic views to religion and ethics, but they represent those views both in content and form. Even more strikingly is this true of the *Confidential Letters on Schlegel's Lucinde*, which was more an independent essay on love than a commentary on Schlegel's work. Schleiermacher himself, although a thoroughly upright man, was no great respecter of conventions and his treatment of the relation of the sensual to the spiritual must have been somewhat shocking to his contemporaries. Hegel never forgot this aspect of Schleiermacher's "subjectivity," that he did not ascribe sufficient importance to objective moral conventions.[61] Schleiermacher's contributions to the *Athenaeum* breathe the romantic spirit. He believes in "infinite humanity," that the power of will and culture bring one closer to the Infinite. In the *Athenaeum's* attacks on the conservatism of the age, Schleiermacher was more eager to go ahead than the rest. He wrote to A. W. Schlegel,

I am entirely of your opinion that there must be rudenesses in the next issue. Only, in order to make it possible, don't limit the battle ground too much. Be generous. Leave Iffland to Tieck, Herder to Bernhardi, and Schiller to your brother, and I guarantee you will get the divinest devilments.[62]

Schlegel felt this unwise, and in a letter of later date Schleiermacher acceded with regret. He was sorry that Schelling's *Heinz Widerporst* was suppressed. Schleiermacher's reviews in the *Athenaeum* were the most annihilating of all. Goethe thought he belonged to the peak of the revolutionary party. Schlegel wrote to him that "the judgment on [Kant's] *Anthropologie* is, as I must boast, held by a certain person to be one of the most atrocious things in the *Athenaeum*."[63]

Five of the romantic ideas which we have mentioned are especially important to keep in mind in examining the *Weltanschauung* of Schleiermacher. First, there is the temper of the movement, the attitude toward the world in general, the conviction that man is by nature good, that the world is beautiful and that man is an intrinsic part of its beauty. This attitude, superficially so antagonistic to transcendental idealism, is really intimately connected with the conclusions of that philosophy. Second, there is the belief that the world is an organism—and the consequent emphasis upon that idea in ethics. This important tenet, coming from Goethe and Schelling's philosophy of nature, was undoubtedly in part the source of the romantic attitude toward the world. Third, the high evaluation of individuality, the belief that this is sufficiently important to have something to do with the fundamental nature of things (and it must be recalled that they believed, along with Schelling, that the universe is a work of art), was an aspect of the romantic creed which Schleiermacher was specially interested in developing. Fourth, Friedrich Schlegel's suggestion that art and its history must be considered along with knowing and acting as necessary for an understanding of the nature of mind is an idea which very likely had something to do with Schleiermacher's somewhat similar treatment of religion and its history. And finally, one must take into account the uncritical effusions of Novalis and his friends, who believed that poetic insight and hypnotic and mystical ecstasy are avenues of acquaintance with the nature of the Absolute. And if this idea finally turns out not to mean what Schleiermacher meant by "religious intuition," it must at least be taken into account in an understanding of what Schleiermacher did mean.

CHAPTER IV

ROMANTICISM AND THE UNITY OF THE UNIVERSE

The first and one of the most important of Schleiermacher's publications, the *Discourses on Religion*, came off the press in 1799, and was followed by the *Soliloquies* in 1800. It is symptomatic of their character that the former book was written partly to fulfill a promise to publish something, made to his romanticist friends at a birthday celebration for him in 1797. Most of it was sent to Schlegel and others for criticism before it went to the printer. Both books bear internal marks of their romantic origin. Written in an artificial style without regard for clarity or simplicity, and savoring of the romantic "subjectivism" which in parts made them almost a history of Schleiermacher's emotions, they did not pretend to be rigorous philosophical works. They were probably particularly intended for consumption by Schleiermacher's own circle of sympathetic acquaintances.

1. Realism and the "Universe"

The central conception of Schleiermacher's whole system is his idea of the "universe." Somewhat paradoxically, however, although typical of the way in which Schleiermacher leaves many subjects not completely elaborated in these books, the reader is allowed to remain in doubt about the sense in which the universe may be thought to be real independently of percipient minds. Schleiermacher does not make it clear whether he believes that physical objects like stars and tables exist in their own right or only through some relation to mind which would make them dependent upon experience.

I am nevertheless convinced that the preponderance of the evidence is in favor of classifying Schleiermacher, in modern terminology, as a dualistic or critical realist in epistemology; and I shall try to lay out the evidence for this view in some detail. But his works are ambiguous—a fact which should perhaps evoke no surprise because the writings of Schelling too (at this time) were so ambiguous on this point that it was not clearly evident whether or not he was in agreement with Fichte. Schelling often speaks of the external world as real, prior to experience; but at the same time he says that this statement is made only from the common-sense level, and that from the level of philosophy this external world is seen to be only a limitation of the infinite activity of mind. So with Schleiermacher. One is not absolutely sure whether the universe exists independently of experience, or whether from the philosopher's point of view it is only a product of mind.

If only it were possible to find some statement which clearly makes out Schleiermacher's attitude toward Fichte, the problem could be definitely solved. But unfortunately all his remarks about epistemology are brought in only as illustrations to help in understanding something else, so that one cannot be sure how much weight he would have laid on them. What he says explicitly about Fichte seems to be self-contradictory.

In 1800, Schleiermacher wrote that he would never become an enthusiastic disciple of Fichte, but his disappointing reason was that "it has never occurred to me to come to religion by way of a formal law"[1]—a statement which is of no value for the question in hand. But in contrast, in the same letter he says that he and others who are usually thought to be followers of Fichte are really closer to Jacobi in spirit; and the faint suggestion is that the letter of his philosophy is closer to Fichte. Again, he writes regarding someone who had criticized his Soliloquies that the critic had found it "highly damning" that he had spoken of

idealism in other than the traditional idealistic terminology, but rather, as he calls it, in a realistic language, because people then have something before them, which they think they understand, without really grasping it. But tell me, whether there is any other way of making oneself intelligible except by expressing the same thought in formulae which are more familiar. I hold that for the great philosophical art, and wish it were true that I had really applied it.[2] [This statement must be compared with another in which he says that his Soliloquies are] an attempt to carry over into life the philosophical point of view, as the Idealists call it, and to exhibit the character which, according to my idea, corresponds to this philosophy.[3]

These last statements would be very important if one could be sure that Schleiermacher meant by "idealism" specifically the transcendental idealism of Fichte, an interpretation which certainly seems natural. A further remark tends to confirm such an interpretation. Describing a conversation with Fichte, he writes that the afternoon dragged because "I have nothing to find fault with in his philosophy, and admiration is not a subject of conversation . . . Fichte is the greatest master of dialectic I know."[4] This sounds very much like approval of Fichte.

Some writers have found in the last mentioned letter a remark which they believe to be an objection to Fichte's idealism, but the contention is not well established. Schleiermacher says:

Philosophy and life are with him quite separate. His natural way of thinking is nothing unusual, and as long as he is on the ordinary stand-point, he is lacking in everything which could make him an interesting object for me. I had thought of speaking to him about his system, and showing him my opinion that he is wrong in separating the ordinary from the philosophical point of view. But I soon drew in this sail, when I saw how embedded he is in the natural way of thinking . . . He is not instructive; he does not seem to have detailed information in the other sciences . . . but only general ideas.

There are difficulties in the interpretation of this passage. But it is not unreasonable to believe that the "philosophical point of view" referred to is that of transcendental philosophy, according to which nature is not real in its own right but only in relation to mind, and according to which morality, which the common-sense man knows only as the demand of his conscience, can be interpreted in a more sophisticated way in the light of the ideally infinite activity of mind. Now, Schleiermacher's objection to Fichte does not seem to be an objection to the *taking* of the "philosophical point of view"; it is an objection to his failure to *carry it over into life*, to do what Schleiermacher himself claimed to have done in the *Soliloquies*. Far from advocating exclusive adherence to the "ordinary" point of view, he says in the *Discourses* that this is exactly what one must get away from if one is to understand religion; and he appeals to the "cultured despisers" of it, because they are the only ones intellectually capable of doing this.[5] What Schleiermacher does object to is that Fichte, being "imbedded in the natural way of thinking," and "lacking detailed knowledge of the sciences" is not the sort of person to whom Schleiermacher's ideas of love, friendship, and marriage would make any appeal.[6] Just as Schelling believed he was interpreting transcendental idealism for physics, Schleiermacher may have thought he was doing so for ethical matters and for religion.

All this evidence suggesting a close relation to Fichte's transcendental idealism has been taken from Schleiermacher's letters. But there is also very strong evidence in his published work, in the fact that there are some passages which sound like Fichte in the books of 1799 and 1800, which he changed and modified when he issued second editions at a time when he clearly did believe that the universe exists independently of experience. I cite some of them.

(1) "Philosophy," he says, "acquaints man with himself not only as creature but as creator too."[7] Of course this sentence is not clearly evidence for idealistic leanings, for if Schleiermacher was a dualistic realist, as I think he was, he could say perfectly well that man is the "creator" of the phenomenal world, that the world of phenomenal objects is the work of the "imagination" just as dreams are, except that real external objects function more intimately as a part cause of that production and are known through it.

(2) "You will know that imagination is the highest and most original part of man, and that outside of it, everything is only reflection upon it; you will know that it is your imagination which creates the world for you."[8] This statement may seem even more pointedly Fichtean, but I submit that it can be interpreted like the former one.

(3) "The birth of everything living in religion is like the first consciousness of man, which withdraws into the darkness of an original and eternal creation, and leaves behind only what it has created."[9] This passage is perhaps not to be taken too literally, but it does seem to suggest idealistic leanings.

(4) "What some people call world, I call man; what they call man, is for me, world. For them, world is always the first, and spirit a little guest upon it, uncertain of its place and power. For me, spirit is the one and only being, for what I recognize as the world, is its most lovely work—its self-created image."[10] This passage is more striking, because it appears in the second edition as follows:

For me, spirit, the inner world, is sharply contrasted with the outer world, the kingdom of stuff and things. Does not mind's unity with body hint at a greater unity with everything corporeal? Do I not grasp the outer world with the strength of my senses? Do I not carry the eternal forms of things in me, and recognize them only as the bright mirror of my inner being?[11]

A comparison of these passages suggests either that Schleiermacher had changed his mind to a realistic view in the second edition or else that he thought he had laid himself open to misunderstanding in the first edition. This latter possibility must not be taken too lightly, for the *Soliloquies* were written in a few weeks, and did not aim at exact philosophical statement. It seems to me, in fact, that, in the light of passages to be cited later, this is what we must conclude about it; the only other alternative is to reject a number of other statements.

(5)

Is there a body without a spirit? Does not the body exist only because and in that mind needs it and is conscious of it? Every feeling which seems to press out of the physical world is really my free action; nothing is its action on me; the effect always passes from me to it. It is not something different from and opposed to me. Therefore, I do not honour it with the name "world," that lofty phrase which implies omnipresence and omnipotence. What I thus honour is only the eternal community of spirits, their influence on each other . . . the sublime harmony of freedom.[12]

Compare this with the second edition:

So the earth is the stage of my free action, and my free action is in every feeling, even in those in which I perceive the kinship of the world and the whole . . . Nothing is simply its action on me. Also there is always influence passing from me to it; and I feel myself limited by it in no way other than by my own body. What I properly contrast with the individual being, what is for me the real world, including omnipresence and omnipotence, that is the eternal community of spirits . . . the lofty harmony of freedom.[13]

Of these two passages from the two editions of the *Soliloquies*, I can only repeat what was said about the previous ones. There is the vague possibility, of course, that at the time of writing the *Soliloquies* Schleiermacher experienced a period of special sympathy for Fichte, but the hypothesis of such a rapid change of mind is not a convincing one. There can be no doubt that Schleiermacher believed that in some sense mind is very important, that man's commerce with friends is somehow more important for the universe as a whole than interaction in the world of inorganic objects. But to claim that he meant more than this seems to me hazardous.

There are many other passages in which Schleiermacher seems to advocate a *realistic* position.* We may begin by noting a statement in a letter in which he says that in the *Soliloquies* he has "deduced formally and explicitly neither the idealism nor the real world, which I will still not allow to be taken from me."[14] This statement suggests as a possible avenue of interpretation of some of the foregoing references to his idealism, that he meant by "idealism" a kind of position which is compatible with the independent reality of the physical world.

But there is evidence which more explicitly requires that Schleiermacher be classified as a dualistic realist.

All intuition [Schleiermacher writes] starts from the influence of what is intuited upon the person intuiting, from an *original* and *independent* [my italics] action of the former, which is then received, synthesized, and comprehended [*aufgenommen, zusammengefasst, und begriffen*] by the latter in conformity with his nature. If rays of light did not—and this is no arrangement of yours—touch your [sense] organs, if the very small parts of bodies did not affect the tips of your finger mechanically or chemically, if the pressure of inertia did not reveal resistance and limitation to your powers, you would not intuit or sense anything; and what you intuit and sense is not the nature of the things, but their action on you. What you know or believe about them lies beyond the sphere of intuition.[15]

This appears to mean that there are objects independent of perception, that they are in a causal relation to an event which is the sensing of sense data, and that the sense data (or better, perceptual world) are in some respects different from these objects (since the effect is synthesized "in conformity with your nature"). It is important to notice that he does not deny that knowledge of these independent objects is possible, since he says only that if there is such knowledge it does not lie within the bounds of pure intuition.

Consistently with this he says, "Your organs mediate the connection between the object and you; [an] affection [of them] reveals to

* Most of this evidence was first pointed out by Süskind, *Der Einfluss Schellings.*

you its being."[16] In comparing sense perception with intuition of the universe, he says that the "appearance" of the universe "is embraced not as a shadow, but as the holy being itself." If he means that this is true also of sense perception, I take it that he believes that whereas what is sensed is the effect of the object, it is nevertheless referred to the object, and in perceptual experience actually taken as the external object.

Some writers who believe that Schleiermacher accepted some form of direct realism have emphasized a passage which I should admit does not easily make sense on the view I am taking. This statement is perhaps best discussed now. Schleiermacher writes that there is a "secret moment, which occurs with every sense perception . . . when sense and its object have flown into one another and become one, before they return to their original places—I know how indescribable it is and how quickly it passes."[17] This statement, as I say, does not seem to make sense when one tries to interpret it in terms of the view I believe Schleiermacher held; but this fact is not to my mind a fatal one, for so far as I can see it remains obscure on any interpretation whatever. For if he believed that objects and brain or mental events are spatially separate, it is difficult to imagine what could be meant by their "flowing together." Possibly he believed that there is some sort of noumenal "contact" between the mind and the noumenal object which is responsible for the generation of consciousness, as Kant seems to have held in his doctrine of double affection. But whatever view one takes of his meaning here, the fact remains that the relation between the external object and the brain (or mind) is prior to and a condition of consciousness, and does not itself get into consciousness, at least to the minds of most philosophers; whereas Schleiermacher in this passage seems to be thinking of an event which can be actually experienced, although it is difficult to introspect and describe.* But the passage is perhaps too brief to repay further suggestions which are incapable of any more elaborate substantiation.

If we provisionally accept the hypothesis that Schleiermacher was

* It is possible that Kant was guilty of a similar inconsistency in saying of the synthesis of imagination that "we are hardly ever conscious of it," B103. Some writers would say that this synthesis is prior to and a condition of consciousness and hence that there can be no consciousness of it.

a dualistic realist (not an agnostic dualist like Kant, for we shall see that he did think knowledge of the independently real objects is possible), we shall find evidence which strongly supports that interpretation.

The most direct criticism of Fichte in his published works is the following:

> And how will it go with that triumph of speculation, the complete and rounded idealism, if religion be not used as a counterpoise, to give it a presentiment of a *higher realism* than that which it so sharply and rightly subordinates to itself? It will negate the Universe while seeming to construct it, it will degrade it to a mere allegory, to an empty shadow image of our own limitation. Sacrifice with me reverently a ringlet to the shades of the holy but repudiated Spinoza! The lofty World-Spirit penetrated him; the Infinite was his alpha and omega, the Universe the one and eternal object of his love. In holy innocence and deep humility he mirrored himself in the eternal world, and observed how he, too, was its lovely reflection.[18]

Two of his affirmations are made clear in this passage. The first is that Schleiermacher believes that what *he* means by the "universe" is real in a way not adequately accounted for in Fichte's philosophy. The second is that some kind of realism (probably materialistic) is even worse than Fichte's system. Spinoza is the object of his praise, I take it, both because he was a realist and because he was a "higher realist," in that the Infinite was the only ultimately real being in his world.

According to Schleiermacher, the real world can be known as it is in itself, not in mere perceptual experience but through scientific and philosophical thought. The physicist can now, he says, "pursue the play of its [the universe's] forces into their most secret recesses, from the inaccessible storehouse of energized matter to the artistic workshops of organic life . . . Mere appearance is fled and the essence won . . ."[19] This is apparently a reference to the speculative physics of Schelling or perhaps of his friends Schlegel and Novalis. "Already," he says, "I see distinguished forms returning from the sanctuary after initiation into these mysteries."

Further evidence for Schleiermacher's realism is supplied by a distinction he draws between aesthetic experience and scientific knowledge of natural laws. The experience of the beautiful or of the

sublime, he says, is of little import to religion because it is only subjective. ("What is it, not in your eye but in and for the Universe?
For this is what you must ask, if it is to be important for your religion."[20]) Knowledge of the causal laws of nature is of significance for
religion, in contrast, because they reveal the "divine unity and eternal
unchangeableness of the world."[21] If Schleiermacher were not a
realist, Süskind has argued, he would not contrast the two in this
way but would probably have pointed out that there is a sense in
which the causal laws of nature are also subjective.

Finally, if Schleiermacher were an idealist like Fichte, why should
he say that the Infinite is indifferent to the destiny of man? The
universe, he says, is far from being simply mankind; its proper nature
rather transcends the being of human experience.

> If mankind itself is something transitory . . . and changes in itself,
> do you not think it impossible that it can be the Universe? Rather, it is
> related to the Universe, as individual persons are related to it; it is only a
> single form of the Universe, a presentation of a single modification of its
> elements . . . some other higher character than his humanity must be
> found in man in order to relate him directly to the Universe . . .[22]

In the light of this passage, it is difficult to believe that Schleiermacher
was convinced that human experience and ethical struggle are so essential to the nature of reality as Fichte thought.*

If this interpretation is correct, what Schleiermacher is saying is
that the universe is real quite apart from its being perceived, that
objects in it affect the sense organs and are part causes of the phenomenal world which is "generated" by the imagination, and that the
nature of the universe can, at least to some extent, be known. Of
course we have not yet considered what he thought to be the nature of
the universe.

It would be a mistake to deny, however, that this interpretation
does leave some loose ends unaccounted for. We do not have a
satisfactory interpretation for the "secret moment" passage. Furthermore, it may be admitted that complete satisfaction is perhaps not to
be found for some of the idealistic statements quoted from the *Soliloquies*. This fact is less serious than it might be, for the reason that

* See appendix at end of sec. 3.

Schleiermacher was not trying to write a rigorous philosophical exposition, as he himself was well aware.*

Of course it is possible that Schleiermacher had not yet committed himself to any epistemological position, and did not intend to allow his book to be attached to any at this time. It may be that he thought the main ideas of his book—the concepts of the universe, of religious intuition, of individuality in its relation to religious intuition and moral self-realization—would stand independently of any such attachment. If this is the case, it may be that the occasional use of idealistic or realistic language is simply an accommodation to the terminology of the day.† This interpretation could be supported by a statement of 1803, to the effect that he is a "neutral" in philosophy.[23] However, his epistemology seems to be more intimately related to the other ideas of the Discourses than this theory would allow, and on the basis of the statements cited and in the light of his occupation with philosophical problems for so long a time, it is impossible to believe that he did not have views of his own on these subjects, however incomplete they might be.

Incidentally, Fichte and Schelling found the philosophy of these works difficult to decipher and said they would wait until he published a scientific work to defend what he had expounded only in a popular fashion in this book.[24]

In order to find out what Schleiermacher meant by calling himself an idealist (by which I think he meant that values, thought, and organization are fundamental to the structure of the universe, in a way which will become plainer as we proceed) it is necessary to examine what he believed to be the nature of the "universe." But first two preliminary comments. It is worth noting that he condemns British philosophy, saying that British thought was not serious with the supersensible, in that it was always devoted to a "wretched empiricism."[25] Second, he is critical of Kant, saying of him that his writings exhibit "incompleteness, confusion, and shortcoming as

* He wrote: "I would suggest that you look not so much at what is actually in it, as at the blanc de l'ouvrage, at the presuppositions behind it, which I—God willing—intend to elucidate in a couple of years, in a really scholarly way." Briefe, vol. IV, p. 59.

† Dilthey, op. cit., p. 303, says he did not have his views fully worked out at that time, but had them only in the form of an "intuition."

regards the understanding of himself."[26] In contrast to this, his letters at this time are full of praise for Plato. These facts are remarkably agreeable to the description of his views we are about to offer.

What is the universe? One is looking for it in the right direction, he says, when one seeks something "beyond sensible appearances and their laws."* The universe in contrast to particular sensory objects is the whole world viewed as "totality, as unity in plurality, as system."[27] Everything, including the sensory objects, is a part of this system.[28] If we are to know what meaning a thing ultimately has in the universe, "it must be observed in its characteristic nature and fullest completeness. A thing can have a place in the universe only by virtue of the totality of its effects and relations."[29] The nature of the universe is best to be learned in the realm of inorganic nature (in so far as it can be descried there) from the laws of chemistry (as he conceived them); but it is also to be characterized through an understanding of humanity, of art, of history, and personal experience. The French Revolution, for example, he declares to be one of the sublimest acts of the universe.[30] In all these matters, one can see the "divine unity and eternal unchangeableness of the World."†

This system, and man's relation to it, are the object of religion, ethics, and metaphysics alike. The moral philosopher studies it in order to discover what kind of conduct is right; the religious man contemplates it in a way to be discussed later; metaphysics "classifies the Universe, divides it into certain essences, seeks the grounds of what is there, deduces the necessity of the real, spins out of itself the reality of the world and its laws."[31]

This universe, this "infinite" system, he connects with the name of Spinoza,‡ although the idea bears witness also to the influence of Goethe, the transcendental idealists, his romantic friends, probably Leibniz,§ and perhaps of Bruno.

* *Reden*, p. 145. The universe is not common sense objects and their obvious modes of behavior. Part of what he means is the unified world known by science.

† *Reden*, p. 83. The reader will find many passages in the *Discourses* which seem to require the reality of space and time, not merely in the phenomenal object but in the world of things. This is a point at which he seems to have broken not only with Kant but with his own ideas as stated in the study of Spinoza.

‡ Dilthey says he acquired firsthand acquaintance with Spinoza's *Ethics* between 1796 and 1799. *Op. cit.*, p. 319.

§ *Ibid.*, p. 320. He was at work on Leibniz at about this time and considered writing a critical article on him.

Schleiermacher's universe includes all being in a harmonious way, organized with a perfection which justifies describing it as a work of art. After discussing the remarkable way in which (according to him) human personalities supplement one another, he says: "This is the harmony of the Universe, this the great and wonderful unity in its eternal work of art."[32] This perfection of the organization of the world, the creation of individual forms which supplement but never repeat each other is illustrated in religion in its various stages and forms, and the individual ways in which it is realized in individual persons.[33] Even in inorganic nature, exceptions to the laws we know point to a greater harmony and perfection of the world. In a work of art, he says, if the sense of the whole picture can be read off from examination of a part of it, we think that the whole is

lacking in what might suggest the presence of a great mind. Where you are to have the feeling of a sublime unity, a magnificently thought out system, there must be, along with the general tendency to order and harmony, particular relations which cannot be fully understood from it. Thus the world is a work, of which you see only a part, and if this were fully ordered and complete in itself, you could form no sublime concept of the Whole.[34]

Even moral evil is not to be despised, because it is the work of the world-spirit, and differences in moral attainment are far better than "the monotonous repetition of a highest ideal."[35]

The universe is not only already a harmonious and artistic system, but it is moving through time to even greater perfection. There is a fate working in the processes of history, bringing in the "end" or "purpose" of the whole. And

if you would comprehend the proper character of all changes and of all human progress, religion will show you how the living gods hate nothing but death, how nothing is to be persecuted and destroyed but this, the first and last enemy of mankind. The crude, the barbarian, and the formless are to be absorbed and recast into an organic culture. Nothing is to be dead matter, which is moved only by an inanimate impact, or offers resistance only through unconscious friction; all is to be individual, complex, connected, exalted life. Blind instinct, unthinking custom, dull obedience, everything inert and passive, all those sad symptoms of the asphyxia of freedom and humanity, are to be abolished. To this is directed the work of minutes and of centuries. It is the ever great advancing work of eternal redemptive love.[36]

In that the universe is a system, harmonious and perfect, organized like a work of art, moving toward an "end" of fuller life and more complex organization, it seems to exhibit a character suggesting that it is in some sense the work of mind. The natural query to be raised respecting Schleiermacher's view, therefore, concerns his belief in the existence of a supreme mind. To this question his answer is that most persons, especially those whose imaginations tend to work in a certain way, will "almost inevitably" have to think of the universe in terms of a personal God.[37] Nevertheless, he believes that this idea is not at all necessary. "God is not everything in religion . . . and the Universe is more."[38] Those whose imagination is such that they can think of the universe more easily without a God have as much justification in doing so as the others, for what one thinks in this matter depends simply on the kind of imagination one has. "For me, deity can be nothing more than one single way of having religious intuitions, of which . . . the others are independent; in my view and according to my ideas the belief, 'no God, no religion,' cannot at all be accepted."[39] In fact, Schleiermacher actually disparages the idea of an unlimited and perfect Creator of the universe, saying that the idea of perfection comes from the science of ethics and the idea of creation from metaphysics, and that the two will not coalesce to give an object suitable for the contemplation of religion.[40]

This hesitation to encourage the traditional theistic interpretation of the universe is paralleled by his attitude to another cardinal principle of traditional Christianity, the belief in immortality. Schleiermacher apparently believes in "eternal life" of a sort, but the "immortality of religion is to become one with the Infinite in the midst of time, and eternal in an instant,"[41] which of course is not the eternal life common to many theistic philosophies. A continuous existence of conscious personality after death seems to be the object of his contempt in the Discourses. He wonders why persons, if they are so concerned about proving their future existence, do not also try to prove their eternal existence in the past. Death is an opportunity to become something more than a human person, and the "pitiful" desire for it is for an immortality that is not worth the name.[42] Rather, one should "strive to negate one's personality, to live in the One and All, to be more than oneself, in order to lose little when one loses oneself"—a passage which is again reminiscent of Spinoza.

Schleiermacher says that when a greater and holier longing than that for the continuation of personal existence is aroused, he will be willing to talk further of the hopes which death gives and of the nature of immortality.* Some writers have taken this to mean that Schleiermacher really believed in personal immortality and disapproved only of the selfish desire which makes men long for it. This interpretation is mistaken. There is a letter written in 1807 by Schleiermacher to his future wife, consoling her upon the occasion of the death of her first husband. Had he believed in personal immortality, he would surely have used this occasion to say something about it. But the following is what he wrote:

Certainty beyond this life is not given to us. Do not misunderstand me. I mean certainty for the imagination, which desires to see everything in distinct images; but otherwise there is the greatest certainty—and nothing would be certain if it were not so—that for the soul there is no such thing as death, no annihilation for the spirit. But personal life is not the essence of spirit; it is only an appearance thereof. How this is repeated we do not know; we can form no conception of it, but only poetic visions . . . Surely you cannot wish that he should return to life, for that would be contrary to the eternal order of things, to which we all cling more earnestly than to any of our individual desires. . . . What would, or what ought to satisfy you in a future life, you cannot know; for you cannot know the order that prevails there. But when you are removed thither you will know it, and then there, as little as here, you will desire what would be opposed to it, and most assuredly it will afford you as full and rapturous satisfaction. But if your imagination suggests to you a merging in the great All, do not let this fill you with bitter anguish. Do not conceive of it as a lifeless, but as a living commingling—as the highest life. Is not the ideal toward which we are all striving even in this world, though we never reach it, the merging of the life of each in the life of all, and the putting away from us of every semblance of a separate existence? If then he lives in God, and you love him eternally in God, as you knew God and loved God in him, can you conceive of anything more glorious or more delightful? Is it not the highest goal which love can reach, compared with which

* *Reden*, p. 133. In *The Christian Faith*, 2nd ed., sec. 84, par. 1, he says that the idea of a divine reward is contrary to Christian feeling.

every feeling which clings to the personal life, and springs from that alone, is as nothing?*

Whatever one may think of the wisdom of Schleiermacher's judgment on these matters, there can be little doubt that he did give up certain beliefs traditionally fundamental to theism. We may therefore proceed upon the assumption that what he says is not to be interpreted in a specially theistic way, and begin a more careful examination of the nature of his universe, a survey which can be completed only at a later stage when other aspects of his system have been described.

Schleiermacher says that the universe is composed of "forces." In this he may have had in mind Schelling's view (close to Kant's) of the nature of matter;† but his view is also illuminated by comparison with Plato's ideas (which Schelling had connected with his work), Aristotle's essences, Kant's discussion of the use of the notion of pure elements in chemistry,[43] and perhaps even with Spinoza's idea of the "infinite immediate modes." Ultimately irreducible kinds of reality (e.g., the elements) are a part of what is denoted by the word "force." He says:

> You know that divinity has compelled itself by unalterable law to cut its great work asunder, to compose every determinate existent only out of two opposed forces, and to bring to existence each of its eternal thoughts in twin forms, opposed to each other but nevertheless possible only through one another. The whole material world . . . seems to the best informed and most thoughtful among you only as an eternally continued play of opposed forces. . . . Everything has its determinate being only in that it combines in an individual way the two primary forces of nature—the attractive force and the . . . expansive force.[44]

Schelling, developing Kant, had said that the essence of matter is to be a point of equilibrium between the attractive force (gravitation) and the expansive force (resistance to pressure). These forces compose and exhaust the nature of matter. Schelling had also applied Fichte's dialectical procedure in order to show that these fundamental

---

* *Briefe*, vol. II, pp. 80-81. In *The Christian Faith*, 2nd ed., sec. 158 ff., he does talk hesitatingly of some kind of immortality as part of the Christian faith.

† So Süskind, *op. cit.*, p. 115 ff. Hunzinger thinks Schleiermacher had the idea before contact with Schelling, *Der Begriff des Gefühls u. seine Wandlungen in Schleiermachers Religionsauffassung*. He could have taken the application of the idea in physics from Kant's *Metaphysische Anfangsgründe der Naturwissenschaft*.

forces eventually imply other phenomena, such as electricity, and are repeated in more complex forms on the organic level. So far Schleiermacher apparently felt attracted by his view:

> See how attraction and repulsion [he said] determine everything and are continuously active everywhere; see how all difference or opposition is only apparent and relative, and all individualization only an empty name; see how everything the same tries to hide its monotony in a thousand different forms, and how you never find anything simple but everything artfully compounded and interlaced: this is the Spirit of the World, which reveals itself in the smallest things as vividly and perfectly as in the greatest.[45]

But Schleiermacher goes a stage further than this; he sees the same phenomena repeated (or at least finds an analogy to them) in the realm of mind—here perhaps influenced by or at least consistent with the speculations of Schlegel and Novalis. So he says:

> It seems that spirits, so soon as they are transplanted to this world, must obey such a law. Every human soul—its temporal acts as well as its inner peculiarities of nature lead us to this conclusion—is only a product of two opposed forces. The one is a struggle to draw everything around it to itself. . . . The other is the longing to stretch out its inner being always wider . . . to communicate itself, without ever being drained. The former seek for pleasure. . . . The latter despise it . . . and want to fill everything with reason and freedom . . . and the perfection of the world of mind consists in all possible combinations of these two forces not only being realized in mankind, but in the actuality of a universal bond of consciousness relating each to all, so that each one, though he cannot be other than what he must be, nevertheless understands every other as clearly as himself, and comprehends all individual instances of humanity.[46]

This realization of all possible kinds of individuals through various combinations of these forces is to his mind one of the chief perfections of the world.*

We shall discover later that Schleiermacher used the concept of "force" sufficiently broadly to allow him to speak of even the religious "instinct" in man as a "force." What exactly he means by the

---

* His view that the world contains every possible type of individual is an illustration of the ancient principle of plenitude, as Professor Lovejoy has recently pointed out. See also pp. 93, 138-140. His idea probably came from Leibniz and the German literary figures.

concept is never made clear, but we shall get much light on it when we study his maturest views of science and philosophy.

Hegel wrote that in contrast to the views of Jacobi,

> in the *Discourses on Religion* nature, as a collection of finite actualities, is done away with, and is recognized as a Universe; so that the longing [of Protestant religion] is recalled from its flight beyond reality to an eternal beyond. The veil between the subject or knowing and the absolutely unattainable object is torn down, the pain atoned for in enjoyment, the endless striving satisfied in intuition.[47]

Schleiermacher's universe is what Hegel recognized as an organic system, which can be known and can be a suitable object for religious affection.

As Hegel says, Schleiermacher's universe is capable of being known. Schleiermacher apparently noted with approval that the new philosophy was attempting to deduce the necessity of the nature of the real.[48] He said of the philosophy which

> raises man to the concept of his relation with the world, teaching him to recognize himself not only as creation, but as creator [that] the anxious wall of separation is broken down. The outer world is only another inner world. Everything is a reflection of mind, just as mind is the reflection of all things. Man can seek himself in this reflection without losing himself or going outside of himself. He can never exhaust himself in contemplation of himself, for everything lies in him. [Thus] natural science sets the man who looks round to discover the Universe, in the center of nature, and no longer suffers him to dissipate himself fruitlessly in the study of small details. He now pursues the play of its forces into their most secret recesses, from the inaccessible storehouses of energized matter to the artistic workshops of organic life. He measures its might from the bounds of world-filled space to the center of his own ego, and finds himself, always in eternal strife and most inseparable unity. Man is nature's center and circumference. *Mere appearance is fled and the essence won.* . . . *He discovers identity under all disguises,* and rests nowhere except in the Infinite and One.*

Although it is clear from the foregoing that Schleiermacher sympathized to some extent with the dialectical deductions of the transcendental philosophers, there is also reason to believe that he took a some-

* *Reden,* pp. 171-172. Italics mine. The phrase, "He discovers identity under all disguises," and some other remarks have made Dilthey and others feel justified in claiming that Schleiermacher was the first to give expression to the philosophy of identity. Cf. Dilthey, *op. cit.,* p. 302.

what more empirical view of philosophical method. At any rate, he seems to have thought that one could learn to know these universal "forces" by a partially empirical study of nature and history. (Probably it was this that he had in mind when he said that previous systems of philosophy had not offered a real system, a "firmer consistency,"[49] because they did not begin with religious intuition.) He welcomed Schelling's publication on the philosophy of nature in 1800, saying that he thought it would bring to light the limitation of the dialectic and leave room for the observation and intuition of the universe, for "mysticism on the other side."[50] The exclusive use of logical dialectic method was probably what he had in mind when he referred disparagingly to Fichte's "ready ability in idealism."[51]

There must have been some sense in which he believed thought eminently capable of knowing nature and the Infinite through sheer dialectic; and on the other hand he must have thought that there is some sense in which it is not sufficient. The world is transparent to thought, according to Schleiermacher, but only to thought in an alliance with experience.

Two problems in interpretation arise at this point, and we shall conclude our discussion of Schleiermacher's system with a consideration of them. First, since he evidently believed that the objects known by science are independent of the knowing of them and not merely a construct of the mind, how is he to explain the possibility of certain knowledge of them? If the object of thought is independent of thinking, how can thought's modes of procedure, its categories and forms of judgment, be known to apply to it? Second, we pointed out in a discussion of Schleiermacher's relation to Spinoza that he at that time believed that there is somehow an unknowable infinite reality which is the "ground" of the world of experience. What has become of this concept? Has it dropped out altogether and if so does Schleiermacher think that experience has no unknowable conditions whatever?

As to the first question, it seems certain that he does not offer any explicit solution in the writings published around 1800. There are several plausible theories about his attitude at this time, however. One is that he did not discuss it because, although he did not have a solution himself, he thought a solution possible and believed it would be forthcoming. Or perhaps he felt that he had a contribution to make in one direction, even if he could not solve all the problems at once. Or perhaps under the magnetic influence of his philosophical environment—Plato, Spinoza, Goethe, Schelling, and the romanticists—the answer to this particular question did not seem of prime urgency. There is another possibility which will be mentioned in a moment.

The second problem is very baffling. The answer which at once springs to mind in the light of his later work is that he believed there is a harmony between the modes of thought and the being of things and that the fact of this harmony requires one to think that both thought and things have a ground which transcends them both. This ground would then be unknowable in its essence, although its existence would be required by the harmony necessary for knowledge. There is great difficulty in determining what precisely he thought to be the relation of the ground to things and experience even in his later works, although he clearly asserted something of this sort. But we are nevertheless restrained from interpreting him in this way by the fact that there is no explicit support for it in the works around 1800; and we shall see that at a later time he himself admitted that in the *Discourses* the idea of God is not explicit, although he claimed it had always been implicit.

If we must have some estimate of his probable view on these points in 1800, much turns on the justification of using his later works to fill in the blanks of these nonphilosophical books. Such a procedure gains some support from the continuity and consistency of his theory on some questions from first to last. And the fact that there is comparatively little explicit metaphysics in these works does not prove that Schleiermacher had not made considerable progress in fashioning his system, for in any case these books were not the place for serious metaphysical argument. His view of the universe as an organic system of "forces," the role which individuality plays in the universe, the important place accorded to thought in science along with his attempts to show that experience is indispensable—these matters are examples of the agreement between the Schleiermacher of 1800 and the Schleiermacher of 1820. If it is legitimate to use his later ideas to fill in blanks, the idea of God as a "transcendental ground" may be the answer to the second question; and his later use of a form of the coherence theory of truth to solve the problem of knowledge may

have been anticipated at least in a germinal way in the early works
for what he says in the Discourses is at least consistent with his late
view and in some ways suggests it. Of course the contention tha
Schleiermacher had these ideas explicitly and definitely before him a
this time cannot be proved and is unwarranted; Schleiermacher can
at best have been groping falteringly for a position he felt intuitively
would prove to be sound. It is misleading to look in these early work
for clear solutions to problems to the clearing up of which he probably
did not think he yet saw the way open.

2. A Methodology for the Philosophy of Religion

The universe, according to Schleiermacher, is a system of "forces"
which constantly manifest themselves in time in individual combina
tions, in concrete, finite individuals. These "forces" are not simply
physical; they comprise all the "essences" necessary for the analysi
of all phenomena. For example, a permanent tendency of human
nature which is the basis of some social institution must either b
included as one of these forces or analyzed in terms of forces.

The belief that religion may be regarded as in some way an "infinite
force" or essential power of the mind pervades the Discourses on Reli
gion and defines Schleiermacher's methodology in his philosophy o
religion. (He seems to have used the word "infinite" to mean "uni
versal" or "essential.")

Religion, he says, is a "function of the inmost and highest life."[5]
"It rises necessarily of itself from the inmost being of every bette
soul, so that a special province of mind belongs to it."[53] It is a "neces
sary and indispensable third" to speculative thought and moral ac
tion.[54] It is founded in "one of the necessary ways of acting, or drives
of human nature."[55] It is a "disposition residing in us all."[56] "Man i
born with a religious instinct as with any other."[57] Since religiousnes
is so fundamental a part of man's nature, it is not something which
can be taught or acquired:

From the inmost being of man's mind must come everything which
belongs to his true life, and is to be an ever active and operative impulse
in him. Such is religion. . . . Everything which, like it, is to be con
tinuously active in the human mind is far beyond the realm of teaching.[5]

Thus Schleiermacher thinks that religion springs from the depths of man's essential being; but its welling forth, he also says, can be repressed. It is difficult, for example, for one who is tied to the needs of the moment to rise to religious contemplation.[59] Religion can be stifled by an education and society which are practical and utilitarian in spirit or by a scientific spirit which insists upon exclusively causal explanations.[60] But repression does not eradicate it, and when the normal functioning of the mind is prevented, religion springs up in abnormal forms. It is effectively present even in the minds of the romanticists who despise it; only they do not recognize it for what it is.[61]

Now Schleiermacher believed that the nature, effects, and relations of these "infinite forces" could be apprehended in either of two ways.

Every creation of the human mind can be examined and comprehended from two points of view. You can look at it from its center, from its inner essence, and then you see it as a product of human nature, grounded in one of man's necessary ways of behavior, or instincts. . . . Or you can look at it from its circumference with reference to the determinate form it has assumed in various times and places; then you see it as a product of time and history.[62]

The method of examining anything "from its center" was later developed into the method of "speculative construction" of a phenomenon; the examination of it from the "circumference" came to mean imply the proper use of empirical material.) Applied to religious phenomena, these methodological ideas meant that religion should be approached and examined from these two points of view. In practice, in the Discourses on Religion, they meant that Schleiermacher was to attempt to understand religion partly by reliance upon psychological analyses and hypotheses, and partly upon the material and classifications afforded by the history of religions.

Saying that experience cannot be expected to offer a pure example of religion any more than it offers one of pure sensation, or understanding, or moral action,[63] Schleiermacher proposed that the scientific imagination can nevertheless "construct" these pure activities and then confirm the validity of such a construction by examining the result of their supposed combined activity. This means, I believe, that he thought it legitimate to set up an hypothesis about the reality of certain "natural" forms of mental activity; and then to confirm this hypothesis by an inspection of the work of these forms of activity when functioning in conjunction.

The manner in which he interlocked empirical with "speculative" considerations in his theory of religion is illustrated by his use of historical material in the *Discourses*. The analysis of history is made to furnish clues to the relation of religion to the other activities of the mind.* For example, he holds that investigation justifies a division of historical religions into three stages (fetishism, polytheism, and monotheism). This historical conclusion he utilized by relating it to three similar levels of conceptual thought; that is, these stages correspond to the periods of human thought in which man has used three progressively more complex concepts for the organization of experience, namely, "chaos," "plurality," and "unity in plurality." Thus logical analysis and history are conjoined in an attempt to understand the religious "activity." Again he conjoins psychological analysis with historical classification in order to make intelligible the division of these three groups of religion each into two further subgroups, according as the divine reality is conceived personally or impersonally (a distinction which on the highest level of religion is that between theism and pantheism). He "explains" this division by relating it to a supposed innate difference in the imaginations of persons, which he believes are involved in the religious activity. Or again, he "explains" the historical fact of the church by showing how it depends on a psychological fact, the natural tendency of man to communicate his experience and to want to discover whether his experience is shared by others. Even the peculiar features of Schleiermacher's own age are "explained" in this way. Deism, he says, can be understood when we see how the natural instinct of religion has been repressed by the scientific and practical interests.

Thus history is made more intelligible in the light of the psychological "forces" or "essences" which combine in the production of it, and it confirms and illustrates the theory of the nature of religion— history and psychological theory are conjoined to make religious phenomena intelligible.

* He thus anticipates the fruitfulness of anthropological study of primitive religion for an understanding of religion, saying that primitive man, with his less complex life, affords a much plainer illustration of these eternal functions.

Religion is therefore, in a sense, that natural instinct of the human mind which in union with the other modes of natural mental behavior gives birth to religious facts and institutions. If the whole realm of possibilities for religion is to be realized in time, this creative activity must become related in all possible ways both to all the other natural tendencies of the mind and to all its possible external "objects."[64] Each concrete actualization of religion is "eternal," according to Schleiermacher, in the sense that it is essential to the complete realization of the system of the "forces," to the fullness of being.[65] Thus "religion" is not a word denoting the characters common to all actual religions; it is not an abstraction, a classification. It denotes both the activity which makes religions possible and the religions which are its products. For this reason, "natural religion," according to him, is not really a religion. It is not an "eternal force," nor a product of one. It is only an abstraction. "Natural religion can make no claim to equality with the positive religions, for it is only an indefinite, poor, and needy idea, which can never really exist for itself."[66] Likewise, religion would not be an "eternal force" if it existed only for the sake of morality or the state. If religion were simply this, it might be "expedient, but it would not be internally necessary; it could remain simply a pious wish, which could never come into existence."[67]

The "forces" are activities manifested in their products, but an understanding of them, according to Schleiermacher, furnishes a norm to which the products should approximate. The harmonious functioning of the various activities can be disturbed, and it must be restored if the world is to be perfect. Although it is difficult to understand how the organic system can go awry, Schleiermacher says that distortion is "inevitable, as soon as the Infinite assumes an incomplete and limited form, and descends into the realm of time and of the universal influence of finite things."[68] But the universe can restore its own perfection as it does when human beings perceive these ideals, and adjust human affairs to permit the system to function harmoniously once more. Thus if religion is known to be a proper activity of man, it should be encouraged in education just as learning and right conduct are encouraged. Or, when the ideal for the church is known, its members should begin to bring actuality into accord with it, for example, by freeing the church from the influence of the state, from responsibility for education and legal marriage, which are not properly parts of the church's life.

These methodological suggestions were one of Schleiermacher's most fruitful contributions to theology and the philosophy of religion. I do not mean to say by this that his idea was an absolutely new one. The general type of approach was in the air at the time and had Schleiermacher not applied it so forcefully to religion, doubtless someone else would have. Furthermore, he had surely derived many suggestions in this direction from several sources—from the writings of Herder, from Kant's *Grundlegung der Metaphysik der Sitten* and probably from the subjective deduction of the categories in the first *Critique*, and from Friedrich Schlegel's work on the philosophy of history and art. But whatever may have been the sources upon which he drew, he made the idea living and forcible in the realm of theological studies. The psychological analysis of religion in our day, and the anthropological study of the religion of primitive peoples are the spiritual descendants of Schleiermacher's work. One does not need to accept his view that religion is an instinct, or "eternal force" in order to credit him with having been on the right track in urging that the study of history, of primitive religions, of psychology both individual and social, is the means by which the nature of religion may be understood.

The significance of his contribution stands out if his work is examined in its historical context, compared with the ideas of his contemporaries. It did not occur to philosophers and theologians that religious phenomena form a distinct group which merits special attention. To them, religion meant the process of being redeemed by the work of Christ or the believing of certain doctrines or moral conduct or obedience, depending upon one's ecclesiastical connections. The phenomena of religious experience, such as mystical ecstasy, did not seem to them to offer subject matter for a study related to the philosophy of religion. Even Kant felt called upon to show how religious faith cannot be based upon the alleged occurrence of miraculous events, and his alternative statement was that "religion is the perception that all our duties are divine commands."[69] He defended the church as an institution based upon a demand of reason, for victory over sin can be achieved only by means of a society founded for the promotion of moral conduct.[70]

Compared with such a rationalistic treatment of religion, Schleiermacher's ideas are meritorious as at least a step toward what are now recognized as scientific methods of investigation. It was a great advance simply to think of religion as a group of phenomena deserving of independent study. Thus, hedged about as it is with presuppositions and beliefs which philosophers today would not accept, and limited as it is by Schleiermacher's own lack of detailed information on the history of religion, his work must nevertheless be regarded as a landmark in the appreciation of religious experience.*

3. RELIGIOUS INTUITION AND MYSTICISM

Religion is an "instinctive" kind of mental activity, an eternal or essential part of human nature, an "infinite force" in the system which makes up the universe. But so far we have not investigated what specifically religion is.

Schleiermacher is definite about what religion is *not*. Perhaps reflecting his Moravian background,† his view is that religion is neither morality nor speculative metaphysics. Religion cannot be identical with moral behavior because some events which we think are religious

---

* The student of Schleiermacher's thought will be repaid by study of his review of Garve's last works (*Werke*, pt. III, vol. I), which contains some illuminating remarks on philosophical method. He reproves Garve for moving only in the sphere of the particular, and never arriving at "anything whole or primary." This is the result of the method of "mere observation," which accepts what is found by "ordinary thinking, as the absolutely given, the absolutely true and conceivable in itself." For such a philosophy, "not only the proper and primary intuition and philosophical thought in general, but also historical thought, becomes impossible." Instead, philosophy should "analyze the individual chemically, separate its internally different constituents from each other, and exhibit them in their quantitative relation; then discover the inner principle of their connection—that deepest secret of individuality—and so reconstruct the individual artificially. But that can occur only if one combines different appearances, and has previously reflected somewhat on the idea of how such appearances may be combined . . ." This requires more than Garve's merely empirical method; it requires higher principles "which are taken over from science and for which a higher view of science is required." This seems to me essentially what Schleiermacher urges in the *Discourses on Religion*.

† Dilthey attributes his separation of religion from morality, science, and metaphysics to his pietistic education, his acquaintance with the spirit of the Christian religion, his study of Kant, and his conviction of the necessity of complete freedom of science and philosophy from interference from religious quarters. *Op. cit.*, pp. 301, 417.

are not morally right; therefore what we mean by "religion" must be different from what we mean by "morality."[71] It is an insult to religion to try to make it the handmaid of morality.[72] Nor is religion metaphysical thought, although the object of the religious activity is the same as that of morality and philosophy, namely, the universe and man's relation to it. Religion is not metaphysics because it does not use the rigorous logical method of the philosopher; religion "dare not posit essences, determine natures, lose itself in an infinity of reasons and deductions, search for final causes, and express eternal truths."[73] And neither can it be a mixture of the two, as it is when the idea of the good is combined with the metaphysical idea of the source of all being, to form the idea of the perfect God who is the author of moral law.[74]

Religion is also not science, and in contrast to science it has affinities with morality and philosophy. The goal of the empirical physicist is achieved when he has obtained information concerning certain measurable relations between events or aspects of processes. Science is interested in the relations of finite objects among themselves, not in their relation to the universe; and it is interested in a partial aspect of them, not in their full individuality. Of course scientific speculation like that of Schelling, Schleiermacher admits, may come very close to religion. Ordinary science does not.

What then is religion? In answer to this question, I shall first venture a brief general statement of what I think Schleiermacher had in mind. I shall then try to support my interpretation by evidence.

The religious man, unlike the scientist, tries to get away from a partial, abstract view of events; he tries to see them in all their individuality, in all their relations. Again, unlike the scientist, and like the moralist and philosopher, he relates them to the universe. The universe, the Infinite Being, seems to him the one true reality, the only independent substance. He regards finite objects and events as acts of or revelations of the nature of the Infinite. He sees the character of the whole in them. Moreover, he responds to these meanings or interpretations by appropriate feelings; he accepts with joy the events which reveal the infinity and perfection of the world-spirit. But unlike the philosopher, he is not actively thoughtful, dialectical, or rational; he is passive, contemplative, lets the universe arouse these interpretations or appreciations in him. They are not reasoned like a syllogism, but immediate like the awareness of a familiar object.

One or two examples from Schleiermacher's letters may serve as an introductory illustration of what he meant.

First, he says in a review of Schlegel's *Lucinde* that the book "is not only poetic, but religious and moral. Religious, because love is everywhere exhibited on the standpoint from which it looks out over life into the Infinite . . ."[75] The book is religious because the phenomenon of love is related to the universe. Second, speaking of a selfish sort of love produced in an acquaintance by adherence to the materialistic system of Helvetius, he says:

But I should not like the world to be devoid of it; it is, as it were, the effervescence obtained from a hard, polished, oyster-shell, which proves it to be in essence lime and putty. Out of it can be moulded the loveliest things imaginable, and the effervescence is the first stage in the process. There is also a proper feeling of reciprocal love for these people, which I should also not want to dispense with. You see, I look at everything with religion.[76]

To be religious is to see in all things, no matter how repugnant they may seem, an underlying relation to the perfection, beauty, and harmony of the universe. "However objectionable something may be in other respects or in itself," he writes, "in this respect it is always worthy of being preserved and contemplated. For a pious mind, religion makes everything holy and valuable, even unholiness and commonness themselves."[77] "The really religious view of things is to seek every trace of the divine, the true, and the eternal, even in what seems to us common and base . . ."[78] Religion is the understanding of the perfection underlying everything. Finally, he wrote to Henriette Herz that he was coming to Berlin "for reasons of religion, for truly, I want to intuit the Universe in you."[79] One's friends offer an opportunity for seeing how the universe has unfolded itself. The chief aim of friendship for some of the romanticists, we have seen, was the discovery of the place and significance which the friend's individuality had in the plan of the whole. Friendship and love acquire a wider meaning for the religious man. "Only through religion," he says in the *Discourses*,[80] "have I learned friendship and love." So he can say that those who seek God outside the world, are very often those who have no appreciation of the world itself.[81] Religion is the discovery of the order, nature, and perfection of the Infinite embodied in the finite.

Schleiermacher uses a number of synonyms to denote the central process in the "perception" of the Infinite in the finite: *Denken, Ansicht, Wahrnehmung, Sinn,* and *Anschauung.* In the central passages he uses the word *Anschauung* (intuition). "Intuition of the Universe," he says, "I beg you to become acquainted with that concept. It is the center of my whole idea. It is the most universal and highest formula of religion . . . from which you can determine its nature . . . most exactly."[82] Schleiermacher describes the religious experience by comparing it with sense perception. In both cases there is an independent object (in religion the Infinite), which exercises a causal influence on the subject (in sense objects by rays of light, in religion by various events, as we shall see), and what is sensed or known immediately is not the independent object itself, but this effect on us. Yet this effect is referred to the object (in religion to the universe), and indeed is accepted not as a shadow (or appearance) but as the universe itself.[83] So he says:

The Universe is in unceasing activity, and reveals itself to us every instant. Every form it produces, every being to which it gives separate existence, every event which it shakes from its always rich and fruitful lap, is an action of it on us; and so, to accept every particular thing as a part of the Whole, everything finite as a representation of the Infinite, is religion.[84]

Religion is no more metaphysics than sense perception by itself is science. "Anything which tries to go beyond this intuitive acceptance, and press deeper into the nature and substance of the Whole, is no longer religion, and when it tries to get itself accepted as religion, inevitably sinks to empty mythology."[85]

So religion is interpretation, the seeing of an event as a part or manifestation of the whole, the perception of its meaning or significance or unique purpose in the plan and order of the whole. But, although it is interpretation, it is not active thought. It is not philosophical or dialectical construction of the nature of the system from the events which manifest it.

Let us temporarily dismiss the problem of how an "interpretation" can be, or in what sense it can be, anything other than part of a system of thoughts or judgments. We shall return to it shortly.

The religious man immediately perceives the Infinite, the unified whole, in the events which are its expressions. These events are not separate appearances, but manifestations or modes of action of what is really *one*—just as the Jews thought that everything that happens is an act of God, the Christians that it is an act of Providence and that everything is appointed by God.

All appearances [he says] are there only, like holy miracles, to lead contemplation to the Spirit which brought them forth. It was religion when ancient peoples, annihilating the limitations of space and time, regarded every individual type of life throughout the whole world as the work and kingdom of an omnipresent being. They had intuited an individual characteristic of the Universe's way of acting, in its unity.[86] . . . Religion is the representation of all the events in the world as acts of God.[87] [The religious man sees the "eternal" significance of every event, through understanding of the Infinite.] Religion knows how to follow and discover the actions of the World-Spirit in everything which concerns human activity, in play as well as in earnestness, in the smallest as in the greatest; so that it finds divine destiny in the very fact that those, in whom the merely moral or legal predominates, want to make religion merely an unimportant appendage to ethics [and thereby undermine morality itself].

This apprehension of events as parts of a unity is illustrated by what Schleiermacher says of the appreciation of character. "There is no other way of getting to know a character than through intuition. You must find the standpoint from which you can survey the whole, and you must know how to construct the inmost being from the appearances."[88] This kind of intuition, when directed to the universe (with the addition of an element of feeling, as we shall see), is religion. We apprehend the manner of action of the universe, and its inner laws, from the events which occur in it. Conversely, we understand the true nature of an event only as we see its relation to the whole.

When any event has been apprehended in its eternal "meaning," the religious man calls it a miracle. Miraculousness has nothing to do with inexplicableness by scientific law. It

simply expresses the immediate relation of an event to the Infinite, to the Universe; but does that exclude an equally immediate relation to the finite and to nature?[89] . . . Miracle is simply the religious name for an event—even the most ordinary and commonplace. As soon as it is so adapted that the religious view of it can become predominant, it is a miracle.[90] [Every event is hence potentially a miracle.] To me, everything is miraculous . . . and if you were more religious, you would see more miracles everywhere.[91]

Our initial brief definition of religion affirmed that religion is close to philosophy and morality in that it relates finite objects to the whole, sees them as part of the universe. Having now sketched out more fully what that means,* we can turn to another part of the definition: the assertion that religion tries to get away from an abstract, partial view of things.

The escape from an abstract view of events is not really separate from the apprehension of them as parts of the whole, because it is not possible to comprehend the full nature of an object until its relations are known—a process which leads to the universe as a whole. Just as the "meaning" of any single part of a work of art is known only through its relation to the whole, or just as one cannot understand one's own individuality as a person without contrasting it with all other persons, so one cannot know what an event really is, or "means," without some acquaintance with the plan of the whole. Schleiermacher even says that a scientist who seeks to know the nature of an object exhaustively, to press below the surface of things, cannot succeed without eventually coming to the Infinite.†

The "total" understanding of an object is to be contrasted sharply with the partial view of persons who have only a practical interest, persons concerned only with the use to which an object can be put, or the control of it for such use, or its causal relations, "the place which an object takes in the series of appearances."[92] The religious sense, he says,

tries to comprehend the undivided impression of something whole; it seeks to perceive what and how a thing is, for itself, and to know everything in its peculiar character. But that is not what is meant by "understanding" [in the bad sense]. The what and the how are too much for it [understanding] . . . Nor does it ask whether and how what is to be understood is to make up a whole. That would lead too far afield; with such a tendency,

---

* The concept will be examined further in Section 5.
† His development of this theory will be examined in Chapter VI.

one would scarcely come away wholly without religion. We are supposed to leave this out, and be content with these dissections and analyses.[93] . . . They think, indeed, that they have the true and real world, and they are the ones who take everything in its right connection. Would that they would see that, in order to understand an object as an element of the Whole, it must necessarily be observed in its individual nature and highest completeness. It can have a place in the Universe only by the totality of its effects and relations.[94]

When an object is understood in its fullness and all its relations, it leads on to a higher order. It leads to the system or unity which is the universe. The *complete* object is not a separate particular, but a part of a whole in which it has a significance other than it has superficially.

So religion escapes from the abstract, partial, practical view of things; it relates them to the universe, and sees their significance in the system of the whole. So far, I think, we are able to follow Schleiermacher's meaning fairly clearly. At least if what he says seems vague, it will be supplemented when we consider some of the concrete products of religious intuition. But whereas his contention so far is essentially intelligible, it is very difficult to reconcile what we have said with other characteristics of "religious intuition," its immediacy, passivity, distinctness from thought, reasoning, and deduction. And again, what he sometimes says leaves the impression that he himself had not clearly decided whether religious intuition "sees" the universe as it is or whether it is only an aesthetically valuable activity whose results may or may not be true.

We shall postpone coming to grips with these problems, however, just as we have postponed consideration of the other element in religious experience, its emotional character.

Schleiermacher has often been called a mystic. In some senses of the word, that is justified. In fact, he sometimes referred to himself as a mystic. But since there are important respects in which it would be a mistake to classify him with the great mystics, we must be clear about what we mean by "mysticism."

If "mystical experience" be defined as "the immediate perception of the Infinite," then I suppose it is perfectly correct to call him a mystic, provided that we mean by "perception" what he meant by "religious intuition," provided we mean by the "Infinite" what he meant by it, and provided we mean by "immediate" what we shall see he meant, viz., given, unreasoned insight.*

In my opinion, when Schleiermacher called himself a mystic he meant just this character of being religious. It is being serious with the view that only the whole is ultimately real, that only the One is truly substance, self-existing being. It is devotion to this reality, in contrast to absorption in the finite world as a collection of particulars on the common-sense level. It is reverent contemplation of the "acts" of the Infinite as manifested in the finite world. It is the happy enjoyment of the scene of world history. It is admiration of the harmony of the world, worship of the perfection of the One. It is being lost in ecstatic rapture from insight into the world order.

This suggestion of an intelligible meaning for "mysticism" in Schleiermacher's system, which is based upon the impossibility of finding any other definition compatible with Schleiermacher's general system of thought, has some support in Schleiermacher's own usage of the word, although it must be confessed that there is no explicit statement of what he meant by it. He occasionally called himself a mystic, but it appears that he would have regarded as "bad mysticism" what is generally understood under that term today.†

There is a scrap in his diary, dated around 1802, in which he says:

The higher life is an unceasing progressive relation of the finite to the Infinite. This put in connection with the relation of finite objects to each other, is true philosophy. To wish to give up the latter procedure for the sake of the former is what can be called *mysticism in the bad sense*.[95]

It seems reasonable to infer from this that he regarded "good mysticism" as identical with religion, viz., the relating of all events to the organism of the universe (without any tendency to disparage science, which would make it "bad"). Other statements are at least not inconsistent with this interpretation. For example, he says that mysticism

---

* On page 74 of the *Reden* there is a long passage which is often taken to be proof that Schleiermacher was a mystic in the traditional sense. The language there is somewhat suggestive of mysticism in the sense of the great mystics, but there is no parallel of such a view elsewhere. It is easy to take the passage as an instance of his extravagant romantic style.
† In *The Christian Faith*, 2nd ed., sec. 100, par. 3, he accepts the suggestion that Christianity is mystical. What he means by this, he says, is "what belongs to the circle of doctrines which only a few share, but for others are a mystery" because they have not had the experiences.

is a "longing for the annihilation of personality,"[96] which I take to mean that although personality is a condition of the value of individuality, it is in some sense a limitation in comparison with the ideal of being merged with the Eternal. Consistently, he says that personal love is a weakness, from the point of view of mysticism, because it is a clinging to the personality.

Schleiermacher contrasts mysticism with rational inference and the dialectical method.[97] But he believes that it is not antagonistic to philosophy. In fact, philosophy needs it. He says in criticism of Fichte, "There is little hope for a philosophy which rests simply on a dialectical basis, without any mysticism, as is the case with the idealism in Fichte."[98] "Without mysticism, it is impossible to be really consistent, because one does not pursue one's thoughts to the Unconditioned, and thus cannot see the conclusions."[99]

His most elaborate description of the relation between mysticism and philosophy occurs in a criticism of Jacobi, for whom, incidentally, Schleiermacher otherwise felt much sympathy, and to whom he felt himself closer than to any other philosopher.[100]

I am of the opinion [he wrote] that not everything in his philosophy is clear, viz., the relation to philosophy of what he really wants . . . What he really wants seems to me to be room and freedom for his subjective mysticism. The apparent conflict of the more recent popular philosophy with mysticism has led him to the false opinion that there can actually be a conflict between philosophy and mysticism, whereas . . . every philosophy leads to mysticism, for those who can see so far. Were Jacobi clear in this matter, he would strike only at philosophies which do not lead to his kind of mysticism, whereas he strikes at philosophy as such. Why? Because he assumes that his mysticism must be deducible from a philosophy, and make up a whole with it—which seems to me impossible for every mysticism and his also. . . . Would he only admit that philosophy and mysticism lie completely outside one another . . . and touch only in their tangents, he would cease fighting uselessly against philosophy, and reveal his beautiful nature in a positive and intimate way, as before.[101]

The novelty of Schleiermacher's view of religion is made clear if it is compared with theological writings from the reformation period to his time. According to the orthodox literature, religion meant the sincere acceptance of certain fundamental articles of faith, and faithful adherence to the Christian ideal for conduct. The act of faith was thought to be accompanied by a divine act of "justification" (involving assurance of well-being in the future life), and to be followed by a happy integration of the self on the level of the new and higher life. Of course there were other notes in post-reformation Protestant religion, elements emphasizing the emotional life or the vision of God, and Spinoza's writings had become known, although until Schleiermacher's day they had been regarded as improper and had had little influence in religious circles. Schleiermacher's idea of religion as intuition, as we shall see, had power to influence the development of theological thought; he was able to change the emphasis in religious literature from objective doctrines to be believed to the subjective religious experience. According to him, it was not so much the specific content of belief which mattered as the fact that the religious person receives the world as the expression or activity of the self-organizing whole (and as we shall see responds to it emotionally as such). The high valuation of this subjective attitude to life (with its more pantheistic temper) is what distinguished Schleiermacher's view from the theology of salvation based on the acceptance of creeds.*

* Dilthey (op. cit., p. 421) and Otto Ritschl (Schleiermachers Stellung zum Christentum, Gotha, 1888) have rightly called attention to the fact that in a volume of sermons published shortly after the Discourses, Schleiermacher speaks from a very different point of view. In the sermons, religion is much more closely related to morality, and the conception of it is of a distinctly Kantian color. Further, the sermons seem to portray a much more theistic idea of God and a greater congeniality to the Christian Church. Dilthey and Ritschl claim that it is the sermons which represent Schleiermacher's personal views, and that the Discourses and Soliloquies are literary presentations adapted to the preconceptions of their audience, which were perhaps intended to prepare their readers for a fuller acceptance of Christianity later.

Ritschl supports this attitude toward the Discourses by citing the following passage: (op. cit., pp. 62-67) "I have indicated only with light outlines some of the most striking intuitions of religion in the sphere of nature and of humanity; but here I have led you to the furthest limit of your horizon. Here is the end of religion for those to whom the Universe and humanity are equivalent. . . . But do not thing that this is also the limit of religion. On the contrary, religion cannot stop here, and only beyond this point does it really see out into the Infinite. If humanity itself is capable of change and cultivation, if it not only manifests itself variously in its particular instances, but is itself here and there different, do you not feel it impossible that humanity itself should be the Universe? It is rather related to the Universe as the single person to it. It is rather only a single form of it, a manifestation of a single modification of its elements. There must be other such forms, by which humanity is to be defined, and from which it is to be distinguished. Humanity is only a mid-point between the particular and One, a stage on the way to the Infinite, and a still higher character in man than his humanity would have to be found, in order to relate him and his appearance directly to the

4. Emotion in Religion

The "mystical" intuition of the universe is always accompanied by emotion. Just as a person may respond with gratitude to an act of generosity toward him, the religious man reacts emotionally to the

Universe. All religion strives for such a presentiment of something outside of and above humanity, in order to be gripped by what is lofty and common to both; but this is also the point where [religion's] outlines are lost to the common eye, where it removes itself always further from particular objects, and where the striving for the highest is most thought to be foolishness . . . For you, any further remark about this would be unintelligible." (Reden, pp. 104-105)

Ritschl takes this to mean that the religion described in the first two Discourses is only religion in general, understanding of which can be expected of all. But a portrayal of the real and deeper nature of the Christian religion is not to be had there, for it could not be understood by the readers. Schleiermacher's own personal view, he argues, was that the Christian religion is inextricably related to the historical revelation of Christ and the ecclesiastical community. To Schleiermacher himself, religion is more than an intuition of humanity; it is a perception of the being of God in the person of Christ, and it is to this "divinity" (in the sense of an absolutely unique "mediator") of Christ that Schleiermacher was referring, Ritschl thinks, when he spoke in the above passage of "the higher character in man than his humanity" which must be discovered before one can really know the Infinite.

There is one exceedingly awkward fact for this theory to face. Schleiermacher was accused by the church leader, Sack, of being unchristian and was asked how he could justify his continued preaching in a Christian pulpit. One would think that if these publications did not reveal Schleiermacher's personal views, he would have stated that most important fact in his reply to Sack. But nothing of the sort occurred. Schleiermacher in fact reiterated his view of the attribution of personality to God, and of the relation of morality to religion. Nothing whatever is said of the Discourses' being adapted to the audience, or not representing his personal views. (See Briefe, vol. III, p. 276 ff., for Sack to Schleiermacher and Schleiermacher to Sack.)

In any case, the long passage I have cited certainly does not prove what it has been supposed to. There is some question in my mind about the object of the passage—whether it was really intended for Schleiermacher's romanticist friends or for subjective idealists. I shall not discuss this point. But if the reader will re-examine this passage after having completed the sections in Chapter VI which deal with the idea of God in Schleiermacher's later thought, I think he will find that this passage, far from advocating orthodoxy or containing a subtle reference to Christ, his unique revelatory work, and the church, is really a reference to the philosophy of identity, which he worked out more fully later. We find here, for example, the notion that the universe is composed of a hierarchy of species, that humanity is midway between the particulars (and presumably infimae species) and the One (presumably meaning the highest species of all, the Absolute Identity). The One is related to humanity, as humanity is to the concrete individual. Religion is interested in other and higher species outside humanity; it wants to know their relations, and what is common to them and the species humanity. If humanity is to be directly related to the One, it must be through finding some "higher" genus realized in man than simply his humanity; in his course of experience in a way determined by the "meaning" of its events for the universe and for himself.

This point in Schleiermacher's doctrine would hardly be worthy of separate mention but for three facts. First, Schleiermacher himself makes much of it, because the presence of feeling is one of the characteristics of living religion which distinguish it from merely intellectually entertained beliefs and philosophy. Second, it is useful to know more about what he meant by "feeling" at this time, in order to note some respects in which he was not a mystic. Third, his idea of the significance of feeling for religion, and its relation to the universe, is subject to gradual change; and it is important to look for traces here of the view he developed later.

There are two usages of the word "feeling," which it is important for the philosopher to distinguish carefully. One might be called the cognitive or intentional meaning of the word. It occurs in such sen-

---

later thought, man's capacity for knowledge and moral action (in which the "ideal side" of his nature is most clearly revealed) and religion would have been the characters which would relate him to the Identity of thought (or the ideal) and being.

The suggestion that he had in mind, even dimly, these tenets of his later philosophy may seem rash; but it seems to me much more reasonable, and more consistent with his other utterances, than these attempts to make of him something more like a theological lamb.

It is possible that the "higher forms" above humanity (referred to more explicitly in the versions of this passage in later editions) refers to the commonly held doctrine that there are forms of reality between God and man—such as the Catholic doctrine of angels, the intelligences of Neoplatonic speculation, and so on. Schleiermacher would be quite right in asserting that the view that man is the highest or only reality in the universe conflicts with the perennial attempt of religious philosophers to talk of a plurality of intermediate forms between man and the Absolute, or God.

The passage, incidentally, is an unfortunate one for Professor Wehrung, who holds that Schleiermacher was a subjective idealist like Fichte, when he wrote the Discourses. He has to call the passage a mystical contradiction. (Der geschichtsphil. Standpunkt Schleiermachers usw., p. 115 ff.)

In the light of his letters, his diary, and the enthusiasm with which he threw himself into the writing of these books, I cannot understand how he can be thought not to have expressed his real views in them. Whether it is to his credit or not, we must recognize that ministers do not always put their most cherished speculations into their sermons. Schleiermacher may well have thought he was discharging his pastoral function most honorably by conforming to the ideas of his congregation and preaching what would actually have the best consequences in his hearers. If it can be argued that he could not talk Christianity to the romanticists and expect to be understood and appreciated, can it not also be argued that he could similarly not preach romanticism to his congregation?

tences as this: "I feel that justice is a lower moral value than forgive-
ness." The other use might be called the qualitative or nonintentional
one. It occurs in such sentences as this: "I feel sad. I have a feeling of
joy." In these latter sentences, although there is a cognitive or intentional element in that the subject is aware of a feeling of a certain sort,
the feeling has no reference to an object beyond itself. In the first
usage, the feeling is a mode of awareness of some other fact—and is
often used as equivalent to "apprehension."

In the book we are considering, Schleiermacher always uses the
word in its second, nonintentional sense. Consequently, there is one
sense in which he cannot be legitimately compared with some mystics.
If the mystic's claim be that there is a "feeling of the Infinite," then,
except in so far as this notion is analogous to Schleiermacher's idea of
intuition, Schleiermacher's claim is different. For here he does not
assert that the feeling is a *feeling of* anything, but only that there is a
feeling of a certain sort "appropriate" to certain intuitions. When he
speaks of feeling, he is denoting such mental events as reverence, awe,
respect, etc.*

As I understand him, Schleiermacher does not believe, in these
books, that there is anything which particularly distinguishes the
psychological causation of religious feelings from any other feelings.
Schleiermacher was not speculating upon psychology, and there is no
reason why he should be particularly interested in the nature and
causes of feeling. Two things he does say. One is that feelings are
connected with awareness of meaning; and we must agree with him
that the "meaning" a thing has for a person defines his feeling toward
it. The second is that feelings have to do with the satisfaction of or
appeal to the instincts and interests. He says, for example, that the
strength of the religious emotion is connected with the strength of
the instinct or drive to "apprehend" the universe.[102] Again, he says
that a feeling is "developed" after the perception has "mingled with
our fundamental drives."[103]

It will be useful to note further reasons for believing that he thought
that feeling is determined by awareness of the "meaning" of events.

* *Reden*, pp. 17, 30, 82 f., 70, 54, 122, 180; cf. Piper, *Das Religiöse Erlebnis*,
pp. 45-46. Schleiermacher did not mean (I think) to refer simply to single affective
states, but also to more permanent moods. This idea will be explained fully in
chapters dealing with his later life.

"Those acts of the Universe," he says, "through which it reveals itself to you in the finite, also bring it into a new relation to the state of your mind. In that you intuit it, you must necessarily be gripped by various feelings."[104] In other words, where a new "meaning" is seen, a new emotional attitude ensues. The "primary intuition" of any religion "determines the character of the feelings."[105] The religious feelings, he says, are those which occur when the self is attending to the universe and the self's relation to it; they are determined by the content of the intuition.[106] Finally, there is a set of passages in which he enumerates first the intuition and then the feeling which occurs along with it. He says, "They are internally connected with those intuitions, necessarily flow out of them, and can be explained only by them." He then enumerates the intuitions and feelings. In four cases out of six, after describing the intuition he says "what could be more natural" than that the feeling in question should occur. In the fifth case, he substitutes the phrase "what could lie closer to mortal being than true unfeigned humility." And in the last one, he says, "How could we restrain a feeling of thankfulness," etc.[107] Schleiermacher is clearly thinking that the emotions which occur in religious experience are determined by the "meanings" uncovered by the religious intuition.

If this analysis be correct, it would seem that Schleiermacher's theory of religious feelings is a relatively simple matter, and in a sense is not important for the philosopher. He himself introduced the notion in the latter part of the second *Discourse* only, as he says, to "complete the general concept of religion."[108]

Schleiermacher insists upon the importance of feeling for religion because he believes that if the self is not implicated in the intuition, there is not living religion at all. Healthy religion must include *both* intuitions and feelings.[109] So he says in criticism both of the too philosophical religious man and of the one who has emotion and nothing more:

One person has intuitions of the world, and formulae which are supposed to express them, and another has feelings and inner experiences, by which he authenticates them. The former braids his formulae, the latter weaves a scheme of salvation out of his experiences, and then there is an argument about how many concepts and explanations one must take, or how many emotions and feelings, in order to put together a sound religion which would be neither too cold nor too extravagant . . . But these are only decompositions of religious sense, which your own reflection was forced to make.[110]

No more than this insistence upon the necessary connection of intuition and feeling in healthy religion seems to be the main contention of the "secret moment" passage which I have already mentioned in connection with sense perception.[111] Before either feeling or intuition comes to consciousness as such, he says, there is in some sense a common prior origin—which I suppose is correct, since the emotion is "generated" as a consequence of awareness of meaning in a way of which we are not introspectively conscious. Therefore, despite the somewhat mystical suggestions of the passage (and perhaps he has Novalis' view of ecstasy in mind), it seems to confirm the interpretation I have outlined.

It must be admitted, however, that there are some passages which have suggested to some writers a rather different idea of his meaning. Schleiermacher is anxious not to give the intuitional or interpretative side of religion any primacy; and he wants to emphasize the passive receptive nature of religion. Religion is not simply a system of ideas which the philosopher might deduce and which might then attain some "emotional" meaning. The whole religious experience must be "immediate" and passive. Since Schleiermacher wishes to maintain this position, he sometimes describes the generation of the feeling as if it were an immediate effect of the universe without any interposition of an interpretation of meaning. To my mind, the fact that he speaks in this way is not at all contradictory to the view I have suggested, and the expressions he uses should be recognized for the metaphorical and elliptical statements they were intended to be. However, if the remarks are taken literally and are read in relation to some statements in his later work which seem to point even more strongly in this direction, one might arrive at quite a different interpretation. Religion, he says,

wants to be gripped by the immediate influences [of the Universe] in childlike passivity, and to be filled by them.[112] [All feelings] are religious only in so far as they are immediately caused by the Universe.[113] [The religious man] lets himself be affected by the Infinite, without any definite activity, and reveals his reaction to the affection in all kinds of religious feeling. [More explicitly, he says] Your organs mediate the connection between you and the object, and the same affection by the latter, which reveals to you its being, must move you in many ways, and produce a change in your inner consciousness [feeling].[114] [So he says that in the religious experience] the eternal world affects the organs of our spirits as the sun affects our eyes.[115]

In the passage referred to above, in which he connects the feeling with the instinct, it is apparently the "effect" of the fact (and not explicitly our awareness of a meaning) which directly "ferments with our fundamental drives" to generate a feeling.[116]

Psychological accuracy was certainly not Schleiermacher's intent in writing this book, and hence too much reliance should not be placed on these passages, in the light of the evidence already adduced. Yet it would be rash to assert definitely that he did not have vaguely in mind here an idea which he seems to suggest later. At any rate, the idea at best plays a very minor role in this argument, and a glance at the amount of space devoted to the two aspects of the religious experience shows that intuition or interpretation is the foundation of his idea of religion and what he is most interested in.

Healthy religion, which comes from one's own insight and is not borrowed, is an intimately connected whole of intuition and feeling. The experience is distorted, becomes less than Schleiermacher means by religion, if either is absent. "Intuition without feeling is nothing, and can have neither right origin nor right strength. Feeling without intuition is also nothing. Both are only then and therefore something, when and because they are originally one and inseparable."[117] This, I take it, is his main contention. At least usually, he thinks that the emotional state wrought in the religious experience is consequent to, a result of, the "meaning" apprehended in the intuition.

5. The Noetic Value of Religious Intuition

What Schleiermacher says about the universe as a unity whose nature or manner of acting is manifested in the temporal world, and what he says about the perception of its nature in these manifestations, leaves the definite impression that he believed it possible for the religious man to have knowledge of that system. To my mind, this assumption is so fundamental to his position that it is impossible to give it up, even were he thereby proved inconsistent on some points. In a moment I shall offer evidence, an explanation of which seems to me out of the question unless we assume that Schleiermacher did believe that religious intuition is a "knowing" of what the universe truly is.

But on the other hand it must not be forgotten that in writing the *Discourses*, Schleiermacher had several other objectives which must have been at least equally important to his mind; clearly he was not concerned so much with proving the deliverances of religious "intui-tion" to be true, as simply in *commending* religion to his audience. And the religion which he wished to commend was not that of a system of dogmas, not the religion of intolerance and persecution. It was a religion like that of the Moravians, one which was primarily a valuable state of mind. In order to commend such a religion to his audience, the best strategy of attack was obviously not to show that it is an excellent means of getting hold of a unique kind of fact, but to indicate how it is a valuable subjective state, a natural part of human nature which contributes to the fullness of the individual life.

In this, incidentally, Schleiermacher is not alien to a more modern spirit in religion. And surely there is something to be said for one who approves of religion because it is valuable, and thinks that this part of religion justifies support of religious institutions whether the dogmatic claim to supernatural truth be valid or not.

If Schleiermacher's purpose be kept in mind, we shall be able to see the reasons why he occasionally ignored or even disparaged the noetic value of religion. Of course, to say that he had some reason to disparage the knowledge claims of religious intuition is not to say that it does not get his system into trouble, for I think we shall be convinced that it is as important for him to claim its noetic value as for anyone holding a more orthodox view of religion. But it is useful when examining some passage which emphasizes the difference be-tween religious intuition and philosophical or scientific knowledge, to know that one can usually find a motive lying behind the view expressed.

Moreover, the very method by which he undertook to determine the nature of religion involved him in a difficulty at the very outset. For in assuming that religion is a unique activity of mind, an "infinite force" whose nature is to be discovered by reasoning and analyzing history, he was also assuming that religion is, at least essentially, different from other activities of the mind. He was forced to try to make out a case for the reality of some mental activity beside scientific and philosophical knowing, morality, and artistic creation, an activity which is different from them not merely trivially, but in such an important way that the religious activity could deserve an equal amount of respect. This necessity was probably in part responsible for an undue tendency to ignore the noetic element in religion—a tendency which one must admit has probably been historically fruitful in encouraging impartial investigation into the nature of all the aspects of religion.

It is impossible to believe, however, that it was simply the method of investigation which caused Schleiermacher to separate religion so sharply from systems of knowledge. The main reason probably was Schleiermacher's conviction that religion is a valuable state of mind, and that the value in question is not merely, or even primarily one of knowledge. He was brought up among the Moravians, it must not be forgotten, and wrote that these folk, with the exception of their theology, have "a really good cause in religion," and that indications of this influence were obvious in his Discourses. He himself, he said, was a Moravian "of a higher order." Apparently what he thought especially valuable in Moravian religion was its "mystical tendency," the germ of his own view of mysticism and religion. For them as for him, religion was the center of life; it consisted in seeing the finger of God in every event and. in responding to this awareness with a rush of emotion. In like vein, Schleiermacher said that the most important things in his life, his friendships and his loves, acquired their full meaning for him only because of their relation to his religion. For him, religion meant the "inward and higher" view of the world. Thus, to his mind the important thing in religion was not the dogmas but "sense and taste for the Infinite" in the finite. So he wrote in his diary just before publishing the Discourses: "Dogmas arise only when religious sense is amputated, and there usually remains behind only the caput mortuum [of religion]."[118]

Religion in its subjective aspect is thus primarily an attitude to life, an accompaniment of experience with intuitions of "meaning" and responses to them in feeling. Its value is the richness it gives to life.

For this reason, the passages in which Schleiermacher comes nearest to offering a "proof" for religion are not concerned with the noetic value of religious intuitions at all, but with the value of a mind attuned to the Infinite. Religion, he says, restores balance both to onesidedly egoistic or hedonistic and to onesidedly active and moral spirits. It is a source of tolerance.[119] It saves from the chains of opinion and desire.[120] It supplements and broadens a morbidly moralistic attitude toward humanity.[121] It supplies harmony to life in that one learns to love the world-spirit. It provides an infinite and therefore satisfying object (just like the aesthetic object to the minds of others of the romanticists) for the devotion of those whose powers exceed the finite objects of their creative activity.[122] As longing for the Infinite, it is a counterpiece to the development of and appreciation for individuality.[123] Yet it also allows and encourages the development of individuality.[124] And more especially in relation to metaphysics and ethics, its intuition and accompaniment of feeling supply the natural counterpiece to the feeling of infinity and likeness to God created by them, which, in itself, is only a onesided response to reality.[125] Schleiermacher was convinced of the value of the religious mood, and was interested in safeguarding all which is essential to secure subjective religion as a really living thing.

Therefore, on the one hand, Schleiermacher says that the "secret moment" is the highest bloom of religion, because it is this moment when the individual person "sees" for himself out of his own experience that secures vital personal religion. And on the other hand, dogmas, which do not have this intimate personal character, are not really a part of religion. Dogmas, religious concepts, and didactic propositions are not "the real elements of religion, but contain abstractions" from it. They are

signs of similarity of result, in all . . . the final chorus, after the individual [aspect] has been communicated . . . in art.[126] [They are] the shadows of our intuitions and feelings, and unless the religious man can share these with us he does not understand what he says, nor what he believes he thinks. Intuition itself cannot be taught.[127] . . . Some dogmas are only abstract expressions of religious intuitions. Others are reflection on the original nature of the religious sense, i.e., results of a comparison of the religious outlook with the ordinary one. But it is a common error to mistake the content of a reflection for the essence of the event being reflected on.[128]

Thus one may have a great deal of religion without ever having the concepts of miracle, revelation, etc.

There is no suggestion here, one must note, that dogmas are not true. He is simply denying that they are identical with religion. But it must be admitted that he does seem, at least superficially, to disparage the noetic value of religion when he especially treasures the individual and unique aspect of a person's religion, and suggests that this is the part it is most valuable to communicate to others. Doubtless he esteems this individual part and the communication of it partly because it embodies the living core of the religious intuition, and partly because he thinks that anything which is individual is valuable and good. At any rate, he notes with approval that religious intuitions reflect the circumstances of their origin and the personality of the person who has them: "Another person may stand close beside you, and everything will appear different to him."[129] Schleiermacher wants to conserve these differences in intuition, because in doing so he is conserving the vital part of personal religion and the values of individuality.

Schleiermacher had other (I think less important) reasons for making the objective side of religious knowledge secondary. First, he wanted to protect religion from charges of intolerance and the spirit of persecution. And if religion is the passive contemplation of the universe, if religion has nothing to do with system building, if there are differences amongst intuitions and if these individual characters are of the very essence of the vitality of religion, then surely there cannot be any spirit of intolerance in religion itself. Only when philosophy and system (which are not part of its essential nature) are brought in, does religion become distorted and intolerance and persecution begin.[130] The religious man has no desire to make other persons see the universe just as he does; he is interested only in "opening the eyes of those who are not yet capable of intuiting it" for themselves.

Second, Schleiermacher believed that the universe and the number of individual forms manifested in it are infinite, and I believe therefore doubted the adequacy of a system of thought to exhaust it—although one might think that a system of thought could at least adequately represent the outline, which contention I think Schleiermacher would hardly have been disposed to deny. At any rate he says that in the universe, as in the starry heavens, everything is "indeterminate and infinite." So "you cannot say that your [special] horizon . . . encompasses everything, and that beyond it there is nothing more to intuit . . . You find limits nowhere, and you cannot conceive of any . . . Religion is infinite."[131]

These various causes—the exigency created by the belief that religion is an "infinite force" and hence unique, the conviction that the essence and value of religion are its subjective nature enriching the life of individual persons, the belief that religion, like all the other "infinite forces" must individuate itself into unique and interesting forms, the desire to defend religion against the charge of intolerance, and faith in the infinitude and inexhaustibleness of the universe—contributed to the separation of religion from any system of knowledge such as science or philosophy. Schleiermacher does not at all deny the possibility of a system of knowledge about the universe. But he is led sometimes to say that religion is not that. It stops short at intuition. It is not active systematizing; it is a passive state of being moved by the universe.

So Schleiermacher sharply distinguishes religion from any system of knowledge:

Intuition is and always remains something particular, unique, separate, the immediate perception and nothing further. To bring it into a connection and put it into a system is not the business of the senses, but that of abstract thought. Similarly with religion. It goes no further than the being and action of the Universe, than the particular intuitions and feelings. Religion knows nothing of deduction and logical connection. These, out of everything that could happen to her, are what contradict her nature the most. In religion, not only a single fact or event which could be called the primary and fundamental part of it, but everything is immediate and true for itself. . . . A *system* of intuitions! Can you imagine anything more remarkable? Can opinions [*Ansichten*], even opinions of the Universe be brought into a system? Can you say that because a person sees one thing in a certain way, he must see another thing in a certain way?[132] . . . Every intuition of the Infinite is fully for itself, is dependent on no other one, and also leads to no other one as a necessary conclusion . . . There is an infinite number of them, and in themselves there is no reason why they should have any given relation to other intuitions.[133]

Striking at any attempt to combine these intuitions into a system, he goes on to say that when the religious man (as distinct from the philosopher) combines the intuitions, his combinations are not comparable to the astronomer's objective grouping of galaxies, but rather to the childlike efforts of primitive man to group the stars into constellations—"the aptest and highest sensory image of religion."[134] Here all the divisions are arbitrary and indefinite, and new stars are continually discovered between the old groups, which shows the arbitrariness of the divisions and relations. Here, as in religion,

only the particular is true and necessary. No one thing can be proved, in religion, from another, and every kind of universal, under which the particular might be comprehended—every connection of this kind—either lies in an alien sphere, if it is related to the inward and the essential, or is a work of playful fantasy and the freest caprice.[135] [Religion stops at the particular intuition and when reflection goes beyond that point, it has transcended the sphere of religion.] [So the] religious man will subordinate any apparent connection to the particular, and will not sacrifice to the former the smallest interest of the latter.[136]

This confining of religion to particular intuitions, the denial that religion can have anything to do with a system of thought, this praise of the individual in religion (which, according to him, is what is to be communicated at religious gatherings), have earned for Schleiermacher the reproach of having made religion simply a matter of subjective caprice.* Hegel criticized Schleiermacher for it and always held it against him. In Schleiermacher's system, Hegel said,

The virtuosity of the religious artist is to be allowed to mingle subjectivity with the tragic earnestness of religion . . . And . . . this subjective part in the expression of one's own intuition of the Universe . . . is to constitute its essential truth and vitality . . . and the freedom of the highest intuition is to consist in this particularity and having something for oneself. . . . The [religious] community is to have the purpose and intention of allowing the inmost part of intuition to be influenced [by the priest] as a virtuoso of edification and inspiration. And instead of abolishing the subjective peculiarity of an intuition . . . it is to seek it, so that little communities and individualities get validity and are multiplied to infinity.[137]

* For parallels to these statements in his later work, see pp. 188-189.

It is not necessary for us to pass our own critical judgment on Schleiermacher here, for the reason that, as I shall argue, he must have been aware of the importance of objectivity or knowledge in religion. But it is perhaps worth while to reflect that if it turned out that religious statements are only produced by subjective fantasy, or are just the expression of feelings—conclusions which would be heartily embraced by certain radical empiricists in our day—it would almost certainly be true that religion would eventually lose even its emotional significance. Only what is believed to be true, I think, can arouse the "religious feelings." At any rate, the philosopher of religion would be relieved of his onerous task, for if religious statements are not meaningful propositions asserted to be true, there is no need for one to defend or formulate them. The field is left to the psychologist.

Before diagnosing Schleiermacher's weakness, in order to show how one or two incorrect assumptions allowed him to admit this subjectivity into religious intuition, and also to obscure his very notion of the intuition itself (which seems to me to have been a valuable suggestion), we must produce the long-promised evidence that Schleiermacher did believe that religious intuitions furnish objective knowledge of the nature of the universe.

(a) Schleiermacher denies that any response to the merely beautiful or sublime in nature can be a religious intuition.

What is this, [he says] not in your eye, but in and for the Universe? For you must put the matter thus, if it is to be something for religion. . . . You must remember that if you want to think of these things as in the Whole, you will find that these appearances, strongly as they move you, are still not suitable to be intuitions of the world. Although, perhaps, from a higher level [they could be viewed as such].[188]

This seems to mean that religious intuitions are not matters of fancy, not mere impressions. They are a serious interpretation of the meaning of an event or fact for the whole. And the suggestion is that what, because of present limitation, cannot be successfully interpreted as a part of the whole, may nevertheless be intelligible upon a higher level, presumably where more knowledge is available.

(b) Some of the intuitions of religion, according to Schleiermacher, are to be based upon the results of science. The religious man, he says, discovers the laws of the whole in the laws of nature discovered by the scientists.[139] The progress of physical science makes possible more varied and richer intuitions than were possible in the earlier stages of religion. "A richer age has allowed us to press deeper into [nature's] inmost being."[140] And although religion gets its highest intuitions not so much from the orderly events in nature as from the anomalies which suggest a higher unity, these anomalies also have a "rule which could be discovered from a higher standpoint."[141] Religious intuitions thus seem sometimes to be interpretations of the results of science, and where they concern the higher unities which science has not explored, they are intimations of an order which is truly there and would be known on a higher level. There is no reason to believe that he thought this process simply the construction of imagination; it is a construction, but it is also a searching for what is really there.

(c) Prophecy is a part of religion. History, he says, is the understanding of a moment in the universal process, after it has occurred. Similarly, prophecy

is the anticipation of the other half of a religious event, when the first half is already given. And it was religious of the Hebrews to measure the divinity of the prophet not by the complexity of the prophecy, but simply by the outcome [fulfillment]. For we cannot know whether a person has understanding in the sphere of religion, until we see if he has rightly comprehended the religious view of precisely that particular event which has affected him.[142]

Thus religion, like history, seems to be concerned with an actual "movement" of the universe, and if the beginning of a movement is understood, its conclusion can be anticipated. Apparently religion perceives facts, and sometimes its assertions can be verified, like those of science, by fulfillment of prediction.

(d) Although "sense" is not concerned with the logical system of science, he says of it that

the scope and the truth of the intuition depend on the sharpness and breadth of sense, and the wisest person without sense is no closer to religion than the most foolish who has the right insight.[143] The healthier the sense, the more clearly and definitely it will apprehend every impression. [Moreover, "sense" apprehends something which is missed by science:] It strives to grasp the undivided impression of something whole; it strives to intuit what and how everything is for itself, and to know

it in its individual character.[144] [Schleiermacher can even lay down definite experiences which condition the possibility of such a "sensing" of the
nature of the whole.] In order to intuit the world and have religion [he
says] one must first have discovered humanity, and one discovers it only
in and through love.[145]

Religion thus seems to be an apprehension of the nature of the world
in its interconnection and significance as a system, from a level where
the false view of objects, as given separate particulars, has been
given up.

(e) Religious intuition, he says, is not biased or one-sided.

The moral world is not the Universe, and what were valid only for that
would be no religious intuition of the Universe. Religion knows how to
discover . . . the acts of the World-Spirit in everything which belongs to
human conduct, in play as in the serious, in the small as in the large.
What religion is able to perceive, it must perceive everywhere.[146]

It is not an emotional reaction to one event or special set of events;
it is an apprehension of the whole universe as a system, and of events
as having significance in that system.

(f) Furthermore, he believes that when some single intuition has
been made the foundation of some positive religion (and this always
occurs), all the other intuitions become so modified as to form a
whole with it. "When for anyone the sense for the Universe is opened
up in a definite intuition and a clear awareness, one afterwards relates
everything else to this . . . and through this moment that person's
religion is determined . . ."[147] This seems to mean that the intuitions
stand in logical relations of significance to one another, so that when
one of them is made fundamental the others must be altered in order
to fit in with the central intuition. If so, then what he says here is not
strictly compatible with his denial that religion has anything to do
with *systems* of thought. If he does not mean that the other intuitions
are altered because of their logical relation to the central intuition, I
do not know what he possibly can mean.

(g) Finally, a number of expressions occurring in the book could
not sensibly be used unless he thought that there is some difference
between intuitions, with respect to truth or interpretational value.
The trouble with certain viciously subjective religious people, he says,
is that

a light and various play of lovely . . . but always accidental and entirely subjective combinations satisfies them, and is their highest; a deeper and more inward connection offers itself to their eyes in vain. They are really seeking only the infinity and universality of attractive appearance— which is either far less or far more than that for which "sense" is really adequate.[148] [Second, the central intuition of Judaism, he says, is] child-like. It could work only on a narrow scene, without complications, when, the whole being simple, the natural consequences of actions would not be disturbed or hindered. The more the adherents of the religion advanced on the scene of the world, and had relations with other peoples, the more difficult became the confirmation of this view. Imagination had to anticipate the word which the Almighty would speak, and, transcending space and time, bring the second part of the moment before the eyes from out of the far distance.[149] [The central intuition of Christianity (of reconciliation through mediators) on the other hand, is] more worthy of adult humanity, and extends itself further over the whole Universe.[150] [Third, he says that the value] of your religion depends on the way in which you intuit the Universe, and on the principle which you find in its actions.[151]

Thus a religion, through superiority in this respect, is "better" than an inferior one, even though the latter were distinguished by having the idea of a God. The intuitions of polytheism are "infinitely more dignified" than those of fetishism. One who intuits the world as a plurality has more religion than the worshipper of a fetish. The universe deserves its name only when it is viewed as a totality and unity, as system, and one who intuits it as such has more religion, he says, than the most refined polytheist. If religion were concerned only with a subjective experience or response of any kind, one intuition would presumably be as good as another.

On the basis of this evidence—and of the coherence of the interpretation of it with further evidence to come later—I shall assume that Schleiermacher did believe that the "interpretations" of the religious man do put him into touch with the truth. I shall therefore hypothetically reject what seems to me to be the only other reasonable alternative, namely, that he thought it a good thing that these intuitions, as psychological events, should occur, although they are only creations of the subjective imagination, and have no claim to truth, or indeed, make no claim to be knowledge. Our problem, then, is to understand the nature of the religious intuition sufficiently clearly to be able to see how it is possible for the "subjectivist" strain in Schleiermacher's system to exist beside his "objectivist" conception of religion.

In order to make the matter as clear as possible, I shall first of all state in my own words what I believe Schleiermacher thought on this point (though I am not sure how clearly or explicitly he had it in mind), and in doing so shall state briefly but nevertheless in more detail than heretofore my final conception of what he means by "intuition."

A religious "intuition" seems to be almost identical with an hypothesis or theory in science, although it differs in a way which I hope to make clear in a moment. These "intuitions" are hypotheses about the nature or behavior of the universe as a whole system. As such, they assume without proof that the universe is such a system. The assumption that the universe is such a system might be said to be the postulate of religiousness, part of the definition of what is meant by a religious man. That postulate is certainly the center of what Schleiermacher means by religiousness. Religion only comes to itself when the world is viewed as a system, as unity in plurality. A person on this level of "insight" is "more religious" than someone on the lower levels.

The nature of this "postulate" and its relation to religious "hypotheses" can be made clearer, I believe, by comparing it with the principle of the uniformity of nature, or the inductive principle or postulate discussed by some recent writers. Physical science apparently proceeds on the assumption that there is a simple constitution of nature, with a finite number of different kinds of entity related to one another in a few fairly simple ways. It assumes that certain kinds of evidence can justify it in the assertion that it is quite probable that some hypothesis correctly represents, or at least comes within a fair measure of accurately representing, the structure of that system. The claim of the religious man, according to Schleiermacher, is analogous to this. He assumes that there is a regular order or system of the universe as a whole, and that in some cases he has grasped the nature of that order, in the religious intuition of some event.

But there is a further analogy between science and religion. Some logicians have believed that the initial assumption of the uniformity of nature is itself to some extent confirmed and strengthened by the building up of a science of nature, by the fulfillment of predictions and the accumulation of a system of as yet unrefuted hypotheses. This again, although it is not an explicit contention of Schleiermacher, I believe is really a part of his system. The religious man's faith in the universe as a system is strengthened and confirmed by his ability to discover the signs of system, of the teleological whole which he thinks the world to be. For example, Schleiermacher thinks that the central intuition of the Jewish religion was the universe's award of penalties for sin in this life. And if it were true that the religious man could discover order of this sort in the world (which Schleiermacher denied in this case), the confirmation of this particular hypothesis in given cases would also strengthen the fundamental assumption of the unity of the whole.

It might be objected that if the religious intuition were an hypothesis about the Infinite, Schleiermacher could never have called it an "intuition," nor argued that it is immediate. But from the point of view of the psychology of discovery, there is immediacy even in science. One recalls the events surrounding some of the great mathematical discoveries of Hamilton and Poincaré. According to the testimony of these men, the solutions to their problems came all at once, in a flash, although of course they had apparently been thinking of the problems at intervals for some time previous. The solution seems to have emerged complete from the "subconscious." I submit that part of what Schleiermacher had in mind when he called intuitions "immediate" was something of this sort. They appear unsolicited in the minds of those who are accustomed to contemplate the universe. Just as, in fitting together a picture puzzle, the structure and outline are "seen" in a flash, religious intuition may be regarded as an immediate "seeing" of the pattern of the Infinite, as it is manifested in the finite. In this, religion might be said to be like mathematics, except in that its results, as we shall see, are not verifiable in the same way.

A description of the content of a number of Schleiermacher's "intuitions," which will be undertaken in the next section, will tend to substantiate the above interpretation. We shall see how Schleiermacher discovered the universe in its lavish production of individual forms, in its being a work of art, in the adaptation of nature to the existence of organisms, in the progress of humankind through history, in the reconciliation of human minds to the universe, by the universe, through the coming of "mediators." I think Schleiermacher believed, as I suppose many religious people have believed, that not only is the nature of the universe to be discovered in these events, but these events in themselves confirm belief that the universe is a self-organizing, "teleological" whole. In Schleiermacher's system, I suppose, the teleological argument for the existence of God could be interpreted as a religious intuition. For this argument claims to discover the adaptedness of nature to organic and human nature, to the existence of beauty in nature itself, and to the development of moral character. And this argument claims that these "intuitions" confirm or point to the goodness and power of God, which Schleiermacher would have described by saying that the universe "takes account of" values and highly developed forms of consciousness.

The difference between religious intuition and science is evident upon examination of the nature of the hypotheses elaborated by each. Physics asserts that, for any event of such and such a character, such and such will also be true or will happen. Newton's laws, or their modern mathematical equivalent, furnish an example. These hypotheses admit quantitative testing, usually in the laboratory. In contrast, in religion, except in cases where what Schleiermacher would call prophecy is involved, I do not see how this kind of confirmation could take place. The kind of event in question cannot be reproduced in the laboratory, for the religious man asserts something about the way of acting of the universe as a whole, not something about the behavior of any part of it taken by itself. Schleiermacher said that history is the "sublimest object of religion"; it is clear that statements about the course of history cannot be tested in the laboratory. Moreover, there cannot be any quantitative testing of a religious assertion. One might try to confirm the supposed Hebrew idea that the universe is a system of award for moral or immoral conduct. One might undertake a statistical study correlating known sins with known misfortunes among the subjects of the study, although such a study would obviously not be accurate. But in the case of intuitions such as the adaptedness of the inorganic to the organic, or the production of beauty in the world, it is impossible to arrive at any exact quantitative estimate, partly because there is no method for comparing values, and partly because it is as yet impossible to agree about the antecedent probability of the world's being just as it is, even if the religious hypothesis is false. I suppose that ultimately this difficulty of quantitative measurement arises for the same reason as the impossibility of laboratory experiment, that religion is dealing with the universe as a whole.

Another difference between religious intuitions and science (a difference which is again a part cause of the described availability of confirmatory methods for science) is the abstractness of the procedure of science.* Physics is interested in measuring only certain relations of bodies, e.g., mass and acceleration. This abstractness is in part a consequence of the desire for information relevant to practical control. Were the scientist to introduce himself to the problem of discovering how, for example, Henriette Herz was different from everybody else (the intuition of the universe in her individuality), he would probably find the problem one to which the methods of physics are not adapted.

It seems to me that what Schleiermacher meant by religious intuition can legitimately be separated from the empirical hypotheses of science, and Schleiermacher was quite correct in contending that this kind of religion is not the same thing as science.

An analysis of the relation between this "religious intuition" and rational philosophical thought must be undertaken in order to complete our description of Schleiermacher's concept. But before attempting to deal with this, I shall try to indicate the relationship between this "objective" view of religious intuition and the passages quoted previously, in which religion was connected with particular, passive intuitions, which are the very opposite of a system of thought.

Schleiermacher's belief is that the religious intuition is like sense perception. It consists of immediate, separate data. Each one is independent of every other. It is the opposite of abstract thought. It is mistaken to hold that because one sees one thing in a certain way, one must also see another thing in a certain way. Any system among them is purely arbitrary.

The first thing to notice about Schleiermacher's contention is that

* A vitalist in biology might hold that biology is like Schleiermacher's "intuition" when it has to face problems of organization.

he seems to be mistaken about the nature of even sense perception. Of course, there is one respect in which what he says is true. When a person looks on the shelf for a favorite book, he does not go through a complex train of reasoning when he recognizes it. The book as such, with all its "meaning" of enjoyment contained therein, is directly and immediately "perceived." But there are two respects in which logical thought must be said to enter into this case of sense perception. First, recognition of the book, along with its "meaning," is largely dependent upon previous experience. Whatever the physiology of it, or despite the fact that certain complex properties of the seen book such as its being extended in three dimensions are not a result of previous experience, the fact remains that some of the most significant characters of the perceptual book are dependent upon past experience. The "meaning" and recognition of the book are now (phenomenologically) unmediated, independent; but genetically, the experience is mediated and dependent upon the past or "interpretations" arising out of it. In its unmediated aspect, the sense perception does seem to be the opposite of abstract thought and logical system; it does seem to be independent of the processes by which anything else may be perceived. In its mediated aspect (which is the aspect we get at through critical thought), it is not the opposite of thought and system, and it is not independent of the means through which anything else is perceived. Schleiermacher seems to have been mistaken in what he says about sense perception, if he really meant his account to be a complete one. A second defect will appear in a moment.

The same criticism can be made of Schleiermacher's treatment of religious intuitions. It is true that, as has been pointed out above, these intuitions (like scientific hypotheses) may be immediate and passive in a sense. What is intuited may take on "meaning" in an instant, and not at the end of a conscious and laborious process of deduction. Phenomenologically, the meaning may be unmediated. But genetically, a religious intuition is at least as mediated as a sense perception. It is highly improbable that such an intuition would occur in a mind not devoted to "intuiting the Universe." As Schleiermacher himself says, it requires "sense" and "imagination." What is more, he admits that the "objects" of religious intuition manifest the work of imagination in a way in which the ordinary objects of common-sense experience do not;[152] imagination is to go out actively to construct the world, though there is a sense in which its work is "passively" rewarded by an intuition. The religious view of the world, the intuition already adopted as central in a religion, in fact all one's previous intuitions, it appears, are involved in the genesis of the new intuition. Every "interpretation" must be a member of a system of "interpretations." On Schleiermacher's own showing, I believe, this is more true of religion than of sense perception; religious interpretation is closer to a system of thought.

There is a further sense in which both sensory and religious perception involve a system of thought. For when one judges, "There is a book," just as when one judges "The Universe punishes all sin during this life," there are legitimate reasons for questioning the truth of the assertion. All the facts which have been used as a basis for epistemological dualism and phenomenalism call for a systematic justification of the claim that the object of perception is existentially independent of the act of perception, and that at least some of its properties which are possessed independently are truly perceived in that perceptual experience. The claim of perceptual experience requires a metaphysical justification. Similarly, any more complex judgment, such as the religious intuition mentioned, will require an even more elaborate justification, both as to the reality of the unity, and the truth of the judgment that the property in question is possessed by the unity. Religious intuitions, as much as or more than perceptual judgments, require the justification obtainable only from a system of thought.

If Schleiermacher did intend to maintain more than the phenomenological immediacy, passivity, and independence of perceptual and religious judgments alike, he was mistaken. Any further kind of immediacy is as much in conflict with the rest of his system as it is with the facts. My belief is that if he did really hold these incompatible subjective and objective positions at the same time, this inconsistency must have been caused by a failure to recognize the mediation of perceptual and religious "intuitions" alike, a failure which, however, is scarcely conceivable.

The objective strain in Schleiermacher's thought is fundamental. The subjective strain has motives, good ones, from the point of view of one who is convinced of the value of the religious activity. But it seems that the subjective element can be made fundamental, at least in its extremer form, only at the price of what Hegel called "the tragic earnestness of religion."

Perhaps Schleiermacher's instincts were right in impelling him to maintain the independence of particular religious judgments, their separateness and disconnection from any system of thought. For so soon as they are recognized for what I believe they are—hypotheses about the Infinite—they cannot escape becoming parts of the one system of truth, and calling for support upon that system for ultimate substantiation of their validity. This means that religion is ultimately not separable from philosophy—a conclusion which, however, I do not believe Schleiermacher himself completely denied, since he always believed that materialism is incompatible with religion.

Let us now turn to his view of the relation of philosophy and religion. There are some passages in the *Discourses* which suggest that he was not prepared seriously to deny *all* relation between religion and philosophy, as he sometimes seems to do. For example, in the very middle of a "subjective" passage, he says that "every connection and combination of this kind either lies in an alien sphere, if it is related to the inward and essential, or is a work of playful fantasy and the purest caprice."[153] This means that the religious intuition can be included, perhaps ought to be included, within the system of knowledge, but that this is the business not of religion but of philosophy.

Dialectical reasoning such as Fichte's is sharply contrasted with religion. Philosophy "deduces the necessity of the real," whereas "religion dares not lose itself in an infinity of reasons and deductions."[154] Philosophy starts with the "finite nature of man, and seeks to determine . . . from the scope of his powers and receptivity with consciousness what the Universe can possibly be for him and how he must necessarily see it,"[155] whereas religion starts with the Infinite, and intuits it lovingly. Philosophy is abstract:

It is the limitation of [only bad or of all?] philosophy to separate self-intuition and intuition of the Universe . . . Their . . . philosophy is a lifeless picture, if they must first quench the light of life, in order to portray their inner being in the narrow space of an abstraction.[156] [As opposed to this, he praises Schelling for showing the limitations of dialectic, and for] leaving room for mysticism beyond the limits of philosophy.[157]

But although religion is not philosophy in that it is not dialectical reasoning, not epistemology, not abstract, Schleiermacher seems to relate them by going on to say that religion is indispensable to philosophy, a statement hardly possible if he thought them quite unrelated.

There is little hope for a philosophy which rests simply on a dialectical basis, without any mysticism.[158] . . . Without mysticism, it is impossible to be strictly logical, because one does not pursue one's thoughts to the Unconditioned.[159] Ethics can be only a bare traditional skeleton without religion, for it requires religious intuitions to teach it the value of individuality.[160] [In the absence of religious intuition, metaphysics becomes an empty play with words:] Everything must begin with intuition, and if you lack the desire to intuit the Infinite, you have no touchstone, and really need none to know if you have really thought about it.[161]

Fichte's transcendental philosophy, he says, has negated the universe, because it has not been taught a higher realism at the feet of religion.

But let us suppose there could be a philosophy which attempted to show the necessary relations of the Infinite and the finite, which included within its scope not merely the abstract aspects dealt with in physics, but dealt with society, art, history, and values. Suppose it attempted to show that the manifestations of the Infinite in all these form a system, and that the Infinite could not have being outside of such a system. Let us suppose that such a philosophical system were possible. How then would religious intuition be related to it?

Schleiermacher wrote, in discussion of the effort of the transcendental philosophy to provide a unified basis for metaphysics and ethics, that one must be careful, or "you will get a religion which stands far above philosophy as it exists at the present time." But how would religion be related to a philosophy which tried to show that the universe is a system, and to elaborate that system? This is not an idle question, for only a short time later, he himself praised Plato and Spinoza because their thought, according to him, began with the Infinite and asserted that the sciences must be deduced from a highest science, apparently a science of the Infinite. It is deduction from a highest science, I think, that he is praising in the *Discourses* when he says that the ideal philosophy and science sweep away "appearance and attain the essence; its glance is sure; its view is clear—recognizing an identical being under all disguises, and resting nowhere except in the Infinite and One."[162]

The suggestion seems to be that the content of Schleiermacher's religious intuitions was very closely related to the philosophy of Schelling, and the later elaboration by Hegel. And yet he emphasizes the difference. In his diary he wrote:

Philosophy and religion are concerned with the ideal activity, ethics and aesthetics with the real. Thus what religion intuits cannot be a production of philosophy, but of ethics and aesthetics. Really it is thus: There is only a philosophy of nature and of humanity, and a religion of the world and of art; but no philosophy of religion and no religion of philosophy.[163]

Religion and philosophy have the same subject matter, but are different. My conjecture is that Schleiermacher here had in mind the subjective, imaginative character of religion as opposed to its character as knowledge—a difficulty discussed above.

There is reason to believe, as has been pointed out,[164] that Schleiermacher is sometimes confused on this matter; sometimes he seems to confuse religion with the philosophy of religion, and not to be certain whether it is religion or the philosophy of religion which is so valuable for speculative and practical philosophy. We find a close similarity between his *method for investigating religion* and his descriptions of religious intuitions. When he says that the religious view of things is to seek for "every trace of the divine, true, and eternal,"[165] he is not describing anything essentially different from his own method of treating religion, i.e., the view that religious phenomena are products of the "forces" in the universe, that the whole is moving within it, that religion is individualized like everything else in the universe. His *method* of investigation does not seem to be different from what he calls "viewing religion with religion."[166] The religious man, it is said, regards every event as an act of the universe; the French Revolution is one of its divinest acts. But is this different from Friedrich Schlegel's analysis of the history of art? Could not the religious man regard art as an act of the universe, and trace out stages in its development, thus getting insight into the nature of the whole? In fact, in the first edition of the *Discourses*, history is said to be the greatest object of religion, the most convenient show-place where the acts of the universe can be contemplated. For all this going behind the realm of common-sense objects, for all this discovery of "real" wholes or unities, for all this discovery of the Infinite in inorganic nature, in the organic world and in the human mind, it is hard to believe that one need not have reflected philosophically, but only have "open senses."

Schleiermacher's "religious intuitions" are closely bound up with a theory of the universe, and in their character as objective knowledge they can be vindicated only by being incorporated in a whole system of philosophy. This assertion, of course, does not deny that, phenomenologically, religious truths are "given" and not reasoned, or that, psychologically, religious beliefs arise where no philosophical proof has been offered. Again, Schleiermacher is probably right that feelings are an essential part of religion, whereas they are only accidental for philosophers. For religion, "seeing with one's own eyes" in such a way that what is seen is bound up intimately with personal experience and attitudes is necessary; whereas for philosophy, so long as the facts, arguments, and their implications are understood, it does not matter how they were learned or whether they are connected with personal experience.

6. The Content of Religious Intuition

A description of some of the religious intuitions which Schleiermacher thought important will enable us to fill in the sketchy outlines of his view of the world. The following discussion of them presupposes as its framework what we have already said about the nature of the universe, its "composition" out of "forces," its unity, its perfection, its harmony, its transparence to thought. What our discussion will add to this framework is merely a more complete account of Schleiermacher's attitude to nature, to minds, to history, to moral conduct, and to the development of individuality. In all these matters it is impossible to draw any line between what Schleiermacher apparently "thought," and what as a religious man he "intuited." The only difference between the religious and the philosophical here seems to be in the psychological setting in the mind of the subject. What he recounts as the most striking examples of religious perception tell us what he thought about the world.

It is rather surprising to find that he disparaged what he called the religion of nature. For it is an important characteristic of his view that it gives nature a reality which had not been ascribed to it by Fichte. Moreover, he seems to think that any event may become a fruitful object of religious intuition. "Religion," he says, "is to view all events in the world as acts of God."[167] He thinks that a highly specialized study of any object must eventually require consideration of the universe, because the more thoroughly it is studied, the more impossible it is to regard it as something separate and independent; specialization leads to the unity and system of the whole.

Despite these facts, however, Schleiermacher had comparatively little interest in nature. As he expressed it to his sister, his interest was in "the inward and higher."[168] He wrote to Henriette Herz:

> You, too, have always regarded nature as dead stuff. . . . Friedrich [Schlegel] has special ideas about nature, which I do not understand—but I do understand my own treatment of it. . . . I am in bitter earnest with my belief that chemical processes exhaust nature, and I lose many a joy on that account, but in any case I hold that kind of enjoyment to be an inferior variety.*

Consequently Schleiermacher had little sympathy for any kind of religion which consisted chiefly of awe at the sublimity of nature or an appreciation of its beauty. Awe at the sublimity of nature is a feeling which is inappropriate when the true character of nature is understood, he thought. Nature is not a worthy object of awe. Its size, immense though it is, can be comprehended in a little formula. "To see the Infinite there," he says, "is a childish way of thinking."[169] Sometimes it exercises unrestrained power of destruction; yet fundamentally it is something to be understood, mastered, harnessed, and made the slave of man. Nature has its place in the system of the world, but its place is not one which justifies fear. The religious attitude appropriate to nature is "to love the World-Spirit and to view its actions joyfully; that is the goal of our religion, and fear is not in love."[170]

The emotional response to beauty in nature has equally little to do with religion. The reason for this is that the collection and arrangement of secondary qualities, the colors and sounds which evoke aesthetic enjoyment, do not have any reality outside the human mind.

---

* *Briefe*, vol. I, p. 239. This seems inconsistent with his tendency to take a more organic view of nature.

They "disappear as an accidental appearance, so soon as you think of the all-pervading stuff whose developments they accompany. Think of how a dark cellar can rob a plant of all its beauties, without destroying its nature." The colors of the sunset are "really" only the same kind of light which is so unpleasantly dazzling at noon. "These appearances, strongly as they may move you, are not suited to be intuitions of the world."[171]

Schleiermacher's judgment that the feeling of awe or the enjoyment of natural beauty is not itself religion seems to be a sound one. He might very well have given better reasons for the distinction, however; it would be easy to show that the religious experience, as he defines it, is not to be identified with them. One cannot but feel, however, that he might have made more of the beauty of nature. It is true that he says that perhaps "on a higher level"* we may be filled with a genuine religious feeling at the intuition of the unity and all-pervasiveness of material force. But surely, even though it be granted that aesthetic enjoyment itself is not religion, the religious man does not have to ascend to some "higher level" to see that the beauty in nature may also be an expression of the nature of the universe. So far as I can see, the beauty in nature has as much claim to be regarded as an "act of the Universe" as does the French Revolution. The physical conditions of the aesthetic enjoyment of nature could be regarded as an instance of the adaptation of the inorganic world to mind, as well as other facts which he brings up elsewhere. Such an interpretation would fit in perfectly with his system. It is an odd fact that he should on the one hand be accused of making religion practically aesthetic enjoyment of the universe, and on the other hand be so depreciatory of the religious value of inorganic nature.

I have already suggested one or two clues which might account for his attitude: his interest in the "inward and higher," his conviction that inorganic nature is exhausted in chemical processes. A remark about Hülsen's philosophy of nature (in which he was moderately interested) serves to some extent to confirm what we have said. Hülsen's treatise in the *Athenaeum*, he says, "is nature-religion, and I doubt, therefore, whether it will have much effect on me. My reli-

* Perhaps he is referring to the possibility of a science of beauty or of the judgments of beauty.

gion is so through and through a heart religion, that I have not room for any other"[172]—an attitude which may well represent the lingering influence of Moravian religion.

Certain other aspects of the natural world, he says, are better suited to be objects of religious intuition. These other events afford insight into the nature of the whole. Its law-abidingness both in the inorganic and the organic world is the first and simplest intuition of the character of the Infinite. A more penetrating insight into the higher unity of nature is secured through its anomalies; these apparently baffling obstacles to insight eventually prove to be indications of a loftier order in the Infinite, whose nature could be known on a higher level.* Observe, for example, the relation of the organic to the inorganic, how inorganic matter furnishes an abundance of nourishment for the forms of life. Christ's sublimest intuition of nature was expressed in that phrase, "Consider the lilies of the field, how they grow: they toil not, neither do they spin. . . . Wherefore, if God so clothe the grass of the field . . ." The results of science secure to our time a more complex knowledge of this organization of nature: the universal operation of the forces of attraction and repulsion, the concretion of the identical substances in a thousand individual forms. This, he says, is the spirit of the material world.[173]

Schleiermacher believes the fundamental nature of the Infinite to be revealed much less in subhuman nature, however, than in the human mind. "The real object of religion is thus the spirit, and it is from it that religion gets its intuitions of the world. The Universe is reflected in the inner life, and the outer world becomes intelligible only through it."[174] And the human mind can be found, in its full nature, only by examining human experience in society.

For Schleiermacher, life in society, friendship, and love are the fountainheads of religious knowledge. They were the favorite objects of his contemplation, probably not only because they enriched his personal life in Berlin (where he himself was praised as a virtuoso in friendship), but because they were intimately connected with what he regarded as the most fundamental problem of philosophy, the

---

* *Reden*, pp. 83-84. I presume he refers to biological events such as the birth of a physiologically abnormal child as at least one case of "anomalies" in nature. He is right that these are anomalies only on the level of common sense, not on that of scientific genetics.

problem of individuality. To his mind social intercourse was one of the most fundamental values; and it was there that he discovered the best revelation of the nature of the universe.

In comparison with the emphasis placed upon moral conflict by Kant and Fichte, it may seem that Schleiermacher was only superficial and artificial in evaluating social intercourse so highly. Criticism should be withheld, however, until we see more fully his view of the significance of human friendship and love. In any event we must credit him with being a consistent determinist; he did not try to avail himself of the values and concepts which are the special property of those who believe in the freedom of the will.

Somewhat paradoxically, Schleiermacher talks a great deal about "freedom" in the *Soliloquies*, and it is precisely through an understanding of what he meant by this word that we can best appreciate the relationship between his determinism and this high valuation of social intercourse. For this reason it will be worth our while to digress for a brief space and consider his doctrine of "freedom."

Schleiermacher's view on this matter may be anticipated from the fact that he praises Spinoza for having the right basis for an ethical system, and at the same time criticizes Fichte for being an indeterminist.[175] His view comes out explicitly in a review of Fichte's *Vocation of Man*, which he wrote shortly after the publication of the *Discourses*. In this review he says that the dominant motive of the indeterminist is only "interest in himself, in his personality as a finite being," desire to be something for himself. This selfish motive is what lies behind insistence upon the ideas of moral imputation, guilt, and merit. This is one side of Fichte. But he says there is occasionally a different spirit in Fichte's book, according to which

all these indeterminate concepts and petty tendencies have disappeared . . . since he has destroyed the monstrous concept of an Infinite as nature in itself, and knows the Infinite as ultimately mental. His ego now sees that there is no such thing as guilt or merit in particular matters, but only in that one is what one is. It knows that, with this application of the concept, [the problem] falls into the absolutely incomprehensible. . . .[176]

In a similarly deterministic vein, he says in the *Discourses* that religion "sees man from the point of view, from which he must be what he is, whether he wishes or not."[177] "Everyone," he says, "is a work of the Universe, and religion can regard him only thus."[178]

What then is the "freedom" of which he talks so much? Schleiermacher would have defined it, I believe, in the words of Spinoza: "That thing is said to be free, which exists by the mere necessity of its own nature and is determined in its actions by itself alone. That thing is said to be necessary or rather compelled, when it is determined in its existence and actions by something else in a certain fixed ratio."*

If we assume that Schleiermacher defined "freedom" in this way, most of his remarks about it then become intelligible. Examine the following passage, for instance:

Ethics proceeds from the consciousness of freedom, seeks to extend its kingdom to infinity, and make everything subordinate to it. Religion breathes where freedom itself has become nature again. It comprehends man on the other side of the play of his particular powers, and of his personality. . . . [179]

It may be that in the first part of this statement Schleiermacher is borrowing the language of Fichte, but what he seems to be saying is that while, from the point of view of action, what is done is determined without constraint by the acting self, from the point of view of religion from which the self too must be considered in its place in the system of nature, the self which determines its actions freely must be regarded as itself a consequence of the nature which brought it forth. From the point of view of the acting individual, each agent is free; from the point of view of the whole system, only the world as a whole is ultimately what it is because of its own nature. This, I believe, is his reason for saying that freedom "has meaning only in and for the particular being."[180] Freedom for the individual self, then,

* Ethics, Bk. I, Def. 7. Cf. his definition of "freedom" in later life in The Christian Faith, 2nd ed., sec. 81, par. 2. (English trans.) He says: "The very phrase 'freedom of the will' conveys a denial of all external necessity, and indicates the very essence of conscious life, the fact, namely, that no external influence determines our total condition in such a way that the reaction too is determined and given, but every excitation really receives its determinate quality from the inmost core of our own life, from which quality, again, proceeds the reaction, so that the sin proceeding from that core is in every case the act of the sinner and of no other. In like manner, the expression 'freedom of the will' negatives the idea that the individual is in all cases pre-determined by the common nature of man." Cf. also sec. 119, par. 1, and sec. 55, par. 3.

means that despite the determination of the nature of itself by the source of its own being, the self is always able to develop and express its own peculiar nature even in the face of obstacles; the self can never be prevented from realizing its own proper nature. Ethical necessity, then, is external limitation of self-realization, an interpretation apparently confirmed by the following statement in which he is denying that there is really any "necessity":

Where is the limit to my power? Where does that fearful alien sphere begin? Impossibility lies only in the limitation of my nature by the first act of freedom: only what I gave up as I determined who I wanted to become—only that lies beyond me. Nothing is impossible except what would reverse that original volition. . . . Always to become more what I already am is my only desire. Every action is a specific phase in the unfolding of this single will . . . and I am always able to act in this manner.[181]

In a similar vein he says that the only one who need feel himself a slave to ethical necessity is the sensualist who regards himself as a collection of "fleeting appearances," and therefore is more subject to external circumstance than he who aims to realize himself as an individual being.

Freedom, then, is the (externally) unrestrained development of the personality. Sometimes, he admits, outward events make the normal development of the personality impossible, just as his own (up to that time) unmarried life prevented him from developing his individuality in certain specific relations. But even in such a case, he thinks, the individuality can be developed by letting the imagination dwell upon the relations which are not actually possible. Nothing can prevent the self from becoming what is its nature to be. Its only compulsion lies in the fact that it is what it is, and cannot be a different self. Its freedom is the possibility of the realization of its individual nature.

"Freedom" is a central idea in Schleiermacher's ethics. Verbally, his theory resembles that of Kant and Fichte. "Be free" is the chief command of reason. But the command, for him, does not mean simply to free oneself from the chains of sense desire, to act according to universal law. "Be free" means "Be yourself," "Be in every relation of your life the self that you are implicitly." It means, "Develop your

personality in all its relations to other persons and the world, so that
it becomes more completely what it is already."

This command to be "free" gets content only if it is possible to
know what the "self" is which is to be realized. This information,
apparently, is to be supplied by religion, which includes an appreciation of the "meaning" of the individual person in his relation to the
whole. Every person has an appointed place as an organ in the universe, and it is the fulfillment of this unique place which is the goal
of "free" action. Religion sees the meaning of the individual person
not only in his relation to the universe in general, but in its articulation, in the person's relation to particular institutions. The failure of
ethical systems, he says, lies in their mistaken independence of religion; they lack religion's intuition of the nature of man, its appreciation of manifoldness and individuality.

The value which Schleiermacher sets at the heart of his ethical system, and which is the most important aspiration of his moral man, is
borrowed from Leibniz,* the poets, and romanticists, although doubtless shaped by Schleiermacher's own originality—that of *individuality*. To be free means, in the first instance, to be one's individual self,
to be different from everyone else, to be a unique combination of the
"infinite forces" which make up humanity, so as to exhibit one of the
infinitely many different combinations in the world.

Schleiermacher says that this is one respect in which his system of
ethics differs fundamentally from (and is an improvement upon) the
theories of Kant and Fichte. He says: "I asked why I should have
personality and the unity of the fleeting stream of consciousness. I
was impelled to seek a higher kind of ethics, to give them meaning.
It did not satisfy me to view humanity in . . . raw masses, inwardly
quite alike." So there came his "highest intuition,"[182] an intuition
connected with the most fundamental problems of philosophy, that
"every man ought to express humanity in a special way, combining its
elements uniquely, so that it may reveal itself in every way, and there
may become real, in the fullness of unending space and time, all
which can issue from its womb."[183] This intuition, he says, revealed to
him a more difficult moral task. The ethical demand of Kant and

* Dilthey says that Schleiermacher's first statements about individuality occur in
a notebook on Leibniz. *Op. cit.*, p. 326.

Fichte might be satisfied, in a given case, in any one of many different ways. But the higher intuition made clear that most of these ways are not compatible with the fulfillment of the task of developing one's own individuality. In order to know what act is just the right one, one must know one's individual place in the process of the universe. Only this knowledge can make possible perception of one's duty in selection of a vocation, in social gatherings, in religious circles, and in life altogether.

We are now in a position to understand why the religious intuitions of friendship, love, and social intercourse are so important for an appreciation of the universe. The significance of separate personal life to a great extent lies in the fact that it makes individuality possible. Religion is interested in personality because of its cosmic significance: it is the bearer of the value of individuality. Schleiermacher had asked in his essays on Spinoza, "What is the point of individual existence?" His answer now is that the value of separate existence is that it makes possible the realization of individual forms—the manifestation of the perfect work of art which is the universe. Finiteness is not merely the negation of the Infinite; it is the means by which the Infinite can express its perfection, the means by which its perfect work of art is made possible. But individuality is not possible outside a society of minds. Only in a society are various combinations realized. Only there is it possible for each one to be aware of one's own place in the system, to contrast oneself with others, to intuit the whole magnificent system of the universe. The "religious" intuition of one's friends is to discern their individuality, to see how each one supplements the others, by helping to fill out the panorama of the whole of humanity. This is what he meant when he said he was coming to Berlin for religious reasons, to intuit the universe in Henriette Herz.*

Ethics, he says, is interested in the attempt of man to discern what he ought to do, the character of his moral task. The truths of ethics are truths only for and within this specific context: the situation of the individual who is making decisions about what he ought to do, and estimating the value of what he has already done. For the moralist, responsibility for the future rests on this person choosing. But

---

* *Briefe*, vol. I, p. 207. This idea is present, but with less emphasis, in his latest work. See *The Christian Faith*, 2nd ed., sec. 125, par. 2.

religion, which views everything in the context of the whole, escapes this limited point of view. It does not regard men "as vessels of honour or of dishonour," but rejoices in everything as it is.[184] Religion intuits every person, including his behavior, as an expression of the universe, so that although for ethics each man is responsible for his obligations, for religion man is only a part of the universe which is working in him. It is thus a narrow judgment to say of a man only that he falls short of the moral ideal. Religion sees the work of the universal Artist even in what is evil and imperfect. Everything is individual, and the less ideal creations give life and fullness to the whole, and make the perfection of others the more impressive. "What would be the uniform repetition of a highest ideal . . . in contrast with these infinite varieties of human phenomena?"[185] Religion sees the caprice of the Creator in the depraved and wicked, a caprice which shows how the elements of the best can become the vessels of evil. Conduct is at once a dealing with moral responsibilities and a manifestation of the inner working of the Infinite.

Schleiermacher's view of ethics, in its relation to religion and the evaluation of the individual forms realized by the Infinite, stands out in sharp contrast to the philosophy of Fichte. Fichte contended that man is a finite being, because the infinite nature of the self must be limited if it is to realize its own nature as activity. Thus the world is a theater for moral conflict; the meaning of the world is the duties which it places upon one. The ideal for the self is freedom—freedom from all the desires of the sensual self, freedom to obey the demands of reason. For Schleiermacher, finitude and limitation are not simply conditions of moral activity or obstacles to be overcome. Finitude is one of the greatest instruments of value, because it makes possible individuality and hence the artistry of the universe. If limitation did not occur, he says, being could not be individual and all distinction would be lost in the uniformity of an abstract ideal. Therefore personal limitation (including the sensual self) is not something to be overcome; the moral task of the self is to become more fully what it already is. Man's being is a holy creation of the Infinite and it must be treasured as such.

The universe of the *Discourses* is therefore different from that infinite ego of Fichte, which is known only through the voice of conscience, and in moral conflict. The meaning of life is no longer exclusively moral conflict: religion is not exhausted in moral resoluteness. The sensual self is not merely something to be subdued, but something to be united with spirit and developed in its individual character. And religion is enjoyment, a love of the world-spirit. The apprehension of absolute reality comes not through conscience alone but through a perception of an "eternal order" in all things, even in morality itself. This was Schleiermacher's meaning when he said: "I have displaced philosophy from ethics into religion."[186]

We return now to a continuation of our review of the content of religious knowledge. The universe can be intuited most significantly, according to Schleiermacher, in the realm of human minds, and especially through the study of history. "The highest occupation of religion is to connect the different moments of humanity together, and to divine from their course the spirit by which the Whole is guided. History, in the real sense, is the highest object for religion. . . ."[187] History is simply the understanding of an act of the universe in its place in the system. One can see, for example, how the world-spirit often recreates the same individuality at different periods, so that the reaction to it may be compared, and it may be seen how the times have changed. The greater effectiveness of a great mind at a later period may show how the climate of humanity has improved. The religious man discovers a divine destiny in history, a fate manifesting sometimes rough, heartless power and sometimes inward love, so that it alternately calls forth the emotions of childlike devotion and powerless defiance. But if

you really want to comprehend the proper character of all changes and of all human progress, religion will show you how the living gods hate nothing but death, how nothing is to be persecuted and destroyed but this, the first and last enemy of mankind. The crude, the barbarian, and the formless are to be absorbed and recast into an organic culture. Nothing is to be dead matter, which is moved only by inanimate impact, or offers resistance only through unconscious friction; all is to be individual, complex, connected, exalted life. Blind instinct, unthinking custom, dull obedience, everything inert and passive, all those sad symptoms of the asphyxia of freedom and humanity, are to be abolished. To this is directed the work of minutes and of centuries. It is the ever great advancing work of eternal redemptive love.[188]

The final meaning of existence on the level of human beings is thus, I believe, twofold. On the one hand, there is the value of the ever-recurring individual combinations of the forces comprising the whole. On the other hand, there is the progressive organization of "death into life," of a dull and sensual humanity into the active possessor of the freedom which alone gives man worth in the eyes of religion. This twofold meaning of history indicates, I believe, a twofold ideal for conduct: first, as we have said, to manifest the individual nature of the universe, as actualized in any single person; and second, to share in the task of abolishing the inert and the dead, of organizing the world for the ends of freedom.

The most recent expositor of Hegel, Professor Haering, has stated that this idea of a universal history—the idea that the process of history is itself a revelation of the universe, and that history is religion's highest object—is, along with the use of the word "universe," one of the ideas of Schleiermacher which may have had some influence upon the development of Hegel.[189]

What Schleiermacher calls the central intuitions of Judaism and Christianity are also to be taken as examples of interpretation of history as the act of the universe. The main theme of the Jewish religion, according to him, is the award of punishment for sin in this world. The universe reacts to every free act of man by another event, which cannot be regarded as accidental, but as according to a law of the universe.[190] The loftier and deeper intuition of Christianity is that

of the universal opposition of everything finite to the unity of the Whole, and of the way in which the deity deals with this opposition, how it reconciles this opposition to itself and sets limits to the ever growing estrangement by single points scattered over the whole, which are both finite and infinite, both human and divine. Corruption and redemption, antagonism and reconciliation—these are the two indivisibly related sides of this intuition. . . .[191]

Thus an analysis of the nature of these religions (and one must admit he has offered rather apt descriptions of Judaism or the Christian idea of the incarnation and redemption through the mediation of Christ) reveals that they are founded essentially upon an interpretation of history.

It would not be difficult, I think, to interpret Greek religion in the same way, through the idea of Fate or the activity of the Olympian gods (as in the account in the *Iliad* or the *Odyssey*). In fact, even in animistic or animatistic forms of religion we find the general belief that events are due to the action of spirit or spirits; it is an interpretation of history in terms of supposed supernatural beings. On the highest level, this interpretation becomes an interpretation of history as the acts of the unity in plurality—the universe.

An account of the ideas of religion and the universe contained in the *Discourses on Religion* would not be complete without some description of the emotional values their author associated with them.

The *Discourses* were in a sense a product of the romantic movement. His use of the idea of individuality, for example, was influenced by the romanticists. Moreover, his methodology for the philosophy of religion was doubtless to some extent dependent on Schlegel's view of the history of literature, and there is an unsolved problem of ascertaining how far he saw transcendental idealism through Schlegel's eyes. We have already seen how enthusiastic a member of the romantic circle he became, and we emphasized how sympathetic he was with the ideas of Schlegel. On the other hand, it would be a mistake to let him be swallowed up in this movement. One must do justice to his own thought, the problems he wrestled with before he came in contact with the romanticists, the temper and intellectual outlook which he had acquired from the Moravians or from his study of Kant, Greek philosophy, Spinoza, and others. Schleiermacher also had an individuality of his own, and once said that his philosophy was due to his own nature more than to anything else.[192]

The religion of the *Discourses* has often been called poetic pantheism, and its intuition a kind of aesthetic appreciation. Kattenbusch says that such an assumption is necessary if Schleiermacher's theology is to make sense at all.[193] The world is an artistic drama; it is the pantheism of Goethe. Professor Oman speaks of his view as an "artistic conception of religion," and says that, according to the *Discourses*, the universe is a "glorious, eternally active whole."[194] Kroner says that "a Spinozism translated into the poetic"[195] underlies his conception of religion, and points out as evidence the fact that Schleiermacher carefully distinguished religion from metaphysics and ethics but not from the sphere of art. He mentions a number of passages in which religion and artistic feeling are mentioned as closely related.[196] The universe is an object of aesthetic appreciation. It is a "work of art." The genius of mankind is an artist. The religious man must be able to understand the "beauty of the world." Therefore Schleiermacher finds it a mistake to seek the Infinite outside the finite. Kroner compares the tendency of the *Discourses* with that of Schiller's *Aesthetische Erziehung der Menschen*, or the new element in Fichte's *Vocation of Man*.

There is evidence to support the contention that the aesthetic element bulked large in Schleiermacher's thought. Especially in his enthusiasm for individuality and the finding of it in his friends (an enthusiasm which I suspect most readers, like myself, will find it difficult to understand) there is a kind of "aesthetic interest," or at least something perhaps not inappropriately so called. The problem of evil, too, is not at all in the foreground of the *Discourses*, or religion would not have regarded immorality as a lovely caprice of the supreme artist. In a letter to his wife in later years Schleiermacher said that "religion and art belong together as body and soul."[197]

Of course it is difficult to estimate the importance of such statements as that the universe is a work of art, without knowing what Schleiermacher meant by a work of art. Neither do I know exactly what kind of experience either Schleiermacher or his critics have in mind when they speak about "aesthetic feeling." Is reverence for the perfection of God, for example, an aesthetic feeling? I have no desire to disparage the view that a kind of artistic appreciation was the very foundation of religious experience for him, but there is some evidence against that hypothesis, which I present for what it is worth.

First, Schleiermacher wrote: "I always picture Christian piety, as I have described it in the *Discourses*, as something that arouses pain. But it is the sweet pain of melancholy, so well calculated to soothe other pains."[198] Second, his religious nature received its training among the Moravians, for whom he never lost sympathy, and traces of whose influence he said could be found in the *Discourses*. Third, although it might be said that religion teaches that everything is part of a great work of art, he says religion has "taught me to regard as holy myself with my virtues and errors in my undivided being."[199]

Does this mean that the perfection of the universe carried the emotional values ordinarily associated with the notion of the holy; or does it mean that the word "holy" came, for him, to carry the emotional values of artistic appreciation? Fourth, although Schleiermacher emphasizes a close relation between religion and art, the fact that he thought that artistic feeling, like self-intuition or intuition of the world, could become religion, suggests that it is something different from religion. Fifth, he disparages nature religion, both in the form of appreciation for the beauty in nature and awe at its sublimity. His religion, he says, is heart religion; it is related to the "inward and higher." Sixth, he says expressly that a friend "had the misunderstanding that I hold artistic feeling itself for religion."[200] And finally, even Schlegel wrote to him: "It is very clear that Goethe has no religion and Fichte a great deal, however stunted and philosophical it may be."[201] If Schlegel could say this, is it not likely that Schleiermacher would have said it too—although of course Schleiermacher does say that Schlegel thinks more highly of Fichte than he does.

An interesting passage suggests that religious contemplation and moral endeavor comprise the ideal life: "A person is lovable who loves [has religion], i.e., who seeks the Infinite everywhere in the finite. He is great, who gives away the finite for the sake of the Infinite [does his duty]. He is perfect, who unites both."[202]

CHAPTER V

TRANSITION: RELIGIOUS FEELING AND THE PHILOSOPHY OF IDENTITY

wwwwwwwwwwwwwwwwwwwwwwwwwwwwwwwwwwwwwwwwwwwwwwwwwwwwwwwwwwwwwwwwwwwwwwwwwwwwwww

1. The Changing Intellectual Environment

Schleiermacher's second period of important literary activity centered around 1806, when he had entered upon his work as newly appointed occupant of a chair in theology at Halle. It was roughly a half dozen years after the *Discourses* and *Soliloquies*.

These years after his earlier publications were a time of quite continuous occupation with philosophy and related subjects, if we may trust the indications scattered throughout his scientific diary. The outcome of his study was the formulation of the general outline of his mature philosophy. He worked out more systematically and in greater detail his views on subjects touched upon more sketchily in the *Discourses*—his view of the universe, of God and his relation to the world, of the nature and scope of philosophy and the various sciences (including natural science, ethics, theology, and aesthetics), and of the significance and nature of religion, art, knowledge, and moral conduct.*

Among the philosophers whom Schleiermacher studied and was influenced by at this time, Plato is probably to be mentioned first. In

---

* One obvious change in his outlook at this time was the cooling of his enthusiasm for romanticism. Of course, there were many ideas expressed in his first works which, despite origination under romantic influence, remained important for his system for the rest of his life. One of these was his emphasis on the value of individuality. Nevertheless, there was a subtle change in temper. He became much less intimate with Friedrich Schlegel, and after a time had no further correspondence with him whatever. Moreover, he became involved in a great many other matters so that his interests had other directions. He had a heavy burden of teaching; he became implicated in church affairs; and in the distress of Germany in its struggle with Napoleon he became very active in matters of state. In addition to his other studies, he assumed responsibility for a translation of Plato. It is not surprising that he lost touch and sympathy with his friends and enthusiasms of previous years.

1800 Schleiermacher had written that "there is no writer who has had such an influence on me, and has initiated me into the holiest not only of philosophy but of men in general, as this divine man."[1] After 1800, it will be recalled, Schleiermacher became engaged upon an analysis of the *Dialogues* with a view to determining their composition and relations, and the plan of his own projected translation. Many of Plato's ideas are paralleled more or less closely in Schleiermacher's later work, and it is likely that they were correspondingly influential in shaping his thought. Particularly deserving of mention are Plato's views of the relation of dialectic to the sciences of ethics and physics, of the contribution of mind and ideas in the knowing process and especially in judgment, of the ideas and the harmony of the principles of knowing and of being, and of the relation of the ideas to the concrete particulars.*

Schleiermacher could scarcely have been so influenced by Plato, however, had he not found the scientific and philosophical situation of his day favorable for it.† More specifically, it is possible that Schleiermacher's philosophy of identity (the nature of which will be more fully explained in the remainder of this and in the next chapter) and his use of Plato's ideas in it were facilitated by his attention to the work of Schelling. I say "possible" because the nature and extent of Schelling's influence on Schleiermacher is a controversial matter. It will become clear, I think, that in important respects Schleiermacher's philosophy was different from Schelling's (although both of

---

* For his interpretation of Plato, see his *History of Philosophy* (*Werke*, pt. III, vol. IV, pt. 1). This was written in 1812, so that of course we cannot assume that he had all of it in mind as early as 1806. In it he pours scorn upon all nominalism, atomism, and empiricism (including Newton's physics). Even Aristotle, the Christian ideas of the creation and the personality of God, and the whole idea of a first cause come in for a share of disparagement, in comparison with the great penetration of Plato's work. The book makes excellent reading, if one wishes an understanding of Schleiermacher's biases, judgments, and attachments as expressed in his criticism of others. Schleiermacher prefers Plato to Aristotle; he sympathizes with Origen and Augustine; he prefers Scotus Erigena and Anselm to Abélard; he has only faint praise for Aquinas; he finds Bonaventura interesting but he strongly dislikes the mysticism of Boehme; Locke, Hobbes, and British empiricism generally are not to be compared with the continental rationalists; and Spinoza is the flower and crown of the movement beginning with Descartes.

† That philosophical thought in general was prepared for new influence by Plato is attested by the fact that the writings of Schelling and Fichte after 1800 also showed Platonic tendencies.

them are difficult to interpret precisely even with respect to central conceptions). Moreover, the extent of Schelling's influence on him is further limited by the fact that (as we shall see) on some matters where they agreed Schleiermacher seems to have conceived at least the outlines of his theory before he was acquainted with a similar development in Schelling's theory. But it would be perverse to believe that Schleiermacher got nothing at all from Schelling; he must have found many suggestions, and Schelling's detailed work in science must have provided him with valuable material in a field where he felt himself to be less competent.*

It will be recalled that during the early years of the last century Fichte's pre-eminence on the German philosophical scene gradually diminished, and he was to some extent eclipsed by Schelling and Hegel. Schleiermacher followed this change closely. He seems not to have been much impressed by the works of Hegel, and in fact seems to have been little influenced by him either at this time or later, except perhaps by way of negative reaction. His diary does contain a reference to Hegel's Latin dissertation of this period, and to the *Glauben und Wissen* (in which Schleiermacher was mentioned). But apparently Schleiermacher regarded him less as an independent thinker than as a mere satellite of Schelling. In making a comment upon philosophers who have disciples around them, he wrote: "See how Schelling hangs himself with Hegel."[2]

Schleiermacher had already become acquainted with the work of Schelling at the time he composed the first edition of the *Discourses*, it will be recalled. Moreover, we know that in 1800 or shortly thereafter, he read the *Weltseele*, the *Bruno*, and the *System des transcendentalen Idealismus*, two of which he considered reviewing. He read and reviewed the *Lectures on the Methods of Academic Study*. The ideas in these books are mentioned upon a number of occasions from 1800 to 1804 both in letters and in his diary.

It is useful for an estimate of the influence of Schelling on Schleiermacher to take note of an intimate friendship between Schleiermacher and a scientist-philosopher named Heinrich Steffens who was not only

* Schleiermacher read Bardili's *Logic* at this time, and it is possible that he was influenced by it.

a close personal friend of Schelling but an ardent devotee of his natural philosophy. Steffens thought that Schelling's deductive treatment of science could be developed profitably in his own special field (geology and mineralogy), and he set himself the task of doing so. Some of his suggestions so influenced Schelling that credit must be given him for the development of certain aspects of Schelling's view of nature. When Schleiermacher came to Halle in 1804, he found Steffens there, and there began a close friendship which apparently rested at least in part upon a very considerable agreement on philosophical matters. Schleiermacher wrote that his ethical theories and Steffens' natural science were complementary and that they agreed on almost all matters where the two sciences are related.[3] After he was called to a chair at Berlin, he tried to obtain the selection of Steffens as lecturer in philosophy because he felt that Steffens' natural science and philosophy would furnish a foundation and complement for his own system of ethics.[4]

This friendship points to the fact that Schleiermacher did not feel himself at odds with the general framework of the Schelling philosophy, although of course there were matters on which Steffens did not follow Schelling.

However much Schelling may actually have influenced Schleiermacher, I believe that Schleiermacher's work is illuminated by reading it in the light of Schelling's system, and for that reason I propose to outline briefly Schelling's views developed during and immediately after 1800. Most persons will probably think that no theory can be made comprehensible by reference to Schelling; but Schleiermacher's work becomes, I think, more intelligible, because his scattered allusions make a fairly coherent unity when fitted together according to the general plan of the Schelling philosophy. Doubtless Schleiermacher would have referred a reader to Schelling for a treatment of some subjects (such as natural philosophy) not touched on extensively in his own writings.

Before proceeding, it is of some interest to notice that possibly there was some influence in the opposite direction, e.g., in Schelling's use of the word "intuition" after 1800. Schelling wrote of him to A. W. Schlegel as follows:

I must tell you that I have become a very ardent admirer of the *Discourses on Religion*. You know how it was with me before because of unpardonable neglect or laziness in the matter. I now revere the author as a spirit whom one can regard only as on equal level with the very first original philosophers. Without this originality, it were impossible so to have penetrated to the inmost speculation without leaving behind a trace of the stages through which one had to go. The work, as it is, seems to be sprung out of itself . . . but nevertheless anyone who wants to produce anything of that sort must have made the deepest philosophical studies, or else have written with blind divine inspiration.[5]

Again, the *Lectures on the Methods of Academic Study*, although they contain a criticism of Schleiermacher's view of religion, show traces of influence by Schleiermacher's *Discourses*.

It will be recalled that before the turn of the century there had been some doubt of the compatibility of Schelling's excursions into the philosophy of nature with the transcendental philosophy of Fichte. For Fichte the ultimate reality was the "activity" of mind; for Schelling, at least as it appeared on the surface, nature had an independent existence in its own right and indeed was one of the conditions of consciousness. Of course Schelling said that this difference was only apparent and due to a misunderstanding of his claims; he declared that his philosophy of nature was only a subordinate part of transcendental philosophy and that nature was not really independent of mind. But beginning about 1800, Schelling promoted nature and demoted the subject of experience; the philosophy of nature ceased to be a mere department and received independent standing. He critized Fichte for being too subjectivistic.[6] Dialectic and the laws of logic, he thought, lead to the heart of reality, but this reality is not merely the activity or experience of a subject. Idealism, he said, is the only fruitful method of philosophy; but there is both an idealism of the ego and an idealism of nature.[7] Philosophical reflection or dialectic is capable not only of uncovering the nature of mind but of revealing the system of forces in equilibrium which constitutes nature.

But neither mind nor nature is independent or conceivable by itself; both are derivative from a reality which is their "indifference." This reality is reason, abstracted from any thinker or from concrete embodiment in the particulars of nature. Its basic principle is the law of identity, $A = A$. It is timeless, spaceless, empty of particular existents; yet it has being. Schelling wrote of it:

The truly ideal alone is, without further mediation, the truly real, and beyond it there is nothing. Philosophy cannot prove the existence of this essential unity, since it is the entrance to all scientific procedure; it can only be proved that without it, there is no science at all, and that essentially this Identity, or the complete resolution of the real into the ideal, is intended by everything which makes a claim to be science.[8]

Dialectical thought can reach the essence of things, because this reason is the reality from which mind and nature alike are derived. Criticized scientific knowledge is therefore ultimately about this identity, which Schelling called God.

If this reality is to know itself, to become self-conscious, it must "posit itself infinitely as subject and object"; for there can be no knowledge without a knower and an object known. Therefore it apparently follows from the nature of God that there must be knowers and objects of knowledge.

Since ultimate reality is one, subjective knowing and the object known must be identical in essence, but since experience requires a relative distinction, they must differ with respect to form. This distinction is coeternal with the identity. But if the subjective and the objective are to be identical in essence, they cannot differ qualitatively; the only possibility is then that they should differ quantitatively. Hence "the form of subjectivity-objectivity is not actual, if a quantitative difference of both is not posited."[9] This means, in effect, that the self-consciousness of the identity requires that there be modes of being, some of which like matter contain much of the objective and little of the subjective principle, whereas others like the human being contain relatively much of the subjective principle and little of the objective.

Schelling went on to say that even this quantitative difference cannot literally be said to be the truth about the identity, but must in some sense be regarded as ouside it. This realm "outside" the identity, which is not ultimately real, is the world taken as finite. The only true being is the identity as such, as the indifference of subjectivity and objectivity. The world as finite, or as a quantitative antithesis of the ideal and the real (subjective-objective), is not self-sustaining, and can be thought to be so only if taken to be what it is not, viz., something independent of the One. So he wrote:

The force which pours itself forth in the matter of nature is essentially the same as that which manifests itself in the world of mind, except that it there has to struggle with a preponderance of the objective principle, while in mind with that of the subjective principle. But further, this antithesis, which is not an antithesis in essence but solely in potency, appears as antithesis only to one who is "outside" the Indifference, and does not regard the Identity itself as primary. . . . But how it is possible that anything should be apart from this absolute totality, or should be separated in thought, is a question which cannot here be answered, since we are rather proving that such a separation is not possible in itself, and from the standpoint of reason is false, yea, the source of all error.[10]

As I have remarked, species of finite objects can be ordered in a series according to the degree of preponderance of the subjective or objective principle. No object is purely one or the other. In the whole series of objects subjectivity and objectivity are necessarily balanced, for the totality must be an absolute identity. Therefore every stage of the preponderantly objective must have as its counterpiece a stage of the preponderantly subjective. Each stage can be shown to be necessarily related to the other stages; and each stage occurs both in the subjective and the objective series. The whole system is necessary for the self-manifestation of reason by which it comes to consciousness of itself. As Hartmann says:

In matter we have the lowest potency, which is also the greatest preponderance of objectivity. In the truth of knowledge and the beauty of the work of art we have the highest potency, along with the greatest preponderance of subjectivity. Between these extremes lies the chain of finite being.[11]

Upon this foundation Schelling claimed to be able to erect a detailed philosophy of nature and of mind. He claimed to be able to show how the forms of being are the necessary modes of the absolute identity. He deduced the three dimensionality of space, matter, attractive and repulsive force, gravity, light, magnetism, specific gravity, chemistry, and so on. Each form or process can be assigned its necessary place in the system; he said that animal and plant in the organic world correspond to iron and water in the inorganic, and he likewise deduced the duality of the sexes. He believed, as in earlier years, that his speculation could decide problems incapable of experimental solution. As he said:

> What up to now was mere anticipation, or rather only hope, i.e., to be able finally to reduce all these phenomena to a single theory, now is certain, and we have reason to expect that, after we have found this universal key, nature will gradually open to us the secret of its particular operations and phenomena, which accompany the dynamic process and which are all simply modifications of one fundamental phenomenon.[12]

Schelling explained his view of the proper nature of science, philosophy, theology, religion, and art—naturally determined by his general philosophical conclusions—in his *Lectures on the Methods of the Academic Study*. It is of some use to us to notice what he there said, partly because Schleiermacher, as we shall see, gave the book a full and favorable review, and partly because it is illuminating to compare it with Schleiermacher's ideas on the same subject.

The business of philosophy, according to Schelling, is the reconstruction of the nature of the universe, of the absolute identity in its necessary forms. Philosophy deals with the eternal forms of existence, with the prototypes, the modes into which the identity must differentiate itself. It seeks the system of reality, and thereby seeks to be identical with God's knowledge of himself. Since reality is so eminently one, the discipline which studies the nature of that reality should perhaps also be one. Nevertheless, philosophy does inevitably get separated into several sciences, each of which specializes in one special aspect of reality. Theology is devoted to the "indifference point," to the Absolute as it is in itself. History or jurisprudence is devoted to the ideal or subjective forms of the identity, whereas natural science (medicine) is concerned with the real or objective ones. Natural science thus requires an understanding of the modes of being of the identity in nature, along the lines of Schelling's "dynamic" deductions. Similarly, the science of mind should include an examination of the necessary forms of the identity realized in the organized life of the state, although Schelling sometimes seems confused on this point.

These "sciences," as Schelling conceived them, are not to be confused with what is ordinarily meant by science. In order to be a scientist in his sense, one must have

raised himself to the intellectual intuition of nature.[18] [It requires] the general capacity for seeing the universal in the particular, the infinite and the finite combined in living unity.[14] To comprehend something rationally [he says] is to grasp something . . . as an organic member of the absolute whole, in necessary connection with it, and thereby as a reflection of the absolute unity.[15]

Consequently Schelling tended to disparage "empirical" science such as Newton's physics. Empirical science, he said, takes the symbol for the reality, falsely abstracting it from its meaning in the whole. It tries to get knowledge by observation only of parts of nature. It attempts to explain one event through its relation to some other particular event, such as in the notion of causation at a distance (which Schelling thought absurd); but the organic systematic character of the universe cannot be known by this method. Empirical science is properly limited to description, and while its descriptions may make prediction possible, they are incapable of getting at the inner nature of the reality with which they deal. Empirical science is necessary, but it is not the highest kind of knowledge of nature; the "higher" physics, through dialectic and intellectual intuition, is able to exhibit the forms of nature as necessary modes of the whole, to get at their nature by indicating their place in the whole.[16]

The history of science, according to him, is the record of the development of the self-consciousness of the Absolute.[17]

Schelling's Lectures outline a view of the nature of religion according to which, as might be expected, this philosophical knowledge of the relation of finite objects to the Infinite comprises the cognitive side of religion. In this chapter Schelling was apparently aiming a criticism at Schleiermacher's Discourses which he believed separated religious experience too sharply from philosophical knowledge. He asserted that if religion becomes separated from the objective content with which philosophy alone can furnish it, it becomes simply an unenlightened brooding over the world. At best, the religious man who eschews philosophy may be able to achieve a harmony of personality which is beautiful. But such a subjective religion cannot claim the objectivity which belongs exclusively to the products of reason, and certainly cannot take philosophy's place.[18] Schelling thought that the cognitive element in healthy religion is concerned (as is theology) primarily with the appreciation of the meaning of history in the cosmic picture. It is an "intuition" (presumably an "intellectual intuition") of the providential character of reality as revealed in history; it is specifically an intuition that our world is a moral order.[19]

It is worth bearing in mind that Schelling's philosophy of identity, which I have just outlined, does not represent a line of thinking sharply different from that of Schleiermacher at the very beginning of the period we are about to discuss, or as expressed in the first editions of the *Discourses* and *Soliloquies*. In fact, there are very considerable and striking similarities. Schleiermacher's idea of the universe as a unity in plurality, as an organism of "forces," finds an analogue in the absolute identity and its necessary articulation into certain forms of being. Again, the *Discourses* emphasized the misleading and distorting abstractness of considering a particular object out of its relationship to the whole; his "higher realism" was an affirmation of the reality of the Infinite. For this reason he disparaged empirical science in so far as it is abstract analysis of particular causal relationships. The *Discourses* maintain that ultimate knowledge must not stop short of the whole, and that the universe is the proper subject matter of philosophy. The *Discourses* do not outline any dialectical "deduction" of the necessary modes of being, but we have seen that there are hints that it is possible in principle to supply one, although he did not precisely agree with Schelling on the nature of "deduction." Finally, what Schleiermacher called the "intuition" of or "sense" for the whole is strikingly similar to what Schelling seems to have meant by the phrase "intellectual intuition." Both men referred by this word to the becoming aware of the interrelation of finite objects in the Infinite, in some way or other. The similarity is so striking that it has been suggested that Schelling's usage was due partly to the influence of Schleiermacher, and that Schleiermacher's inclination to dispense with the term "intuition" in later years was because of his recognition of the fact that Schelling was using a similar term in a way sufficiently similar to brook confusion.[20]

So much solid agreement existed between Schelling's identity philosophy and Schleiermacher's views in 1800. Other points of agree-

ment might have been mentioned. Of course, temperamentally the
two men were far apart. Schelling apparently was not specially interested in Schleiermacher's ideas of friendship, individuality, and so on;
in short, he did not acknowledge the same values. Schleiermacher
wrote scathingly of Schelling's "loveless wisdom."[21] But comparison
with Schelling places the outline of Schleiermacher's views in a clearer
light. It is even possible that without Schelling's influence, Schleiermacher's philosophical views could not have developed in the way in
which they did.

2. THE UNIVERSE IN GOD

Schleiermacher's views changed considerably in the years following his first publications. It may be useful first of all to state what in
my opinion were the most important of these changes: (1) the development of a theory of the Absolute very similar to that of Schelling's, (2) the development of a parallel view of the nature of philosophy and its relation to the sciences, and (3) the identification of
religion not any longer with intuition and feeling but with feeling
alone. That these were changes in his thought I shall attempt to
establish; and the assumption that these changes did occur will make
intelligible passages in his works, particularly in the case of the second
edition of the Discourses, which to my mind are otherwise very
obscure.

I have stated that Schleiermacher's diary and letters from 1801 to
1805 contain references to Schelling. The comments in question are
not extensive or elaborate; in fact they are extremely terse to the
point of obscurity. But the matters referred to are significant for our
understanding of his thought. First of all, at a time before he was
acquainted with Schelling's expositions of his identity philosophy,
Schleiermacher was puzzled by the relation between Schelling's philosophy of nature and his "transcendental philosophy," which Schelling asserted to be of equal dignity and counterparts to one another
without saying exactly how. These two parts of his system, according
to Schleiermacher (and here he was quite right), did "not run on all
fours."[22] If they had, he said, Schelling would have been able to
deduce the world of spirit (presumably social institutions, etc.) in the

one, just as he was able to deduce the material world in the other.
He wrote:

If transcendental philosophy and the philosophy of nature are to be the
eternally contrary but entirely corresponding views, then the philosophy
of nature must explain the reality of the ego for the external world, just
as the transcendental philosophy explains the reality of the outer world for
the ego. Schelling tried to do this in the *Weltseele*, but has he succeeded?
Further, if there is to be a speculative physics, elaborated on the principles
of natural philosophy, as a special science, must there not also be a speculative science of mind, which is developed from the principles of idealism?
Does Schelling have something of this sort, and if so, what could it be?
Somehow ethics, in my sense?[23] [Again, he remarked on the as yet unex-
plained relation between the philosophy of nature and transcendental
idealism:] And what will he call the higher discipline (in so far as it is
knowledge) in which both these disciplines are united?[24]

In these comments Schleiermacher was perfectly justified. Even
in the later identity philosophy, according to which, as we have seen,
there is a preponderantly objective realm and a preponderantly subjective one, for each of which there is to be a special branch of science,
Schelling did not make very clear what was to be the science of the
subjective side which was to correspond to his earlier transcendental
philosophy. Schleiermacher's judgment was apparently correct, that
there must be a theory or deduction of the world of mind to parallel
the science of nature.

Almost immediately after the above comments, Schleiermacher
wrote down his own view: "Physics and ethics are the two sciences
which proceed from the *Elementarphilosophie*. History is the result
in which they end."[25] He seems to mean by this that there should be
a highest discipline from which the philosophy of nature and the
philosophy of mind should be "deduced," and that there should be
developed a kind of empirical natural science complementary to the
philosophy of nature, and also an empirical "history" complementary
to the philosophy of mind.* Presumably this division of the sciences
of both nature and mind into a more speculative and a more empirical

---

* He said about this time that everything in history must not only be exhibited
in its causal relations but as a part (presumably of the self-differentiation of the
identity), and that all philosophy must culminate in history. Dilthey, *op. cit.*,
Appendix, p. 129.

part is identical with the distinction between "speculative" and "empirical" science which he elaborated later.

It is worth noting (as Süskind has pointed out) that these comments were made before his acquaintance with Schelling's expositions of his identity philosophy, and are therefore not directly dependent on Schelling, although doubtless suggested by the difficulties in his system.

There are also some scattered comments which suggest points of disagreement with Schelling. He wrote that he was considering composing a dialogue attacking him, patterned on Plato's *Parmenides*.[26] He repeated his mentioned criticism, that Schelling's system did not really have a place for ethics (in his sense), just as Fichte's philosophy had no room for physics. Somewhat later he said that Schelling's criticism of Fichte and his general work were good up to the point where he "always comes to grief," namely, in showing how in his system there can be any error.[27] This last criticism is a suggestive one, and it is unfortunate that we have no explicit information about what he had in mind.

A final and obscure passage is the following:

Is then the whole world anything but an individuation of the Identical? And can one then reach it, if one, as Schelling does (in spite of his boast about the Indifference), places himself only on the one pole? But if now strict philosophy is the antithesis of poesie, what should you call that indubitably higher thing, which combines both?[28]

This means, I take it, that Schleiermacher agrees that the world *is* nothing but the individuation of the identity, but that Schelling does not get at its nature because of his one-sidedness. There is a temptation to think that the one-sidedness in question is Schelling's interest in nature as opposed to mind and ethics; and that may be what it means. But I am inclined to think that Schleiermacher believed that philosophical thought itself (like religious intuition in the *Discourses*) should contain an element of subjective imagination, whereas Schelling is exclusively rational and dialectical.* This interpretation of him is consistent with what he says of Jacobi in the same letter, with his lecture notes of 1804,[29] and with part of his review of

* This idea may be related to the passages stressing the subjective individual side of religious intuition, in the first edition of the *Discourses*.

Schelling's *Lectures*.[30] The idea reappears in a slightly different form in his later works, but does not seem to play an important role.

As might be expected from what has been said, Schleiermacher's review of the *Lectures on the Methods of Academic Study* was very favorable, and expressed admiration for Schelling's system as a whole. This brief outline of his philosophy, Schleiermacher said, placed Schelling's views in an unusually favorable light. And although Schelling had professed not to have "deduced" anything in this book, Schleiermacher said that he had really accomplished more than he claimed. Moreover, he wrote that Schelling's chapter on Christianity was excellent and made out clearly its mystical nature and its relation to history, although he said (hinting at the *Discourses*) that some people might not regard the substance of it as particularly new. On the other hand, he was critical of Schelling's general arrangement of the sciences. Religion, for example, does not have the relation to the sciences of mind and nature which Schelling thought it had; nor does art. Moreover, he did not agree that theology can be a science of the "indifference point." And in line with the comments already cited, he thought that ethics should replace jurisprudence and history as the science to be coequal with natural philosophy.

All this evidence taken together strongly suggests that Schleiermacher to a large extent (although not in detail) shared Schelling's views about the absolute identity, its self-manifestation in the worlds of nature and of mind, and what follows from these assumptions for a theory of philosophy and science. Of course the agreement is in very general terms, and much room must be left for differences. But the evidence establishes a large measure of agreement, and that evidence will be strengthened by an examination of Schleiermacher's views in more detail. This more complete statement I shall now begin.

There is no reason to believe that Schleiermacher's view of sense perception had changed from the dualistic theory we have already expounded. Of course he came to believe in a more completely defined way that this causal interaction is not a complete or wholly true account of the reality involved, but he also believed this in 1799. It is true that one of the most important passages supporting my interpretation is omitted in the second edition of the *Discourses*, but the reason for this was that, as we shall see, he no longer believed that religion

is "intuition," and hence there was no point in a comparison between sensory and religious intuition. There are other new passages,
however, which confirm the interpretation I have offered. Sense
experience, he says, is "in harmony with the . . . outer world."[31] In
sense perception "the organic being, by means of a definite influence,
coalesces with the whole" so that the sensation "becomes a representation of the object and by means of it the organic being becomes one
with the object."[32] Elsewhere he speaks of sense perception as a
"relation between the individual being and the world."[33] In the
revised form of the "secret moment" passage,[34] he describes more
elaborately how the rise of consciousness is determined by a preconscious interaction between the mind and its object. But, as in the
first edition, there are difficulties in this passage, so that it is unwise
to attempt to derive any precise theory from it.[35]

So he was an epistemological dualist. But, as before, he was not an
agnostic; he believed it possible to know the nature of reality at least
within limits. All those statements adduced as evidence for this belief
in the first edition of the Discourses are retained in the second.
Philosophy, he says, tells us about the "nature of things";[36] natural
philosophy seeks

to know things in their peculiar natures, to indicate the special relations
through which each is what it is, to determine for each its place in the
whole and to distinguish it from others, to place all of actuality in its
reciprocally determined necessity, and to make clear the identity of all
phenomena with their eternal laws.[37]

So far we have found agreement with what was said in the first
edition of the Discourses. There is an independent world which affects
the sense organs and makes sense experience possible; scientific knowledge pierces at least partially into the inner nature of the real world.
The agreement goes much further. The universe, according to the
second edition, is still that system of "infinite forces," that organism
which is in some sense really a unity; and that organism is harmonious,
worthy of reverence, the supreme work of art.

The aspect of this unity which Schleiermacher most emphasizes at
this later time is the agreement of the order of ideas with that of
things. He speaks of the "higher consciousness" (religious or scientific) as the consciousness of the

identity of the ideal and the real worlds.[38] . . . The inner content of every philosophy is the same [he says] and it is the intuition of nature and reason, which are everywhere objectively identical.[39] . . . The primary object is the Whole . . . and the fundamental universal is nothing but the mutual absorption of the real and the ideal [in each other].[40]

He does not say why he believes that thought and things must somehow be of one order; but the probable reason (which is the one he himself gave later and which Schelling gave in the *Lectures*) was that science and thought seem to presuppose it in their claim that thought can be knowledge about independently real things.*

Schleiermacher next proposed the hypothesis that the identity of thought and the world is somehow dependent upon an absolute identity (itself unknowable in its essence), which in some way is real in finite form in natural phenomena and thought, in an infinity of particular events—a theory similar to that of Schelling. A passage (somewhat obscure) in the *Ethics* suggests this:

Objective knowledge consists of a system, an organic whole. For not only is it the totality of the relations of the world to man, who is himself an organic whole; but it is the whole of the manifestation of the unity of the world in the infinity of the particular, and so an infinitely articulated being in which there is one soul—so an organic whole.[41]

Our interpretation of this is confirmed by some sentences added to the second edition of the *Discourses*. There, consistently with Schelling's view that the identity is presupposed by science but cannot itself be deduced, he says that philosophy

puts God at the peak of all science, as the basis of knowledge.[42] [And] there is an immediate knowledge of God in science, which is the source of all other knowledge.[43] [In a similar vein, he says:] Is not God the sole and highest unity? Is it not God alone before whom and in whom all particularity vanishes? And if you regard the world as a whole and a totality, can you do it otherwise than in God? Otherwise, tell me of some way by which to distinguish the supreme nature, the fundamental and eternal being, from the particular, the temporal, and the derived.[44] [Again, slightly later:] Philosophy proper begins when sensation, as it tries to exist for itself apart from higher knowledge, is repudiated . . . This happens

---

* See the discussion of this problem in its relation to the first edition and the study of Spinoza, Chap. IV, sec. 1, at the end.

in "dialectic"* when the root of both the physical and the ethical, the animating principle thought of as God, is raised from the lower potency of plurality and antithesis to the higher potency of unity.[45]

Moreover, the absolute identity is not to be conceived as thought any more than as objective being (for the reason that the identity logically is prior to the differentiation into the subjective and the objective). So he criticizes a view of God according to which God

is supposed to be the highest and stand above everything and still is himself involved in an antithesis of thought [which is impossible for the absolutely highest being], and subordinates being to thought. There is another concept of God opposite to this, which expresses the converse relation [of thought to being] and is just as inacceptable.†

Schleiermacher does not deny all reality to the world of particular events whether subjective or objective as Schelling sometimes seems to. He does say that it is impossible to understand the "significance" of the finite object or to know what it "really" is, without understanding the place it has in the whole system of things. He seems to say that the particular object, taken separately by itself is partially unreal, fragmentary in meaning, and that it gets reality only in its place in the whole. Yet he does not say that the undifferentiated identity is the sole reality, and that finite objects are mere illusion, as Schelling sometimes does. Although the identity of the subjective and the objective is the most fundamental fact about Schleiermacher's world, yet he clearly says that there is an actual process going on in time, and that history itself is the record of the organization of the objective world by reason for its own ends.

Schleiermacher's view seems to require a doctrine of degrees of truth and reality.

For Schleiermacher, the universe is real. Mind can know its character. The absolute identity is its ground. The identity transcends all distinctions of thought. It is in some sense the unity of the world,

---

* A technical term referring to a fundamental discipline composed of parts of logic and epistemology; see Chap. VI, sec. 1.
† *Reden*, Pünjer ed., p. 123. Schleiermacher's idea of God will be much more fully described in the following chapter, where his mature work is considered. It does not seem to me unwarranted to read the preceding paragraphs in terms of his later view that God is, as the highest genus, somehow the source of the various species of being, although it would probably be mistaken to find in this earlier work the details and more elaborate structure of his more mature thought.

but the world is also real, although it is a realm of distinctions and multiplicity, of space, time and finitude.

The absolute identity cannot, in Schleiermacher's opinion, be the object of a science, and for this reason he rejects Schelling's suggestion that the identity is the subject matter of the science of theology. There can be a science (as we shall see) only where there are data (viz., experienced events) to be organized into a system. This is not true of the Absolute, and hence there can be no science of it, although he says there might be a pure philosophy of the Absolute.*

Schelling affirmed that the absolute identity "differentiates" itself into preponderantly subjective and preponderantly objective entities. Among the finite objects none is merely subjective or objective; everything is a combination of both and entities differ only in the proportions. In this way the identity of the Absolute is not abolished even in its manifoldness. This thought, difficult as it is to make much of, is apparently what Schleiermacher had in mind in the following statement. Love, he says, is related to the

longing-to-be-spirit through which Reason becomes one with matter or with nature in general. Love is the most immediate turning-point between the physical and the ethical. The ascent to organism is the will-to-be-body of matter. Thus the old intuition, that love is the principle of being of particular things. This is true also in ethics. Without love there would be no identity of being and becoming, no going out of itself by Reason as an objective being.[46]

I understand this statement to mean that the subjective aspect of material nature is at least in part its self-organization to produce consciousness; that the phenomenon of love may be said to be the point midway between the preponderantly objective being of nature and the preponderantly subjective being of rational mind; and that love is that character of subjective mind which impels it to organize nature into more and more rational forms ("to go out of itself as an objective being").

According to Schleiermacher, the ideal or subjective side of reality is the proper object of the science of ethics; and the real or objective side of reality is the object of natural science. Each of these sciences

---

* Review of Schelling, *Briefe*, vol. IV, p. 584. Knowledge of God could be at best an ideal on his theory—like the adequate knowledge of anything else.

is again to be divided into a more theoretical and a more empirical part.

Natural science was not Schleiermacher's field. His subjects were ethics, theology, and the philosophy of religion. It was for this reason that he wanted Steffens in Berlin as a "complement" to his own work. As a result, there is no place at this time in which he makes any extended reference to the philosophy of nature. He does say something about it in the later *Dialectic* (which he wrote when it was apparent that Steffens would not be able to lecture in Berlin), and we shall discuss this later. But because of the fact that he did not regard ethics as a science of a quite different character from natural science (viz., not as a normative science in the sense of some contemporary intuitionists), it is possible to learn something of his view of scientific method from what he says about ethics.

According to his view, ethics and natural science are both to be deduced (i.e., their principles and procedures shown to be necessary, in some sense not very clearly defined in the writings of this time) from the "higher science" (a kind of philosophical logic) which

cannot, like the other special sciences, itself rest upon a highest principle; but it is to be conceived of as a whole, in which any part can be the beginning, and everything, being reciprocally determined, depends upon the whole, such that the whole can either be accepted or rejected but not proved or demonstrated.[47]

This higher science (to be identified with what he later called *Dialectic*) is concerned with the relation between thought and its objects, and their identity in the absolute being. This basis for all knowledge is presupposed by the particular sciences and is common property to them all. So he says: "What unifies scientists is the consciousness of the necessary unity of all knowledge, of the laws and conditions of its rise, of the form and character by virtue of which, really, any perception or thought is actually knowledge."[48] The highest science thus seems to be practically epistemology. He praises Spinoza and Plato for having used this "deductive" method, at least in principle; in this, he probably had in mind their making ethics dependent on an understanding of the relation of man to the universe, which relation is investigated by philosophy.

It is not quite clear whether Schleiermacher believed that there is some sense in which this "highest science" can be developed and systematized only along with the advances of the derived sciences or whether he thought that "philosophy," as a discipline *different* from the highest science, is a system which includes it and the derived science; so that *it* can be fully developed only with the growth of the real sciences. At any rate he says:

> The scientific spirit, as the highest principle, the immediate unity of all knowledge, cannot be set up for itself alone . . . in mere transcendental philosophy, like a ghost. . . . It is not possible to think of anything emptier than a philosophy . . . which waits for real knowledge to be given, as something lower, from an entirely different direction. . . . But philosophy can be exhibited only in its living influence on all knowledge, and its spirit can be comprehended only along with its body, viz., real knowledge.[49]

Science is thus to get its logical foundations from the highest science; a kind of epistemology is to make possible the proof of the "necessity" of the highest sciences.

But science is also empirical in that in its "deductive" discovery of the system of "forces" which are the reality of the finite world, it is dependent upon empirical knowledge to some extent. A combination of deduction and induction (which is more exactly explained in the *Dialectic*, as we shall see) is the essence of scientific method. Schleiermacher clearly did not advocate empiricism like that of Bacon, which he says would make science impossible. Nor is it empiricism like that of Locke who he says did not understand the part played by active thought in the rise of knowledge. Science is possible only through the order introduced into experience by mind, because of the system of relations which is the work of thought.

Thought begins with the most fundamental epistemological principles on the one hand and the data of sense on the other, and weaves them together into a system. When this is accomplished, the system of "infinite forces" is discovered, in its relation to the absolute identity, to particular existence, and to sense experience. When this system comes into being, the possessor of it has an "intuition" of the nature of the universe. Schleiermacher says that "scientific intuition is present where appearance and law are given as the same."[50] The content of philosophy is the "intuition of nature and reason."[51] In his criticism of Fichte, he says: "Fichte knows nothing of an intuition in which the temporal and the eternal, the universal and the particular, form and essence, 'that' and 'how,' are in each other and one, so that speculation and empiricism form one knowledge."[52] Schleiermacher sums up the general aim of science in these words:

Insight into the necessity and scope of all real knowledge is to develop from the *immediate intuition* of reason and its activity, so that from the very beginning the supposed antithesis between reason and experience, speculation and empiricism, is abolished, and so true knowledge is not only made possible but, at least in an undeveloped way, is actually produced.*

This "intuition," furnished by the system of science connecting the absolute identity with particular entities and sense experience, is the analogon in Schleiermacher's philosophy to the "intellectual intuition" of Schelling.

The relation between this scientific "intuition" and the "religious intuition" of the first edition of the *Discourses* lies on the surface. There is one difference which concerns what we decided to be a fundamental misunderstanding of Schleiermacher's earlier period. For the "intuition" of 1806 is related to the system of thought, whereas the "intuition" of 1799 was supposed to be logically independent of other intuitions. Corresponding to this change, in 1806 he thought sense perception to be what it is partly because of the activity of thought, whereas sense perception in 1799 was apparently thought to be independent of thought, like "religious intuition." But the similarity between the two ideas is what is most striking. In both cases, intuition concerns the relation of the finite objects to the universe, not simply their relations (e.g. causal) to each other. Intuition does not concern the common-sense world, but the "significance" of events in the "life" of the Infinite. Intuition involves the claim that the universe contains an "order," and that thought has grasped that order, and can confirm its beliefs by pointing out how that system reveals itself in particulars and can make sense perception capable of intelligible organization. Moreover, there is a sense in which intuition, in both periods, is immediate; one can "see" how a proposed

* *Werke*, pt. III, vol. I, p. 572. My italics. His use of the word "immediate" should be noted.

theory of the nature of the universe weaves fundamental principles and sensation into an organic whole. This kind of science, this intuition of the system of the world, cannot be tested quantitatively or in the laboratory for reasons I have already elaborated. In fact, the "intuition" of 1799 seems to be identical with the scientific intuition of 1806, except for the subjectivity and individual imagination supposed to constitute part of the very essence of the production of intuitions in 1799, and their logical independence of each other. That the science of 1806 and the religion of 1799 should be so similar ought not to be surprising, since we saw that in 1799 Schleiermacher was unable to make clear any important distinction between the intuitions of religion and the content of philosophical thought. "Intuition," at both times, meant seeing the Infinite and the finite in each other, in his sense.

The explicit development of his view that science uses "intuition" and the better understanding of its relation to logical thought were important for his conception of religion. It meant that science had taken over what had been a fundamental and distinguishing character of religion. It meant that if this were retained in the definition of religion, religion could not be sharply differentiated from science and thought. But the character of his course on ethics, as we shall see, required that he distinguish the "nature" of religion from science, art, and morals. Moreover, it is very likely that Schleiermacher was anxious not to have his view of religion associated with Schelling, who had now pre-empted "intuition" for his own purposes. So it is not surprising that he felt it necessary to redefine religion. He did this around 1806, and his conclusion was that religion is a kind of feeling.

3. The Practical Reason: Ethical Conduct

Schleiermacher's ethical theory is a useful object of study not only on its own account but because it is an illustration of what he called "deductive" method and because it contains a sketch of the outline of his science of mind or the subjective aspect of the world. It will be recalled that ethics is for him the speculative science of the preponderantly subjective side of reality; physics is the complementary speculative science of the preponderantly objective side.

Moral philosophy, it will be remembered, was Schleiermacher's first interest, and it was the part of his thought which first matured, even though his various manuscripts in later years show that he was dissatisfied with his positive results. As a whole it is not now tenable, but Schleiermacher was well acquainted with the literature of the subject, and many of his critical strictures and clarifying analyses were and are quite valid. For example, he criticized the abstractness of Kant's categorical imperative and showed that it required supplementation in order to be concrete enough to decide on the morality of suggested maxims. He showed the difficulties of the distinction between perfect and imperfect duties. He showed that there cannot ever be a conflict of duties, but only a conflict between the obligations which conjointly determine one's duty. He accented the neglected concept of moral value.[53]

Schleiermacher was also well aware of the difficulties of method facing the moral philosopher. He did not manage to avoid all the pitfalls himself, but he was clear that valid moral ideals can not be discovered simply by a straightforward analysis of common beliefs on moral questions, although he also felt that ordinary moral ideals must in some way be comprehended in a satisfactory moral system. He approved of Plato's ethical work because he thought Plato had illustrated the proper balance between induction and deduction in this matter.[54] Schleiermacher insisted that the moralist's own culture should not be surreptitiously introduced into his system as the uncriticized but valid standard; there must be "deduction" and room for real ethical criticism. His own theory of scientific method, as we have seen, demanded that the principles of ethics be ascertained both by deduction from the "higher knowledge" and by inductive analysis of the given data of history, of human behavior, individual and social. The ideal of this dual procedure was a "scientific intuition" of that aspect of reality.

How close to this ideal was Schleiermacher himself able to come? In answering this question, because his lecture notes of 1804-1805 and 1805-1806 do not provide a very complete statement of his "deduction" of ethics (and because I shall not say anything further about his moral theory), I shall make use not only of the notes of the period we are considering but also of those of later years and of some lectures read to the Academy from 1819 on, which are perhaps the best brief statement of his views.[55] The deduction from the "higher knowledge" is fairly completely outlined in the *Ethics* of 1812-1813,[56] and elaborated in the *Ethics* of 1816[57] which deduction is the one I shall follow.

Schleiermacher proceeds as follows: After explaining what he means by saying that "thought expresses being" and that "being expresses thought," he begins by asserting that the Absolute can be spoken of as either the highest knowledge or the highest being, since in either case the one expresses the other (and the Absolute is the indifference of both). The Absolute, which we have said is the ground of the relation of thought to being and of distinctions within them, itself transcends such distinctions, and hence can be thought of neither as a thing nor as an activity. Thus, although it is the ground and source of all other knowledge and being, it cannot itself be represented in consciousness (meaning, presumably, that we can know *that* it is real, but not *what* it is, viz., its nature). After some preliminary discussion of his belief that finite knowledge must consist in the relating of opposites, Schleiermacher raises the question of the nature of the most general and fundamental logical division within reality. He decides (without offering proof) that the most fundamental division is between being a thing and being a mind, the latter being the principle of conscious knowing, the former that of being an object of knowledge. Each of these principles taken by itself, he says, is only a barren abstraction; concrete reality exhibits them only in combination (a view to be compared with Schelling's idea that every real entity must be a combination of both the ideal and the objective in order not to abolish the indifference of the Absolute). The concrete reality exhibiting a preponderance of the principle of mind is *reason*; that with the preponderance of thinghood is *nature*. But there is mind in nature just as there is thinghood in reason. Mind is present in nature in the actuality of *form*; thinghood is present in reason in the form of *consciousness*.

So far Schleiermacher has "deduced" a double distinction or division in reality: reason, as a quantitative relation of the ideal and the objective with the ideal element dominating, and nature, a similar quantitative relation with the real element dominant. In order to get more divisions, Schleiermacher introduces a new principle. He says that any object may be examined in either of two ways, first, with respect to its essence, or second, with respect to its actuality (*Wesen* versus *Dasein*). The assumption corresponds to the distinction already noted between the speculative or more deductive aspect of a science and the empirical or more inductive part. Schleiermacher relates this distinction to the logical division already at hand, and manufactures a fourfold division of the subject matter of thought. This constitutes his deduction of the four fundamental branches of science: the speculative science of nature or *physics*; the empirical science of nature, or *natural history*; the speculative science of reason, or *ethics*; and the empirical science of reason, or *history*. It is apparent from this division that he regards ethics as a science of rational conduct in the same sense in which physics (not in our sense but in a sense resembling Schelling's view) is a science of nature.

This completes his "deduction" of ethics from the higher knowledge. The deduction of the rest of his ethical system is just like it: a division of the activity of reason into the phenomena where reason is predominantly active (industry, agriculture, commerce, etc.) or is predominantly passive (knowledge, aesthetic contemplation, etc.). These divisions are again subdivided according as the phenomena manifest reason in its universal aspect (industry, science) or in its more individual, personal, imaginative aspect (personal property, artistic creations, aesthetic enjoyment). In this manner, Schleiermacher produces four general divisions of ethics, which form the basis for his study.

It may be useful to explain what is the justification for calling this procedure a "deduction," since there is no strict logical necessity exhibited anywhere along the line. Schleiermacher made no pretense of having offered a deduction in the modern sense. In fact, he would have disparaged the value of such an undertaking, just as he disparaged the scientific value of formal logic in general.* His kind of nonformal scientific "deduction" he regarded as more important, for he thought it a method of discovery, a method for establishing new general classifications and the framework of a science. He regarded it as significant precisely because it was not merely formal, because it

* Cf. his account of Aristotle in his *History of Philosophy*, Werke, pt. III, vol. IV, pt. 1.

was true and not merely valid, because it was constructive, a basis for further procedure, supported not merely by deduction from other propositions which must then themselves be validated, but by an appeal to the whole of knowledge, including sense experience. His "deduction" is really simply a systematic laying down of a logical scheme or system for making experience intelligible; it is meant to be a coherent organization of experience in a form which he believed to be a fruitful one for scientific thought to pursue. Schleiermacher did not intend it to be pure *a priori* deduction; he criticized Fichte for writing as if he thought he could effect a deduction by sheer dialectic, without reliance upon the whole structure of experience and knowledge. It is possible that he exaggerated the efficacy of his scheme by thinking that he had shown his system to be in some sense necessary.*

An important feature of his view which I have already hinted at is that it is of only secondary importance to him to develop the concept of ethics as a normative science. Schleiermacher objected strongly to the idea that the natural sciences deal with the "is," while ethics and the normative sciences in general (theory of education, theory of politics, etc.) deal only with the "ought to be."† To his mind the science of ethics is strictly parallel with the other sciences. Ethics is a systematic understanding of the organizing activity of the intellectual (or ideal) principle in nature, just as biology is a science of the activity of the vital principle. This intellectual principle, or reason, is just as real as are the vital principle and the chemical principles. Moreover, he thought that there is analogy to moral error, to falling short of the ideal "aimed at" by the organizing process, on these lower levels of organization as well. He did not claim that exceptions can be found to the laws of mathematical physics on account of their abstract character, but he believed that certainly on the level of chemistry and biology it is possible to find cases where the principle organizing the material of a lower level in the form of the higher level is unable, for some reason, to control its material. Consequently there are sports,

* His view of deduction will be more fully discussed in the next chapter. He was misled by his distinction between a speculative and an empirical science—a distinction common in his day.

† Of course he distinguished between the ethical and the purely descriptive sides of these sciences.

monsters, abnormalities. The same is true on the ethical level. The rational or "higher" principle does not always prevail, and when it does not, the individual may give way to biological passion or selfishness—principles operative on the lower vital level.* So there is not a great gulf between ethical behavior and biological de⸺lopment; Schleiermacher had little sympathy with Kant's idea of the categorical imperative as an ideal itself psychologically powerless to operate. "Reason" is a "force" of which there can be speculative and empirical sciences just as there can be sciences of inorganic and organic nature. Morality is unique not in having to do merely with powerless ideals or "oughts," but in that it has to do with a principle organizing reality on a higher level.

On this basis, Schleiermacher's "deduction" of the branches of ethics achieves a division of the directions of the activity of this rational principle, of the fields of actual accomplishment of the organization of reality on a "higher" level. Industry, agriculture, commerce, science, art, religion, and friendship are all illustrations of the impact of the "ideal principle" on the world.

Schleiermacher says that his idea of rational activity as a higher principle of organization has nothing to do with his metaphysics, although he adds that even if reason is only a result of the evolution of organic life "its having come into being is the turning point in the history of the world, at which morality begins, and after which there can for the first time be talk of a 'good.' "[58] But there is no difficulty in seeing how conveniently his ethical views fitted in with his system as a whole. This will become clearer later on.

The normative side of ethics, I have said, is only secondary in Schleiermacher's theory. But it is there. "The ideal," he said, "is the total effectiveness of reason in all the being of the earth."[59] There is to be a perfection of that organization which has already begun. "The goal is the greatest possible organization of all nature for the spiritual functions of man."[60] The resources of the earth are to be completely and economically exploited; commerce is to distribute the materials smoothly. Science is to flourish freely. The emotional life is to be developed especially in its higher (religious) phases. Artistic

* Werke, pt. III, vol. II, p. 410 ff. The ethical essays in the latter part of this volume are the best source of information about his developed ethical views.

expression is to be encouraged, and everyone will express and understand his own individual self.

From the point of view of much modern ethical literature, there is a large begging of the question in this part of Schleiermacher's theory. For he seems to be assuming that it is possible to infer the nature of the ideal, or what ought to be done, from an analysis of the process of "rationalization" actually going on. Some writers would hold that he committed the "naturalistic fallacy," for the reason that the ideal can never be inferred from the actual (but must be known by direct insight). At best, if the ideal is to be inferred from the real, the answer is to be had not by Schleiermacher's simple architectonic schemes (which too easily fitted into the already accepted ideals of the German culture of his time) but by a psychological and biological understanding of human behavior. Moreover, Schleiermacher did not offer a clear definition of "the rational," and often seems arbitrary in his discussion about what really is the work of "reason." For him, "rationality" meant that reason in some sense becomes the animating principle of all reality: of external physical nature, of sense experience, of feeling, of the materials molded by aesthetic creation. For example, sense data are "rationalized" when they get organized into a system of science; or emotion is "rationalized" when (as we shall see) the ultimate meaning of events, as contrasted with their superficial meanings, control the emotional reactions with which persons respond to them. From the modern point of view, these statements appear uncritical. There is undoubtedly a certain amount of truth in what he says, but as has been abundantly demonstrated (and as he said in criticizing Kant), mere "rationality" is not a principle sufficient by itself for the derivation of the nature of the ideal for conduct. Schleiermacher seems to have proceeded loosely and rather arbitrarily from vague principles to an ideal which by tradition and inclination he had already accepted.

It is to be noted that in this more mature elaboration of his ethical views, everything he says is perfectly consistent with relevant statements in the Discourses and Soliloquies, and also with the early essays written just after he left the university. There is nowhere any distinction between the "freedom" of moral acts and the necessity of the rest of nature, except in so far as moral decisions are partially determined by a new factor, the rational principle activating the human mind. There is no utilitarian consideration of means and ends, and in particular no decision about the rightness of some line of action on the basis of its pleasure-producing effects. Schleiermacher seems to leave happiness and satisfaction out of account and to believe that the ideal for conduct can be detected on the basis of "rationality" alone.

It is to be noted that Schleiermacher believed that part of the rationalization of reality was the expression of individuality and the development of individual forms.*

Schleiermacher interpreted the traditional ethical concepts in a fashion defined by these general assumptions. The "good" was defined by him as simply whatever is produced by rational moral activity in the broadest sense.† Anything which is produced in the process by which the reason in human nature organizes its world or expresses itself therein is good. Hence wealth, education, and art are all good. The economic order, as moral, is to achieve "the greatest possible organization of nature for the spiritual function of man."[61] A work of art is good in that through it reason expresses itself in nature. Any aspect of human life is good in so far as it has been brought within the sway of reason, in so far as it has become the organ of or the symbol for reason, to use his terms. Every act which promotes this organization is a moral act; and everyone who works toward that end participates in the good itself.

Virtue is the quality of a person, which is that he is a potent producer of goods.

In the concept of virtue, the ethical process is exhibited as a force which has its seat in the individual life. For we all speak of virtue as something in man from which his actions not only do proceed but from which

* This view is a continuation of his ideas in the Soliloquies. Cf. supra, Chap. IV, sec. 6. Schleiermacher himself considered his development of the concept of individuality in morals one of his greatest contributions to the subject. He pointed out that many writers had ignored the fact that the individuality of persons and circumstances should be considered in determining a person's duty. Some persons are fitted to perform a function or make a contribution or realize a value impossible for others. Only when such facts are taken into account can ethics decide precisely what an individual in a certain situation ought to do. The realization of the individual is a good in itself, according to him. Cf. Grundlinien, Werke, pt. III, vol. I, pp. 59-66, 109, 257 ff.

† Werke, pt. III, vol. II, pp. 455-460. He proposed this definition as early as his first critical essay on Kant's ethics. Cf. his Grundlinien, pp. 68 f., 130 ff., 149 f., where his view of the relation of good, virtue, and duty is discussed.

actions of a certain kind must follow. . . . It is the source of life from which the particular actions follow. . . .[62]

Virtue, like the good, has degrees according to the extent to which the source of human actions is dominated by reason; the degree of virtue is the extent to which the higher (rational) principle commands and the lower (animal) principle obeys.

"Duty" has to do with the formula for the moral act. The act which is my duty is the act which expresses intelligent human nature in some specific situation. "Let each one, on every occasion, achieve with all his moral strength as much as possible for the completion of the total moral task in fellowship with all."[63] One's duty is to take part in the rationalization of the world in such a way that what the act brings about is an extension of the kind of rational organization which has already been accomplished.

I have said that the ideal or subjective side of the identity is the object also of an empirical moral science, viz., history. There are, he says with respect to this, two false methods of historical research: first, treating history as a mere collection of unrelated details, and second, explanation of the present by means of the past, which is really mere psychology.[64] The true view [he says] is related to these as the organic potency to the mechanical and the chemical.[65] . . . History is the whole of what science contains, viewed as in time. Thus the organization of nature, as becoming, is natural history; and the organization of mind, as becoming, is the history of culture. The identity of both, as becoming, is universal history. Its nature is the absorption of time into idea. In it, every antithesis between speculation and empiricism is abolished.[66]

History shows how the ethical process has brought about its products. And since the ethical process must be regarded as ideally a system, the historical process must be regarded as an organic whole. "In history," says Schleiermacher, "everything is really one, and something is to be set apart only in so far as, in observing an organism, one can separate one system of living activity from another. The single organic parts of the ethical construction are related in just that way."[67] History is the study, from the point of view of time, of that object which the speculative sciences study with regard to the system of "forces" involved.*

* For a general discussion of Schleiermacher's view of history, see H. Mulert's *Schleiermachers Geschichtsphilosophische Ansichten in ihrer Bedeutung für seine Theologie*, Giessen, 1907.

The foregoing account of his view of ethics and history is the clearest example available of his view of science and scientific method, and of his theory of the nature of the one side of the identity, the organization of nature by mind.

4. RELIGION AS FEELING

The pressure on Schleiermacher to alter or refine his conception of religion, brought to bear by the development of his view of scientific "intuition" which he did not want to identify with religion, has already been pointed out. The change was made urgent by the fact that one of his duties at the University of Halle was to deliver lectures on ethics. His ethical theory required that he distinguish clearly between the several areas in which it may be said that nature is being organized by or being made a symbol of reason, e.g., science, agriculture, art, and religion.

A new analysis of religion was proposed in the second year of his professorship,* and whatever its disadvantages, it set forth a distinction of religion from other activities of mind, especially science and philosophy. According to it, religion is not intuition and feeling (primarily intuition) as he thought in 1800, but is feeling alone. The introduction of this analysis and the philosophical ideas I have already outlined constitute the difference in outlook between the first and second editions of the *Discourses* (the second appearing in 1806).

If the two editions of the *Discourses* are compared, the alterations introduced in the second will be found to support the view that Schleiermacher intended to introduce these changes into the new edition. He reworked thoroughly the passages dealing with the relation of religion to science and morality, with the nature of religion as intuition and feeling, those describing the nature of feeling and its connection with intuition, knowledge, and action, and those describing the object of religion in a way not easily reconciled with the new identity philosophy.

A comparison of the structure of the argument in the two editions points to the same result. The first edition moves as follows: First, religion is isolated as a function of mind different from and largely independent of science and ethics. Second, religion is declared to be

* He did not have it in the first year, as will be seen by examining the notes of his first series of lectures on ethics. See Appendix I.

composed of feelings and intuitions. Third, he says that intuition determines the character of the religion. And fourth, he argues that religion is not normal unless both intuition and feeling originate in a moment of unity, in which the two are aspects of one experience.

All this is changed in the second edition. First, religion is a distinct function of mind, but it is not separate or independent. Second, it is essentially feeling, not intuition. Intuition is given over to science. This implies, of course, that if the two editions are to be parallel, science must be as closely connected to religion or feeling in the second edition as intuition was in the first edition. Consequently, third, he says that religion (feeling) is normal only when it arises from a moment in which feeling and knowledge are one (this taking the place of the unity between feeling and religious intuition). But finally, must we hold, in order to maintain the parallel, that the results of science and philosophy are to determine the character of religion? This problem is a difficult one and it is one of our main purposes to solve it.

Feeling, then, is the essence of religion, according to Schleiermacher at this time. Religion is a particular kind of feeling. But what is feeling? The statement that Schleiermacher thought religion a kind of feeling is vague until we know what he meant by feeling. And what he did mean by "feeling" is by no means easy to decide.

I have already distinguished* between cognitive or intentional and qualitative (or nonintentional) uses of the word "feeling." The cognitive use of the word occurs in such sentences as "I have a feeling that honor is better than life." In such cases, "feeling" is conceived to be a mode of awareness of some fact or content. The qualitative or noncognitive use occurs in such sentences as these: "I feel sad. I have a feeling of joy." In such cases the feeling is not primarily a mode of awareness of some fact or proposition. Several different forms of the noncognitive usage may be distinguished. For example, "feeling" may refer simply to the hedonic tone accompanying cognitive (or other) states. Or it may refer more broadly to the affective side of experience, to complex emotions.

We shall find that what Schleiermacher means by "feeling" is not quite identical with any of these usages, but for the present these

* Cf. pp. 106-107.

distinctions will suffice to enable us to state the difficulty in understanding him. Primarily, it is this: either religious feeling is of cognitive or of noncognitive character. If it is the former, then (whatever
the difficulties of maintaining the position) it might be legitimate to
assert that religion has an ideal content, that it makes assertions about
the world. On the other hand, if it is noncognitive, then the religious
feelings by themselves cannot be the apprehension of a fact capable
of being stated, although it might be true either (1) that there is a
"meaning" cognitively apprehended which is so inseparable from
religious feeling as to make separate discussion a vicious abstraction,
or (2) that one might be able to say that the occurrence of the feeling
itself has some specific significance which could be noted by someone
observing it. Now if Schleiermacher meant that feeling is noncognitive
in character (and in the main I am convinced this is what he did mean
at this time), then he should have pointed out either that religion qua
feeling has no ideal content, makes no assertions about the world, or
that religious feeling is always related to an ideal content cognitively
apprehended in science or philosophy (in which case religion would
be partially dependent on these disciplines), or that the content of
religious doctrine arises from interpretation of the feeling but is not
contained within the feeling itself.

At least some of these distinctions should have been made by
Schleiermacher and kept in the forefront of his discussion. But even
to the end of his life and in his most influential works, he did not
go out of his way to do so.

Once the foregoing distinctions are recognized, the reason for the
obscurity of the second edition of the Discourses is obvious. The first
edition was written upon the assumption that religion is a combination of intuition and feeling. Religion contains a cognitive element;
it is the interpretation of an event as part of the universe. But according to the second edition, religion is only feeling, and moreover "feeling" in the noncognitive sense, as it appears. On this view, he ought
not to speak of the "religious view" of the world at all; what he should
mean by these words is just the kind of philosophical conclusion
which is most congenial to religious feeling. Hence, to have been perfectly accurate in the expression of his view he should have rewritten
the book completely. But he did not wish to do that, for two reasons.

First, he did not think he should change the entire character of the work. "Important alterations I should, in any case, hesitate to make, lest the character of the book be changed."[68] Second, he was pressed for time. The printer was anxious to get the work to press, and Schleiermacher was forced to make the changes within the space of a few weeks.[69] Consequently, much went unaltered that would otherwise have been changed. He wrote to Gass[70] that he was expecting to revise much of the second and third *Discourses*, but actually the third one, which represents religious intuition as the activity which in 1806 he thought was scientific, was little changed. It could not have been changed without revising the work extensively.

This explains the very odd way in which he has altered the sentences which referred to religion as intuition. In the part of the second *Discourse* which was completely revised, the new view is stated fairly carefully. But in the other *Discourses*, he has simply substituted for the word "intuition," the word "feeling" or some other general word such as "view" or "idea," without altering the sense of the passage. In some cases, he has let the word "intuition" remain. One might be tempted to conclude from this that the divergence from the first edition is only verbal; but we shall see that this view is mistaken.

We have said that in the main, Schleiermacher accepted the non-cognitive view of feeling. But neither at this time nor at any other did he fail to say that religion makes assertions about the world. That is, religion contains a kernel of idea, meaning, and assertion. We shall reserve for later discussion the reasons for believing that he thought religion involves such an element, and the discussion of his attempt to reconcile it with the subjective noncognitive character of feeling which is the essence of religion.

We are now in a position to examine profitably what he means by "feeling" and by saying that religion is a matter of feeling.

Feeling, according to Schleiermacher, is to be contrasted with any activity of the self on the one hand, and with the objectivity of sense perception on the other. He elaborates his conception briefly in the second edition of the *Discourses*. Consciousness, he says, is generated by a preconscious event involving a relation between the individual and the environment. Now the causal efficacy in this relation may assume either of two directions: the individual may alter the world, or the world may cause a change in the individual. Suppose the latter occurs. Then the change in the individual will be one of two sorts. Either it is such that the empirical consciousness generated presents the generative event primarily as the representation of an object (sense perception); or it is such that consciousness presents the event primarily as an affection of the self (subjective feeling). By means of the former, science attempts to reach through to the object which is independent of the objective experience. The latter is the feeling of the "significance" for life of the event in question.[71] So he says:

The experience through which the organic being, by means of a definite affection, coalesces more with the Whole than in itself, now becomes a representation of the object. . . . The experience through which it rather finds itself than loses itself, viz., distinguishes itself more clearly and becomes one with its momentary state, is feeling.[72] . . . What we affirm as intuition, we affirm to be identically related to subjectivity in general. . . . What we regard as feeling, we affirm to be personal, individual, local, temporal subjectivity. We view the former as unconditionally identical in all; of the latter, we are content to say that it is in no one else entirely identical with the way it is in us.[73] [One aspect of the subjective consciousness is the hedonic tone due to the enhancement or depression of life by the given relation to the world:] The common character [of all types of feeling] is the immediacy of consciousness determined as a state which, outside its determinateness, also appears as enhancement or depression of life in pleasure and pain.[74] [Elsewhere he says in a similar vein:] Feeling is just the immediate consciousness of life.[75]

Feeling is thus an immediate conscious state, the result of an interaction between the individual and his environment, a mirroring of the effect of that interaction on the individual, its enhancing or depressing his life in a specific way; and feeling is either pleasant or unpleasant in tone.*

* The concept of feeling was only beginning to be made definite at the beginning of the last century. Feeling, as a specific experience, had been emphasized by Tetens, Sulzer, Mendelssohn, and Kant. The Leibniz-Wolffian school regarded it as a perception of perfection, or lack of it. J. A. Eberhard (Schleiermacher's teacher) said it is a mass of unclear perceptions. Philosophers were much occupied with the moral, aesthetic, and religious feelings, and especially with the works of Hutcheson and Shaftesbury. These considerations complicated their problem immensely. The influence of this situation is illustrated in the works of Friedrich Bouterwek. In 1800, he said (Anfangsgründe der speculativen Philosophie, art. 78): "So far as we think of impressions as subjective, viz., changes of ourselves, they are called Empfindungen or Gefühle. So far as we think of them as objective, i.e., as representations, or in relation to an object, they are called sensory intuitions

Religion is a species of this genus. It is not a specific feeling or emotion, although religious feelings tend to have a peculiar character, a melancholic tone. A religious feeling is any feeling which occurs in the experience of the religious person. And the religious person is one who has a certain emotional system, so that any feeling occurring in the experience of a person with this emotional system can be called a religious feeling. Sometimes Schleiermacher calls this emotional system itself religious feeling.

Being religious is having a certain emotional set or system of sentiments, as a result of which experience has a character it would otherwise not have had. He says:

> The whole religious life is composed of two elements: that man give himself up to the Universe and allow himself to be moved by the aspect it reveals to him, and that this contact which, as such and in its definiteness, is a single feeling, is made inward and absorbed into the inner unity

or representations." So in 1810 he objected to the tendency to speak of the "faculty of feeling as the faculty of subjective states in their relation to pleasure and pain" in large part because this tendency was not in accord with usage which "gives the word feeling a much wider meaning." Thus with the older psychologists, he preferred to "reduce the faculty of feeling, as a faculty of pleasure and pain, to the general concept of the faculty of perceptions (*Empfindungen*)," thus making the distinction between feeling and perception logically posterior and subordinate to the more general one between thought and sensibility. Yet he disliked putting all feelings together under the general notion of sensibility, "for the higher feelings, which belong to the possibility of inner perception and of real thought itself—the feelings which accompany our representations of the true, the good, and the beautiful, and without which we are incapable of our moral self-determination—are sharply distinguished from the animal feelings which one usually thinks of, under the term 'sense.'" (*Op. cit.*, 2nd ed., 1820, pp. 40-41.)

Kant treats feeling as an experience expressing the state of the subject (*Beobachtungen über das Gefühl des Schönen u. Erhabenen, Werke*, vol. II, p. 245). "Pleasure is the representation of the agreement of the object or the action with the subjective conditions of life." (Second *Critique, Werke*, vol. V, p. 9, note.) The experience reveals only how the object affects the subject. Pleasure is the feeling of the improvement of the bodily condition. Similarly, G. E. Schulze wrote: "The pleasant or unpleasant affections pertaining to sensation have been distinguished from the cognitive element by the word 'feeling'" (*Psychische Anthropologie*, 1816, pp. 281-282). He finds feeling to be an immediate, unanalyzable perception of the state of the whole being of the person.

Schleiermacher was certainly acquainted with the literature on the subject. He reviewed Kant's *Anthropologie* for the *Athenaeum*. He also read Bouterwek and the English writers, and was interested in theories of aesthetic feeling.

Eisler's *Wörterbuch der philosophischen Begriffe* contains a good discussion of the subject.

We shall see that in his final stage he apparently regarded feeling as sometimes a mode of inner perception.

of his life and being. The continual repetition of this procedure is the religious life.[76] [Thus, the particular feeling] is relieved of its temporal character, does not indwell the individual any longer as something particular or strongly moving, but as something eternal, pure, and peaceful. From this inner unity there arises action, as a proper part of life . . . and as a reaction of feeling . . . and every particular act . . . exhibits the whole inner unity of mind, but does not correspond . . . to any single emotion.[77]

To have religion, I take it, is to possess an emotional system of such a nature that the observation of the events of the universe arouses "pure, eternal, and peaceful" emotions.

It is worth remarking at this point that, although no one would deny that emotional systems such as he describes do occur or that the "pure and peaceful" feelings to which they give rise are immediate in the sense of being phenomenologically given qualities, nevertheless the question of the conditions of the formation of such a disposition are a matter very relevant to Schleiermacher's occasional claim (as we shall see) that religious feeling is immediate. If thoughts, beliefs, and assumptions are actually involved in the formation of this emotional set, then Schleiermacher would have to admit that in that sense, at least, religious experiences are mediated by beliefs. But the relation of cognition to feeling and emotion must be reserved for later discussion.

First we must examine more fully what is meant by saying that the emotional disposition is religious. It is the kind of disposition one has, he says, when God or reason has "entered feeling."

Religion, according to Schleiermacher, is part of the "morality" of feeling. Now feeling is "moral" if and only if the character of the feeling can be correlated, not with the particular enhancement or depression of the separate life of the feeling individual which may have been caused by the event which evokes the feeling, but with the enhancement of or significance of the event for the "life" of the universe as a whole.

The thoroughgoing morality of feeling [he says] is simply in that the unity [of subjective experience] is recognized for what it is, for the product of the higher capacity [in that, as we have seen, subjective feeling is not distinguished except through the work of thought]; and in that everything which occurs in it is related to the identity of reason and organization.[78]

This means that the standpoint from which things are valued according as they bring physical well-being to the individual is transcended; moral feeling is feeling made universal in the sense that its character fits the fact that it is a relation between an individual and the universe. "Only in this way," Schleiermacher says, "is feeling raised to the potency of morality, and this process is nothing but what we call religion."[79]

In other words, the religious person has achieved universality even in feeling. "The higher disposition always expresses itself as opposition to egoism, and lives in the larger whole."[80]

Schleiermacher's view that the religious man transcends egoism in feeling in this sense, and has love for God and the universe and therein is rational and universal is only the recognition that religion is the fulfillment of a process moving toward it. As he points out, the personality is never isolated. The individual personality is organically related to the family, the state, the social group, the scientific organization. In all of these respects, the self has already become part of a larger whole. It is already on the way to being religious. For the person who is related to one of these organizations already reacts to events with feelings which show that their life is his own; he is pleased with their success, he is displeased at their failure.[81] And true religion is only carrying this process further. It is having God or the universe in one's feeling in the same way in which the family, the state, or the social group is "in" one's feeling.

Schleiermacher says a person has religion "in so far as feeling and its response [the inward side of action, viz., decision of will] are animated by the higher principle of life; that is, enjoyment and its reaction are not related simply to the [individual] personality."[82] So "the higher life is unceasing progressive relation of the finite to the Infinite."[83] In this sense the religious man is said to have "communion with God."[84] And only rational beings can have it: "Animals . . . have commerce only among themselves or with animate nature in general or with particular inanimate objects, but not with God. This occurs only on the higher level of life, where the Absolute is absorbed into the activity of the particular in a special way."[85] Religious feeling "expresses a common higher life."[86]

Schleiermacher's view, at this time, might be summarized as follows: The religious man is one whose emotional system has become so ordered that it responds to an event, not for its immediate value to himself as an individual but for its "significance" in the whole, as an "expression" of God. The religious man feels everything as "in God," and that feeling is the being of God in him. The religious man is himself in a sense divine, because he responds to everything as a part of the universe; he has made the universe his body. As a result, the emotions which occur are "pure and eternal." There is a kind of religious mood which permeates all his feelings. So he says that the holy melancholy which is the character of Christian feeling "accompanies every joy and every pain, every love and every fear; yea, it is the chord of pride as of humility, and everything is related to it."[87] It is a temper which qualifies all experience. And yet there are special moments when it reveals itself in concentrated form, when "all single activities are repressed or abolished, and the whole soul is resolved in an immediate feeling of the infinite and eternal and its communion with it."[88]

If this interpretation be kept in mind, the important new passages in the second edition of the *Discourses* seem to me to become intelligible. It is clear why he should believe that this subjective character is different from and perhaps more important than intellectually entertained beliefs. For a person might believe himself to be a part of the Absolute without being religious in his sense. Schleiermacher says: "Do not think that I count God and immortality the chief thing in religion, for what is that must be feeling and immediate perception."[89] An atheist is one "who does not have the deity immediately present in feeling."[90] Atheism is a religious term and refers not to belief in propositions but to the actuality of a character of the mind. Again he says: "The one and all of religion is to feel everything moving us in feeling, in its highest unity, as one and the same, and everything particular and single as mediated by it: thus our own being as a being in God, and our life as a life in God."[91]

Although they do not add anything new to our understanding of his view of religion, it is useful to be able to confirm what I have said with some other statements which are among the more important additions to the second edition of the *Discourses*. Religion is actual, he says, "if the eternal unity of Reason and nature, the universal being of all the finite in the Infinite, lives in you *immediately*."[92] Again:

Religion is the totality of all relations of man to the deity, in the Universe, as he *feels* them immediately as his own life.[93] . . . Your piety is your feeling, in so far as it expresses the being and life common to you and the Universe.[94] . . . A feeling can be called an excitation of piety only when there moves us [emotionally] not the particular as such but the Whole in and with it: thus there enters our life not a particular and finite object, but God himself . . . and so there is aroused immediately in us not just some function or other but our whole being . . . viz., the divine in us.[95]

I shall make no criticism of this account of religion which Schleiermacher gave during the years succeeding 1806, except in one particular, the reliability of his analysis of the relation of religion, philosophy, and science, of the dependence or independence of religion with respect to knowledge. We want to know whether this kind of religion can flourish apart from belief in propositions about the world and God; and if it cannot, whether it is held that in religion there is somehow immediate intuition of some of these facts, or whether there must be a dependence upon science and philosophy for this ideal content.

Whatever our conclusion may be in this matter, there can be no doubt that Schleiermacher's conception of religion has been not only historically influential but very suggestive. Its originality is more doubtful, for there is much like it in religious and philosophical literature, for example in Spinoza's *Ethics*.

5. RELIGIOUS FEELING AND RELIGIOUS BELIEF

Two questions require an answer before Schleiermacher's idea of religion will have been completely described. The first one is: in what way if at all is belief or assertion about the world and God essential to or presupposed by this religious experience? The second one is: if it be granted that belief is involved in religious experience, in what way if at all is this belief dependent upon a whole system of beliefs, such as presumably would be the content of the sciences and philosophy?

The first edition of the *Discourses*, it will be recalled, made intuition central. Feeling was introduced only "to complete the picture" of religion. Feelings were regarded as determined by the intuition and as in a sense posterior to it. An intuition of the universe was said to involve various emotional responses. Feelings were said to be necessarily connected with intuitions, to follow out of them, and to be explicable in relation to them. But in the second edition the place of meanings, interpretations, or beliefs is not made so clear. For feeling is made the essence of religion, and intuition as the determinant of feeling, is dropped out. Our problem is to ascertain how far an ideal element is involved in religious feeling, and in what relation it stands to the system of philosophical and scientific knowledge.

The approach to our problem may be gained least awkwardly by raising two issues. First, is religious belief essential to the religious experience we have described (a) in point of fact, or (b) according to Schleiermacher? Second, does Schleiermacher's description of religion include reference to an element of belief, independently of the previous issue of whether this element of belief is *essential* for religious feeling? These two issues are rather difficult to untangle, but if we can answer them we shall be well on our way to an understanding of the relation between religion, science, and philosophy in Schleiermacher's thought.

I shall discuss the second of these issues first, since it is the simpler and admits of an unambiguous answer. Schleiermacher does clearly and unmistakably believe that religion includes (even if religious feeling does not necessarily involve) ideal content. I shall present the evidence for this assertion in a moment, but first I must answer a possible objection. One might argue: "Since you have yourself admitted that Schleiermacher revised the *Discourses* very hastily, and did not alter passages he should have revised in order to make his view consistent, of what value can quotation from the *Discourses* be, as proof that religion, for him, still retained ideal content, assertion about the world and God?" My answer is, first, that one can draw for evidence upon passages which have been very largely rewritten. Second, in his later books on theology he still indubitably admits the importance of ideal assertion for religion. Third, it is impossible to believe that he held that his religion was compatible, for example, with belief that the world can be exhaustively described by the concepts of a materialistic atomism.

There is a further answer to the possible objection. If it were true that Schleiermacher no longer believed at all that ideal content or beliefs are involved in or intimately related to religious experience, why should he have issued a second edition of a book which maintained the importance of intuition for religion, since intuition, as we saw, meant a kind of assertion, belief, or knowledge? Or if he thought it best to have it reprinted, why should he have muddled it, have made it a patchwork by introducing sentences based on an entirely different view of religion? Furthermore, it will be recalled that a number of passages were mentioned in the previous chapter, which point clearly to the objectivity and noetic value of religion. Now, if he were to try to revise the book at all on a quite different set of assumptions, why did he not at least do something with these passages, above all? Yet, of those cited, all but one are either unchanged in the second edition or have undergone only insignificant alterations of wording. All this would not make sense unless Schleiermacher believed in 1806 (despite the fact that he defined religion as a kind of emotion or sentiment) that belief and affirmation are somehow a part of or related to religion.

Concrete evidence for this contention is supplied by the following passages selected from the second *Discourse*, which was largely rewritten.

(1) He had previously said that religion intuits the divine in nature not only in its unchanging laws but more especially in the anomalies of nature, which point to a higher unity, the rule for which could be known from a higher point of view. He now says of this:

> We easily distinguish in our feeling . . . as something higher, that wherein the relation of the particular to the most remote combinations of the Whole, the determination of the particular by the as yet uninvestigated universal life, is revealed—those wonderful, awesome, secret emotions which take possession of us when imagination reminds us that what has already taken shape in us as knowledge of nature does not yet correspond at all to her action on us; and they are the same in all even if among the scientists they pass over into a more living activity of knowledge.[96]

Here he suggests not only that ideal interpretation is relevant to religious experience, but that the interpretation actually determines the character of the feeling. We feel in a certain way when imagination "reminds us" of something, viz., reminds us of his view of the universe, as applied to a certain set of facts.

(2) After describing his view of nature, and saying that the history of religion would have more inspiring data as its object if that idea had penetrated to ordinary people from the very beginning, he goes on:

But now it is really come to pass through the gradually effective fellowship between feeling and knowledge, that all those who want to be called cultured have this already in immediate feeling, and find in their being nothing but the work of this Spirit and a manifestation and execution of its laws, and everything which enters their life is, by virtue of this feeling, truly a world, formed and penetrated by the deity, and One . . . And this would be the essence of religious feelings from this side [viz., from that of nature:] to feel a oneness with nature, and to be entirely rooted in her, so that in all the changing phenomena of life, even in the change from life to death, we should await with approval and calmness only the execution of those eternal laws.[97]

Apparently religion is the actuality of the attitude and feeling toward the universe which are appropriate to a certain belief about it. Moreover, this character of "feeling" is "worked by the gradual efficacy of the fellowship of knowing and feeling." This does not mean, I take it, that every individual who has the feeling has necessarily arrived at the belief by independent thought, or even that he has the belief explicitly in mind. The occurrence of the feeling in any given individual might be a result of the atmosphere, the general intellectual climate of the age. But the point is that there is belief of this kind related to religious feeling, and that through the relation of feeling and belief, the feeling fitting to that belief is eventually brought about.

(3) If religion were only a matter of emotional disposition or sentiment, and cognition were irrelevant, Schleiermacher's statement that history in the proper sense is the "highest object" of religion would be hardly intelligible. "The finest and tenderest in history can never be comprehended scientifically, but only in the feeling of the religious spirit."[98] Although it is clear that Schleiermacher is here somehow contrasting religious knowledge with scientific knowledge, he apparently does believe that "comprehension" of some sort is involved in religion.

(4) Finally, we must compare what he says about the stages of religion, in the two editions. In the first one, he says the stages of

religious development are determined by the principle of intuition which they embody. Upon the lowest stage, the universe is regarded as a chaos in which there is no manifold and no real unity. On the second stage, a manifold of aspects or properties has been distinguished, but there is no all-embracing unity; thus there is plurality but not unity. This is the stage of polytheism. On the highest stage, the universe is viewed as unity in plurality, or totality: pantheism or theism.

Now observe how he translates these distinctions into his theory of religion as feeling in the second edition.[99]

Where the feeling of man is still a dim instinct, where his whole relation to the world has not yet come to clearness, the world can be nothing for him but a unity in which no manifold is distinguishable, as a chaos . . . without division, order, or law, in which nothing specific can be differentiated, except as it is arbitrarily separated in space and time . . . After further progress, the feeling becomes more conscious; the relations are distinguished in their manifoldness and determination. Thus there becomes predominant, in the feeling of the Universe, the plurality of the heterogeneous elements and forces, the continual and eternal strife of which determines its phenomena . . . Now let us go higher, to the place where all conflict is reconciled, where the Universe exhibits itself as totality, as unity in plurality and as system . . . Should not one, who first perceives it in this way, as one and all, and so is most perfectly the antithesis of the Whole and also one with it in feeling [should he not be more valued for his religion than persons on lower stages?] [The higher level] exhibits to us a more vital and beautiful life of the Universe in feeling—most beautiful where the manifold and the indwelling highest unity are connected in the most intimate way.

If religion and its emotional disposition were totally unrelated to thought and ideal elements, Schleiermacher could not possibly have written in this way. It may be that Schleiermacher had not thought out exactly the relationship between religion and thought, but that there was an ideal content in or related to religious experience there can be no doubt.

Of course in apparent contrast to all this, he says that religion has nothing to do with systems except in the sense that there is an organic relation among the aspects of any particular religion. But system in the sense of a proof why one must feel in one way, if one also feels in a certain other fashion, is repugnant to the nature of religion. The feeling itself is what is essential to the religious experience, and along with the immediate feeling there is no feeling of the *necessity* of any feeling.[100] For this reason Schleiermacher says there can be no such thing as a universal religion, to which all other religions are related as false to the true. In fact, the distinction of true and false does not apply to religion, for

all this is valid only where one has to do with concepts, and the negative laws of logic can be of some avail, but not elsewhere. Everything immediate in religion is true, for how could it have been anything other than it is? But only that is immediate which has not yet gone through the stage of conceptualization, but is developed purely in feeling. Thus everything which occurs in a religious way is good, for it takes place only because it expresses a common higher life.[101]

These statements in which, contrary to what I have argued about the presence of an ideal element in religion, seem to separate not only systems of thought but conceptual thought in general from religion, correspond to that part of the first edition of the *Discourses* which tried to make out the logical independence of every religious intuition. The argument of the second edition, however, is more acceptable than that of the first edition. For, in holding that religion is *essentially* a matter of emotion and sentiment, as he does in the second edition, Schleiermacher could consistently contend that the distinction of truth and falsehood does not apply to the *essential* matter of religion, for it of course applies only to propositions. Nevertheless, in obscuring the relation of this emotional disposition to belief, and in emphasizing the immediacy of religion in the sense of unmediatedness by thought, this passage is inconsistent with what he says elsewhere and misrepresents the nature of his system.

The evidence so far adduced seems to me to justify the assumption that Schleiermacher believed that ideal content, or assertion about the world and God, is somehow related to or a part of religion. With that in mind, we can now turn to the other issue mentioned, viz., is religious belief essential to or presupposed by the religious experience we have described, (a) in point of fact and (b) according to Schleiermacher?

The factual issue is a purely empirical one. It is simply a question of the possibility of the sentiment or emotional system of religion without the entertainment by the subject of certain beliefs, desires, expectations, and so on—without experience having a certain "meaning" for him. One need not deny that it is possible for a person to develop the sentiment in question without the understanding of theological doctrines. For, as Schleiermacher says, "every disposition, the scientific as well as the religious, is formed and perfected in life, i.e., in community with other persons."[102] It would be unwise to deny that the religious sentiment could be produced by a religious atmosphere without understanding of any dogmas; and again it is probably true that much the same emotions are produced by religious groups having quite different theological bases. Nevertheless, the occurrence of an emotion is bound up with the "meaning" of events for the subject; and these "meanings" are in the long run dependent upon the hopes, aspirations, or assumptions which creeds make possible. In other words, it may be true that the world may possess emotional meaning for an individual (so that the religious disposition can be developed) apart from an explicit adherence to any creed or belief; but if over a period of time the seriousness of belief in creeds has abated, the support of the religious meaning of the world is drained away and the religious disposition becomes impossible. This is what I suppose has happened in many places in the last few decades.

Whatever Schleiermacher says about the matter, it seems fairly clear that religious experience is dependent upon beliefs, and that beliefs (if they are to be taken as seriously as is necessary for religion) must be in the long run organically related to the system of thought elaborated by the sciences and philosophy. Religion, as a matter of empirical fact, is in this sense inseparable from knowledge.

Schleiermacher himself, I think, accepts this conclusion in the main, despite some vacillations and an understandable hesitation to embrace the conclusion which abolishes the complete independence of religion as a mental phenomenon. But we must first consider evidence suggesting a contrary interpretation.

Our discussion of Schleiermacher's doctrine of feeling in the first edition of the Discourses emphasized the fact that at times he speaks as if the religious feeling were produced as an immediate effect of the universe, without any interposition of interpretation or meaning. He sometimes writes as if he thought that in the preconscious moment of interaction between the self and the world, the feeling of the self is determined directly, apart from or largely independent of any awareness of the meaning of an event. And this theory seems at times to have been carried over into the second edition of the *Discourses*. Consider, for example, the following sentence: "If a man is not one with the Universe in the immediate unity of intuition and feeling, he remains eternally estranged from it, in the derived unity of consciousness."[103] Superficially this passage seems to mean that if there is to be religiousness or relation to God in empirical consciousness, God must have been in some way specially present in the preconscious moment of interaction between the self and the world—a view that suggests an immediate relation between the Absolute and the feeling of religion.*

In view of passages like this, it is impossible to exclude absolutely the possibility of Schleiermacher's having thought that the religious feeling is immediate in the sense of being altogether unmediated by thought, directly brought about by the contact with the universe, and hence independent of scientific or philosophic knowledge.

On the assumption that he may have toyed with such an idea, we must next ask whence then comes the ideal content which he thinks is in some way a part of or related to religion. Schleiermacher's answer (and this is his theory of dogmatic theology, both in 1806 and later) is one which anticipates his views of later years, and which we shall eventually have to examine in more detail. Religious doctrines are "the result of the inspection of feeling, or reflective comparison . . . the common expression for a definite feeling."[104]

On this reply, two comments must be made. First, it may be that Schleiermacher did not understand the nature of an emotional expression. If he meant by religious feelings just the bare qualities of emotional tone produced by the religious sentiment, but apart from the "meaning" of the object which arouses the feeling, then the feeling may be "expressed" by an ejaculation, but not properly by a judgment about the object. In other words, although an object might arouse a certain peaceful emotion in a person, he would not be simply giving utterance to the emotion by saying, e.g., "That is the work of

* I believe the actual meaning is that if one is not religious in permanent disposition, emotional system, or attitude, one's conscious moments will not be religious in character; the feelings will not be pure and eternal.

Providence." Any judgment is far more than a mere expression of feeling. Of course some writers have argued that moral judgments are only expressions of feeling, a judgment that a person is bad being only the expression of resentment at his deed. But although it is possible in this sense for a set of words in the form of a judgment to be only the expression of a feeling, it is to be noted that once the true character of this occurrence is recognized, it is seen that this kind of sentence can make no claim to be either true or false and hence cannot be a proposition. And I take it that this was not what Schleiermacher wanted for religion. What he says seems to leave little doubt that the religious man is at least making assertions about the world and God.

We shall go into this matter more carefully in the next chapter. But it does seem that if Schleiermacher did really believe this at this time, he was mistaken about the nature of emotional expression.

The second comment is this. It is barely possible that he was sometimes using the word "feeling" in such a way as to include *both* its noncognitive and cognitive significance. He might be meaning that the religious experience which is directly and unmediatedly produced includes both noncognitive feeling and a direct (perhaps emotionally conditioned) intuition of a religious fact. There are a few stray remarks which show that he sometimes uses "feeling" in a cognitive sense, though not in the sense of intuition. For example, he occasionally uses the word to denote a general impression, or a proposition which cannot be clearly established.[105] In one place he says that when ideas have not yet come to the clarity and precision of verbal formulation, they must be called feeling.[106]

If Schleiermacher did mean that religious feelings include such intuition which is an independent act of the religious consciousness, then he could consistently believe that religion is independent of science in that it is experience independent of thought which may nevertheless be expressed in judgments which may be true or false. Unfortunately for this view, it is difficult to see of what importance certain judgments would be even if they did somehow express religious intuitions of this sort. For the religious man would have little reason to believe these judgments to be true. At best they could be only a crude kind of opinion, which could not enjoy the high degree of probability or confirmation of judgments integrated with the whole system of thought and knowledge. And if conflicts arose between these judgments and scientific thought, the latter would have all the advantage due to the logical weight of the whole integrated system of which it is a part. It is difficult to believe that Schleiermacher meant this, although some passages do suggest the interpretation. But even if he inclined to do so at some points, the suggestion is of little use in extricating him from his logical difficulty.*

The evidence seems, however, to be overwhelmingly weighted toward the view that at this time Schleiermacher himself, although he recognized the possibility of religious experience apart from knowledge in some circumstances, believed that religious experience ultimately cannot occur without interpretations of the world which are bound up with scientific and philosophical thought. I shall begin by citing a passage from the *Weihnachtsfeier*, which seems to me to put in a nutshell his view of religion at the time:

What is the human being in himself but the World-Spirit itself, the Knowing of the world in its eternal being and its ever changing becoming. As such, there is no corruption in man, no fall, no need of redemption. But the single individual, as he relates himself to the other productions of the world and seeks his knowledge in them, since indeed they can be known only in him—the single individual is only becoming, and in him there is fall and corruption, which is discord and corruption; and he finds his salvation only in the [ideal] man-in-himself. Salvation, viz., in that the identity of the eternal being and the becoming of spirit, as it can reveal itself in the world, becomes clear to him, so that every man sees all becoming and also himself in the eternal Being, and loves it as such . . . and has no desire to be anything other than a thought of this eternal Being, and wishes a foundation in no other eternal Being than in the one which is identical with the ever changing and recurring becoming. . . . Only when the individual . . . exalts humanity as a living community of individuals, carries its spirit and consciousness in him, both loses and rediscovers in it his separate being, only then does he have in him the higher life and the peace of God. But the community in which the being of man in himself is both made clear and restored is the church. This is related to everything else . . . as the self-consciousness of mankind in individuals, to unconsciousness. Thus everyone in whom this self-

---

* Some philosophers would dispute these statements, especially when applied to values. If some kind of perception, they would say, reveals a special aspect of reality, how can you reject this because it is not supported by some other kind of experience? I believe my remarks are correct, however, although I cannot defend them here.

consciousness arises comes to the church. Hence no one can truly have science in him in a living fashion without being in the church at least in spirit. . . . Of course, some who are not scientists can be in the church, for they possess that higher self-consciousness in feeling, if not also in intuition—what is usually the case with women.*

There are many statements in which he discourages anyone who wants to separate feeling sharply from knowledge. The subjective and the objective have a common origin in one undivided act.[107] He speaks of a faith which is higher than knowledge, when feeling and knowledge have become one.[108] Since feeling and intuition always arise in the same act, each must be on the same "level"; hence where there is empiricism in science there must be hedonism in feeling. If it sometimes seems otherwise, the appearance is due to the fact that the objective knowledge was not really one's own work, or that moral feeling has been confused with convention. Wrong feelings are due to lack of self knowledge.[109] Ethical feeling (in his sense) is incompatible with wrong intuition, and vice versa.[110] And I take it that one of the main purposes of the "secret moment" passage, in this edition, is to make out the inseparability of knowledge and feeling, which always come together and are the expression of one event. The various functions of the mental life make up an organic unity, and no one can be developed without the others: "There is no feeling which is not pious, unless there be some diseased or impaired state of life, which is also communicated to the other functions."[111]

On occasion Schleiermacher even explicitly agrees with the first edition of the Discourses in holding that feeling is determined by knowledge. In our discussion of feeling in the first edition, we cited several passages stating this view. Some of these have been omitted altogether in the second edition, but some have been retained or only slightly altered. For example, the first edition reads: "The primary intuition of that from which all these views are derived determines the character of the feelings."[112] The second edition reads: "The original view [Ansicht] to which all other relations are related also determines in the individual the character of the feelings." Again, we called attention to several passages[113] in which he seemed to assume

* Werke, pt. I, vol. I, pp. 521-522. This statement is made by a character in the dialogue, but in the context it seems reasonable to believe that it expresses Schleiermacher's own view.

without question that idea determines feeling, and spoke of the "naturalness" with which a feeling occurs if a given idea is present. This
passage has been removed in the second edition, but its parts have
been re-inserted almost in entirety in other places.[114]

The main passages in which he discusses the relation between religion, science, and philosophy seem to lead to the same conclusion,
that religion cannot flourish without meanings and interpretations
placed upon the world, without beliefs, and hence eventually without
the support of and harmony with the system of knowledge which
would substantiate these beliefs.

Of course he distinguishes between religion and philosophy. It is
not the business of religion to "know things as to their peculiar nature, to show their particular relations, through which each is what
it is, to determine the place of each in the Whole, and to distinguish
it from all others . . . to exhibit how each phenomenon is identical
with its eternal laws."[115] Again, "the degree of knowledge is not the
degree of piety."[116] A man may be pious even though he is not a
scientist and knows only scraps of scientific conclusions. Moreover,
even if science regards God as the crowning idea of its ideas, as the
fundamental basis of all knowing, this is not religion's way of knowing
God. Religion is not concerned with the relations of finite objects,
but with the being of all finite objects in the Infinite; it has all life
and being, as such, in immediate feeling.[117]

But this does not touch the fundamental issue. Granted that religion is emotion or sentiment, and granted that it can sometimes exist
apart from scientific knowledge, we want to know if it is or is not
true that religion can endure without certain claims about the world
and without these being harmonized with the rest of thought.

His most interesting statement on the subject occurs in a passage
in which he discusses the interrelations of religion, science, and morality. They are all connected, he says. One cannot be moral without
being religious, nor can one be religious without being moral. Nor
can one be scientific in the full sense without being religious.[118] When
he then discusses the dependence of religion on science, he speaks
very cautiously. He denies that he asserts in the book that a person
can be religious without some science; he says he has only gone so far
as to say that there is no correlation between the degree of piety and

the amount of scientific knowledge. Finally, he permits himself to say that a person may combine religion with ignorance, but not with false knowledge. That is, the religious man must not make the mistake of taking for reality what is only appearance.[119] This statement, I believe it is legitimate to infer, must be interpreted in the light of Schleiermacher's own views. I take it that it means that, for example, it would be a mistake to take particular objects in space and time as completely and independently real; and that a person who made that mistake could not be religious. According to Schleiermacher, the full meaning of objects can be comprehended only in their relation to the whole. Their relation to that system, which is grounded in God, is essential to their nature. "Not to know falsely" would seem to mean that the religious man may not take the world, or himself, to have an independent reality which it does not have. He may not know how the appearances are comprehended in the Absolute. He may be ignorant of the details of philosophy and science. But he may not accept the common-sense world as the final reality. Such is the "ignorance" which the religious man is allowed to have.

Suppose we assume, then, that according to Schleiermacher a man cannot be religious unless he believes that the finite world and its common-sense order are not ultimate, and that complete knowledge of them involves the idea of God. This means, I think, that for him religious belief, philosophy, and science must eventually make up a harmonious whole, in which there are no contradictions and no double-truths. "True science," he says, "is completed intuition; true conduct is self-created culture and art; true religion is feeling and taste for the Infinite,"[120] a statement not meant to emphasize their difference but to show how when what is implied by each is fully understood, each requires and depends on the others, for all are parts of one unified whole life.

The ideal life of the community, according to Schleiermacher, contains science, morality (in his sense), and religion, each in its individual distinctness, and each in its proper relation to all the others. Religion is the immediate "being of God in feeling"; but this immediate being in feeling cannot occur apart from belief about God and the world, and this again cannot be substantiated apart from science and philosophy. The necessity of this harmonious unity creates no problem for one who, like Schleiermacher at this time, believes that God, the identity of thought and being, is the very presupposition of all thought.

6. The Content of Religious Belief

There is one major alteration in Schleiermacher's account of the scope and content of religious experience which deserves special consideration, largely for the reason that the change is so strikingly coincident with his philosophy of identity. It concerns the treatment and dignity accorded to nature.

The second edition of the *Discourses*, consistently with the identity philosophy (according to which the subjective and the objective are equal and opposite differentiations of the absolute reason) accords to nature a more important place than hitherto. Not only are those passages altered which savored of Fichte's ethical idealism, but there is quite a different estimate of the importance for religion of appreciation of natural beauty, of sublimity and awesomeness in nature, and of nature in general.*

Of course, even in the second edition, the intuition of humanity and individuality remains the center of religion. But where he had said before that nature is only "the outer forecourt of religion," he now says it is *almost* only that.[121] The second edition omits that striking phrase of the first: "How far we still are [in the religion of nature] from that which would be the highest, and how incomplete this intuition remains."[122] He speaks with approval of the cheerful joy in nature which characterized Greek religion, and points out that if that joy had been spread among all peoples, the religions would have had sublime forms from the very beginning.[123] So he says that one side of religion is to feel oneself entirely rooted in nature, so that one can witness with approval the execution of her eternal laws.[124] Finally, whereas he had said in 1799 that the categories by which we give nature meaning can be had only in the sphere of mind and are then carried over to nature, and that human spirit is what religion is properly concerned with, the second edition remarks only that the categories are not to be found so easily in nature as in mind, that the

* Some comparisons of passages in the two editions of the *Soliloquies* which have the same effect have been supplied in Chapter IV.

religious sense *inclines* to the side of mind, and finds these concepts predominantly there.[125]

According to the first edition, individuality is to be found mostly in the realm of mind; in 1806, individuality in nature is the basis for that of mind. There is spiritual individuality because reason must individuate itself in a person compatibly with the organic, nonrational, and nonmoral individuality of his temperament and constitution. Similarly, but on a larger scale, climate and living conditions form the basis of the spiritual individuality of a nation.[126]

The dignity accorded nature in 1806 is best illustrated by the treatment of the relation to religion of emotional responses to the awesomeness or beauty of nature. He adheres to his earlier view that fear is not a legitimate response to nature; but then he adds that fear has never been a religious attitude toward nature. Religion has always regarded the kindlier aspects of nature as of equal importance. The "Fate" of ancient Greece included both the friendly and the destructive. And the holy reverence with which the Greeks beheld it was not servile fear.[127] It was, if we understand what it meant to them, the first element of religion. Fear of nature is not religious, but there is a holy reverence for it which is. This kind of religion of nature, he allows, is a real element of religion.

In a similar vein, he admits that enjoyment of the beauty of nature can be a religious joy. If one accepts nature like a child or a sage but unlike a philosopher (who is troubled by the distinction of appearance and reality) then "the joy would be a true and pure feeling, a moment of living . . . contact between one and the world."[128] On the other hand, he still believes that there is an artificial joy in natural beauty which is not religious. "Do not give out as an emotion of piety that empty affected thing . . . which is but a wretched mask for cold, hard refinement."[129] To go out and find delicate beauties in a flower or in the sunset, and to be ravished by the thought that no human instrument could have devised them so well, is not religion. To do this is to be deceived, for, he says, beauty is only subjective appearance and piety cannot be genuine when it has been aroused by mere appearance.

The steps of this argument by which he tries to prove that the enjoyment of natural beauty experienced by the child or sage is a part of religion, whereas that of the philosopher or aesthete is not, are by no means clear. My belief is that he thought that the experience of the latter is perverted by false beliefs and expectations and is based on false assumptions.

However this may be, the emotions aroused by natural beauty, or by nature's conformity to law, or its awesomeness, are now regarded as religious. That is the kernel to be preserved from his treatment of nature in the second edition. Nature is given a place beside man as a proper object for religious experience.

CHAPTER VI

MATURITY: THE SYSTEM OF PHILOSOPHY
AND THEOLOGY

1. THE THEORY OF KNOWLEDGE AND SCIENCE

At the outset of an analysis of Schleiermacher's latest writings, which contain his philosophical views in their most mature form, it must be emphasized that Schleiermacher had become a well-equipped and able philosophical thinker. His work on the history of ancient philosophy marks him as an excellent scholar in that field. Moreover, his published lecture notes on the history of philosophy (written in 1812) show that he was well informed in modern philosophy, even though they contain some errors (his weakest point being the empirical philosophers of England) and diverge on some points from the most recent and reliable interpretations now available. Although these notes were written at the very beginning of his twenty-five years of academic life in Berlin and hence presumably represent his least adequate comprehension of the history of philosophy, they reveal the product of very patient and thoughtful analysis. The manuscript breaks off with Spinoza (there are a discussion of Locke and references to Berkeley and Hume), but there is no reason to doubt that he had a competent grasp of the more recent philosophers, and especially Kant, on whom he had spent so much time—at least an understanding as adequate as could be expected at his time. For this reason I hesitate to pass by any statement of his with the assumption that it is the result of crude thinking, misunderstanding, or confusion. My experience, in fact, has been that many passages which at first appeared merely crude or confused later turned out to be perfectly intelligible and valuable. Thus the parts of his work which are still obscure to me (and there are many of them), I suspect, remain opaque partly because we are forced to rely mainly on his lecture notes imperfectly edited, and partly because of an imperfect grasp of his system as a whole. I do not mean to assert that everything he has said can be excused on these grounds, and I shall later mention some important defects in his work. Nor should I assert that Schleiermacher was a first-rate philosopher, although I am sure his was a much more able philosophical mind than he is generally given credit for in English-speaking countries.

The main outlines of Schleiermacher's mature thought are to be found with more or less explicitness in several of his works composed during this later period, but they receive a connected exposition in the series of lectures which he called "*Dialectic*." These lectures (a series of notes dating from 1811 to 1831) were written with the intent of giving a suitable philosophical foundation to students of ethics and theology. They are epistemological in that they contain an analysis of the forms, development, and presuppositions of scientific thought. In this they are similar to Kant's first *Critique*, but they differ widely in that they assert the possibility of knowing the independent reality which causes the given matter of sense perception. His metaphysical system is "critical" in the sense that it is based upon an analysis of the knowing process. Like Kant, he was interested in furnishing a theory of constructive scientific thought; this, he thought, would result in the eduction of rules of scientific method. Moreover, he thought his theory would supply (like Kant's) an epistemological basis for the sciences, as well as an actual "deduction" of the two highest sciences, ethics and physics.

His lectures culminate in an epistemological proof of God's existence, and a discussion of God's nature and relation to the world. According to him, the possibility of knowledge (or moral will), as we shall see, involves a kind of fundamental world unity, a unity especially of reason and nature. This unity is God (with some reservations to appear later).

There are several stages in his argument which lead eventually to the various results outlined.

The first stage in his analysis of scientific thought consists of a distinction of two important elements in any piece of scientific thinking. First, he thinks that such thought always refers to something external to itself. Scientific thought or knowledge is always *about* something, and what it is about is always different from the thought which is about it. There is always some fact or entity in such a way independent of the thought about it that the thought must adjust itself to it if that thought is to be knowledge. "In every thought," he says (distinguishing scientific thought from the play of fancy), "some object outside thought is assumed. To think means not only that there is determinate thought, but that there is a relation of it to something assumed to be outside it."*

Schleiermacher places no restrictions on the nature of this entity "outside thought." It may be the consciousness of the thinker itself, the experience of other persons, or a common real world; but in any case it is an entity independent of the thought about it. In general, the most important objects of knowledge are those with which, directly or indirectly, the thinker is in causal contact through the sense organs.

Thought comes to its object or stuff through the fact that mental life is open toward the outside—through the sense organs. . . . Everyone grants of thought relevant to experience that we get the material for it through the sense organs.[1] [And this] receptivity to the external world is not confined to awareness of thinking beings, but extends to non-thinking objects which we call the common world. . . .† A thing [he says] is something that can affect the sense organs and can subsist through a manifold of sense impressions.‡

The second point in his exposition of the nature of scientific thought is that it claims to correspond with the object to which it refers. What we mean when we say we know something is that we have a system of concepts or judgments which corresponds or accords with the entities to which it refers. The degree of correspondence with the object defines the degree of truth value of the thought.[2] So he says: "Knowledge is agreement of thought with being. What this agreement is, since both remain outside each other, is not to be explained further."[3] "Thought is knowledge . . . if it is represented as

* *Dialektik*, p. 48. For a discussion of the meaning of "being," see pp. 386 and 450. Relation to being, he thought, is presupposed by any difference of opinion. Cf. p. 449, also p. 386.

† *Ibid.*, p. 491. He occasionally suggested that the reality of other persons is known more immediately than that of things. Cf. p. 453.

‡ *Ibid.*, p. 59. For a general account of the causal relation between the sense organs and the object, see *Psychologie*, pp. 418-420.

corresponding to the object referred to."* If thought successfully discriminates the unities of being, and really copies [abbilden] it, it is said to be knowledge.[4]

Schleiermacher's account of the nature of truth does not include any considerable discussion of or defense against the objections which might be raised against his statements. But he does anticipate and answer one or two possible criticisms. I quote what he says.

Some people think that the correspondence of thought with an object is an empty idea because of the absolute difference of nature and incommensurability of both. But in self-consciousness we can know by inspection that we are both—thought and thought about. . . . And this is necessarily supposed if one assumes that there is a plurality of individuals.† But second, some will say that we beg the question in assuming an object outside the knowledge itself. But they ought to remember that knowledge itself is, in consciousness, embodied in being, as something different from it; and the assumption of the difference of the two is the very presupposition of the attempt to find the distinguishing characteristic of knowledge. Finally, some will argue that there cannot be any relation of thought to being, for the two are absolutely separated. But in self-consciousness we experience the reciprocal change of each through the other in reflection and volition, and no one can really believe that the two move along without any connection.[5]

Although Schleiermacher accepts the correspondence theory of truth as a correct analysis of the meaning of truth, he deserts it in favor of a form of the coherence theory when he discusses the criteria by which true judgments may be recognized. For he does not claim that, in general, thought can be compared with its objects.‡ Hence, whether it corresponds or not can be known only indirectly. His view in brief (we shall discuss it more fully in a moment) is that a judgment is confirmed if it can be made part of a whole system of judgments which makes possible the organization of sense experience on the one hand, and is "deducible" (in a sense to be explained) on the other hand. If this condition is fulfilled, Schleiermacher thinks it likely that there is a respectable degree of correspondence, although

---

* Ibid., p. 43. Cf. p. 43 ff. also for other properties of true judgments.

† Some realists would agree with Schleiermacher that one of the strongest arguments for the correspondence theory is the case of a statement about the content of some person's experience.

‡ He would contend that there are exceptions, e.g., in the case of self-awareness.

he recognizes that the truth claim of a judgment cannot be satisfactorily substantiated until the whole system of thought is completely set up. Since this never has happened and never will happen, he admits that it is not possible to be perfectly certain about any part of "real" (to be explained later) or synthetic knowledge. There is always some idiosyncrasy in systems of thought; perfect objectivity cannot be had. Thoughts only relatively correspond to things; and we can be only relatively sure that they do correspond. But he thinks there is no doubt that the system of science is able more and more adequately to approximate to ideal correspondence.[6]

The next stage in Schleiermacher's general analysis consists of an account of the parts played respectively by sense experience and reason in the construction of the system of scientific judgments which constitutes knowledge. Science, he says, is possible because of the interplay of these two factors, and the nature of science can be appreciated only through an understanding of the contribution of each. The product of this interplay is the sphere of "real" or synthetic knowledge.

Although Schleiermacher ascribes an unusually large share in the production of knowledge to the activity of reason, he does not believe that there is any certain and a priori knowledge except (in a sense) in the case of the idea of God, that is, in the case of our knowledge that the identity of the real and the ideal (in a sense to be explained) is the presupposition of knowledge. As a consequence of his denial of pure a priori synthetic knowledge he says that the assertions of arithmetic and geometry (such as $2 \times 2 = 4$, or the angles in a triangle equal $180°$),[7] or the logical laws of identity and contradiction are either merely analytic judgments, or else involve reference to sense experience. Schleiermacher tries to make out that since, as he argues, the law of identity has content only when it expresses the form of the knowledge activity or else a condition of knowledge (the identity of the subject), therefore it "has a sensuous side."[8] These remarks should be compared with a scrap in his diary, written around 1801, in which he says that "all previous mathematics has really been idealistic . . . because it has deduced the necessity of the application from that of the representation. It were time to produce a realistic theory."* There

* Dilthey, op. cit., Appendix, p. 130. In The Christian Faith (2nd ed., sec. 100, par. 3) he says of proofs "that things must have been so," that "they are possible in the realm of experience only in so far as mathematics is applicable."

does not seem to be any evidence concerning his knowledge of the foundations of mathematics, but it is just possible that we have here an anticipation of some modern theories, according to which the theorems of mathematics follow from a system of postulates which cannot themselves be known a priori to apply to the actual world, as in the case of non-Euclidean geometries.

In this connection Schleiermacher takes pains to make clear the difference between his view of the system of knowledge and that of the speculative idealists with their deductive systems. He says he does not "deny that such a deduction [presumably like those of Schelling and Hegel] is possible," but he himself makes no claim to set up, for example, a speculative science of physics in that way.[9] The idealists, he says, make a sharp distinction between their deductive knowledge and the ordinary knowledge of common-sense science, but this distinction is neither possible nor fruitful.[10] He goes on to say:

It is the general impression that philosophy must begin with one principle, which must then be divided into several principles for the different fields of knowledge, and the entire content of every science must then be produced from its first principle according to the rules of deduction of the second element of the philosophy. This view has often been tried out, but one can scarcely say that a real science has ever been produced in this way. And the idea of the highest principle has always been a deception; there are always many hypothetical elements lying behind it, and there must needs be, if there is to be a deduction out of one first principle.[11]

In other words, although Schleiermacher himself emphasized the role of reason in scientific knowing, he did not believe it possible to start from necessary first principles and derive the whole system of knowledge out of them, without explicit recourse to sense experience. In any case, he believed, this kind of deduction leaves no room for historical, temporal, or causal judgments.[12]

All scientific thought, then, contains a reference to sense experience and could not occur independently of it. In a sentence reminiscent of Kant's remark that concepts without percepts are empty and percepts without concepts are blind, Schleiermacher says: "Without unity and plurality [thought] the manifold would be undetermined; without the manifold the definite unity and plurality would be empty. The business of reason in experience is the introduction of determination [Bestimmung]; that of sense is to give content [Belebung]."[13]

The error opposite to idealism is that of the pure empiricists or sensationalists. The error consists in believing that knowledge can come out of sense experience without the activity of reason, or eventually without "deduction" in Schleiermacher's sense. The thoroughgoing sensationalist, he says, can have no criterion for truth and falsity, for the only method of testing is that of examining the coherence of judgments, whereas the mere influence of objects in sense experience does not give any unities capable of analysis, but only an infinite chaos.[14] Mere sense experience is simply a flux of qualities which contains no "meanings." The "meaning" of sense data is due to the interpretation and organization by thought; the same sensation may first "mean" simply a colored object, then a kind of crystal, and finally a stone with certain properties. The "meaning" of the sensation depends upon thought and its organization of experience through a system of concepts.[15] "The activity of the sense organs without the work of reason is not thought, for it cannot attain to the fixity of an object, but is only the chaotic manifold of impressions."*

Experience in the simplest form in which we can actually inspect it is already the result of the activity of reason, of its organization of the manifold of sense into a plurality of unities, namely, of objects.† But this determination of a quality or set of qualities as one object occurs, he says, in conjunction with the development of a system of concepts, so that the sense experience is defined as a certain object only as the object or "meaning" of the sense experience is related to an organic system of "meanings" or objects, namely, the system of thought.[16] Thus he says that the fixation of the sensory image corresponding to the concept of the object is the formation of the schema, which is the sensory objectification of the concept. When, for example, a person who is acquainted with buildings sees a tower for the first time, the sensations derive their meaning by being subsumed under the concept of "building." The image is regarded as the sensory objectification of a kind of building,[17] and a new concept (that of "tower") is formed.

A further stage in Schleiermacher's analysis is occupied by his dis-

* *Dialektik*, p. 57. His use of the word "chaotic" is misleading. In his theory the sense data must have an *order* to be capable of rational interpretation.

† Gestalt psychologists would deny that we know that the organization of experience into objects is the result of "interpretations."

crimination of two general forms of thought and by his claim that the nature of these forms entails certain restrictions upon the objects of knowledge.

According to him there are two fundamental forms of scientific knowledge: that which consists in the relations of a system of concepts, and that which consists of a system of synthetic judgments (the exact meaning of both terms to be explained).* He does not say that either system can occur independently of the other; he asserts only their relative difference. Concepts introduce unity and plurality in that the concept is a unity and its instances a plurality; or in the case of the concept of an individual object, the concept of it as object unifies its appearances which then become the plurality.[18] In either case the pure manifold is organized. Much the same is true of synthetic *judgments*; they differ in that judgments involve a kind of unity different from that of a system of concepts. Concepts have logical relations to one another, e.g., that of species to genus, etc. In a synthetic judgment, however, the predicate is not a part of the definition of the subject; the subject "contains" it only in the sense that it is a possible mode of being of the subject. The unity it expresses is that of matter-of-fact relationship.†

The import of this division of thought into the conceptual and the judgmental becomes clear only in connection with the system which he thinks to be the result of thought. Conceptual thought is embodied in what he called "speculative science" which consists in a system of thought exhibiting the relationships of the essences of the various types of reality. The system of speculative science, in his view, resembles to some extent the tree of Porphyry: there are very general concepts, which are divided on a certain principle to produce more determinate concepts, and so on down to the concrete individual. This system, ideally, represents the essential nature of every entity. As such, it is not complete, and indeed the complete definition of any entity whatever cannot be given, since this can be accomplished only when the system as a whole is complete.

If the complete definition of any one concept were available, the

---

* Dilthey, op. cit., p. 298, says he drew on Plato for this general idea.

† Schleiermacher's view can be usefully compared with that of Kant in the *Critique of Pure Reason*, section "On the Logical Use of the Understanding," 2nd ed., p. 92 ff.

whole system of science would be found to be implicit in it.[19] Take, for example, the idea of sculpture. Understanding of the essence of this concept involves, according to Schleiermacher, knowledge of the nature of feeling and its relation to artistic creation and the whole activity of symbolism, of the characteristics by which this art is distinguished from the other kinds of art, on the one hand. And on the other hand, the nature of sculpture is not fully apprehended prior to an understanding of the physical material which the sculptor uses. For practical purposes, of course, this need not go very far. But since knowledge of any item is complete only in the whole system of knowledge, Schleiermacher believes that this understanding of the physical material ultimately requires an understanding of the whole of the order of the physical world. In other words, sculpture can be understood only when and in that everything else is understood.[20]

I have said that the system of essences and definitions which is the result of conceptual thought resembles to some extent the tree of Porphyry. But there are two important differences. The first is that Schleiermacher will not allow dichotomy, which he calls a negative principle of division of genus into species, in that, e.g., animal nature is divided into the rational and irrational, and rational nature into the mortal and the immortal, and so on. The principle of division, he says, must be positive, and hence will not be discovered apart from inductive study of the individual facts. The second difference is in that Schleiermacher will not allow what he calls a simple division, as of any genus A into the species b and c, upon some principle. A simple division of this sort is, he thinks, logically untenable.

If we think of A [he says] as divided into b and c, this presupposes that in A there is a relation to b and c, in virtue of which common relation to A, b and c must be related to each other. But just this reciprocal relation would be abolished by the [simple] division. Thus another division must be introduced, so that there is a double antithesis.*

In other words, every essential nature involves at least two elements, and the nature must be divided into species by setting up such a relation between these two elements that the genus is divided. Take, for example, a musical instrument. This object can be regarded from the

* *Dialektik*, pp. 556-557; cf. pp. 244, 249. This is similar to some recent idealistic logics. His view is that an understanding of the genus involves an understanding of the necessity of the several species.

deductive system, he says, as the "identity of vibrating body and vibrating air." The genus can therefore be divided as follows: either the body is set in vibration and it in turn moves the air (stringed instrument), or the air is set in vibration and it in turn moves the object (wind instrument). This gives us the division of musical instruments into stringed and wind.

This discussion of the way in which the relation of genus and species ought to be conceived is of particular interest because of his application of the idea in the plan of his own scientific analyses. His "deductive" divisions in ethics, for example, were obviously modeled upon this theory. Moreover, a system of concepts of this sort is to his mind the goal of "speculative" science. We do not have any extended statement of his view of the proper manner of developing the natural sciences in this fashion, for he wrote nothing on the natural sciences, but it is legitimate to draw some conclusions about the ideal he had in mind for the physical sciences despite his hint that the methods of the sciences of mind and of the objective may well be somewhat different.[21] It is perhaps not rash to suppose that in the case of physics he would have started with the notions of attractive and repulsive force, as Schelling (following Kant) had done and as he himself had done earlier, and would have tried to develop a system of the concepts of science somewhat in the manner of Schelling. It is also clear that there would have been important differences, partly in the extent to which experience is explicitly relied upon, and partly in that the relations of the concepts which Schelling deduces cannot easily be identified with the genus-species relation which Schleiermacher describes. Schleiermacher doubtless looked on the natural philosophy of Steffens and Schelling as the complement of his own, but it is not necessary to believe that he agreed with them on other than general matters.

As a consequence of his correspondence theory of truth, Schleiermacher naturally goes on to assume that if the logical system of a speculative science is to deserve the title of being knowledge, there must be a systematic relation of real entities corresponding to it. He believes that the relation of the genus and species by means of which thought organizes experience is identical with a real relation of genus and species in nature. He uses some curious terminology in expressing this, and I quote what he says:

Just as the possibility of the lower concept [species] is based on the higher [genus], and brings the higher concept to intuition in the manifoldness of greater determinateness, while the higher one is a productive comprehension of a plurality of the lower; so the lower existence is one bringing the higher to intuition, or is the appearance of it, but its possibility is grounded in the higher one. . . . Thus the living forces . . . correspond to the species and genera as universal concepts, and appearances correspond to the particular representations, as lower.[22]

Thought, he is saying, must necessarily proceed by its conceptual and judgmental methods, which involve the relating of species to genus, and so on; nature submits to this kind of interpretation in that its character is suited to this kind of ideal organization. We shall see later that this fact is the foundation of Schleiermacher's argument for the existence of God.

This description of "speculative science" is his final statement of the science of the system of "infinite forces" described in the first edition of the *Discourses*. Speculative science has as its object for study the system of "forces" or essences which appear in space and time. He adheres, incidentally, to his earlier comment that the actualizations of these "forces" sometimes do not exhibit the proper nature of the "force," for he says in his *History of Philosophy* that if Locke had had a proper understanding of the idea of substantial forms, and of "the organic and the elementary forces and their reciprocal perturbations," he would not have used the birth of defective infants to prove that species are not eternally productive forces in nature, but would have understood how "the rule is present even in the exception."[23]

It will be useful at this point to pause and take our bearings, so that we do not miss the significance of Schleiermacher's analysis of the forms and structure of knowledge, when taken in conjunction with his correspondence theory of truth. As I understand the movement of his argument, it has a striking similarity to the argument of Kant, especially in his "metaphysical deduction" of the categories. For Schleiermacher begins by urging that thought does and must proceed by the use of a certain form. According to Kant, the necessary forms of thought are revealed in the logical analysis of the forms of judgment, and in the categories derived therefrom. Schleiermacher does not commit himself to exactly this analysis of the forms of thought, but he does agree that thought has its definite way of working, which is independent of the organic and inorganic world with which it is in contact. He begins with an analysis of concepts and judgments, and claims that if there is to be scientific thought at all, it must be by means of them.

In this general contention Schleiermacher, like Kant, seems to have taken a plausible position. For, as has recently been argued by commentators on Kant, if thought is to be possible it must be by means of universal concepts which enable us to think of a plurality of instances as a unity or whole. Or again, if there is to be thought at all, it must be possible to predicate something of a logical subject, or to assert relations between two or more subjects. Schleiermacher would go farther than this. He would say that if the world is to be intelligible there must be coexistent entities so related that they determine one another's characters reciprocally.[24] He would go on to say that there can be no scientific thought unless experience can be arranged in a hierarchy of forms, related as genus and species.

Thus far, Schleiermacher's argument closely resembles Kant's deductions of the categories of the understanding. However, the use to which he puts his contentions is quite different from Kant's. For on the basis of his realism and his correspondence theory of truth, he goes on to urge that unless the structure of the real world is such as to conform to these laws of thought, there cannot be science. Kant, in contrast, made no such assumption about the independently real world; he found it necessary to assume only that the mind-constructed phenomenal world must answer to the demands of thought, and the responsiveness of this phenomenal world to the forms of thought, he believed, implies nothing about the character of the independently real.

Another part of Kant's *Critique* is in some ways even more similar to Schleiermacher's idea. In the appendix on the "regulative use of the ideas of pure reason," Kant suggests that science must proceed on the assumption that diverse individual objects can be organized in terms of species of identical properties, then again in terms of higher genera (from which the species can be derived by "further determination"), and that eventually all of them can be comprehended under one highest genus, of which all the lower ones are divisions.[25] This assumption, of which he gives illustrations from the procedure of chemists and astronomers, is "a logical principle without which no use of reason could occur." (There are difficulties in Kant's theory here similar to some in Schleiermacher's.) But Kant separates this principle (although it is rationally necessary) from the principles of the understanding. The former is only for "regulative" use; that is, it is an ideal which guides the scientific organization of knowledge of objects; but there can be no strict proof that nature conforms to it. There can be no deduction of the validity of the regulative ideal.

Schleiermacher's idea diverges from this theory of Kant's in two major respects. First, he would I think not recognize any sharp distinction between this idea as a regulative principle for thought and principles of thought regarded as more certain.[26] Second, while Schleiermacher would agree that there can be no theoretical "proof" of the principle, he would emphasize its implication even in the simplest kinds of knowledge, and the magnitude of what would have to be given up if it were seriously doubted.

It is unfortunate that Schleiermacher does not furnish a discussion of some of the categories like substance. It is possible that he did not, partly because the theological outcome of the argument at which he was primarily aiming did not require it, and partly because he thought that what he did say implied a great deal about this subject. Some facts are clear. He found flaws in Kant's logical table and it is almost certain that he regarded Kant's list of categories as an instance of artificial architectonic. He accepted the universal applicability of the concept of cause and believed that the characters of objects are determined exhaustively by these causal relations. About the category of substance it is impossible to speak with any confidence. In one place, he asserted that there is only one true substance, i.e., the universe as a whole. It is clear that he did not believe that individuals' minds are indiscerptible substances.

Schleiermacher's contention, then, is that scientific knowledge is possible only if the nature of the world is conformed to the forms of thought. In particular, as we have seen, he thinks that in conformity with the system of concepts of speculative science, there must be a kind of hierarchical organization of "forces," and that these "forces" must be related to each other by the kind of "double division" I have previously outlined. Schleiermacher does not anywhere elaborate his view of the exact form which physical nature must have in order to meet these demands of thought. That is, he does not even sketch a "deduction" of the main ideas of physics. Nor does he give any examples of what he means. Presumably the various kinds of inorganic element and the various organic species are what he has in mind. It seems a reasonable assumption to believe that he had in mind a treatment of these subjects somewhat on the lines taken by Schelling, Steffens, and Hegel, although as I have suggested there would doubtless have been differences. It is also clear that the human mind with its modes of behavior is among these "forces," and any of the types of being which seem necessary to explain social behavior. That is, it appears that religious experience, aesthetic creation, political organization, commerce, education, and the church—in fact all the institutions involved in social life—would be regarded by him as somehow among the "forces" operative in the world (which are deduced in his ethics).

To the modern reader this claim about the external world must seem strange, because of the world picture of modern science. Chiefly on account of the atomistic theories in physics, chemistry, and even biology, the present scientist believes that the various kinds of "substance" are related in a manner very different from what is here suggested by Schleiermacher, which seems much better adapted to an older type of chemistry and biology. Schleiermacher, in contrast, believed atomism to be an impossible view of nature.[27] (Most of his philosophical contemporaries, including Kant, also rejected atomism.) On that account the present theory of the different elements and compounds and their properties (identical properties of complex arrangements of atoms or of subatomic entities), or of the properties of organic systems, was not open to him. He apparently believed that the different types of being are the appearance of a system of essences in some way related to each other as genus and species (and in accordance with his "double divisions"). But it is difficult to see what sense he could make of the table of elements, for example, without departing widely from his scheme. In any case it is a significant fact that there is today no natural science occupied with the problems assigned his "speculative physics." The theoretical physics of today on this account would have to be classified by him as a part of "natural history." That is exactly where he placed the "so-called [empirical] physics" of his own day, which he had to contrast with the "speculative" physics.[28] Schleiermacher's attitude toward modern science is nicely expressed in what he has to say about Newton. The Newtonian philosophy, he remarks, "is full of true discoveries, but still always only from the observation of single functions of nature, and thus a mere aggregate, without any tendency to bring forth a whole."[29]

I do not mean to suggest that atomism in physics involves the physical insignificance of the concepts of "form" or "pattern" in somewhat the sense in which Schleiermacher used them. Some modern tendencies among physicists seem to be quite in the opposite direction.

The theological significance of Schleiermacher's argument is obvious. God is introduced as an explanation of the harmony between nature and the necessary forms of thought. We shall return to this later.

So far we have said nothing about that second form of knowledge, in judgments, which according to Schleiermacher is equal in dignity to the speculative system of concepts. Judgmental knowledge differs from conceptual knowledge by being more closely bound to sense experience and being less "deductive." This is illustrated by the fact that, except in analytic judgments, we cannot know that a given subject is to be qualified by a given predicate through a mere analysis of the essence of the subject, but must rely on sense perception. Of course he believes that sense perception would be "meaningless" apart from thought's construction, but nevertheless judgment is relatively more dependent upon sense perception.

The system of concepts of speculative science expresses the timeless relationships of various natures, genera, and species. In contrast, the object of judgmental knowledge is the realm of particular events and objects, their spatio-temporal and causal relations to one another. Judgment has to do primarily with the concrete actualizations of the universals whose relations are examined by speculative science. The concept of an object may contain reference to the possibility of whatever mode of concrete existence it can have;[30] or the concepts of two objects taken together may include information about the possibility of some relation between them (e.g., knowledge of the natures of A and B may explain why they love each other[31]). But the matter-of-fact relationships of particulars are the proper object of judgment. "To judgment," he says, "corresponds the matter of fact. The matter of fact is the change of identical being in its unity, as moment of activity and passivity."[32]

Schleiermacher believes that his view that judgment, in his sense, is a valid form of knowledge is a fact distinguishing him from the idealists, who think that the system of concepts is the only true knowledge and that particular objects are unreal because their being cannot be exhaustively described by a system of concepts.[33] It must be remembered of course that however valid his criticism of others may be, he himself would be bound to say that the judgments of common sense about particular objects are always to some degree illusory and misleading, on account of his doctrine that there is no true knowledge except in the complete and final system of knowledge.

The dignity accorded by him to judgmental knowledge is related to his view of space and time. These are not merely the forms of subjective experience but relations of the independent objects. "Space and time," he says, "are modes of being of the things themselves, and not only of our representations—a view which follows from our general idea of knowledge, that all real knowledge is also quantitative. The forms [of space and time] are both in the representations and in the things."[34] Apparently he believed that space and time are involved in coexistence or even in the existence of different forms of being. At any rate he says:

Everything which stands under the form of antithesis is also under the forms of space and time. [God, as we shall see, is spaceless and timeless.] These forms are posited along with divided or relative being. Space is the mutual externality of objects, time the mutual externality of bits of activity. Inner space or filled space represents the manifoldness of the thing in the unity of its being. Every filled space represents an inner antithesis, and when this is abolished, as between soul and body, there is no spatial relation.*

The suggestion is that if the Absolute is to "develop" antitheses out of itself, and with them the realm of finite being, then space and

* *Dialektik*, p. 336. These passages come from the earliest set of lectures, delivered in 1811. For his comments on Zeno, see his *History of Philosophy*, p. 68.

time, as the condition of the coexistence of finite objects, are necessary and must be real.

The sum total of scientific thought in the form of judgment comprises the historical or empirical sciences. These are concerned with the particular actualizations of the "forces" in their space-time adventures. Physics and the other natural sciences, in our contemporary sense, are a department of natural history because of their emphasis on space, time, and functional laws. The various departments of anthropology, in our sense, are a division of the history of mind. These sciences are all primarily interested in laws of causal relations between events, rates of change, quantitative relations, dates, places, developments, and so on.

Schleiermacher's claim for empirical science is identical with his claim for speculative science; if empirical science is to be true knowledge, there must be an objective reality related in a way which answers to the form of synthetic judgment. That is, the kind of relation which must obtain between the subject and predicate of a judgment must also obtain in nature. In all judgments, he says, something is attributed to the subject which only partially follows from its nature; the predicate follows from the essence of the subject only in that the subject concept includes the possibility of its having a mode of being such as is predicated of it. Logically, the reason for the attribution of the predicate must come from outside the subject. Moreover, he says, predicates or universals are attributed to many subjects, but they are never asserted except in relation to a subject. Now something corresponding to this relationship must be the case in nature if thought is exhaustively to apply to things. The character of reality which fills this requirement, he says, is just the coexistence of things, in virtue of which each thing is "in" all others, and acts upon and is acted upon by each of them.[35] This is his deduction, I believe, of the categories of cause, reciprocity, and plurality.

This argument, to which applies what has been said about his discussion of the implications of speculative science, is later used as a basis for his argument for the existence of God, as was the case with his argument from an analysis of conceptual thinking.

It remains only to make some concluding generalizations about his view of knowledge. The organization of sense experience into this system of conceptual and judgmental knowledge is the work of thought. Thought tries out definitions of substances, finds necessary divisions of the genus into the species, unifies the appearances into the object, separates the being of the object from its acts, moves back and forth from system to experience and experience to system in order to fit system and experience to each other, and finds analogies between a portion of the construction of one kind of experience and the outlines of the construction of another and uses that analogy to make a provisional construction where theory is lacking. In this way, knowledge is the product of the union of reason and sense experience.

The verification of any particular assertion within that system of knowledge consists in its making possible a self-coherent system. The ideal of science is "to comprehend the manifold into a self-cohering unity."[36] Thus any true assertion can be related both to the "deductive" system and to the manifold of sense experience.

Knowledge [says Schleiermacher] is that act of thought which, without the necessity of changing anything posited in itself, can go over from thought to sensation, and vice versa.[37] . . . We must distinguish correct thought through the exact agreement of the corresponding sensation with the organic [sensory] element already contained in that thought.[38]

Verification by appeal to experience is a part of the appeal to the coherence of the system, for the system is nothing but the intellectual organization of sense experience.

2. THE PROOFS FOR GOD

Several different lines of argument are offered by Schleiermacher to establish the reality of what he calls the transcendental unity of thought and being. As we shall see, this unity does not always seem to be identified with God, in his writings. But it will become clear as the argument proceeds that it is practically unavoidable to regard the arguments as arguments for the reality of God. The line of reasoning he develops differs considerably from the traditional arguments for the existence of God, although he himself claimed that his proof represented the truth of the ontological proof.[39] Schleiermacher apparently had little sympathy with the traditional formulations of the cosmological and teleological proofs.

Schleiermacher's arguments in the main depend upon his discus-

sion of the nature of thought and knowledge and may be regarded as
the consequence of his epistemological position. There are three lines
of reasoning, two of which involve his belief that the possibility of
knowledge requires a transcendental unity, and the third that the possibility of moral action requires it. We shall postpone this last argument until the end. Schleiermacher apparently never quite made up
his mind as to the exact logic of any of them. They take a slightly
different form in each of the various editions of the *Dialectic*, and one
of them, which we shall call the "Argument from the Limit," changes
shape in a confusing fashion throughout the several sets of lectures.

The first and, to my mind, most effective argument is as follows:

We have already seen how Schleiermacher believed that knowledge
arises through the synthesis of the manifold of sense experience by the
forms of reason. Thought, or the activity of the rational principle in
consciousness, introduces unity and plurality into the manifold of
sense experience. It does so both in the form of concepts with their
subordinate and superordinate concepts and their instances, and in
the form of judgment and its relation of subject and predicate. There
is no experience in the proper sense, no "meaning," except as a
product of these two stems. There are no pure percepts independent
of the activity of thought; there are no pure concepts without a
sensuous element or at least a relation to the process of sensing. But
although experience always contains both the sensuous element and
the element of thought or reason, in a unity, and although neither
the pure unity of concepts nor the pure manifold of sense is ever
experienced as such, it is a necessity of thought to regard sensation
and thought as independent elements, in a very important sense. For
the sensory element in knowledge is ideally distinguishable from the
rational element. The sensory and ideal elements enter into particular
examples of knowledge in quite different degrees. Some perceptual
judgments such as "This tree is green" contain a relatively low degree
of rational activity and a relatively high degree of dependence upon
sensation, whereas some of the more abstract statements or concepts
of science depend very largely on abstract thought and very little (at
least directly) upon sense experience. The degrees to which these two
elements are present vary and therefore we can conceive, as an ideal
limit, of such entities as the pure manifold of sense and the purely

rational activity. To think of these as the conditions of knowing makes the knowledge process intelligible.

The sensuous element Schleiermacher calls the "organic," because it is determined by the activity of the sense organs; the rational or intellectual element, in contrast, is determined by the activity of an organizing principle called reason or mind. Knowledge, therefore, depends upon two forms of activity, first of sense reception which is an activity on the biological level, and second of thought which is a more complex form of organization on the higher, rational level.

Now truth, as we have seen, means the correspondence of concept or proposition with the fact to which the thought refers. The knowledge which is the product of the synthesis of the sense manifold by reason must be such as to conform to the reality which it represents.

This implies that if there is to be knowledge in this sense, rational activity must be such as to make possible the representation of the facts to which the thought refers; that the content of the sense manifold must be capable of making possible this representation of the objective world; and that in this joint venture, reason and sense content must be so far complementary that the characteristic activity of the former is successful in giving intelligible organization corresponding to the objects represented to the content of the latter.

The argument may be clarified by a comparison with Kant. Kant is in agreement with Schleiermacher that thought has a characteristic form. Consequently if anything is to be thought, understood, or made intelligible, it must be such that the form of thought can apply to it. That is, any object of experience must be a substance or a quality of a substance, and in causal interaction with other things. But how can we know that the objects of experience will be intelligible? Kant's answer is that they must be, for common-sense objects of experience are products of imagination and understanding working upon the material of sense, and the forms and principles of thought are involved therefore in the construction of such objects and hence must be applicable to them. Where there is not intelligibility, there can be no experience. But how can we be sure that the data of sense, which are after all a necessary constituent of the phenomenal world, will be of such a character as to make possible the construction of a world out of them? Kant's answer to this question seems to be extremely obscure; at any rate, he argues, *if* there is to be experience, there must be intelligibility and we do admittedly have experience.

Now for Schleiermacher too, thought and intelligibility have a characteristic form. Thought can occur only in the form of concepts or judgments. If there is to be an intelligible system of knowledge, these necessary forms of thought must organize the sense content to form that knowledge as the product of both. So far he agrees with Kant, with the exception of Kant's claims about what are the necessary forms of thought. But how can we be sure that the content of sense is capable of being organized in this fashion? If sense experience and the real world are independent of the forms of thought, how shall we be sure that the forms of thought can make an intelligible system out of it? Schleiermacher's answer is that we cannot be certain, but that the complementariness of the two is a presupposition. If there is to be knowledge, then sense content must be such as to admit of organization by thought. There must be a kind of identity between thought-form, sense data, and things, if an intelligible system of knowledge is to be the result of the knowing process. So he says:

> The foundation of all thought which claims to be knowledge is the relation of these two processes to each other. . . . The fundamental assumption of the complementariness of these two poles, and of the relatableness of everything in the one to everything in the other is incapable of proof. But whoever denies it must give up thinking; for in every thought he starts with it.[40] [Again] The same thing must be capable of being contained in thought, in reference to being, as in perception, and vice versa. Thus, the same thing must be capable of being posited in the activity of reason, under the form of unity and plurality, as is posited under the organic activity as indefinite manifold. That act of thought is knowledge which, without the necessity of any alteration, can pass over from thought to perception, and vice versa.[41]

Moreover, since one of the properties of knowledge is its universal validity, and since the scientific knowledge of all persons must thus agree, it is necessary to postulate the identity of both the sensory and the intellectual functions (in their relevant aspects) among all rational persons whose knowledge product is to be the same.[42] "With the idea of knowledge," he says, "is posited a commonness of experience and of principles among all, by means of the identity of reason and sense organization in all."[43]

Let us now summarize the various threads of this argument. Experience is the synthesis of the manifold of sense experience by the activity of thought. But thought uses certain characteristic and necessary forms of organization. If the synthesis of the manifold into an intelligible whole of experience is to be possible, the forms of thought and the content of sense must be complementary, i.e., the "object" must be given in each in its own fashion. Furthermore, if true thought must correspond with the facts to which it refers, there must be such an identity between the forms of thought, the content of sense, and the facts, that thought is capable, ideally, of corresponding with what it claims to represent. Finally, if there is to be universal validity of knowledge, this relation between thought, its objects, and the sense content, must be identical for all persons, viz., all rational knowing beings.

Schleiermacher then proceeds to formulate the theological implications of the foregoing argument in the following statements. He says:

Since this activity of reason is grounded in the ideal [presumably as a principle of organization contrasted with biological organization], and the sensory element, as dependent upon the impressions of the objects, is grounded in the real, therefore being is posited in an ideal fashion just as in a real fashion, and the ideal and the real are parallel modes of being. . . . The Ideal is that in reality which is the principle of all rational activity (in so far as this does not originate in the organic side); and the Real is that in reality by virtue of which it is principle of the sensory function (in so far as this does not originate in the rational activity). . . . This highest antithesis (of the Real and the Ideal) is the border between the transcendental and the immanent, and just as it comprehends everything in which the system of antithesis is extended, so, because it would be an empty mystery if one went no further, it can only be comprehended by and reduced to the One Being, which develops it, and with it all comprehended antitheses, out of itself. This transcendental Being, to which we have come, is the idea of Being-in-itself under two opposed and related kinds or forms and modes, the Ideal and the Real, as condition of the reality of knowledge.[44]

In this argument the principle or ground of the active organization of the content of sense in the form of unity and plurality is taken to be one form or mode of reality, in contrast to other modes of activity, e.g., on the biological level.[45] Second, the being, the reality to be found primarily in nature, is taken to be another mode or form of reality. The principle of thought is thus contrasted with the principle of objective being. The ideal and the real are the most fundamental differentiae of being, which is divided on these principles into the realms of nature and mind; they are the characters defining both nature and mind, nature being endowed with a preponderance of the real, mind with a preponderance of the ideal. Now since reason and sense content must be identical in the sense that the forms of the one must be capable of organizing the content of the other, so as to represent the real world, the ideal and the real must be looked on as different but parallel modes of being. But this parallelism between the two fundamental modes of being, which constitutes the "highest antithesis" or the most general logical division in nature, would not be intelligible, would remain a mystery, unless there is a Being which is one, which comprehends this division of parallel modes of being, and "develops" it and all other forms of being out of itself.

Schleiermacher's argument will be made clearer if notice is taken of an important assumption on the basis of which he is arguing. This is his belief that there are certain essences in nature (not distinct from the particulars in which they are embodied, but in them). This fact is what makes conceptual thought possible, for if reality were not a system of this sort, thought could not proceed by means of concepts or the logical system of genera and species. Now certain types of being operate on certain principles and other types of being on certain other principles. For instance, chemical processes are of one type. Biological processes exhibit a different and more complex form of unity. There is thus reason to classify organic beings together and to distinguish them from the inorganic, on account of the different forms regularly (or at least almost regularly) operative in the two types of being. The same is true of mind. Mind is a form of being, in which certain unique principles are operative. The principles operative in mind are very different from those operative in other forms of reality. Their product, conscious experience, is so significantly different from the nature of the objects of that conscious experience that the scientist is justified in making a very general classification, in distinguishing the primarily "objective" modes of being on the one hand from the "subjective" mode of being on the other, viz., the ideal from the real. Now, as I have said, Schleiermacher is assuming that the principle of rational activity involved in mind is quite independent of the principle of real activity involved in nature. Nature does not make reason what it is any more than subjective reason makes nature what it is (except within certain very limited spheres, e.g., in artistic production or ethical action). They are in causal interaction, to be sure. And nature acts on mental reality through the affection of the senses of the body. But the remarkable fact is that the rational principle, operating along its own independent line, introduces a kind of organization into sense experience, such that it is possible for objective reality to be represented in thought as it is, or at least approximately as it is. Mind and nature are independent modes of being, and yet they are so far complementary that the one is able to represent the other. (As a result of ethical action, nature is also able to "represent" mind.) Schleiermacher's argument is simply that this complementariness requires explanation. There are two types of being so related that we can say that the real principle and the ideal principle actually express the same forms, each in its peculiar way. Certain forms get realized in nature or are operative there; those same forms are so operative in mind that experience can represent nature. Schleiermacher's explanation of this difficulty is that mind and nature must be somehow derivative from a Being which is their unity, and which "develops" them both out of itself; they are not ultimately independent.

Let us examine this argument further. Schleiermacher is urging that the world would be "mysterious" unless the reality of the unity be granted, and I suppose he means that a world which met the requirements of thought would be a very improbable affair unless this transcendental assumption were made. In other words, he seems to be saying that the world conceivably might be different from what it is, unresponsive to the demands of thought. Nevertheless, out of the various possibilities, it happens actually to be a world which is responsive to the requirements of thought. And the realization of precisely this fortunate one amongst the various possibilities requires a reason. Such a reason is supplied by his suggestion that thought and the world are both "comprehended" by one Being.

For the sake of argument, we can grant him some of his assumptions. We can grant that conceptual thought is possible only if its objects are of a certain sort; we can grant that human beings using conceptual thought are a "mode" of reality relatively independent at the present time of the formative influence of nature, i.e., that thought proceeds on a certain established line laid down by itself and not by the nature on which it works; and we can grant that nature at least thus far seems to have lived up to these demands of thought. But what is thereby proved? Has it been proved that this complementariness requires the kind of explanation he offers (assuming that some explanation is required)? Or, if his contention there be granted, does his theory really furnish such an explanation? Or is it possible to show that there is no other theory which would fare better than his? There can be little doubt that the answers to these questions are not all in Schleiermacher's favor.

Of course Schleiermacher had an immense advantage in his day because he was not an evolutionist. As we have seen, he did believe in development and progress in world history, but there is little evidence to suggest that he seriously believed that new organic forms, much less a thinking human being, are evolved as the result of natural processes. Or, even if we assume that he was agreeable to the idea that human thought is a recent arrival on the cosmic scene, Schleiermacher clearly believed that, far from being an accident, thought is somehow a fundamental aspect of the universe, essential to and involved in the nature of the whole.

It is clear that Schleiermacher's demand for an explanation is much more forcible for one who believes that the universe has "eternally" been a going concern of certain "forms" of being. For one who puts his faith in evolution, the situation is much less difficult. The evolutionist can argue that it is no surprise at all that nature and human nature are so complementary, for human nature is a product of nature and if nature had not happened to be so ordered that conceptual thinking could be successful in it, conceptual thinkers would not have appeared on the scene. Schleiermacher could of course carry the argument a stage further back. He could ask whether after all we do not have to explain the fact that nature happened to be of just that character that conceptual thinkers could emerge and successfully cope with it by means of their conceptual thinking. This new step raises a great many questions, which I shall abstain from discussing.

There are difficulties for Schleiermacher on other fronts, however.

The most obvious one is that he claims that the complementariness of
nature and mind would remain "mysterious" unless both are comprehended in one Being, and yet the assumption of this one Being is
by no means shown to explain the mystery. Had Schleiermacher
shown how it follows from the nature of the transcendental unity that
there must be just such a parallelism between thought and things, his
position would be plausible. But he expressly insists both that the
nature of the unity is for various reasons unknowable, and that any
attempt to deduce from it the parallelism of being would be "mytho-
logical."[46] In these circumstances, it is difficult to believe his assumption a useful one.

Schleiermacher of course recognized that there might be other theories in explanation of the facts in question, such as a more theistic
theory of pre-established harmony, for example. Schleiermacher had
objections to all such formulations, and it must be admitted that these
theories have their own difficulties, especially when they attempt to
become more explicit than Schleiermacher was.

One might raise an objection to the thesis that the complementariness requires any explanation, even on his nonevolutionary grounds.
Certainly this particular adaptation does not seem to require explanation more than many other adaptations in nature. Much depends, of
course, upon the intricacy of the harmony demanded. If the possibility
of knowledge requires only that some events in nature be similar to
others or that there be some amount of law-abidingness in nature, the
demand for an explanation of the harmony is not so pressing as it is
if it can be shown that the possibility of knowledge requires more.
The more harmony there must be, the greater the demand for some
basis for the harmony.

In some passages Schleiermacher seems to go so far as to say that
all the concepts which human minds ever use must be in some sense
innate. Schleiermacher does not believe that there are any concepts
present in the human mind, as concepts, before they are thought of,
and in so far he holds that the doctrine of innate ideas, as it has sometimes been conceived, is crude. But he says:

If there is to be knowledge, then the system of all the concepts constituting knowledge must be in the one Reason which animates all persons,
in a timeless way.[47] [Reason, he says, is] the source of all true concepts in

just the way in which God is the source of all living forces.[48] [Again, he remarks that] the truth in the idea of the microcosmos [Leibniz?] is that man has all the stages of life in himself, and forms his representations of external reality therewith.[49]

These remarks, based on the Platonic idea of the function of "reminiscence" in knowing, might be taken to mean that the human mind is of such a nature that it is ready to form a certain concept on the occasion of the presentation of a sensory datum with which that form is to be connected or which can be organized by it. In this case, one would have to think of the mind as an incredibly complex structure, stored with a practically infinite number of different ideas waiting to be produced at the right moment. If such were his idea, we should probably have to admit that the correspondence of this great conceptual system with the system of nature required some kind of explanation. But I cannot believe that he did have anything so crude in mind. All that he actually meant by his talk of innate ideas, I think, was that in fact these concepts have been developed by the mind in its interaction with the perceptual world, that they could not be simply read from the sense data, that mind produces the concepts in accord with the logical system of genus and species required by any discursive thought and makes them concrete by relation to sense experience, and that therefore it is not exaggerated to say that these concepts are innate to or grounded in reason. In one of the later series of lectures, he says: "This groundedness [of concepts in reason] means nothing but that reason as a living principle, as activity in thought, is predetermined to produce these concepts and no others. Just this is expressed by the statement that it is the source of concepts."[50] With the exception of the prefix "pre" in "predetermined," which may very well have been a slip, this sentence means simply that the human mind has succeeded in producing a system of science which organizes experience to the extent that science does organize it, and that these concepts are grounded in it in the sense that they are the result of the organizing principle's being just what it is.

In criticizing Locke's view of innate ideas, Schleiermacher says that he should have regarded them only "as the perfectible productions of concepts dwelling in us in an ideal way as tendency."[51] It is not necessary to assume that he meant by this anything more than that the system of concepts is implicit in reason in the sense that the system of genera and species by which it must organize experience will actually acquire concrete content of a certain sort as the process of knowing proceeds. He once remarked that both Descartes and Kant regarded innate ideas as "only forms of construction,"[52] and if he allied himself with them on this point, that would mean that mind's general method of procedure is innate, but not the specific concepts.

If this interpretation of him is correct, then it is not necessary to assume that there is a detailed and far-reaching correspondence between a complex innate mental structure and the structure of nature. It may be, however, that the other and less sophisticated view ought to be ascribed to him.

It must be kept in mind throughout this argument that Schleiermacher is assuming that the distinction between the principle of thought and the principle of things is somehow of great cosmological significance. It is on this account that he believes the transcendental unity to be fundamentally a unity of reason and nature, and thinks that this "antithesis" is of great importance for the construction of science. Thought has a dignity and importance equal to nature. To many people this assumption will doubtless seem a gigantic anthropomorphism.

Schleiermacher himself sensed the difficulty about this "highest opposition" within reality and attempted to defend it. He offers only a very feeble argument, however. He first assumes that he has been justified in distinguishing between an intellectual and an organic principle in knowledge. Then he says: "Since being is for us only in relation to thought, this antithesis is also the highest for us, so that it exhausts all being which can occur in scientific thought"[53]— an argument which appears to be nothing more than a form of the misuse of the egocentric predicament. Schleiermacher recognizes that he has not really proved that there are two quite different principles of activity in the knowledge process itself. This, he confesses, must be a matter of "disposition."[54] But he has some arguments. For, he says, if we do not make the distinction, we must hold either that we ourselves are only the "puppets" of nature or that nature is produced by ourselves. In general, he says, "If anyone seeks an intuition of life in general, he must accept this dualism."* Of course his argument will carry weight only for someone to whom the conclusions he points out will prove distasteful.

One additional fact should be recalled in connection with the argument. It is that the distinction of the ideal and the real does not coincide with the distinction between consciousness and body. For Schleiermacher, both consciousness and body contain an element of both principles.

Later we shall consider more carefully the nature of the transcendental unity, in particular its relation to the world of science and the legitimacy of identifying it with God. I have now said all I have to say about the first argument for the reality of this unity, and I turn with some reluctance to the second argument, which I have called the "Argument from the Limit."

This argument is only briefly sketched,[55] and is much inferior to the first argument both in clarity and plausibility. Its nature is greatly obscured by the fact that Schleiermacher is trying to prove several things at the same time. His reasoning is an attempt to prove, first and foremost, that the unity is unknowable and only secondly that it is real; and in addition it is intended to establish that both speculative idealism and empiricism are one-sided, and so on. Moreover, he does not stop to make some very important distinctions, and had these distinctions been made, his argument might not have fared so well.

As I have said, the main purpose of the argument is to show that the kind of entity arrived at by the preceding epistemological argument cannot be a proper object of knowledge. The reasoning proceeds through an analysis of the nature and relations of concepts and judgments, and ends with the discovery that the transcendental reality which is the condition of knowledge, while it is a necessary limiting "idea," is of such a character that there can be neither a concept of it in the proper sense, nor a judgment about it. In this way Schleiermacher allies himself with the agnostic side of Kant and opposes himself to the speculative ideals. He holds that we can know that there must be a transcendental reality which is the identity of thought and being, but that its nature cannot be descried. Schleiermacher also allies

---

* *Dialektik*, p. 77. This antithesis was important to him as the basis of his fundamental division of the sciences into physics and ethics.

himself with those theologians who hold that there is no positive intellectual apprehension of God. For example, he cites his agreement with Augustine's view that "essence and quality are identical in God, that he is wholly substance and has no accidents, and in general has nothing but only *is* absolutely."[56] There can be, he says, only negative judgments about this unity.[57]

Schleiermacher's agnosticism about the nature of the absolute identity lays the foundation for his treatment of theological dogmas as expressions of our relation to God, in feeling. It seems to me possible, however, that psychologically the order was the opposite of this. That is, it may very well be that Schleiermacher was inclined to attempt to prove that God is absolutely unknowable by his prior belief that religion is primarily a matter of feeling, and that speculative metaphysics destroys it and should be kept out of it. Schleiermacher himself was not insistent upon the unknowability of God in his earlier years, and stated that although there can be no science of God there might be a pure philosophy about God.

The argument, as remarked, proceeds by means of an analysis of concepts and judgments, which however is very imperfect in the light of modern analysis, since it ignores a number of distinctions. I shall omit as much as possible of the detail of the argument. Schleiermacher emphasizes two properties of concepts, their determinateness and their generality. For example, the concept "fox terrier" is more determinate than "dog," because it implies a greater number of properties or a more defined meaning. For this reason, the more determinate concept admits fewer synthetic judgments about it than the less determinate concept. "Smallness," for example, can be synthetically predicated of the subject "dog," but it can be predicated analytically only of the concept "fox terrier," since the meaning of the concept includes the notion of smallness. Concepts can be made more and more determinate, and the ideal of determinateness is a concept the meaning of which is so complete as to include the possibility of everything that could be judged of it, leaving to synthetic judgment only the statement of the actual temporal realization of these possibilities.[58]

The subject concepts of which Schleiermacher is talking are apparently those of natural kinds, although he does not say so.

These concepts are related to each other by relations of subordination and superordination. That is, the more general or higher concept is superordinate to the less general, and in some sense includes it within itself. Schleiermacher does not give a satisfactory analysis of this relationship, but we can gather a general idea of his meaning from what has been said concerning his view of the nature of logical division and the tree of Porphyry.

Suppose now we envisage the pyramidal hierarchy of these concepts, the two very general concepts of the objective and the ideal constituting the highest antithesis. (We have already seen why he thought this to be the case.) If we attempt, however, to go on one more stage in generality, we no longer have a concept before us. The reason for this lies partly in that we have abolished the antithesis of thought and its object, and partly in that (as he has declared elsewhere) a concept can be defined and made determinate only through a system of judgments, whereas there can be no judgment about this subject. For these reasons, he says, there can be no discursive knowledge about the absolute identity as an identity of the ideal and the real.

Before commenting on this argument as a whole I state a second line of reasoning which leads to the same conclusion. This begins with the assertion that the predicate of a synthetic judgment, which is by definition not grounded in the essence of the subject, must be grounded in some other subject, and is therefore said to express the nonbeing of the subject. The judgment is thus the "identity" of the being and the nonbeing of the subject. Schleiermacher goes on to argue that the more being is posited in a subject, the less can be predicated of it, by which he must mean to say, if I understand him, that (as stated above) the more determinate concepts admit of less synthetic predication than do the less determinate. But he goes on to urge* that the absolute subject (the identity of the real and the ideal) is "that wherein all being is posited, and of which, therefore, there can be no predication." On this account, the Absolute is a limiting "idea" for the system of judgments and there can be no knowledge of it in the form of judgment.

The general cogency of Schleiermacher's argument is diminished, as I have said, by his failure to make a number of distinctions. For

---

* *Ibid.*, p. 91. It is not clear to me how this argument is easily reconcilable with his view that judgment expresses only action or matter-of-fact relations.

example, he does not seem to distinguish predication about a particular concrete entity from predication about a universal or species.* As a result of this, it is sometimes not clear whether he is talking about the most general universal possible, or reality taken as a whole. The conclusion itself is much less likely to be quarreled with. It is clear that there cannot be knowledge of the transcendental identity in the same sense in which there is knowledge of natural kinds or particular objects comprehended within it. In fact, in my opinion he could have reached such a conclusion much more simply (as he occasionally does elsewhere), and it appears to me that the choice of this method was perhaps due to an overfondness for architectonic, for which his work was once condemned by Hegel. On the other hand, it is clear that Schleiermacher is wrong in asserting that there can be no thought about it whatever, so long as he thinks himself able to offer arguments for believing in its necessity. It is difficult to see how there can be reasons for believing in the reality of the Identity, in the absence of any information about what is being believed in.

So far I have dealt with this "Argument from the Limit" only as a means of establishing the unknowableness of the Absolute. I now translate Schleiermacher's very brief special argument for the reality of this absolute subject. His intention is to show that there must be a reality corresponding to these "limiting concepts." He says: "For if nothing corresponds to these limits of thought . . . but yet the real thought, which we can represent as continuous with these limits, really corresponds to something, then the corresponding must have come from the not-corresponding, i.e., something from nothing, which cannot be true."[59]

I shall say of this argument only that it seems to me very much confused.

In the later series of lectures, Schleiermacher seems to distinguish between these "limits of thought" (e.g., the absolute subject) and God, and to identify the limits rather with an ideal for the knowledge of the world. That is, these limits seem to represent an unattainable ideal for knowledge which it is important for the scientist to hold before him. The significance of this distinction is diminished, however,

---

* Ueberweg suggests this confusion is to be traced to Aristotle's discussion of substance. *System der Logik*, pp. 156-157.

by the difficulty of distinguishing God from the concept of the world, on his system. This difficulty will be discussed shortly.

It remains to say something briefly of Schleiermacher's moral argument for the identity. This he thinks to be parallel to the first of the arguments we have cited. In so far as there is a parallel, it lies in the fact that, in the argument described, a transcendental being is said to be required in order to account for the possibility of ideas (purposes) getting themselves expressed in the form of things. He states his brief argument as follows: "The ground of the agreement of our will and [external] reality, so that our activity is really effective outside us, and so that external reality is receptive for reason and the ideal form of our will,—this ground lies . . . only in the pure transcendental unity of the Ideal and the Real."[60] Schleiermacher does not work the proof out in any further detail, and hence I shall say no more about it.

3. God and the World

The transcendental identity of the ideal and the real, I have said, may legitimately be identified with what Schleiermacher means by God, despite some remarks which seem to point in the opposite direction. It is now necessary to go into this matter somewhat further, and to attempt to determine more precisely what this identity is and what its relation is to the world of common-sense and science.

Two factors in the situation make this problem more difficult than it need have been. The first one is that, possibly out of a desire to favor his theory that God is "possessed" only in religious feeling, Schleiermacher continually stresses the agnostic side of his philosophy. Consequently he often excuses himself from making positive statements where in my opinion they are certainly called for. In the second place, in his later years Schleiermacher became quite anxious to be as conciliatory as possible to the church. It must be remembered that he was regarded as the leading Christian preacher in Germany, and he therefore wished to avoid any suggestion of being unchristian in his views. He was particularly careful to avoid being called a pantheist. As a result, he went out of his way to conform his language, at least, as much as possible to the views accepted by his contemporaries. This conciliatory tendency can be clearly seen at work if one compares the first edition of The Christian Faith with either the second edition or with his letters to Dr. Lücke.[61] It also appears to have had an effect upon the formulation of his *Dialectic*, and it is not clear whether certain alterations of statement really signify important changes of thought, or merely illustrate his capacity for setting forth his views in an unexceptionable terminology. Certain of his statements have provoked a considerable amount of discussion in Germany,[62] and it is unfortunately impossible to reach a completely convincing solution.

The situation is roughly as follows: Schleiermacher clearly did not believe that God is an individual self-conscious being, capable of distinguishing Himself from the world. On the other hand, he continually insists upon a distinction between God and the world. Neither God nor the world is conceivable without the other, but nevertheless God is different from the world. But to insist upon the distinction of God from the world is not necessarily to dissociate oneself even from pantheism; the pantheistic God can be different from the world in the same way in which the three-sidedness of a triangle is different from its property of containing angles equal to 180°. "God" and "world" could be words having different meanings, which yet denote only different aspects of the same individual reality. Moreover, it would appear from many passages that God is related to the antithesis of the real and the ideal in the same way in which that antithesis is related to the next most general opposition subordinated to it, but other statements deny this. In general, an important advance would have been made if we could know exactly what Schleiermacher thought to be the relation between the species and the genus, but it is very difficult to decide just what he did have in mind.

Schleiermacher's earliest views were more straightforward and less complicated. The impression left particularly by the first edition of the *Discourses on Religion* is that the object in which religion is interested is the universe as a whole. The idea of God occupies a very secondary place. When he disparages belief in the personality of God, when he says that pantheism and theism are not really different in the eyes of religion, he seems to place the emphasis on the system as a whole, in fact to make no distinction at all between God and the world except in that he differentiates between the universe as an infinite organism and the finite particulars which are its products, and which are taken on the common-sense level to be the world.

One might claim that there is at least the germ of a distinction between God and the world in his concept of the universe as a "unity in plurality." If one were to lay emphasis on the "unity," one might discriminate an aspect of the universe particularly entitled to be called God. Whether or not Schleiermacher did have some such idea vaguely in mind cannot be known; at least he did not make it explicit.

In 1806, however, he had begun to insist upon a distinction between the world and God. It will be recalled that he had made the "infinite forces" of the first edition of the Discourses (one aspect of the plurality of the universe) the object of the sciences. Of these and their relations it was possible to have scientific knowledge. He pointed out now, however, that distinct from them is the unity which is their ground, which "develops" the antitheses out of itself, but itself transcends antithesis. This unity, he said (as early as his review of Schelling), cannot be made an object of scientific investigation, for scientific method can be applied only where there is distinction and differentiation. This Being, however, is "the basis of all knowledge." It is the "sole and highest unity." He says of it, "If you are to regard the world as a whole and as a totality, can you do it otherwise than in God?"* Knowledge, he says, must be an organic system because it is "the manifestation of the Unity of the world in the infinity of the particular, and so an infinitely articulated being in which there is one soul."[63]

Yet even at this time he certainly did not make his position clear, and doubtless had not worked it out carefully. It is notable that Schleiermacher himself, in the third edition of the Discourses, felt it necessary to apologize for some of his expressions on this point. For example, he added a note in the third edition in which he wrote of certain passages in the earlier editions:

What will strike most people here is this. The Infinite Being here seems not to be the Supreme Being as cause of the world, but the world itself. But I would suggest for consideration that, in such a situation, it is impossible not to assume God along with it. And I challenge anyone to try to represent the world as a true All and Whole, without God.[64]

Schleiermacher began to lecture on Dialectic in 1811. It is very likely that it was the stimulus of giving these lectures which induced

* Cf. supra, pp. 160 ff.

him to work out and attempt to clarify his idea of God. As we shall
see, there are some important differences between the earlier and
the later sets of lectures.

In several passages throughout the *Dialectic*, Schleiermacher identifies God with the transcendental unity of thought and being. (Sometimes he speaks of God as the ground of this unity.) This identification also corresponds to the logic of his general argument, and it is
difficult to see what God could be if he is not this unity; nor does one
find any arguments for the reality of God apart from the arguments
for this unity. It is therefore difficult to avoid believing, despite Jonas'
objection,[65] that Schleiermacher must have identified God with the
reality the necessity of which is proved by the epistemological and
moral arguments already outlined, and that the seemingly contradictory passages must be understood as attempts to prevent misunderstanding or hasty identification of his view with pantheism.

It will be recalled that Schleiermacher had argued for the reality
of God on the ground that such an assumption is necessary if the
"mystery" of two harmonious parallel modes of being is to be avoided.
This mystery can be explained, he says, only if the two modes are

comprehended by and reduced to the One Being, which develops it [this
highest antithesis] and with it all comprehended antitheses, out of itself.
This . . . Being . . . is the idea of Being-in-Itself under two opposed
and related kinds or forms and modes, the Ideal and the Real, as condition of the reality of knowledge.

This statement leaves a great deal to be desired in point of precision,
but the last part of it suggests strongly that he thought the relation of
the unity to the highest "antithesis" to be that of genus to species, it
being understood that he had his own special view of the nature of that
relation. There are other statements which seem to support this interpretation strongly.*

He says:

The idea of the Absolute is the first step [in the deductive process]. In
this, we find the principles of division: being and action, the Ideal and the
Real. The relative unity of these is the world, or the second step. The
former [the Absolute] is unity, necessary, not given; the latter is plurality,

* It is not clear whether he meant to identify himself with what he believed
to be the view of the transcendental philosophy, *History of Philosophy*, p. 270.

conditioned, given. These characters repeat themselves on every stage. Every stage outside the first is the identity of these, representing the first stage as unity and necessity, the second as a manifold and given. . . . The totality of the particular is identical with the Absolute.[66] [The identity, he says] comprehends the fullness of the antitheses under itself and in itself.[67] [Again:] In the Absolute, there is a falling apart into a totality of antitheses from the primary life, in which all actions are reduced to and grounded in it, and through which the Absolute and the total coexistence of all single objects are one and the same.[68]

Moreover, the "Argument from the Limit," which was intended to prove the unknowableness of God, at least by discursive thought, makes the assumption that the idea of God is an attempt to go one stage further in the hierarchy of being, beyond the highest antithesis, presumably in the same way in which this highest antithesis comprehends the lower antitheses involved in it. Schleiermacher clearly identifies these "limiting ideas" with the transcendental unity established in his first argument, and if the two were intended to be different, the point of the argument would apparently be lost.

Let us assume hypothetically that Schleiermacher's God is somehow the genus of which the ideal and the real are the species. We must attempt to define this relation more accurately. In the first place, we recall that he urged that there is a sense in which the higher concept always has "more being" than the lower one. This claim is to be compared with a number of other statements. God, he says, cannot be regarded as a

mere indifference of consciousness and the unconscious[69] [presumably meaning by this that "God" cannot simply denote the properties that are common to the notions of the ideal and the real]. [God, he asserts, is] not merely an empty unity, viz., nothing, and the world the full unity. Rather God is the perfect unity, and the world, taken by itself, is the one plurality.[70] . . . The Absolute Unity is not a unity because of want, because it could not be a plurality, but because it is infinity, and an infinity which is not a confused manifoldness, but a unity.[71]

Whatever else Schleiermacher means by these statements, it is clear that he does not want to make God unthinkable because the concept of God is so abstract that it cannot properly be thought at all, so abstract that it denotes only those properties common to the pure thought and the objective.

We may proceed by pointing out that there are two ways in which the determinateness, ideal content, or intension of higher concepts may be thought of. First, we may hold that the higher genera, with greater extension, have less intension than the species they comprehend. For example, "animal" has a greater extension than "man"; and some logicians hold that it has less intension, because what we mean by "animal" is more abstract, less defined, than what we mean by "man." This view of the relation of genus and species is irreconcilable with at least many of Schleiermacher's statements. A second view, however, seems to be closer to what he means. That is, some logicians would hold that when the genus is really understood, it is seen to contain within itself the possibility of the various species in all their determinateness so that its concept is not simply an abstraction from the concepts of the species, but contains the system of them; so that the intension of the higher concept is greater than or at least as great as that of the lower concept.* This view would be compatible with Schleiermacher's idea that no one concept can be completely understood without an understanding of all the rest. On this theory we could say that in the case of God or the highest genus, if we understood its nature perfectly, all its species and their subordinate species down to concrete individuals could be seen to be involved by it and in this sense it might with some show of reason be said to have more being than the lower concepts. This would mean also that we might agree with his statement that there is no room for predication, in an ordinary sense, about the Absolute.

Let us assume, then, that "God" is the name of a concept which, if its meaning were fully understood, would be seen to involve all other concepts.

Schleiermacher often speaks of God as the "ground" or even as the "cause" of the world. He certainly did not mean by this that God is temporally antecedent to the world, or that there is a causal relationship between God and the world analogous to that obtaining between particular objects. I presume that he meant to assert that the highest concept stands in such a relation to the lower ones that it can be said to be their ground. The following sentence is the clearest expression I

---

* Schleiermacher's view has points in common with the doctrine of the concrete universal.

have found of his view that God is the ground of the world: "God is the presupposition lying still further back, thus the source of all the activity in the world given as the unity of 'force.' "[72]

But Schleiermacher apparently believes that any genus is the source or productive ground of its species. And if so, there seems to be no reason for distinguishing the relation which God has to the highest antithesis from that which any genus has to the opposed forms of being which it "comprehends." He says:

> Just as the lower concept is grounded in the higher in respect of its possibility . . . but the higher is a productive comprehension of a plurality of the lower, so also the lower being . . . is grounded in respect of possibility only in the higher, and the higher is the productive ground or the force for a plurality of appearances.[73]

On the basis of the foregoing considerations, I suggest that Schleiermacher's following statement of his idea of God is not misleading:

> Let us consider the character of knowledge—that a being corresponds to every thought as concept—from its transcendental side. If there is to be knowledge under the form of concept, then being, like the concept, must bear within itself the contrast of the higher and the lower. The lowest form of being is the particular things, and there are infinite stages from there through the species and genera up to the highest. So, just as the single thing corresponds to the single representation, which is only a unity for a manifold of judgments, a higher being corresponds to the concept of species and genera—which has been called the doctrine of the reality of ideas—and, assuming this higher being, we ascend to the Absolute, or God, the transcendental source of all being and ideally also of all knowledge, so that everything as being and thought is in us only as rooted [gewurzelt] in the Deity, who is superior to the higher being of the particular things, just as the higher being is superior to the particular things themselves.[74]

God, then, is the genus which is the ground of all the species. Presumably this is what is meant when Schleiermacher says that God "develops out of himself" all the subordinate oppositions of the world. If God could be completely understood, it would be seen how all reality follows from His nature; God is the ground of the world, just as any genus is the ground of its species.

But what exactly is meant by saying that any genus, so conceived, is the ground of its species, and what is meant by saying that, in this same sense, God is the ground of the real and the ideal? In what way is the harmony of the ideal and the real (which was the problem which set Schleiermacher in search of a higher unity) explained by such an ideal? In the previous chapter, in discussing the relation of the identity to the world, I suggested that God "articulates" himself in the world. But what does this mean?

I must confess that I am at a loss to answer these questions; Schleiermacher himself certainly does not supply the material for the answers. It has been suggested that Schleiermacher's idea is similar to Plato's view that the "Good" is the source of all reality; and this suggestion may offer clarification to some readers. The most plausible suggestion I can make is that for Schleiermacher "God" denotes just the fact that the universe as a whole (including both the ideal and the real aspects) is an organic, logically ordered, rational system; it denotes the character of reality in so far as it forms such a system. I am not sure that I see in what sense such an ideal explains the harmony of the forms of thought and the forms of things; what this "explanation" is saying is simply that organic logical structure, which is "expressed" in both subjective thought and objective being, is the most fundamental fact behind which it is impossible to go any further. In this sense, to say that God is the ground of the world or the genus is the ground of its species is simply to denote partial aspects, which when taken in the system of which they are inextricable parts are identical with each other.*

But this suggestion seems to me incompatible with statements which Schleiermacher makes elsewhere, and we must now consider some passages which seem to contradict what I have said about his view of the relation of God to the world.

In the lectures of 1814, referring to the discussion of the absolute subject in the "Argument from the Limit," he surprisingly denies the correlation of the "highest concept" with the "highest force" (or genus) because, he says, an identification of the two would be pantheism, for the highest force does not exist outside of the forms in which it is manifested, so that it does not really escape the world of "anti-

* On this view, the difference between God and the world would be a difference of point of view. God would be everything viewed as a unified system; the world would be the related individuals. The distinction is comparable with that of Spinoza.

thetical being."[75] At a slightly later stage in the same series of lectures, Schleiermacher reverses his contention, and now affirming the identity of the highest concept and the highest force, he denies that either of them can be identified with God.[76] Schleiermacher's reason for this, again, seems to be that the highest concept, like the highest force, can not be regarded as really free from the realm of finitude and antithesis. As he expresses it in a later series of lectures, God cannot be merely *natura naturans*, or

as the totality of the appearance, i.e., *natura naturata*. . . . For force does not appear otherwise than in the totality of its appearances, and thus conditioned by them in a certain sense. It is impossible that the conditioning being should be related to the totality of what is thought, as something within that totality to something else. Thus we have not accomplished the transition from the real into the primary basis. . . . If the *natura naturans* would secure the unity in the transcendent, it is still not transcendent enough.[77]

In other words, Schleiermacher seems to have discovered that the genus is not separate from its species, and its being is in some sense exhausted in them. This being the case, God and the world are brought into very close relation, a relation which Schleiermacher must have been anxious to deny for religious reasons.

It is on account of these statements that Jonas has been inclined to believe not only that the "limiting concepts" in Schleiermacher's second argument, but even the transcendental identity of the ideal and the real of the first argument, cannot be taken to be what Schleiermacher meant by God. The difficulty with Jonas' view, however, is that if we introduce a distinction between these ideas and the idea of God, Schleiermacher's whole system, leading up as it does to his idea that God is present to man in feeling, simply does not make sense. Despite these denials by Schleiermacher, I am unable to find any statement in which he makes clear what he means by God if it is not to be identified with these concepts, nor can I find any reason offered for believing in any further reality than these.

It is true that, as Jonas urges, Schleiermacher does seem to distinguish God from the world, and to say that the ideal for knowledge, the system of things, is the idea of the world and not the idea of God. "The idea of deity," he says, "is the transcendental *terminus a quo*, the principle of the possibility of knowledge in itself; the idea of the world is the transcendental *terminus ad quem*, and the principle of the reality of knowledge in its becoming."[78] His idea here seems to be that, although neither God nor the world can be conceived apart from the other, they are to be distinguished; and God is the full but undifferentiated unity which is the ground of the unity of the world, while the world is the spatio-temporal world without unity.[79] Their relation cannot be further defined, he says; all the metaphorical suggestions that have been offered are unsatisfactory. We can say of their relation only that it is one of coexistence.[80]

One fact which tends to ease the apparent contradiction between all these more theistic statements and the view I have suggested is that Schleiermacher occasionally remarks that it is "in thought" that God and the world are to be distinguished. It is possible that he is using theistic language to describe what seems to him to be only different aspects of the same individual reality.[81]

Schleiermacher probably had religious reasons for this about-face, whatever his other reasons may have been. He wished to avoid any appearance of pantheism. He wished to hold that all finite objects are conditioned by God but that none of them are in turn conditions of God. And he wanted to preserve a kind of agnosticism with respect to God, in order that speculative philosophy be kept out of religion. Perhaps he was encouraged in this latter tendency by a dislike for Hegel's *Logic*, which had appeared in 1812. This would account for the fact that these changes occurred first in 1814. In the first series of lectures, there is no distinction between God and the absolute subject or transcendental identity of the real and the ideal. There is clearly not the same attempt to distinguish God from the system of the world in these first lectures that is to be found in the later series. Similarly, as we shall see, there is not the same insistence upon the unknowableness of God. Of course, the suggestion that Hegel's publication was of influence is rather speculative; the changes may have been due simply to the natural development of Schleiermacher's own thinking.

I do not know of any satisfactory reconciliation of the main body of Schleiermacher's argument with these more theistic formulations of the relation of God to the world. The best suggestion that I can make is that Schleiermacher believed that the absolute identity would necessarily be misrepresented if it were thought of as just the topmost link in the chain of the types of finite reality. He apparently believed that to think of it in that way would mean the distortion of its nature—a distinction of it from other things as if it did not transcend all distinctions, a resolution of it into particulars instead of the retention of its organic wholeness.

It is possible, of course, that Schleiermacher himself did not think he had a perfectly consistent line of argument at this point. It may be that he saw that one line of reasoning brought him close to a kind of pantheism, while another set of facts convinced him that the idea of God must somehow be kept distinct from the idea of the world. It may be that he preferred to let an apparent inconsistency remain, rather than retract either conflicting position where he felt it was necessary to maintain it.

A number of passages emphasize the distinction of God from the world and attempt a negative definition of their relation. So far as I can see, however, they can be interpreted compatibly with either of the views that have been mentioned. God and the world, he says, are not the same.[82]

The deity [he says] is always regarded in thought as unity without plurality, the world as plurality without unity.* The world fills space and time; God is spaceless and timeless. The world is the totality of antitheses; God is the real negation of all antitheses.[83] [Or, as he puts it at a later time:] God is the unity with exclusion of all antitheses; the world is the unity with inclusion of all antitheses.[84]

God and the world are distinct, but neither can be conceived without reference to the other. The "formula for the world is inadequate and not up to our demands, apart from the idea of God."[85] On the other hand, the idea of God is meaningless apart from its relation to the idea of the world.[86] God is not the creator of the world; if he were thus independent of it, the world would have to be viewed as accidental, which is erroneous.[87] The creation cannot be conceived as a free act of God, for that would involve God in an antithesis, that of freedom and necessity.[88] Nor can God be thought of as a form defining matter, for that would make God conditioned by matter.[89] The world cannot

---

* He argues elsewhere that unity and plurality are notions which have meaning only in relation to each other.

be a system of emanations (or otherwise derived, as the partially real, from the Infinite), for then God would have to be thought of as conditioned by it, viz., "through his non-being."[90] That is unthinkable.

Schleiermacher is willing to make one slightly more positive affirmation. Materialism, he says, is incompatible with the nature of his God. As the source of the ideal and the living, God cannot be purely material or mechanical. God must be regarded as in some sense living. (In one passage, he says that the essence of the concept of life is "the activity of the ideal.")[91]

If the transcendent ground is to be thought at all [he writes] it is quite impossible to regard it as dead, although this notion has always occurred in the view of materialism and atomism. The being which is the ground of all thought is [there] assumed to be matter . . . But therewith must always be exercised a kind of sleight-of-hand, if something else is to be evolved from what is dead, as when one postulates a kind of impact, or something of the sort, by means of which everything is set in motion.[92]

Of course the actual positive insight into Schleiermacher's views afforded by these statements is very slight; the point is simply that Schleiermacher's world, and consequently its "ground," cannot be fitted at all into a crudely mechanistic world picture.

Throughout the major portion of his life, Schleiermacher insisted that there can be no scientific knowledge of God. All of his utterances in his later years—even in the apparently least agnostic period around 1811—are agreed upon this point. In 1811 he said:

The absolute knowledge is the expression of no antithesis, but of the absolute Being which is identical with itself. . . . As such, it is not definite knowledge in the finite consciousness, viz., one which could be expressed adequately in a number of concepts or propositions, but only the foundation and source of all particular knowledge.[93]

Nevertheless, at this early date he did believe that there is some information about God to be gained by a general knowledge of the sciences.

There is no *isolated* intuition of the Deity [he says] but we intuit it only in and with the whole system of intuition. . . . Our knowledge of God is completed only with the intuition of the world. As soon as there is a trace of the latter, we discover the outlines of the former. In so far as the intuition of the world remains incomplete, the idea of God remains mythical.[94] [Again:] We are thus engaged in the construction of the living intuition of the Deity, in so far as we work at the completion of the real sciences. This does not occur, if one particular is added to another only as a collection, but only through systematic treatment, in which the totality is at least sought for.[95]

I am not sure just what these statements mean, but they seem to me quite compatible with my suggestion that at that time he thought of God as the highest genus which is the ground of the species, and which therefore can presumably be known to some extent through a knowledge of the system which they constitute.

The later series of lectures emphasize man's ignorance of God. He now denies that the progress of science makes possible a closer approximation to comprehension of God.[96] Even if it were possible to know the world adequately as it is in its plurality (which is not possible, according to him), knowledge of God would still be unattainable. For

we should have to have the idea of God in one act, because there is no plurality in it. This is not possible, however, for all knowledge is organic [involves sense perception] but the idea of God is not to be understood in this way.[97] [Were such knowledge to be attainable] there would have to be a sense impression related to God as he is in himself; and this is impossible. For that reason, the terms "Absolute," "Highest Unity," "Identity of the Real and the Ideal," are only *schemata*. To make them living, we should have to return to the sphere of finitude and existence as we do when we think of God as *natura naturans*, or as conscious absolute ego.[98]

The formulae which can be given have a "symbolic value," but they do not adequately express the transcendental ground.[99]

Nevertheless Schleiermacher admits that there is a sense in which we know what God is, viz., we know what he is well enough to know what he is not. He says: "We have not failed to apprehend the transcendental condition. . . . We have failed only to bring it to a unity of real consciousness. But we do have it; in fact we recognize the insufficiency of one-sided and antithetical formulae."[100]

What has been said of the nature of God so far has been derived exclusively from Schleiermacher's metaphysical works. This material will now be supplemented briefly from his chief work on theology, *The Christian Faith*. An introduction of matter from this book, however, must be prefaced with a warning that the use of it may be misleading. As we shall see, Schleiermacher believed that the office of theology is to depict the content of Christian conviction or experience (in a way to be described later) and is therefore not primarily intended to serve as objective knowledge. For this reason it is possible that dogmas expressive of Christian experience may not coincide with the affirmations about God which Schleiermacher himself believed to be theoretically justifiable. It is evident, for example, that Schleiermacher sometimes gives weight in theology to doctrines supported by the Bible (which is to him the most reliable expression of Christian religious experience), which are hardly compatible with his philosophical views or at least do not follow from them.* Nevertheless, in point of fact the dogmatic statements about God are closely related to his philosophical ideas (although the expression tends to be more conventional), and it will be pointed out later that he believed that the two forms of expression must "agree." For this reason the doctrines explained in The Christian Faith are of value as an explication of his idea of God, even if they must be used with care. This book seems to be more theistic, at least in language, than some of his philosophical works (especially the earlier ones), and pantheism is repudiated; but it is not so easy to be sure that Schleiermacher says anything incompatible with the kind of "pantheism" we have outlined.

I shall first describe the view of God expounded in The Christian Faith, and then inquire whether the doctrines in it require us to change our conception of his idea of God.

The central point of his theological view is that religious people are justified (in a way to be explained) by their religious experience in saying that they are conscious of being dependent (along with all finite beings) upon a reality which is not itself finite.[101] God is therefore said to be the ground, or "timeless eternal cause" of the world.[102] This "causality" is sharply to be distinguished, of course, from the causal relations of finite objects among themselves, although it is coextensive with them and conditions them.

In saying that God is "infinite," Schleiermacher means that God's attributes may not be formulated in a way which would be appropriate only for a limited being, viz., one which is subject to limitation or

* See his teaching on the Last Judgment and related subjects.

determination by other objects.[103] The being of God transcends every antithesis of thought.[104] Furthermore, God is "unconditioned and absolutely simple," in contrast to finite objects.[105] By God's simplicity is meant "the unseparated and inseparable inherence of all divine attributes and activities."[106] Simplicity implies that there can be no separation between the attributes defining God as he is in himself and the attributes defining his relation to the world.

God is eternal. By this Schleiermacher means to contrast God's causal activity with that of finite objects, which involves change and reciprocal influence.[107] God is not merely endlessly enduring, but is out of time altogether. Schleiermacher does not think it possible to make wholly clear just what this means, but he says there is an analogy to it in the realm of the finite. The analogy he suggests is to the "ego, which is the permanent ground of all changing states of mind, viz., of all decisions."[108]

God is also omnipresent. This attribute, again, expresses primarily a contrast between God and finite objects, whose causal efficacy tends to diminish with the increase of spatial distance from their center. God is not just everywhere in space in the sense in which a finite object can be larger or smaller; it is more proper to say that God is out of space altogether, or spaceless.[109]

God is also omnipotent. By this he means primarily that "the whole system of nature, comprising all spaces and times, is grounded in the divine causality, which is eternal and omnipresent in contrast to everything finite."[110]

God is omniscient. In discussing this attribute, Schleiermacher contrasts his view with mechanism. The Infinite, he says, is not to be regarded as a "dead" force. By this I believe he means to distinguish the operation of mechanical force from the operation of (for example) organic "forces" which mold the inorganic material into a form subserving purpose and realizing values. Schleiermacher suggests that the essence of God might be expressed by the phrase, "Absolute Vitality."[111] Denying that God can be a "dead and blind necessity," he urges that such a view would amount to the equation of finite and divine causality. On the other hand, he denies that the divine omniscience can be regarded as "perception or experience, a thinking together or viewing together" (Zusammendenken oder

Zusammenschauen). God's knowledge is not like finite knowledge, which is the result of passive reception of influence from a finite object independent of the knower. God's knowledge is different in that its objects are identical with the result of his own purposive activity. Therefore the divine thinking is identical with the divine will. Furthermore, there is no distinction between God's purposes (or his execution of them) and what He knows; for everything He proposes is real. Moreover, God does not know a realm of possible existents which He contrasts with the realm of the real; for to God, everything that is possible at all is real, and everything that is unreal is impossible.

There is no distinction between perception, memory, and fore-knowledge in God. Otherwise a change from one to the other, in relation to some finite object, would occur whenever an object comes into being and passes away, which is incompatible with God's eternity. Rather, God has an eternal knowledge of the inner law of development of any object, and of the influence of other things upon it.[112]

There are four further attributes which are particularly important for religion: God's holiness, justice, wisdom, and love. These attributes are arrived at by considering the fact that God is the ground of everything in the world, in connection with some character of world history or human nature which is important for the religious consciousness. "By the holiness of God," he says,[113]

we mean the divine causality, by virtue of which in all human corporate life conscience occurs along with the state of need of redemption. By conscience, we mean that all modes of activity issuing from our God-consciousness . . . get validity in our self-consciousness in such a way that deviation of action from them is apprehended as . . . sin.

God's "holiness" refers to the fact that He is the ground of conscience, of awareness of the moral ideal which itself is regarded as holy.

The attribute of justice is defined and supported in the same way. "The justice of God is the divine causality, by virtue of which, in the state of general [gemeinsam] sinfulness, a connection between actual sin and evil is ordained."[114] In other words, God is the ground of the process in which evil is the result of sin, either through natural causes or through human decision. The function which this divinely ordained process serves is that it makes it possible for conscience to make headway in a mind which is dominated by sense desires.

The most important of the religious attributes of God is his lovingness. This attribute is, like the others, derived from a consideration of an aspect of the world process, here the redemptive process, in connection with the doctrine of divine causality. Lovingness is the quality attributed to a person's character if he tends to form bonds of unity with others. The process of redemption is precisely such an activity; it is the union of the divine essence with human nature. The divine nature upon which this process is based must then, in analogy with human persons, be regarded as loving.[115]

Of importance second only to the divine love is the divine wisdom. If lovingness is analogous to human motives or character, God's wisdom is analogous to the understanding which enables human beings to give expression to their love in a complex world. "By wisdom we understand the correct conception of purposes and plans, considered in their manifold determinateness and in the totality of their relations to each other."[116] God's wisdom is an aspect of his timeless knowing, and refers to the aspect of forward-lookingness, whereas his omniscience refers to the aspect of looking back. It is the aspect of God's causality by virtue of which we must regard the finite world as "an absolutely harmonious divine work of art."[117] God's work is like the behavior of the ethically perfect man whose "plans of activity . . . form a complete whole of communicative self-representation."[118] So "the divine wisdom is the Supreme Being considered as in this not compositely, but simply and originally perfect and absolute self-presentation and communication."[119] The divine wisdom is not to be regarded as a faculty of finding suitable means for attaining certain desired ends, for the contrast of means and ends holds only for a finite, non-omnipotent being.

The divine wisdom and the divine love are not to be regarded as separate attributes, but are aspects of the one divine act of timeless causation.

The religious attributes are the final characteristics of God considered by Schleiermacher in The Christian Faith, and they conclude this brief outline of his theological doctrine of God (as distinct from his metaphysically elaborated theory of God). We must now consider whether this book has added anything materially to the description of God contained in the *Dialectic* and the *Ethics*.

One is first of all struck with the similarity between his theological treatment and the philosophical one. The fundamental idea of God's timeless causation of the world of finite objects, based upon the religious "feeling of dependence," is so similar to his metaphysical theory that God is the "transcendental source" or ground of all finite being that one is led to suspect that Schleiermacher came to emphasize the "feeling of dependence" in religious experience (which we shall see was not very consistent with his theory of religion) chiefly for the reason that it enabled him to derive a theological doctrine, supposedly as the expression of religious experience, which was congenial to his metaphysical theory.

If we examine the list of attributes which Schleiermacher discusses in this theological book, we find that most of them are contained in his metaphysical works also. That God is the timeless cause of the finite world, that he is eternal, infinite (in the sense explained), simple, spaceless, and omnipotent: all these attributes can legitimately be ascribed to the Deity described in the early part of this section.

Schleiermacher comes nearer to breaking away to a more theistic conception of God when he considers the attributes involving something analogous to intelligence and will. He there sets up redemption through the work of Christ as the crown of world history, and seems to assume something like purpose or intention in God, in relation to it. (Of course, Schleiermacher is careful to point out that God's knowledge and will cannot be distinct from each other, and that knowledge cannot be a matter of experience, or passivity, or the result of discursive thought, any more than God's will is a result of need or desire. But this would be admitted by most theists.) Schleiermacher evidently means to say that the world is not merely a mechanical system and that the values of the world-process are not merely accidental phenomena, but somehow central to the system as a whole. The universe is an organized system, and the process of redemption through Christ is no chance circumstance, but the culmination toward which all creation has been straining. We must, I think, assert that at this time Schleiermacher still held to the philosophy of history of his earlier years: that the world is progressively realizing more values in the course of the "ethical" process and that it is also a system of individuals, each of which is supplementary to the others and essential for the perfection of the whole.*

The question is whether the fact of the realization of value in the world, combined with what Schleiermacher says about divine knowledge and wisdom, implies that the "timeless cause" of the world is a personal being independent of the world who in some sense can have knowledge and purposes and apprehend the process of realization of those purposes. Such a view would be equivalent to theism.

It may be said in answer to this question that it is perfectly clear that Schleiermacher did not countenance the idea of a God who performed miracles or answered prayer other than as a part of His eternal plan. Schleiermacher's God's providential activity is limited to the products of the natural order. In fact he says,

It has always been recognized by the most careful theologians that the divine preservation, as the absolute dependence of all events and changes on God, and natural causation, as the complete conditioning of all events by the universal [causal] nexus, are the same thing, only viewed from different angles, and neither is to be separated or limited by the other.[120]

Of course Schleiermacher did not mean in this statement to give up the distinction between God and the natural causal order.

Moreover, there are several facts to be considered which encourage reluctance to ascribe to him more theistic views than are justifiable on the basis of his more metaphysical books. In the first place, Schleiermacher in his book on dogmatics is admittedly describing Christian feeling on these matters, and is not necessarily representing his own point of view in philosophy, although there is no reason to doubt that he combined them as far as possible.

In the second place, if one examines carefully the language which Schleiermacher uses, one finds that he has avoided definitely committing himself to any of the more anthropomorphic features of theism. (In this, of course, he was in accord with some of the best tradition of the church.) He abstains from defending doctrines such as that God's creation is an act of freedom and that He might, consistently with His own nature, have refrained from creating. He will have nothing to do with the idea of a God selecting from among

* See *The Christian Faith*, sec. 125, par. 2.

numerous possible worlds. But here as in other doctrines it may be that he is defending only a more plausible and consistent form of theism than many have defended. Perhaps his defense of the attributes of omniscience and wisdom ought to classify him as a theist. But when he has pared away the anthropomorphic features of these attributes, it seems necessary to say that he believed that nature is somehow organized "for" ends and values, but it is by no means clear that he believed there is a personal being able to comprehend purposes and devise a plan to realize them, or which is conscious of itself and of its distinction from the world. Schleiermacher thought that the nature of an Infinite Being excludes this distinction between means and ends.

Finally, it must be recalled that Schleiermacher himself believed that theology is justified in speaking in more anthropomorphic (presumably theistic) terms than the philosopher can strictly allow. His view on this matter is presented clearly in a letter to Jacobi:

With reference to your second proposition, that "there is no third alternative between deification of nature and anthropomorphism" . . . because you can see no third alternative, and because you will not deify nature, you deify human consciousness. But in my eyes, the one is as much a deification as the other, and this view, that both are deifications, is in my opinion the third alternative. We can in no way escape from the antithesis between the real and the ideal, or however you may choose to designate it.

Are you better able to conceive of God as a person than as *natura naturans*? If you form a living idea of a person, must not this person of necessity be finite? Can an "infinite reason" and "infinite will" be anything more than empty words, when reason and will, by differing from each other, also necessarily limit each other? And if you attempt to annul the distinction between reason and will, is not the conception of personality destroyed by the same attempt?

On the other side, the same is true. Anthropomorphism, or let me rather say ideomorphism, is, however, unavoidable in regard to the interpretation of religious feeling. Whether hylozoism is not equally indispensable in natural science I cannot say, because I am not sufficiently well acquainted with the subject. But I can make use of the first . . . within the domain of religion because of the view I take, while within the domain of philosophy, I maintain that one expression is as good and as imperfect as another, that we cannot form any real conception of the Supreme Being; but that philosophy properly consists in the perception that this inexpressible reality of the Supreme Being underlies all our thinking and all our feeling, and the development of this knowledge is, according to my conviction, what Plato understood by dialectic.[121]

It is possible that a deanthropomorphized theism is hardly distinguishable from the metaphysical view of God outlined in the earlier part of this section, and that the aspect of organized unity in the universe, whose nature implies the development of the highest forms of life, is a perfectly legitimate meaning for theism. If so, Schleiermacher can have been quite consistent. On the other hand, it may be that he was more theistic in the later years of his life than his metaphysical arguments for God could support.

It is worth while to emphasize one fact which has already been mentioned. It is reasonable to believe that Schleiermacher's decision that religion is essentially a feeling of dependence upon God did not rest merely upon empirical analysis of historical religion but upon the basis of his metaphysics, according to which God is the "source" of all finite being.

We shall have to leave our definition of his view of God in this rather unsatisfactory state.

4. REASON AND NATURE

In contrast to a deistic view which describes God as external to and not essentially required in the process of the experienced world, Schleiermacher's philosophy involves far-reaching reinterpretation of the sensed world in order to reach ultimate truth about it. When reinterpreted, Schleiermacher thought, when understood for what it really is in its relation to reality as a whole, the ordinary world can be the source of religious inspiration; if not so reinterpreted, the religious "instinct" in man will cause him to seek a God beyond it. Schleiermacher wrote: "It is clearly a mistake to look for the Infinite outside the finite, the eternal and higher outside the mundane and sensory; but is that not most natural for those who know the finite and sensible world almost entirely merely superficially?"[122]

It is perhaps worth while to make some supplement to the account already given of this world.

The religious interest in the nature of reality is usually directed, I believe, predominantly toward the problem of the nature and status of mind and value in the world-process. Thus theism sets valuation and the willing of the valuable at the ground of the world; it sets the perfection, sin, and reclamation of mind at the center of history; Christianity envisions the triumph of spirit over nature and the body at the end of time, so that the "coming of the Kingdom" is the goal toward which the whole of creation is moving.

As I understand Schleiermacher, his emphasis was somewhat different from this. For him, the duality in the world-process is not between conscious spirits and nature, but between the ideal and the real, or between reason and nature. And to him, the goal of the world-process is not the reclamation of the human spirit from sinfulness and the coming of a kingdom of spirits in any other sense than through simply the organization of nature by reason, through commerce, industry, agriculture, government, art, science, and religion. It will be recalled that in the first edition of the *Discourses on Religion*, he prophesied that since the gods hate nothing but death, Fate in history is moving toward the elimination of the dead and the inert, the supremacy of life, the organized, and the rational. So far as I can see, this view was never changed in substance. History is, for him, the process by means of which the active reason in human individuals "moralizes," viz., organizes rationally or in accord with the "intent" of the universe everything with which it is confronted. Complete "moralization" would be perfection.

Coherently with his general position, I believe, Schleiermacher has a doctrine of mind which does not require that mind and matter be different substances. I propose to say something about his view of mind and matter, although, as usual, it is to be wished that he had left more explicit statements on the subject.

As I have said, there is no doubt that he was an epistemological dualist. He believed that the objects we perceive are not the independently existing objects themselves, but something that is the result of an interaction of our self with the object.

The activity [he says] during which the living being seeks an affection [by the objects] terminates in a change according to the nature of the living being, in which, however, the affection by the things is reflected; these objects have been preponderantly active on this occasion, and such states are therefore the being of things in the living subject. . . . In every sense impression something of the nature of the object is copied. . . . At first, only their temporal relations are copied in sense; but to this are related all the so-called higher activities of the understanding, which constitute knowledge of the nature of objects out of combinations of these impressions.[123]

Epistemologically he was a dualist. As such, one might think that the problems which arise might incline him also to accept an ontological dualism of substance between mind and body. As a matter of fact, however, nothing of the sort seems to be the case.

Schleiermacher's view, which at least verbally is similar to Schelling, is that reason and nature differ only quantitatively. That is, the fundamental principle of the logical division of reality is the distinction between the real and the ideal. Both nature and reason are, as embodied in existent particulars, a combination of the two principles; reason has "reality" just as nature is in a sense "ideal." Reason is "quantitatively" different from nature in that it has comparatively more of the "ideal"; nature has relatively more of the "real." He says: "The subordinate and incomplete character of the division is illustrated by the fact that reason must immediately be viewed as nature, if it is to be an object and be known, and just so that nature must be viewed as reason, when it is regarded as carrying and exhibiting ideas as purposes in itself."[124]

As a consequence, the world, according to him, is not divided into mental facts and physical facts. Both the mental and the physical have both the "ideal" and the "real" in them, and their difference is in the proportion of these two factors, viz., is a quantitative difference. So he says that "the act of the spiritual [ideal] in nature is its form; the effect of the objective in reason is consciousness."[125] Without the ideal, he says, the physical world would be mere formless stuff; without the real, or consciousness, the "soul" would be only the nameless counterpiece of stuff, the empty source of concepts.

Body and soul in man is the highest tension of the antithesis, a twofold interpenetration of the objective [real] and the spiritual [ideal]. We see it diminish in the animal and the vegetable world, but we never see it quite disappear. Where there is form, there is also consciousness corresponding to it, and vice versa. This antithesis, which was first found in our own being . . . extends through the whole of reality.[126] . . . The most universal antithesis . . . is that of the ideal and the real. The interpenetration of all conceived antitheses under this highest one . . . with a preponderance of the real, is posited for us as nature; with a preponderance of the ideal . . . it is given to us as Reason. The function of the ideal in the particular object of nature is *form*. The function of the ideal in the particular object of Reason is *consciousness*. As expressing both . . . in the immediate individual life, it is innate in us in the form of soul and body.[127]

Subjective experience is also on this account ideally separable into its ideal and real aspects. It is the product or combination of the predominantly ideal activity with the real material. So he says that "thoughts are not Reason itself, but only its expression in the conscious life, and every single thought is such a single expression and hence a symbol."[128] Just as the ideal principle is expressed both in mind and in nature as form, the real principle occurs both in nature and in experience as the space-filling and the time-filling, respectively. While writing on this subject, he seems to contrast matter with mind as if he thinks them to be simply the indeterminate and pure form. He says: "When we refer to it [matter] we are speaking not only of what is ponderable, or fills space, but of the *intellectual matter*, viz., what fills time in mere consciousness. These two are rather to be compared."[129]

The world in general presents a series of differing proportions of combination of the ideal principle and the real principle, from the point where the smallest part of the ideal is combined with the real, to the point where the ideal principle vastly predominates. For example, take a series of fractions, of which the numerators stand for the ideal principle, and the denominators for the real principle. So long as neither numerator nor denominator is allowed to be zero, we can order these fractions into two groups, those greater than $1/1$, and those less than this. In the former group will be those whose numerator is larger, and which represent the preponderance of the ideal; in the latter group there will be represented the preponderance of the real principle. To Schleiermacher's mind, the universe is such a system as this. However, so far as this world is concerned, at any rate, the preponderantly real series is much larger than that of the preponderantly ideal, for there is only one class in the latter group—that of human beings, who are the "turning-point" between the real and the ideal, and alone express the proper nature of the ideal principle.[130] The ideal principle is present, however (although not in its explicit nature), in the subhuman world, but there "the distinction between the ideal and the real is blunted, and the activity of the ideal principle in its special nature is not to be found."[131]

The nature and manifestations of the "ideal principle" are the object of the mental sciences, especially psychology. In fact, Schleiermacher says that the only reason for making psychology a separate science is "in order to intuit the spiritual principle, which pervades all life, on a definite stage—the only one which is really given to us—, and from there to go on to generalization. Speculative insights are thus the real purpose of psychology."[132] The two data for psychology in which the ideal principle is revealed in its purest form are the formation of concepts and the decisions of will.[133] The reason for this seems to be that in the one act the content of sense is organized according to the form or set of relationships which are embodied in a system of ideas, whereas in the second act, ideals are actively propagated or embodied in nature as a result of the moral decision. But the whole knowledge process, in which thought organizes experience into science, is to be regarded as one manifestation of the ideal principle; and on the other hand, aesthetic creation and the organization of nature in general can be viewed as the other aspect of it. Thought and ideals, the work of reason, are what make possible the prevention of utter chaos in conduct, the promiscuous clash of purposes. The organization of the state, of commerce, of business enterprises for the exploitation of natural resources for the ends of reason, shows the rationality and universality of purpose which are characteristic of advanced social life. These forms of organization exhibit the gradual transcendence of the standpoint of individualistic egoism, so that the social life slowly loses the aspect of being divided into little centers, each seeking something for itself. The world-process rather shows reason and order triumphing over the personal and the selfish. The moral person keeps nothing exclusively for himself; even one's most intimate and individually expressive possessions are offered for the enjoyment of others in social hospitality. Personality enters into the process only in so far as it is part of the moral task to develop one's personality and communicate its individual character to other persons, so that it is in a sense made universal.

Ideal organization is also involved in aesthetic creation. Art is possible because of the fact that persons naturally and spontaneously seek to express their feelings and moods. These expressions become artistic when and in that a principle of order comes between the feeling and the expression.[134] In art, balance and harmony are introduced. Each part of the aesthetic creation "refers to" every other part, and in this sense the work becomes an organic whole. In this way, the activity of reason transforms a purely psychological reaction into an aesthetic moment.

We shall see shortly how the ideal activity is manifested in human feelings—how the consciousness of the identity of the individual with some or all members of the species is expressed in feelings of sympathy, and how religious feelings express the consciousness of the identity of the self with the world, in that both are conditioned by and dependent on the Absolute.

What then is the ideal principle, which is to be found manifested in all these activities? Briefly, it seems to me that Schleiermacher means by the "ideal principle" the principle of rational order, logical system, and organization, which makes knowledge possible. In the activity of the human mind, this principle works actively and obviously, introducing its kind of order into the sense data which confront it, or in the aesthetic materials or the material and social world awaiting human action. In nature it is less obvious, but I take it he means that the same principle is exhibited on a cruder level where animate nature realizes consistently complex organic forms, and in a still cruder and less distinct way by vegetable nature and finally on the level of the inorganic.

There is to my mind a great deal more obscurity about what he means by the opposite or "real" principle. At times it seems that he means simply what I have described as the ideal principle working in nature. That is, it is those forms or principles on account of which nature, especially organic species, is what it is; and he says that it is on account of a fundamental identity of this "real principle with the ideal principle that there is a harmony between the two such that knowledge is possible." But sometimes, as I have suggested, he extends the "ideal" principle so widely that it is identical with the formal aspect of anything, so that in so far as anything is knowable, that is precisely because of the efficacy of the "ideal" principle. In that case, the "real" principle seems to be demoted to obliviousness to forms or ideals, to action by impact, to mere coexistence in space and time, to matter of fact, to the manifold of change and qualities. This assumption would explain why he says that empirical or historical science and judgment are closer to the "real" principle, while the speculative sciences and the system of concepts are closer to the intellectual or "ideal" principle. The "real" principle sometimes seems to be very near to "chaos," by which he presumably had Plato's *Receptacle* in mind.

If the "real" were to be identified with the "chaotic," however, further difficulties would arise. For Schleiermacher's God is supposed to be the basis of the harmony of the ideal and the real, and at the same time God is also regarded as the complete opposite of chaos. The implication is that the "real" principle must be different from chaos.*

5. The Feeling of Dependence

The metaphysical doctrine of God which we have been discussing has not been the point of Schleiermacher's chief historical influence in theology. This position is held by another and quite contrary aspect of his thought. The moving power of his theological ideas historically has been what may be called his "empiricism" in theology, that is, his claim that in some sense religious experience and the theological doctrines which express it are independent of the results of metaphysical speculation and indeed of intellectual formulations in general. Beliefs (even those in accord with traditional theological doctrines about the justice of God, the work of Christ, God's promises, and so on) are to be distinguished, according to him, from religious faith. Religion is not essentially concerned with these beliefs; it is essentially a matter of a kind of feeling, or (as he more precisely states it in *The Christian Faith*) of a feeling of absolute dependence. This religious feeling, he claimed, can occur independently of metaphysical theories and indeed of any supposedly revealed theological system; and the theological discipline called dogmatic theology is also

* For Schleiermacher's comments on "chaos," see the *Dialektik*, pp. 60, 116-121, 138-140, 455.

able to arrive at a statement of Christian doctrines (in his sense) without dependence upon anything but this religious experience itself. It is Schleiermacher's assertion of the independence of religious life (and religious experience is independent of the later dogmas which formulate it) and of the dependence of religious dogmas on nothing but the religious experience itself, which has made for him the place he holds as the founder of an important branch of modern Protestant theology.

Schleiermacher's idea was a new departure not only among religious philosophers but theologians who would themselves tend to avoid proofs by natural reason. The theological writers who influenced the development of Protestant thought believed that ideas and thought have a great deal to do both with religious experience and theology. To be sure, they did not claim that philosophical belief will produce Christian religious experience; the hearing of the Word through preaching and the sacraments are required for this. They did not believe that natural reason will produce theology, for which revelation is necessary. But it was believed that natural reason, especially when including in its survey the facts of the natural moral consciousness, was able to do something toward the production of religious experience. In any case, that experience, according to the Reformers, is founded upon ideas: belief in one's own sinfulness, the justice of God, the atoning sacrifice of Christ, the promise of God to remit the sins of all who believe.

Schleiermacher's view, on the other hand, is that religious experience is possible independently of beliefs and particularly of metaphysical ideas (such as the proof for the existence of God by natural reason). And theology, according to him, is independent of both rational scientific arguments and supernatural revelations; it has an experiential basis, and its assertions are founded upon that basis, which is just the fact of the religious experience.[135]

These contentions constitute the essence of what has been called Schleiermacher's empiricism in theology.

There is one point in this "empiricism" which invites preliminary mention because Schleiermacher seems often to have been misunderstood on it. Schleiermacher does not suggest that his "empiricism" supplies a new intellectual proof of the existence of God, based on a more scientific form of reasoning and more direct evidence than the old proofs. His only "proof" of religion is his attempt to show that religious feeling is a normal (sometimes he says it is a necessary) moment in the development of experience, and that religion occupies a place in the harmonious "life" of the universe, without which the perfection of the universe could not be actualized. The human spirit being what it is, religion is required for its perfection, and for the perfection of the world. In contrast to religion there are philosophy and science, which are "natural" developments of the objective side of human spirit in the same way in which religion is the perfection of the subjective side.* All of these phenomena are necessary for the perfect realization of the possibilities which lie within the human mind. They all spring up from the depths of the human spirit and are equally expressions of mind and required for its complete realization. Religion is therefore just as natural, dignified, and valuable as science. And some particular form of religion, developed in a certain historical situation and therefore of a certain individual form, is a "natural" occurrence in the mind of the person who has it, and so commends itself to him by its satisfyingness that that person wants no other religion. These are the only senses in which "proof" of religion can be offered, according to Schleiermacher, although we shall later have occasion to consider some statements which suggest that he thought he had a kind of experiential mystical proof in his theological analysis of religious experience.

Even if he does not offer a new "proof," however, his view, he thought, had the effect of freeing theology from the necessity of offering one. Religion is commended as a "higher" form of life, and theology is given a free hand to proceed without the necessity of defending the traditional religious ideas by means of a difficult and laborious attempt to prove the truth of certain propositions.

In the course of the discussion in previous chapters, some of the reasons which led Schleiermacher to seek a new approach to religion

---

* Cf. George Wehrung, *Die philosophisch-theologische Methode Schleiermachers*, Göttingen, 1911. Schleiermacher says that the way to save the church from the charge of being "illusory" is to show that it is "a necessary element for the development of the human mind." *Kurze Darstellung des theologischen Studiums*, 2nd ed., sec. 22, cf. Gl. B, pt. 6, par. I, for a good treatment of his view.

and theology have been mentioned.* Some of his letters written during this last period of his life are valuable in setting the matter in an unusually clear perspective. These letters reveal the fact that Schleiermacher was concerned over the apparent conflict between the claims of traditional religion and the results of science and philosophy, and he apparently thought that the solution lay in the abating of the noetic claims of religion. There are many assertions which Christians have become accustomed to make, he says, which it is important for them to get on without—such as the statements about creation, miracles, the Mosaic chronology, and so on. For these statements conflict with reliable scientific knowledge, and, he says, it would be scandalous if religion were to ally itself only with a crude and unsound science, while reliable scientists were forced by the unnecessary claims of religion to ally themselves with the irreligious elements of society. Schleiermacher seems particularly to have felt the sting of the results of the (at that time) new internal criticism of the Bible.† All these facts, he thinks, have the effect of putting the religious man in a dilemma and of forcing him to find a way of reconciling his two legitimate interests.

On the other hand, Schleiermacher hesitated more and more to encourage a solution of the religious problem along the lines of speculative idealism. For in this circle, which was professedly favorable to religion, Schleiermacher thought he found a spirit which was uncongenial to it. Among the speculative philosophers there was, he said, "a hierarchy of intellectual culture, a priesthood of speculation . . . which I can never find very Protestant, and wherever I have met it, it has not appeared without a certain taint of popery."‡ In this opposition, again, he felt himself in line with the experience and belief of the church, that faith comes through the church and its teaching and not through the abstract speculation of philosophers.

Thus Schleiermacher believed that religion requires protection from the intellectuals, both from scientific enemies and professed philosophical friends. The particular protection he was prepared to

* Cf. especially Chap. V, sec. 5.

† Werke, pt. I, vol. II, pp. 612-621. It will be recalled that Luther, for example, was free from any intellectual difficulties and experienced no trouble in accepting traditional religious beliefs as true.

‡ Ibid., p. 588. He had a similar objection to proof based on texts in the Bible, The Christian Faith, 2nd ed., sec. 128, par. 2.

offer was in the form of a reconciliation of religion with intellectual claims by segregation. That is, the entire realm of knowledge about the objects in which traditional theology had been interested, whether philosophical or scientific, is to become the province of secular thinkers, and secured from theological or religious interference. On the other hand, the realm of religious experience is to be given to the theologian as a datum for the formulation of doctrine, clear of all dependence on this philosophical knowledge, and theology is to be a scientific expression of this religious experience. The value of this proposal is one of the things we have to examine.

Of course, Schleiermacher does not make this proposal in independence of historical fact. On the contrary, he thinks that he is in a position to show that religion and theology (apart from confusions) have been virtually just what he says they are and that when we examine our thought about them we must find that we have implicitly been assuming all along that religion is primarily a matter of feeling and that theology is its expression.

Schleiermacher does not mean to say that religion and theology have no relation whatever to scientific thought. As a matter of fact, he deals with religious experience in several of his own scientific works—in the *Ethics*, the *Aesthetics*, the *Dialectic*, and the *Psychology*. Religious feeling is a kind of feeling which is to be understood just as much as any other subjective phenomenon. Ideally, psychology should be able to describe its appearance in the human mind and the conditions which determine the character of its appearance. The science of aesthetics should make possible the understanding of the expression of religious feeling, in works of art, for example. In fact, there are numerous passages scattered all through his works in which Schleiermacher deals scientifically with the concept of religious experience. Schleiermacher actually goes so far as to hold that it is possible to "deduce" both religious experience, its several general forms, and theology as a "science" of it in the same sense in which, as we have seen, he thinks it possible to deduce other mental phenomena.

His view of the "deduction" of religion can be clarified by relating it more fully to his idea of scientific method. I have pointed out how he believed that "speculative" science can evolve a system of concepts which expresses the "essences" of the forms of being or activity to which they refer, and that the subordinate species are "deduced" by showing how they are the necessary species into which the genus must be divided by a double principle of division. His *Ethics*, or science of mind, is organized in that way. And he assumes that religion, which is an institution or activity of mind and hence a part of the science of mind, must be understood by relating the concept of it to the other ideas or forms of reality dealt with by ethics, and incorporating it within the system of the sciences of mind as a whole. The deduction, it will be recalled, is not purely a *priori*, but proceeds by elaborating a system of concepts "from above" while at the same time taking into account a mass of material which is organized in terms of those concepts.

Not only religion but various types of religion, Schleiermacher thinks, can be deduced in this way. His "deductions" are not always carried out in the same fashion, but in general he first divides reality into the realms of nature and mind. Then he divides the mental into the active and the passive. (Sometimes, however, he uses a threefold division into knowing, willing, and feeling, as described below.) The passive side of mind is divided into knowing and feeling. Feelings are divided into those in which there is a feeling of partial freedom and those in which there is a feeling of absolute dependence (in *The Christian Faith*). The feeling of absolute dependence is identified with the "essence" of religion. But actual religions must be again divided into groups corresponding to the purity and development of the appearance of the feeling in them. There are three religions on the highest stage: Judaism, Mohammedanism, and Christianity. There are several points of distinction among these. Christianity is most clearly distinguished by being a religion of moral redemption, which fact Schleiermacher thinks is inseparable from its having been founded by Christ.* But there are differences again between Protestantism and Catholicism, the essence of which is concerned with their views about the place of the church in the religious life.

The foregoing is a rough sketch of Schleiermacher's "deduction" of Protestantism. He does not claim that this is formally valid or that it will be convincing to everyone. The science of ethics would have to

---

* There are certain respects in which he thinks Christianity cannot be deduced. Cf. Gl. B, sec. 11, par. 5.

have taken a more complete and generally acceptable form, he thought, before that could be the case. There is or will be, he thinks, a special branch of science within the science of ethics, which will be particularly concerned with a rigorous deduction of religion and (for example) the Protestant church. This branch of science will comprise what should be understood by the "philosophy of religion" and "philosophical theology."[136] Schleiermacher did not think that these sciences yet existed in his day in a developed and convincing form.

Schleiermacher's brief sketch of these matters occupies a large part of the admittedly rather philosophical introductory portion of The Christian Faith.

Schleiermacher's only "proof" of religion is comprised in the foregoing kind of "deduction," which for reasons which will appear later he thought showed that religion is a natural development of human nature.

Dogmatic theology, the nature of which will be explained in the next section, is not one of these "speculative sciences," much less a metaphysical theory of God or a system of doctrines based on revelation; it is one of the "historical" or more empirical sciences.[137] It is, as we shall see, an expression or description of religious experience within a certain religious community, for the purpose of guiding and benefiting the development and life of that community.[138] It is in this sense that theology is independent of science for him.* Its nature will be described more fully later.

I shall now describe more fully one of his "deductions" of the nature of religion. There are several of them in his works, and I shall arbitrarily select the one in The Christian Faith as an example.

He begins by assuming that the sciences of mind should be divided on the basis of a threefold division of the faculties of the mind (this threefold division not being quite usual for him or consistent with his theory of the division of a genus), that is, according to the three faculties of knowing, acting, and feeling. His second assumption is

---

* It is to be noted that this science is dependent on the other sciences for their definition of the proper scientific method, for the definition of its object and so on. Schleiermacher sometimes tends to exaggerate the independence of dogmatic theology, as is illustrated by his attempt to draw a sharp line between the introductory part of The Christian Faith and its main body. See Werke, pt. I, vol. II, p. 607.

that since religion is a mental activity, and since these three faculties comprise the ways in which mind may function, therefore essentially religion must be one of them. That is, essentially religion must be either a kind of knowledge or a kind of action or a kind of feeling. In order then to decide between these three possibilities, Schleiermacher proceeds to eliminate on the basis of a principle very similar to Mill's method of concomitant variation. As he puts it: "Whatever in its increase and decrease is not the measure of the completeness of something, cannot constitute the essence of that thing."[139] In other words, if religion is essentially a species of knowing, then the more knowledge the more religion and the less knowledge the less religion. Similarly with action and feeling. Since he has assumed that there are only three possibilities, he has only to eliminate two of them by showing that the degree of religion does not vary concomitantly with the degree of the mental activity being considered, and to show that the degree of religion does vary concomitantly with the third activity and he will have established the essence of religion. Apparently this is an example of the way in which he thought empirical phenomena should be utilized in constructing a scientific system.

Schleiermacher first eliminates knowledge. If religion were essentially a matter of knowledge, he says, the best theologian would be the most pious, which everyone will admit is false.[140] Next, he eliminates ethical action. If religion were essentially a matter of conduct, the degree of piety would vary concomitantly either with the efficacy of our actions (which we clearly do not believe) or at least with the motives behind the overt action. But the motives, he thinks, should be classified with feeling. So ethical conduct goes out, except in that it is still possible that certain kinds of motive may be correlated with being religious. Furthermore, he believes there are reasons for denying that religion can be defined by any combination of knowledge and action or of knowledge, action, and feeling, unless feeling is given a central place in the definition. These conclusions seem to leave the field open to feeling if only a case can be made out for it, and of course it fares more happily. Schleiermacher writes: "There are states of feeling such as penitence, contrition, confidence, and joy in God, which we pronounce pious in themselves, without regard to any knowing or doing that proceeds from them." Therefore he concludes that religion is "essentially" a matter of feeling, although "there are both a knowing and a doing which pertain to piety, but neither of these constitutes its essence."[141]

In somewhat similar fashion, Schleiermacher arrives at the conclusion that the factor common to pious experiences is a specific type of feeling, viz., the feeling of absolute dependence, or of dependence upon God.[142]

After these introductory remarks about the nature of Schleiermacher's "theological empiricism" we can proceed profitably to an examination of his view that religion is essentially a feeling of dependence. In doing so, we shall first probe into his idea of "feeling" in general, then second, in the light of our findings elaborate his idea of "religious feeling," and third, explain his view that religious feeling is essentially a feeling of dependence on God.

(1) *Schleiermacher's view of "feeling" in general.*—There is no breech with his earlier (1806) idea of feeling at this later time. His understanding of the processes denoted by various usages of the word "feeling" remained the same in outline though it seems to have been expanded and elaborated. Briefly, he thinks that particular affective states (feelings) are generated by the interaction of the individual with his environment. These feelings are subjective; they do not reflect the character of the environment except in so far as its nature is involved in the meaning it has for the subject. What they reveal most is the character of the subject, his goals, ideals, conflicts, and desires. If the environment depresses the life of the subject, there is unpleasant feeling; if life is promoted, the feelings are pleasant. Schleiermacher thinks the character of the self may give a common tone or mood to the feelings; if the character is religious, the feelings will have the mood of contrition or blessedness. The main difference of emphasis between the two periods is in that at the later date Schleiermacher tended to use the word "feeling" to denote not the particular affective states but rather the character, attitude, emotional set, or mental structure which lies behind the feelings and gives them their character (without, however, abstracting this from the common tone in the feelings themselves). "Feeling" is sometimes used to denote the transitory affective state; but it usually denotes rather the permanent conditions lying behind the conscious state, taken in connec-

tion with the kind of mood which reflects them in consciousness. In making this change Schleiermacher doubtless had Protestant religious experience in mind. The feelings and attitudes with which the naturalist or Buddhist faces the world are different from those with which the pious Lutheran views life. By "feeling," Schleiermacher intended to point to that fact and its conditions. It is practically identical with some modern uses of "attitude."

Schleiermacher denies that feeling has the universality and objectivity of sense perceptions. It is rather in some sense a consciousness of the state of the self, and hence the feelings of persons cannot be expected to be similar except in so far as the relevant states of their selves are similar. (He sometimes uses "self-consciousness" as a synonym for feeling, presumably on this account. As we shall see, Schleiermacher sometimes seems to regard feeling as a mode of inner awareness in which the nature of the self is cognized.) He says, for example:

A visual impression can usually be classed as an objective perception. The more perfect it is, the more the whole self is absorbed in the expression of the character of the object. The purest intuition is the most complete forgetting of the self. But if the impression is so strong as to be blinding, the objective perception is lost, and there remains only the state of the self, or feeling, and the purest feeling is the most complete forgetting of the affecting object.[143]

As I have said, in the more important passages he does not use "feeling" primarily to refer to particular affective states. In some cases he definitely repudiates this usage. For example, he says of feeling that

it is different from the affection [Empfindung] which constitutes the subjective personal life of a definite moment, due to affection by an object.[144] [A more positive statement is the following:] The permanence of religious feeling is mood: the tendency to relate the single moments of life to the relation of man to the highest being.[145]

I take this to mean that the religious man's attitude toward everything in life is determined by his faith in God, which defines the mood or common tone of his emotional experiences. Another more obscure statement should, I believe, be understood in the same way: "By 'feeling' I mean the self-consciousness as it is, if not exclusively, still predominantly time-filling, and occurs essentially under . . . the antithetical form of pleasure and pain."[146]

It has been suggested, both on account of statements like the above which imply that feeling may be partially out of time, and statements which imply that feeling is the "unity" of knowing and doing, that he may be using "feeling" to refer simply to the pure transcendental ego. This view is not admissible. Schleiermacher clearly distinguishes between "feeling" and the transcendental ego; he says that the subject manifests itself in the three modes of experience (knowing, acting, feeling), and is their common foundation.[147] But nevertheless it is the case that Schleiermacher thinks that feeling is in some sense the core of man's being, the center of the self, in a way in which perception and activity are not. For example, he wrote into his own copy of The Christian Faith,

It is essential to feeling to arouse knowing and doing . . . and it is the unity of these two.[148] [Again:] A determination of self-consciousness lies at the base of every impulse, and if we want to distinguish one impulse from another . . . we must go back to that inmost being, and that is just feeling passing into activity.[149]

More specifically, he speaks of feeling as the unity which is the point of transition from knowing to acting.

The transition as such [he says] is the consciousness of nothing at all, objectively regarded, but is also the identity of the subject in two moments, i.e., the ego.[150] [Again:] If we consider our life as a series [of moments], it is a transition from thought to volition and conversely. . . . The transition is the point where thought ceases and volition begins, i.e., the identity of both. In thought, the being of things is posited in us . . . and in volition, our being is posited in the things. But our being is what does the positing, and this remains at the zero point. . . . This is the immediate self-consciousness, or feeling.[151]

The interpretation of these passages is somewhat speculative, and I feel confident that my explanation of their meaning does not exhaust all he had in mind. But I believe the main point he wanted to make is that what he meant by "feeling" is not simply an affective state, but has to do with the fundamental nature of the self of which the tone of emotional states and also actions (moral decisions) are the expression.*

* It is this fact which I believe he is trying to express, in a very artificial way, in passages frequently quoted by writers on this subject (*Dialektik*, pp. 152, 429, 524-525), to the effect that in feeling there is an analogy with the absolute identity,

This interpretation fits in with the examples of religious "feeling" which he mentions in The Christian Faith, viz., penitence, contrition, confidence, and joy in God.[152] These words do not refer merely to specific affectional states, but rather to attitudes of mind with their corresponding moods or general emotional sets toward different situations.

There is a statement in the Ethics which contains some interesting suggestions for an understanding of his use of "feeling":

What in general we call feeling is, like thought, the expression of Reason in nature. It is an activity of life, which has come to being in nature only through Reason—which is true not only of moral and religious feeling, but also of physical feeling, so long as it is given as human and as a whole moment of feeling. . . . It is the definite expression of Reason's mode of dwelling in this particular bit of nature. For feeling, even of the lowest kind, always expresses what Reason accomplishes in nature, or fails to accomplish. And every feeling is concerned only with the unity of life, not with something particular. . . . Feeling always expresses what Reason does or does not accomplish in the bit of nature unified with it, in the relation in which this stands to what is not united with it; and this is just the excitation pertinent to every feeling.[153]

This passage expresses several ideas. First, he means that there could be no "feeling" at all except for the organizing activity of the mind—just as he would think that there could be a series of sensations in an animal, but an objective world only for a mind using ideas in thought. Second, and more pertinently, he means that the emotional set or attitude with the specific emotional tone to which it gives rise are the work of mind (the organizing power on the supra-organic level) in the individual; and their character expresses the extent to which the principle (mind) has organized the individual on the new level. For example, if reason or mind has not succeeded in mastering the sense desires and incorporating them into a harmonious system of volitions, that fact is expressed in a person's "feeling." Selfishness will make itself known in the attitude of a subject toward an event that promotes or hinders his personal well-being. Selfishness, jealousy,

because it is a unity of the ideal and the real in which all distinctions are done away. The idea that feeling is somehow the unity of thought and will was expressed in his early essay on value, mentioned in chap. II, sec. 4. It may possibly have come from his teacher, Eberhard. See his Allgemeine Theorie des Denkens und Empfindens, Berlin, 1776.

and envy indicate the failure of reason to subordinate the individual well-being to the well-being of the whole; sympathy, generosity, and love indicate the success of reason in organizing individual interests and relating them to the well-being of a wider circle.

This interpretation is admittedly speculative but if this is what he meant, it seems to me it is intelligible.

I conclude by quoting a remark of Steffens which Schleiermacher said was so like his own view that transition from it to his own idea of feeling was easy.[154] Steffens wrote: "What we here call feeling is the immediate presence of the whole undivided being, both sensory and spiritual; of the unity of the person and his sensory and spiritual world."

This seems to mean that "feeling" is the attitude or emotional responsiveness which is the result of the nature of the whole self or character, although here again the meaning is far from obvious.

(2) *The nature of religious feeling.*—Religion is the highest development of feeling. This contention runs through all of Schleiermacher's later works. What he had in mind can be roughly indicated by contrasting religion with other types of feeling. The lowest stage would be pure selfishness and interest only in satisfaction of the physical needs. A higher stage is reached in so far as the individual comes to care for other persons or groups, or in so far as more "spiritual" objects come to control his interest. One who is insensitive to beauty or dead to the sublime is on only a primitive stage of development. The higher levels of feeling occur when the individual is responsive to the beautiful, the fine, and the awesome; when he cares for human beings just because they are persons. But the highest development of feeling comes only in religion, which is the continuation and fulfillment of all that is good in the human spirit. In fact, he believed moral character and aesthetic appreciation cannot be perfect in the absence of religion.

Schleiermacher is not very precise about the exact nature of this "highest life," but doubtless the spirit he had in mind was that of pietistic Protestantism at its best, with the emphasis on those tendencies which had something in common with Spinoza.[155]

He also believed that this "highest perfection" could be realized only in connection with the Christian community, and in particular through at least indirect contact with the person of Christ. In the pre-Christian state, he says, the self-consciousnes (or feeling) is such that "only sensuous feelings determine the will. When the life is linked to Christ, there is a change of this relationship [so that religious feeling determines the will] and this is what is called 'conversion.'"[156] Knowledge of the personality of Christ, he thinks, deepens discontent with life on the lower level (a discontent called "consciousness of sin"); and the impact of his personality also makes possible the fuller life on the higher level.[157] Such is his interpretation of the Christian idea that "Christ is the second Adam, the beginner and originator of this more perfect human life, or the fulfillment of the creation of man."[158]

The highest perfection of the feeling of man is an extension of the "expansion of life" which occurs in the lover of humanity, but it also includes elements contained in the awareness of the sublime. First it is an extension of love for human persons. Schleiermacher points out that as the mind develops there is a movement from selfishness to sympathy, from individualism to unity with society. This fact is illustrated in altruistic conduct, which cannot be explained on any egoistic theory which would regard it as simply an attempt to get rid of one's own displeasure resulting from insight into another person's need.[159] Egoistic hedonism (or egoism in general) Schleiermacher classes with atomistic sensationalism in theory of knowledge, and thinks that it is as little possible to get a theory of social behavior from the one as an understanding of the fact of knowledge from the other. Schleiermacher thinks that at the level at which a person genuinely cares for others one must believe that the person in some sense assimilates the lives of others into his own, and that as a result his experience is exalted and made richer.[160] When this love for others is perfected, the well-being of others so dominates the feeling that personal considerations do not count at all[161] and moral conflict does not occur. Now religion, as I have said, is to be an extension of this. (He actually believes that even moral perfection is not attainable without religion.)* As he puts it:

* Cf. Gl. B, sec. 121-125. "It was first through Christ (as the founder of a society which can include all men and which, in attaching individuals to itself, has been interested simply in the fact that they are human) that the consciousness of the species, along with the consciousness of God and with reference to the same

The self can also extend itself beyond the consciousness of [love of] its own species. There is already sympathy with [love for] everything animate as such, in our contact with animals. There is sympathy with natural forces, in the feeling of the sublime. . . . Similarly, there may be an extension of the self to sympathy with all particular and finite being as such, including our acquaintance with the whole world.[162]

This fullest extension of "sympathy" to the whole universe of finite objects is religion.[163]

Before developing this notion further, we must note that Schleiermacher rightly points out the close analogy between an aspect of religious experience and the feeling of the sublime. He says that "devotion is a similar [to the impact of the sublime] subjection of the self to an other, a submerging of oneself in the inexhaustible object, and also a being attracted by it. It is losing oneself in the Infinite, with the awareness that here any reaction is entirely inappropriate." Religion is an extension both of the social feelings (sympathy) and the feeling of the sublime in nature.[164]

Schleiermacher points out that the development of the social feeling of "love" or "sympathy" is dependent upon the existence and recognition of a realm of identity between the individual and those toward whom he can develop the social feelings. It is obvious, for example, that the members of a family have much in common. A similar community of being must be recognized as existing within a wider group, if sympathy is to be developed toward its members. Identity of origin, of language, or of customs may form the basis of such a wide community of feeling. Schleiermacher thinks that the widest extension of the strictly social feeling has been reached when what is common simply among human beings as such (e.g.,

---

thing, has become a powerful motive. But just for this reason, this power is not a natural principle, which could have developed itself spontaneously out of human nature, as it would have remained without Christ. On the contrary, we recognize it as the most original expression of the Holy Spirit, as the consciousness of the urgent need of salvation in all, and of the equal capacity of all to be received into living fellowship with Christ; and the universal love of humanity we know only as identical with the will for the Kingdom of God in its widest extension." (sec. 121, par. 3)

Schleiermacher here fastened on the fact of the impetus given by the Christian religion to humanitarian projects, and to respect for the personality, well-being, and right of all men just as men. It is true that religion has led in the development of moral ideals, in the recognition that all persons are the subject of rights, and not merely members of some tribe or group.

their dependence on nature, their scientific interests, etc.) is sufficient to establish love of one person for his fellow men.[165]

The wider (religious) sympathy which extends to all finite objects must apparently also be founded upon the reality and recognition of such identity between them and the conscious self. The assimilation of others' lives into one's own and the consequent exaltation and expansion of experience on the level of human intercourse, requires the recognition of something in common; similarly, if everything finite

is to be absorbed into the self-consciousness, an attempt must appear, after the analogy of the previous development, to form a consciousness of community between the self and nature, and this now becomes the consciousness of the absolute unity of all life, viz., the deity, and the relation of all situations in life to this consciousness constitutes the religious feelings.[166]

Religion, in other words, is a feeling which is possible because of the unity of all beings—conscious and inorganic alike—in God.

I believe it was to this fact that he was pointing when he wrote: "Religion is nothing but the immediate reality of the Absolute in consciousness; similarly love is nothing but the reality of the universally human in consciousness."[167]

This view of the nature of religion is expressed in *The Christian Faith*, especially in the first edition. He says that religion occurs when

the individual regards himself *as a part of the whole world* . . . and after he has assimilated the unity of everything finite into his self-consciousness [feeling], and feels himself dependent on God. But in that he feels himself as only one part of the whole world, *all opposition between himself and other particular finite objects is done away with.*[168]

In the corresponding passage of the second edition, he remarks that the religious feeling is not a consciousness

of ourselves as finite objects of a certain character, but only of ourselves as particular finite beings in general, so that we do not oppose or contrast ourselves with any other individual being; rather, in this feeling, *all contrast between one individual being and another is done away with.*[169]

Religion is the love (or sympathy) for the world, mediated by

the fact that the conscious self ultimately has in common with all
other beings that they are one in this relation to God. In several
passages Schleiermacher states clearly the necessity of some kind of
identity of things through relationship to the Infinite, as the basis
for the development of religious feeling. "This sympathy [the love
of religion]," he says, "can occur only in so far as in each finite being
there is a relation to something outside the totality [of finite things].
If it is to be possible, that Being must lie outside the realm of reciprocal interaction."[170]

In his lectures on psychology in 1830, Schleiermacher connected
this view of religion with the *feeling of dependence* on God. He says:

> We must assume an immediate tendency toward the Infinite. The
> antithesis between conscious being as a genus and the being given to con-
> sciousness must be abolished in self-consciousness [feeling]; hence it must
> be affected by an other. But clearly not by one on which it can react;
> hence the feeling of absolute dependence.[171]

What he seems to mean is that religious love, which is the assimilation of all the world into one's own life so that the contrast is an-
nulled and all is felt as one, requires that there should be some real
(and consciously recognized?) identity between the conscious individual and his world. This identity can occur if and in that both
are parts of one systematic world, conditioned by God. This being
through relation to which the knower and his objects can feel themselves to be identical must not itself be a finite object on which the
knower could react, for in that case it would itself be an object with
which the knower could contrast himself. It must be a being on
which the knower and the known are dependent, without their being
in any way free to act on it. That is, it must be an Infinite Being
which is the source of all finite being, with which a finite object
cannot be contrasted, as it always can be with some other finite
object. It must be, therefore, an object toward which there can be a
pure or absolute feeling of dependence—the feeling which he says
in *The Christian Faith* is the essence of religion. A very similar passage
appears in the *Dialectic*.[172]

There is an ambiguity in his theory that religious love or the feeling of sympathy is connected with an identity between the self and
the object of the feeling. It is not clear whether there must actually

be some kind of "common life," or whether it is sufficient that the subject should think or assume that there is. And, if the latter alternative expresses what Schleiermacher means, it is not clear whether there must be an explicit judgment of the reality of such a community of being or whether a vague assumption of it is enough. A decision between these possibilities is important for an understanding of Schleiermacher's view of the dependence of religious experience on ideas and beliefs. From a psychological point of view, it is difficult to see how the actual fact of such a "union" could serve as the basis for or be necessary to the higher affectional life, unless the subject became aware of it as such. On the other hand, to make religious feeling dependent upon belief would be dangerous to his view that religious experience does not require any ideas of God but (as we shall see) is an immediate fact which is the datum which the idea of God is trying to express.

(3) *Religion as an absolute feeling of dependence.*—The fullest expression of Schleiermacher's view that religion is specifically an absolute feeling of dependence is contained in *The Christian Faith.*

It is not perfectly clear what the relation is between the view of religious feeling which I have been describing and this idea that religion is essentially a feeling of dependence. He must have thought that the feeling of dependence is somehow central to the "religious love." Very possibly he meant, as has been suggested, that the feeling that all finite things are dependent on God and that consequently they have in common their union with God is the basis required for the realization of "love." Obviously he must have thought "love" and the "feeling of dependence" intimately related if not identical.

There are several reasons why he should have chosen to emphasize this particular aspect of religious experience—and there is no doubt that it is a real feeling which he is talking about when he refers to the feeling of dependence in religion. One of the reasons is, as I have already suggested, that his metaphysics affirmed that all finite objects are "grounded," or have their source in God; the religious feeling of the dependence of all things on God is a close parallel to the metaphysical idea. Furthermore, as we shall see, his taking the "feeling of dependence" as the central fact of religion enabled him to set up a system of doctrine not remote from the traditional systems, but nevertheless purified of elements which were objectionable to the modern scientific conscience. This "feeling of dependence," as we shall see, is the hub upon which his whole empirical approach to theology turns. It is because he thinks it possible to begin his theology with the feeling of dependence as an original fact which does not need to be derived from philosophy that he is able to claim that his theology can be independent of metaphysics and that it is simply the expression of religious feeling.

Schleiermacher explains what he means in somewhat the following terms. There are two important types of feeling, he says, the feeling of freedom when the self is predominantly active in its relation to the world, and the feeling of dependence when it is predominantly receptive. When the self is interacting with other finite objects there is always an element of both these feelings present in experience, because there is always a sense in which the self is active and always a sense in which it is passive. However, in contrast to this, inspection of religious experience reveals that religious feeling in all its various forms is always a pure feeling of dependence, so that there is never any element of freedom in it.[173] (In the second edition Schleiermacher calls it an absolute feeling of dependence, meaning by that that there can never be included in it any degree whatever of the opposite feeling of freedom.) But it is always possible to have a feeling of freedom when the self is related to a finite object, for the very nature of everything finite is just that a subject can be active in relation to it. This means that the religious consciousness, which is a feeling of pure dependence, must be a relation of the subject not to anything finite but to "the simple and absolute Infinity. And this is the meaning of the above expression, that to feel oneself absolutely dependent and to feel oneself dependent on God is the same thing."[174] The feeling of absolute dependence, which inspection shows is the feeling common to all religious states, must be the feeling of the self when it is conscious of its relation to God. "It is the consciousness that the whole of our spontaneous activity comes from a Source outside us in just the same sense in which anything toward which we should have a feeling of absolute freedom must have proceeded entirely from ourselves."[175]

These passages in The Christian Faith in which the feeling of dependence is introduced have been the subject of much controversy, for it is not clear just what he meant or what he intended to prove. There are several points, however, which he seems to be making. In the first place, he asserts as an empirical fact to be admitted by all that there is such a religious experience as the absolute feeling of dependence. We shall see in a moment how it is that he thinks that it is necessary and natural that there should be one; but whether or not it is true, as has sometimes been claimed, that he was trying to prove that such a feeling is necessary,* it is indubitable that he also thought it a given fact of experience which must be recognized by all and does not need to be proved. In the second place, Schleiermacher apparently thinks that this feeling is a consciousness of the state of the self. (I have already remarked that he thinks that feeling in general is consciousness of the state of the self.) He believes that there is a feeling of freedom when the self is active and a feeling of dependence when it is passive and determined from without. This correlation of subjective feelings with objective facts is an important step in Schleiermacher's argument, for it is a move away from pure feeling to more objective meanings—a move which was necessary if he was to elaborate a system of doctrines making statements about God and the world. In the third place, because the feeling in question is a feeling of pure dependence it cannot be a consciousness of a relation of the self to any finite object, for it is always possible that there should be a feeling of freedom in relation to a finite object. Therefore the absolute feeling of dependence must be regarded as a consciousness of the self's state of receptiveness in relation not to any finite object but to the Infinite Being, or God. By means of this step Schleiermacher is able to move from the subjective fact of feeling to the idea of relationship to God, naturally a great gain from the point of view of one who is attempting to set up a religious doctrine as the expression of this feeling. Finally, he moves back again from his analysis of feeling to argue that it is a universal and "necessary" element in human experience. The reason for its universality is that, presumably because it is a consciousness of the fundamental meta-

* Sometimes he seems to mean by the "necessity" of something only that it can be deduced (as shown above) in a science, and occupies a place in the conceptual scheme by which experience is organized.

physical conditionedness of the self, "it does not depend upon any particular modification of human nature, but upon the universal nature of man."[176] It is an advantage to him to be able to say this, for he goes on to contend that recognition of this fact takes the place of the traditional proofs for God; religion does not have to be supported by proofs if it can be shown to be necessary.

We shall content ourselves here with raising some brief and obvious objections to Schleiermacher's idea. In the following section I shall analyze further the nature of the "feeling of dependence" and state my view of the legitimacy of basing theological doctrines upon it. But a few remarks may be made now. In the first place, there is the difficulty mentioned about the relation between this feeling and the "religious feeling" described previously. It is possible that a feeling of dependence on God is a part of the highest and most developed affective life of spirit, but it is clear that such a feeling is by no means all of it. There is vacillation here about the very nature of religion. In the second place, as we shall see more clearly later, the "feeling of dependence" is in fact not a feeling in the sense which his theological system demands that it be. Schleiermacher leads the reader astray by treating it as an immediate experience just like certain other affective states which are significantly different from it, and by contrasting it with cognitive states, beliefs, judgments, and so on. It is important for him to do this, for it is his contention that religion is a matter of immediate feeling and not of ideas that enables him to establish theology as a science independent of philosophy and religion as a phenomenon not dependent on ideas and proofs. The "feeling of dependence" is not a feeling in the required sense, as we shall see.* In the third place, his correlation of "feelings" with objective situations (the feeling of freedom with the activity of the self) does hold in some instances, although it is to be noted that the "feeling of freedom" like the feeling of dependence, is a much more complex state, psychologically, than he allows. But there is no reason to believe that it holds everywhere,

---

* As will be pointed out in the next section, it may be that he did not intend rigorously to exclude all elements of judgment from the phenomenon denoted by "feeling of dependence." In that case, the above criticism would not apply. But if so, he is inconsistent and not in a position to say that religion is independent of metaphysics.

and in fact it does not. This means that it is not necessarily the case that a pure feeling of dependence must be interpreted as a consciousness of relation to God. Fourth, his argument to prove that religion is a universal element in the experience of man is invalid for the same reason. (He always held that in fact religion is natural or instinctive in some sense, however.)

In conclusion it is worth remarking that this analysis of religion as essentially a feeling of dependence expresses only one aspect of historical religion. For many persons (like Luther, for example) religion seems to mean less dependence on the Absolute than confidence in God's forgiving grace, in the dependableness of His promises and attitude toward men. I do not see how Schleiermacher could have fitted such religious experience into his system, and he would probably not have thought highly of it because of the anthropomorphic personal idea of God which goes with it.

I do not mean to disparage the importance and value of Schleiermacher's analysis of religion. Both his idea that it is a pure feeling of dependence and his idea that it is "universal love" seem to me useful, even if they need to be clarified and altered in many details. It may be that an idea like the latter one approximates what "religion" can or ought to mean to the modern man. What is to be objected to is only his uncritical use of the notion of the "feeling of dependence," which occurred because of his desire to keep religion independent of ideas, science, and philosophy.

6. Theological Empiricism

It has already been indicated that for various reasons Schleiermacher disparaged the importance of the results of science and philosophy for religion. Religion is feeling and has no direct connection with thought. It can exist in its most vital form without the knowledge of proofs for God and indeed without intellectual assent to doctrines. This view implied a break not only with the new idealistic intellectualism in Germany but with most traditional ways of thinking about religion. The road had of course been prepared by the Pietistic movement which emphasized the importance of emotions and conduct in contrast with intellectual acceptance of doctrines; but it was still generally thought that Christianity was inseparable from certain doctrinal claims, assent to which was necessary for a saving faith.

It was also a break with the earlier periods of his thought during which he had himself admitted that religion and religious feeling involved metaphysical beliefs congenial to them.

Schleiermacher now refused to accept the view that beliefs are a condition of vital religion. He was "opposed," he said, "to the view that the feeling of dependence itself is conditioned by any prior knowledge of God."[177] He made his position very clear in some public letters explaining what he had intended in the first edition of The Christian Faith. One of his opponents, he said,

appears to believe that feeling comes from the representation, and as he clearly expresses it, the ultimate basis of faith always remains the insight into the necessary connection of comprehended ideas; so I must always return to this, that what I understand by pious feeling does not at all come from representations, but is the original expression of an immediate existential relation.[178] . . . The feeling [he says] is primitive, and the thought does not arise until there is reflection on the feeling.[179]

His breach with tradition on the importance of belief in doctrines for religion was paralleled by his disagreement with the past about the nature of doctrines and the method by which they are to be supported. It was generally believed within the church that the cardinal tenets of Christianity were capable of proof either by the natural reason (in the case of doctrines like the existence of God) or of authentication by divine revelation (e.g., in the Bible), the supernatural origin of which could be attested and demonstrated by appeal to the fact of miracles and the fulfillment of prophecy. Schleiermacher did not believe that the doctrines of Christianity could be demonstrated in this way (although we have seen that he thought the existence of God is presupposed by scientific method). Moreover, he did not think that the church ought to attempt to support its doctrines in the traditional way, because the philosophical defense of doctrines is irrelevant to theology. He said that if there is any philosophical knowledge of God,

we who are concerned with the teaching of the Christian faith can have nothing to do with it, because it obviously enough has no immediate relation to piety.[180] [Or again:] We renounce any other proof for the necessity or truth of Christianity, except the one each person carries in him, that he is aware that his piety could take no other form than this one, and that he feels himself satisfied in its historical and internal connection; and that is the proof of faith.[181]

The reason why an intellectual demonstration of doctrines is irrelevant for dogmatic theology is that theological doctrines are not to be presented as propositions to be made palatable to the intellect of the unbeliever for the sake of convincing him of the truth of Christianity; they are instead a description or expression of the religious experience which is prior to them and independent of them. Schleiermacher thought that religious doctrines have always been neither more nor less than this, and that where proofs and philosophy have been mixed with them it has been due to a misunderstanding which ought to be cleared away.

In beginning the discussion of the theory of religious doctrines which is defended in Schleiermacher's historically most important book, *The Christian Faith*, I shall first describe his view of the relation of theology to religion in a few words, and then offer a more expanded account. Schleiermacher's idea was that every human being has an innate capacity for religion, for the most perfect development of feeling. There will be differences in the form in which this capacity flowers into full being according to the tradition and influences under which its development has been nurtured. Thus Christian religious feeling has a unique nature because of the impact of the perfect religious consciousness of its founder upon the development of the religion of those who have become attached to the Christian tradition. Now according to Schleiermacher's view, a system of doctrines ought to be an empirical description or expression of the experience of persons (in the particular tradition of which the author of that system is a member) in which all phases of the religious development are considered systematically both in their historical connections and their relations to each other. Therefore his procedure is to examine the whole fabric of Christian doctrine, show how some parts are adequate expressions of Christian religious experience as he knows it and organize these parts into a systematic whole, rejecting other parts on the ground that they have to do with metaphysics, not religion, or that they are mistaken or confusing expressions of religious feeling.

Such is the essence of his "empiricism" in theology, of his view that theology is essentially a descriptive science whose object is the actual experience of persons who are members of a religious tradition. We must now explain some parts of his view more fully.

According to Schleiermacher's theory of ethics, it is desirable that every subjective experience should be objectified (as in a work of art which expresses it) and thereby communicated, that is, made a possible object of public enjoyment. This objectification may take any of several forms. It may occur in song or dance or in one of the more advanced types of art, such as sculpture, painting, or literature. Now religious "feeling" also, like everything subjective, should be communicated. In the less developed stages of culture and science it has been communicated only by means of art. At a later stage, however, it comes to be communicated verbally. "When the feelings are contemplated," he says, "they develop into thoughts."[182] "States [of feeling] can also be brought together and put under a concept."[183] Thus the form in which religious feeling is eventually communicated is that of verbal expressions (e.g., "I feel dependent upon God," "God created the world"). In the early stages of religion and science, however, these verbal expressions (because they are figurative and deal with the intangible), are likely to convey or communicate the feeling only very inexactly. This fact makes desirable some more developed technique of communication by which the feelings can be conveyed with more exactness. The science which develops and applies this technique is dogmatic theology.

Dogmatic theology, Schleiermacher says, is only a means of exact and systematic expression of feeling; it is "an analytic consideration of the original pious states of feeling,"[184] for the purpose of making possible exact communication. There are two other forms of religious expression in current use besides this "descriptively didactic" form: the poetic and the rhetorical (e.g., hymn singing and preaching).[185] But dogmatic theology has an advantage over these in that "they carry in themselves the vestiges of their one-sided origin, and fall into conflict with themselves, which can be resolved only through manifold connection with that upon which there is agreement, and through setting up a rigorous system."[186]

Dogmatic theology consists of two parts: first, "the effort to exhibit the excitations of the Christian pious consciousness in doctrine, and second, the effort to bring into exact connection what is expressed in doctrine."[187] The first part is an instance of the normal tendency to make all subjective states an object of contemplation, to grasp them in thought, and to communicate them; the second part exhibits the normal scientific tendency, the essence of which is to introduce systematic connection into experience.[188] Parallel to these two parts of dogmatic theology, the ecclesiastical value of a doctrine is in the completeness with which it expresses the feeling.[189] The scientific value, on the other hand, is the "manifoldness of its connections with other doctrines[190] . . . the less it occasions apparent contradiction, and the more significant all that is, to which it points either forward or backward."[191] Thus the proper task of dogmatic theology as a science is to avoid confusion by as rigorous a scientific form as possible.[192] In other words, dogmatic theology is to express and describe religious feeling, and to do so by a systematic connection which makes clear the various types of feeling, their relations to each other and to other facts.

The aim of dogmatic theology as a science is not to deduce the truth of any assertions about the world supposedly contained in it, but simply to organize the communication of religious experience in order that its nature may be understood clearly and completely. So it is not, he says, "deduction from a highest principle," (although as we have seen there is a deduction of the concept of religion) but

its absolutely given is an inward fact, and what we have to develop out of it is only the different ways in which this fact is modified and appears in different relations. The task of organization is only so to construe those modifying relations that they appear as a perfect whole, and thus the infinite manifoldness of the particular is viewed in a definite plurality.[193] [Again he says:] My systematic art, if I may boast of one in dogmatic theology, is not connected with principles and deductions . . . but is simply talent in discovering such formulae of division, that one gets thereby a conviction of the completeness of the treatment, and that one, if not immediately, still mediately is brought back by every dogmatic proposition to the immediate self-consciousness represented in it.[194] [In fine] I have always represented the task to myself, from the very beginning, as a delineation of the self-consciousness developed in the Christian church, as we have it in us, in all its expressions, so that it should appear in every single moment as pure as possible, and so that the single instances which arise in this way can be viewed together and can approximate to unity, just as the feeling itself is always the same, whether it be connected with the consciousness of our freedom, or with that of natural connection, or with historical development. My dogmatic doctrine of God is to be explained purely from this conception of the task.[195]

Since dogmatic theology is simply a systematic expression of feeling, according to Schleiermacher, it is independent of philosophy and the other sciences, at least in so far as any empirical science is independent. Dogmatic theology has religious feeling for its datum just as any other discipline has certain facts as its data. It presupposes no metaphysics any more than any other science. It starts with no proof making legitimate the belief in God. It starts with a given fact and all it does is to describe this fact systematically. Metaphysics and cosmology are not necessary for religious feeling and not relevant to the dogmatic theology which is its expression. This is Schleiermacher's empiricism in theology.

Although it is Schleiermacher's contention that all doctrines should be scientific expressions or descriptions of religious experience in its manifold connections, Schleiermacher's doctrines (omitting the introductory philosophical part on method, etc.) fall into two rather different groups. One of these types of doctrine is really empirical in character (with the exception of some minor inconsistencies). The other part, in contrast, seems to be much more metaphysical, at least on first examination. We shall deal with both of these parts in turn; the second, apparently nonempirical part, is of greater interest to the philosopher.

The empirical part of theology exhibits Schleiermacher's realistic grasp of the religious life and its conditions. The interpretations of Christian doctrine which he suggests have on this account rightly had a wide influence. I shall illustrate his method by examples: (1) The authority of the Bible. Schleiermacher rejects altogether proofs of the Bible's or Christ's authority by appeal to a record of miracles or fulfillment of prophecies in the Bible. He paradoxically puts it the other way about: one will not accept the authority of the Bible unless one already has faith in Christ. Faith is awakened by the direct impression of the personality of Christ and not by external proofs of authority.[196] The Bible is, however, a normative presentation of the Christian faith. It is normative in the sense that its writers were near to Christ and were able therefore to present a pure statement of the spirit of his life and teaching because of their vivid memory of him. There is no foundation for any belief that the Scriptures were written under special supernatural or mechanical influence; they can be regarded as inspired only in the sense that they were written under the influence of the spirit of Christ among the apostles.[197] (2) The Virgin Birth. This doctrine is dealt with quite briefly. Schleiermacher holds that in some sense it is proper to say that there was supernatural activity involved in the conception of Christ, else the union of sinful natures would not have resulted in Christ's perfection. (Possibly he is not quite consistent at this point.)[198] But he does not think that any real explanation of the possibility of Christ's nature is furnished simply by asserting the absence of male participation in the generation. So, to his mind, the doctrine of the Virgin Birth is without any significance for the religious consciousness and he is ready to drop it out. (3) The Eucharist. Schleiermacher thinks that private meditation and public services of worship are necessary for the periodic renewal of the religious consciousness secured through relation to Christ. The Lord's Supper is the supremely effective act of renewal, by virtue of the unique manner of the presentation of Christ to the worshipper.

Not all of Schleiermacher's doctrines are as free of traditional ways of thought as the examples mentioned. Schleiermacher was careful to avoid offense as much as possible. But in general he intended to supply (and to a large extent succeeded in furnishing) an empirical account of the effect of Christ in the Christian religious consciousness, of the place of the church in the development of the religious consciousness, of the process by which the sensuous desires are subdued and the higher religious life introduced and so on.

A second and apparently different type of doctrine is to be contrasted with the foregoing examples. The attributes of God already discussed in a previous section provide an illustration of the second type of statement. These propositions do not seem to be descriptive or expressive of the religious man's "feeling"; they say nothing of the process by which "salvation" emerges from a state of sin or the conditions of that process, like Christ, preaching, the church, or the sacraments. They seem to be straightforward assertions about the objects of metaphysics, about which one might appeal to philosophical argument if one were interested in knowing whether they were true. Nevertheless Schleiermacher claims that they are in some way simply the expression or description of religious feeling.

It is difficult to know what exactly Schleiermacher means by saying that these Christian doctrines are an expression of feeling. For one thing, he is inconsistent in his use of the word "feeling." For the present, I shall assume that he is using the word to refer to some subjective state which is not and which neither explicitly nor implicitly includes a belief or judgment, such as "cheerfulness." Furthermore, "expression" might refer to any one of three relations: first, description, like the statement of an analytical psychologist about the character of some experience; or, second, expression, that is a form of words like an ejaculation which is conventionally attached to certain kinds of feeling (as "ouch" with pain) and which is therefore able to convey or communicate the kind of experience which the subject is undergoing. Or, third, it might refer to the expressiveness of a work of art. If this is what Schleiermacher meant, then doctrines would be a kind of poetry. Actually, it will be recalled, Schleiermacher distinguishes the dogmatic (as the descriptively didactic) form of expression from the poetic (hymns) and the rhetorical (preaching), so that we can be sure that he did not have this in mind, even if we are not clear about what he did mean.

The next step in analyzing Schleiermacher's meaning requires a decision about whether he intended that the statements in his book on theology should or should not mean literally what that form of words ordinarily means. Take the statement, "God is omnipotent." If Schleiermacher intended this statement to mean literally what it normally does, then the statement is asserting that there is some entity, God, and that that entity has a certain property, namely the property of omnipotence. Theological statements have generally been intended to be interpreted in this way (with reservations about analogical predication).

The difficulty with Schleiermacher's view, if he intends his theological statements to be taken literally, is that they cannot then possibly be either descriptions or expressions of feeling in the senses mentioned. At least they cannot if the fundamental propositions of theology are to be about entities like God, a point to which we shall refer again. They cannot be *descriptions* of "feeling," for it is one thing to say that a feeling is of a certain sort and it is another thing to say that God has a certain property. They could be descriptions of the *content* of "feeling," if Schleiermacher were to use the word in its intentional sense, as a kind of intuition (or in the sense of a "conviction") which could have a content. We shall return to this possibility again, but for the moment I am ruling out this possibility and assuming that Schleiermacher used the word "feeling" univocally in the sense defined.

Second, if they are to be interpreted literally, neither can dogmatic statements be considered *expressions* of feeling. Some persons (e.g., logical positivists) hold that theological statements are expressions of feeling and are not to be taken literally. (It has recently been argued* that the only real expressions of feeling are ejaculations like "ah" or "ouch," and that expressions in the verbal form of propositions are never merely expressions of feeling. If this is true, then the statements in Schleiermacher's theology cannot be regarded as solely expressions of feeling, although it is possible that he thought they were.) We can illustrate this view by examining the statement, "The Lord is my shepherd." Traditionally (that is, on the literal theory) this statement would be taken to mean that there is an analogy, or similarity of relation, between the relation of God to me and the relation a shepherd has to his sheep. Interpreted in this way, the statement would be false either if there is no God at all or if God is not a loving God interested in some way in the well-being of human persons. On the non-literal expressive view of meaning, however (which the positivists use in interpreting theological statements), the statement in question would not be made false by, for example, the nonexistence of God. For it is not asserting anything about God. It is only expressing perhaps my feeling of confidence

* Cf. W. M. Urban, *Language and Reality*, and Scheler, *Der Formalismus in der Ethik*, p. 173.

in a situation which otherwise looks very hopeless. One might say that it is a true statement if I really have the feeling which people will think I have if I use the phrase, and false if I do not.

It is easy to see that if a theological statement is to be interpreted literally, it cannot be merely an expression of feeling. It is of course possible that Schleiermacher may not have analyzed very carefully what it means for a form of words to be an expression of feeling, and consequently he may have thought that a proposition could have objective reference and at the same time be an expression of feeling. If so he was mistaken. And we shall see that Schleiermacher certainly must have made either this error or one related to it.

We have thus far only pointed out the problem that is set for Schleiermacher if he tries to say at the same time both that dogmatic propositions are literally true, and that they are expressions or descriptions of human states of feeling. It must now be shown that Schleiermacher does in fact hold that dogmatic propositions are literally true (again with the traditional reservations about analogical predication about God). Reference to Schleiermacher's discussion of the attributes of God in a previous section will probably convince the reader that Schleiermacher's theology is about God and not merely about human feelings. There is a fact, however, which makes one hesitate to infer directly from his discussion of God that his dogmatic statements have objective reference. This fact is that Schleiermacher himself says that dogmatic statements about God and the world have only a secondary and derivative position in theology, and that the only fundamental and underivative propositions in theology are those which describe human states of mind. Propositions about God and the world are not even a part of theology, he says, unless they are "reducible" to propositions of the other kind; and therefore they may be regarded as ultimately superfluous. He even suggests that he has introduced such derivative statements into his book only because otherwise his work would have "no connection with the past."[199]

I do not think the difficulty facing him would be materially decreased even if we dropped out of consideration these statements about God and the world which most obviously seem to be statements not about human feelings but about the world, and dealt with propositions only of the more fundamental type. I shall shortly indicate why this is the case. Nevertheless, what he says to the contrary notwithstanding, when one examines the manner in which he "derives" the secondary statements about God and the world, there does not seem to be justification for drawing a sharp line between the two.[200] And if this is correct, then there are some theological statements which are meant literally and assert objective facts about extramental entities, and in this respect do not differ from philosophical assertions, even if they differ in origin and purpose. An example of such a literal assertion (and it is difficult to take it other than literally) is his statement that the doctrine of preservation expresses Christian feeling better than the doctrine of creation, and that the "creation of the particular things is by the preservation of the species to which they belong, because the renewal of the individual already lies in the concept of the species."[201] How can it be said that Schleiermacher was here asserting only something about the feelings of religious people?

In addition there are scattered remarks by Schleiermacher which indicate that he himself recognized that the statements of his theological work have objective reference, and mean the same as would metaphysical statements of the same verbal form. For example, he said in the *Dialectic* that theological expressions about God can have only a limited *validity*.[202] If they were meant to be only descriptions or expressions of feeling, there could scarcely be any question of their validity or adequacy as descriptions of the nature of God. In the *Kurze Darstellung*[203] he says that speculative philosophy is concerned with "the God of our religious consciousness," thereby indicating that theological statements are concerned with the object thought about by metaphysics. Moreover, in the same breath in which he says that speculative and theological propositions

do not belong together and do not determine each other [he also remarks that they] must agree.[204] [Again he says:] Everyone whose speculative interest is awake must seek to become aware of an exact agreement between the expressions of it and the excitations of his pious feeling, because he can be conscious of the highest unity of his being only in the harmony of these two functions, which together form the highest stage of his being.[205]

But if theological statements are only expressions of feeling and philosophical ones are about reality, what could be the meaning of "harmony" or "agreement" between them? Surely he could not mean merely that they use the same verbal forms. Again, he admits that some systems are unsuitable as foundations for theology. He asserts: "The only views which are primarily unfit for use in dogmatic language are those which make no separation between the concepts of God and the world, admit no contrast between good and evil, and thus make no definite distinction in man between the spiritual and the sensual."[206] This implies something about the nature of theology; there are some views with which doctrine is incompatible, whereas one statement can hardly be incompatible with another if at least one is only an expression of feeling and not an affirmation of some other fact.[207]

I shall now explain the reasons why even Schleiermacher's "fundamental" forms of religious doctrines cannot be either an expression or description of feeling. We may take as our illustration of the most fundamental religious statement, "We are conscious of ourselves as absolutely dependent, or (what is to say the same thing) of being in relation with God."[208] It is clear from the use to which he puts this statement that it is not merely poetry calculated to arouse a certain mood in the hearer, and that it is not intended to be a meaningless statement (in the sense of the logical positivists) which expresses the feelings only like an ejaculation. It is not "expressive" of our feeling, if we use the word "expressive" in the sense defined and if we use the word "feeling" to refer, as I have previously defined it, "to a subjective state (like cheerfulness) which is not, and which neither explicitly nor implicitly includes, a belief or judgment." Nor is it a description of feeling in the senses in which these words have here been given. It may be a description of something, but it is not a description of feeling in the sense defined, for it is clear that there is in the statement a reference which points beyond the feeling and has to do with a kind of reference or content of feeling—suggesting that Schleiermacher is using the word "feeling" in a sense different from that which for reasons which will appear shortly I have chosen to define.

I have been defining feeling as a subjective state which cannot have a content in the way in which a belief or a judgment can. It follows that if Schleiermacher's doctrinal statement includes reference or content in a manner similar to beliefs or judgments, he cannot be describing a feeling in my sense.

Schleiermacher seems to have landed himself in a flat contradiction by believing both that propositions in theology have literal meaning and that they are descriptions or expressions of feeling (it being assumed that he was using "feeling" in the sense defined).*

It is not altogether plausible, however, to conclude that an able theological thinker, after many years of study and reflection, made the mistake of putting such a contradiction at the very heart of his theological system unless one can point to some fact which might easily have misled him. I do not believe that it is impossible in this case, both because at the present time one is able to make use in analysis of materials and distinctions which were not familiar to him and would not have seemed clear to him, and also because his discussions of fundamental issues always seem to be the least happy, a fact which suggests that he himself was less clear about the foundations than about the superstructure. But our conclusion will be more convincing if it is possible to point to some complexity in the phenomena Schleiermacher was describing, which might easily have led him astray.

The reader especially of The Christian Faith will be impressed by what appears to be a simple equivocation in the use of the word Bewusstsein (consciousness). Schleiermacher seems to use the word, as suits his purpose, sometimes to refer to a noncognitive "feeling" (in the sense defined) and sometimes to refer to an act analogous to belief, that is, to refer to a consciousness of something, such as the consciousness of being a finite object conditioned by God. This equivocation appears to go far to lighten his task of explaining how doctrines can be the expression of feeling. For doctrines (even when taken literally) can be an expression of "consciousness" when he is using the word in its intentional sense, and they can also be said to be an expression

* It is possible that Schleiermacher may have been using the word "feeling" to denote a religious conviction, a subjective state including both emotions and beliefs. He may possibly mean that this conviction is independent of philosophy in that it arises naturally in Christianity through the impression made by Christ's personality. In this case, he would have a logical right to talk of propositions as "expressions of feeling." But obviously such an interpretation would make him inconsistent in many other places. And the uniqueness and value of his theory would be sacrificed, for he would then be saying only that doctrines express beliefs or convictions, without attempting to prove them true; the proof of them is given by philosophy and science.

of feeling (as I have defined it), for the word is also used in a non-intentional sense.[209] The plausibility of his argument seems to depend upon his shifting back and forth from one sense to another.

On the assumption that Schleiermacher was unaware of any deceitful inconsistency in the use of language, however, the reason for his apparent self-contradiction must be traced back further to the phenomena themselves. Can it be made clear how an honest thinker could use words in this way while under the impression that he was consistently and honestly describing the phenomena?

My suggestion is that the phenomenon of the religious "feeling of dependence" was not completely analyzed by Schleiermacher, and that this fact is the ground of his difficulty. I do not wish to argue about his inconsistency in emphasizing this aspect of religious experience so much in The Christian Faith, when in other places his description is so different. He had fastened on one real fact in religious experience which he thought would serve his purpose of developing a dogmatic theology, and whether consistent or not this attempt should be judged on its own merit. Schleiermacher is perfectly correct that there is such a phenomenon as a "feeling of dependence" (although psychologists would now regard even the emotional component as complex), and that this phenomenon is a subjective one in the sense that we can know that we have it without going beyond direct experience, in the sense that we are not surprised when others do not have it, and also in the sense that the empirical subject is more intimately related to it than it is to the perception, for example, that a stone is heavy. Nevertheless, the phenomenon is a very complex one and Schleiermacher's error, I believe, lay in a mistaken classification due to failure to take account of all its features. Because the "feeling of dependence" resembles affective states like cheerfulness or sadness or pleasantness in some respects, he seems to have concluded that they must be alike in other respects, or at least in the respects important for his contentions.

The "feeling of dependence" in fact differs from feelings like cheerfulness in that it leads beyond the subject to something outside; it makes a claim on the world which can be contradicted. It is intentional in character. It has an arrow, a reference, which points beyond itself and out of the subject's experience altogether, toward something else. On this account a natural way of expressing it is to say: "I feel that I am dependent on something." Now it is clear that a feeling of dependence is not merely an intellectual judgment. It has its emotional components which are essential to it. But equally essential to it is a certain "structuring" of experience which includes reference to a transsubjective object independent of the subject, a meaningfulness of the situation of myself in my environment. Without that structuring and meaningfulness involving a transsubjective object the emotional components do not occur; they are dependent on it. The "feeling of dependence" makes a claim on the facts.

For this reason a "feeling of dependence" can be "expressed" (at least in part and in a peculiar sense of "express," with which we are perfectly familiar in ordinary speech) by a proposition having objective reference. And it can be contradicted by a statement asserting something discrepant with the proposition which "expresses" it. It is for this reason that Schleiermacher rejects many doctrines as incompatible with religious feeling. He remarks in one place that if a certain (untenable) doctrine were accepted, the "basic feeling of religion would thereby be destroyed."[210] If religion is feeling in this sense, it has to do with ideas, propositions, and claims to know.

The complete independence of theology as a "science" based on the datum of religious feeling cannot be preserved on this theory of feeling. It could be preserved if the religious feeling were some affective state like cheerfulness which makes no claim upon the facts; it was for this reason that I began by trying to understand feeling in this sense, and showing that it is impossible to regard theological statements as an expression of it. There is another possibility which would save the independence of theology; this is that the religious feeling is itself an immediate intuition of the religious object. I shall consider this possibility in a moment.

My view of the logic of The Christian Faith is therefore as follows. Schleiermacher rightly holds that religious people "feel" dependent on God. (At least this was true of persons like Luther or Augustine.) From this fact he derives statements about God which he regards as expressions of the feeling. This view of doctrines is a possible one if he had in mind an analysis of feeling such as I have offered. But this view of feeling makes religion and theology intimately related to philosophy, which is the investigation of the truth of the assertions which the religious consciousness is making. The "feeling of dependence" is an empirically given fact, but because of its very nature it is not a fact which can stand alone, but points toward and makes a claim about something which goes beyond itself.

Of course he could still hold that theology is an independent science in the sense that religion is an instinctive, natural, and "necessary" activity which can be described without any reference to metaphysics; and in the sense that dogmatic theology is a verbal "expression" of religious feeling which is required for the maintenance of the institution which supports that experience; and in the sense that these convictions of religious feeling can be stated without raising or attempting to solve the problem of whether they are true, and that their proof or coincidence with the results of metaphysics is of secondary importance to theology, whose purpose is the nurturing of faith. Perhaps he meant to assert no more than this: certainly many of the passages I have cited are consistent with it, as was his belief that there is not in any case any knowledge of the nature of God. But if this were all he meant to say, then his theology stopped short at precisely the crucial point; it ignored what Hegel called the "tragic earnestness" of religion, the fact that the religious man cannot stop at mere conviction, but must meet the demand of the intellect to know whether the content of his conviction is actually the truth. If he meant that theology is only a description of the content of faith, he stopped short of considering the one problem the intellect believes it is essential for the religious thinker to solve.

It is possible, however, as I have suggested, that he meant to assert that there is an immediate awareness of the divine object in the religious feeling, and that religion and theology are independent of philosophical thought for that reason. He may have thought that the feeling of dependence includes within itself a direct intuition of the fact that we are dependent. He may have believed that one cannot have this feeling of dependence without being dependent, or on the other hand, to use his example, one cannot feel free without actually being free. On his view that feeling is self-consciousness, he may have thought that feeling must, or at least does, contain or express this fundamental metaphysical fact about the self, that it is conditioned by something other than itself. Thus the religious experience would be self-validating. But if he did think so, he should have offered a more extended defense of his idea. It is true that there is a sense in which feeling expresses the well-being of the self; for example, normally pain is felt when the self is being injured. There is a sense in which any subjective experience is an expression of the self's being; that is, if we knew enough we could infer from it something about the functioning of the psychobiological organism. But that is far from saying that a feeling of freedom is invariantly connected with actual freedom, or that a feeling of dependence is connected with actual dependence. It is obvious that people often feel either more or less dependent than they are. The existence of the religious feeling does not relieve the theologian of the task of substantiating the claims of the religious consciousness about the facts, and in order to do so he must do more than simply express feeling; he must justify the claims by laying out the bearing of all knowledge upon them, that is, he will have to justify them (if they can be justified) by philosophy.

If Schleiermacher's view that theology is an independent science is supported along this line of an immediate intuition in religion, there is in the nature of the case no way of making out a defensible case for him. As I have said, I am not at all sure that he meant to take up this position, for he asserts quite often that he is not trying to offer any proofs for the reality of the divine object. On the other hand, in statements he makes about the feeling of dependence it does seem as if he is claiming an immediate consciousness of God in feeling.

I wish to explain a little further the reasons for the indefensibility of the whole concept of supporting theological statements about God (and others of this more metaphysical sort, as distinguished from psychological and historical statements about the religious consciousness as a psychological fact) by an appeal to religious experience, for the difficulty is not peculiar to Schleiermacher's work but is inevitable for any theory which holds that theology, as a science of a nonnatural object, can be founded on·a set of data of this sort.*

The reason for the difficulty is that the claim of the religious man

---

* There is an able discussion of this point in Tennant's *Philosophical Theology*, vol. I, chap. 12.

always transcends what is immediately given in experience, just as any perceptual judgment asserts more than the content or aspect of the object experienced by the observer, and refers to independent but not given reality. In both cases it is clear that the isolated experience by itself is no certain warrant for the truth of the statement which goes beyond it. The experienced content sometimes turns out not to be the aspect of a real object which it was taken to be, and the whole history of modern theories of knowledge is testimony to the difficulty of showing that there are actually such independently real objects at all. Belief in the reality of the not-given, especially in the case of more hypothetical entities like those of physics, rests eventually on the logical system of the sciences, in which experiences and beliefs are made to support one another in a system which cannot seriously be denied as a whole, and the parts of which are so related logically that they in turn cannot be questioned without questioning the whole. The same is true of religious experience. The isolated experience does not afford logical support for a statement reaching beyond it to an independent divine reality. The feeling that a God is present in moments of aspiration does not prove it. If the experience is to be ground for belief in the being of God, it must be incorporated in a logical system of interlocking beliefs, so that it is shown that in the face of the experience the reality of God cannot be denied without calling into question a system of beliefs which cannot seriously be denied or which we at least think is probably true.

The possibility is open that religious experience can be used indirectly to establish the reality of its objects. It may be granted that there is no immediate assurance that a feeling or subjective state is an intuition of a transsubjective divine reality, but it may still be the case that the experience can be used as a datum on which to base an hypothesis in the same way in which the atomic theory is established to account for certain experimental facts.

It is clear that if religious experience is to be valuable for the purposes of the theologian, it must be utilized in this indirect way. But the theologian cannot hope to attain a convincing degree of probability for his hypothesis of a divine object unless he takes into account, along with religious experience, all the other evidence which has been embraced in the traditional arguments for God. The reason for this is to be found in an analysis of scientific method. The reason is, briefly, that an hypothesis about a divine object intended to explain the occurrence of religious experience would not stand in the same relation to the body of scientific knowledge in which the other statements of science stand to each other. The atomic theory, for example, is not justified simply by a few experiments but by its coherence with the entire body of physical knowledge. The objections raised by scientists to nonnatural hypotheses are not simply the expression of prejudice; they are objections based upon the fact that such hypotheses are incongruous with the experience of scientists in the development of their science. It is likely that most psychologists would prefer a naturalistic account of religious experience for the purposes of their science, even if they suspected that the divine object was actual. The nonnaturalistic hypothesis is not a "good" hypothesis; it does not suggest further experiments; it does not simplify the understanding of human behavior but rather brings in a factor not amenable to scientific treatment; it is not coherent with the whole of the science of psychology. For this reason any hypothesis about a divine object cannot be accepted as probable to any considerable degree unless the whole of the evidence for it is systematically marshaled. An argument for God cannot be plausibly based on religious experience alone. If it is to be established at all, it must be shown that the hypothesis of a divine being is a useful one for understanding a wider mass of evidence, for solving major puzzles in philosophy.

Philosophy is precisely the discipline which examines the bearing of our whole experience on these matters, and it would therefore seem that if an argument to a religious object is to be valid at all, it must be through metaphysical thinking. There are no valid short cuts. It is difficult to see how the existence of a science of theology, if this is to be separate from philosophy, is to be justified.

It may of course be argued that religious experience *is* an apprehension of the divine object, even if it cannot be known to be so. It may be said that the logic and methods of science and philosophy are not adapted to the divine object. Perhaps God exists, although the rational net is either not fine enough or not extensive enough to make knowledge of God possible. This may or may not be true, but if it is true theology ought not to be called a science.

We have seen how the attempt to maintain a position like Schleiermacher's, to defend the independence of a science of theology and to derive dogmatic statements from religious feeling, leads to grave difficulties. His earlier views were more correct—when he admitted that the fortunes of religion and theology are ultimately bound up with the system of knowledge. I have already suggested that there are several senses in which religious experience and theological dogmas are independent of science and philosophy. For example, religion often occurs independently of explicitly formulated beliefs. But this or any other kind of independence which might be mentioned does not quite touch the real issue. That is that certain claims about reality seem to be essential to the kind of life historically known as religious, and that these claims are sometimes contradicted by metaphysical systems, and their substantiation cannot be given by some single bit of experience but only ultimately (if at all) by the whole system of philosophical thought.

CHAPTER VII

SCHLEIERMACHER'S INFLUENCE

wwwwwwwwwwwwwwwwwwwwwwwwwwwwwwwwwwwwwwwwwwwwwwwwwwwwwwwwwwwwwwwww

An adequate discussion of Schleiermacher's influence, especially in Germany, would require a separate book. For his work in theology was so significant in bringing about a revision of the idea of the nature and purpose of theology that his books may be regarded as a substantial part of the root of modern theology. It is agreed on all sides that Schleiermacher has been the most important figure in Protestant theology since the time of the Reformation. Seeberg, in his *History of the German Church in the Nineteenth Century*, remarked that "one can say that all the work of the church on dogmatic theology in the nineteenth century acquired its ideals and its direction from Schleiermacher's work."[1] He set the climate of liberal theological opinion for the next generation, so much so that he has influenced even writers who either had not read him or repudiated him, because the influence which he left was in the air they breathed. Almost every theologian at the present time has therefore been affected by him either directly or indirectly.

Schleiermacher's vast influence has been partly due to the fact that his system is very adaptable. (One historian has remarked that, strangely enough, his doctrine of religious feeling and dogma enjoyed a good reception from liberal and orthodox theologians alike, for the reason that his view left the liberals free to stray as far from tradition as they pleased, while the orthodox felt perfectly free to continue using old modes of expression.[2]) But his real distinction rests upon his success in mediating between supernaturalistic theology and naturalism. He showed theologians a way in which they could both accept modern science and defend religion and theology. In this his contribution has been compared with that of Kant; it has been said that his transcendence of the opposition between naturalism and supernaturalism is similar to Kant's transcendence of rationalism and empiricism.

Both, it is pointed out, found solutions along the same line, that is, through an analysis of experience, the one basing a priori knowledge upon the nature of thought, the other basing religious doctrine on the fact of subjective religious feeling.[3] This comparison at least makes clear the outstanding place which Schleiermacher has held in the minds of leading theological writers.

During his lifetime and thereafter in Germany Schleiermacher enjoyed an enormous reputation not only as a theologian but as an historical scholar, a philosopher, and a scientist. His philosophical system (never published) did not have the systematic grandeur, the inclusiveness, and the considered finish of Hegel's, and probably on this account he did not establish a "school." But his lectures were widely attended because of his vast erudition, his original analysis, and his great suggestiveness. Owing to these qualities his ideas have borne fruit in German thought in many spheres outside of theology— a fact attested to by the bulk of the literature on the many sides of Schleiermacher's work.

Of these many lines of influence only two can be discussed here, that on theology and that on logic and epistemology. The impact of his publications in the romantic period can be only briefly mentioned. His contribution to the theory of education was significant in the development of German thought on that subject.[4] I have already mentioned the usefulness of his work on aesthetics, unfortunately little known in England and America.[5] His work on ethics has also exercised some influence in Germany. His share in reviving interest in the study of ancient philosophy, particularly of Plato, was a large one; and his approach to the composition of Plato's Dialogues is to be honored as one of the first attempts at a scientific analysis.[6] His internal criticism of the New Testament, his reconstruction of the life of Christ, and his examination of church history, as well as his endeavors in other fields, played a significant part in the progress of those studies, even though his work has today been superseded. His work on psychology and the theory of the state, however, has made little impression.

Before turning to the points of his major influence, I wish to recall the reception of his earliest publications (around 1800), which have been taken by many to be an illustration of the possible place of religion in the romantic view of life. Friedrich Schlegel praised the *Discourses* publicly in a review in the *Athenaeum* (although he remarked rightly that Schleiermacher had not yet achieved a fully organic view of the human mind); privately he seems to have been less enthusiastic, possibly because of somewhat strained personal relations between them at the time. The *Discourses* seem to have had some influence on his "Gespräche über Poesie," which appeared shortly after the publication of Schleiermacher's book.[7] Schlegel introduced the book to Novalis and Tieck, who read it most enthusiastically of all the romanticists. They planned to write a new book of songs and sermons for Christianity, in accordance with Schleiermacher's suggestion that there could be a new Holy Writ for Christianity.[8] This book was to be dedicated to Schleiermacher. The program was never carried through as planned, but it did result in the appearance of Novalis' religious hymns. Schleiermacher's ideas also found expression in other works of Novalis who because of his sensitive and lonely spirit was initially disposed to religiousness like that portrayed in the *Discourses*. His *Heinrich von Ofterdingen* displayed a religious attitude and an interpretation of religion plainly manifesting the growth from seeds planted by Schleiermacher's book. The same is true of his *Die Christenheit oder Europa*.

I have already mentioned the reception of the *Discourses* by Schelling and Hegel. At first Schelling was unappreciative, but later—despite the fact that he was critical of their too subjective theory of religion—he spoke warmly in praise of them. Both his idea of "intellectual intuition" and his view of religion show traces of the impact of Schleiermacher's work. Hegel's indebtedness to these early works was comparatively slight. His early essays on religion, as published by Nohl, show that his view of religion had been developed independently. There are passages in his *Systemfragment*, written in 1800,[9] however, which are so strikingly similar to the *Discourses* that we must believe that Hegel was at least encouraged by the confirmation he found in Schleiermacher's book, even if he found at the most only a few suggestions which he could use. Professor Haering believes that Schleiermacher's influence on Hegel did not extend at most beyond the introduction of the term "Universe" and suggestions relative to his idea of universal history (an idea which was in the air at the time, and had been emphasized by Herder).[10] Hegel commended the *Discourses* highly, although like Schelling he objected to their subjective tendency—a fault, at least of Schleiermacher's exposition, which Hegel was never able to forget. Commenting on the relation of Schleiermacher's work to the philosophical milieu in which it was written, he said:

> In the *Discourses*, nature is abolished as a collection of finite actualities and recognized as a Universe; so that the [subjective] longing [of Protestant religion] is recalled from its flight beyond reality to an eternal Beyond. The partition between the subject or knowing and the absolutely unattainable object is torn down, the pain atoned for in enjoyment, the endless striving satisfied in intuition.[11]

Hegel's reaction to *The Christian Faith* is discussed elsewhere.[12]

1. His Influence of Protestant Theological Thought

The justification of theologians' high estimation of Schleiermacher's work lies in its relation to the theological movements of his time, and its formulation of a new approach to theology which escaped many objections to the old and bore within itself the capacity for further development along a fresh line.

It will be recalled that after the Reformation several different tendencies had gradually found expression. First there was orthodoxy. After 1600 there was little to distinguish orthodox Protestantism from the Catholicism of the Scholastic period. Its philosophical foundation was similar. It was believed that there are evidences and arguments which enable the natural reason to establish the existence of God, the sinfulness of man, and so on. It was thought that God has, however, acted and revealed himself on man's behalf in a special way. The record of this revelation and action is contained in the Bible. The whole of the Bible is inerrant because of the miraculous inspiration by God of the writers of its several books. The inspiration of its authors, it was held, has been attested by performance of miracles and fulfillment of prophecies. Salvation is to be had by belief in the Bible, and especially in the doctrines of the work and significance of Christ taught therein, but belief must be accompanied by moral conduct (including worship), as it has been commanded by God in his revelation.

In England and later in Germany, this orthodox theology became the target of the rationalistic Deists. The Deists did not question certain fundamental assumptions of orthodoxy, such as its belief in the existence of God, and the future punishment of man for his sin; but they did come to question (encouraged by the development of science and a scientific attitude toward the world) the features of orthodoxy which had more specifically to do with Christianity. There were various grades of heterodoxy among the English Deists, and most of them did not deny the actuality of a special revelation by God in Christ and the Bible. But, tired of theological dissention, they came more and more to whittle away at the special significance of Christianity in favor of the religion of natural reason. They pared away the elements of Christianity which they regarded as mysterious and above reason. They questioned the reality of any work of Christ on behalf of man other than his being a specially clear and needed revelation of the will of God—the nature of which could have been known by human reason from the beginning, but which had been obscured by human sin and therefore needed to be republished. For example, they adduced moral reasons for the impossibility of Christianity's being a new and necessary means of salvation; it would not have been fair, they argued, for God to have withheld the means of salvation until such a recent date. Attention was directed upon factual inaccuracies and evidences of a low moral level in both the Old and the New Testament, in order to shake confidence in the infallibility of the Bible as a whole. The orthodox had based the authority of the Bible on attestation by miracles and the fulfillment of prophecies. The Deists now threw doubt on the reality of fulfillment of prophecies, and they raised questions about the validity of arguments from the alleged occurrence of miracles to the infallibility of the ideas of persons supposed to have performed them. For the Deists, belief in God, virtue, and worship comprised the requirements for salvation.

Two further opposite movements grew up, at least partially as the result of the influence of orthodoxy and Deism. Both of them were skeptical of the capacity of human reason. One of them was theological skepticism; the other was Pietism in Germany (Evangelicalism in England). Hume is the best example of English skepticism; Kant, although he was favorable to religion, held that it was impossible to give a rational foundation to belief in the existence of God along the lines of traditional theological thought, and affirmed that religion is simply the acceptance of the moral law as a divine command. By 1800 the success of the natural sciences and the freedom of thought and discussion had diverted a large element to the ranks of skepticism.

The Pietistic and Evangelical movements also disparaged the capacities of human reason. But they did so in favor of an active commitment to the ideals of Christianity. Like the Reformers (especially Luther) they seem to have suffered but little from intellectual difficulties in Christian theology. For them Christ was not merely a new revelation of God, but a necessary means of redemption from sin. They opposed orthodoxy's emphasis on the importance of intellectual assent; for them a new life through contact with Christ, expressing itself in loving service to others and through emotional experience, was the essence of religion. In England it was the Deists who were theologically farthest removed from the new evangelical group.*

Of these four groups, Schleiermacher undoubtedly felt himself nearest in spirit to the Pietistic movement. He always remained very sympathetic to the type of religion which he had known in his boyhood, and it will be recalled that he said he would gladly rejoin the Moravians if it were not for their theology, which, however, he did not regard as the kernel of their religion. He also once referred to himself as one of them, only "of a higher order." By this he probably referred both to theological differences and also to the molding which his religious experience had undergone as a result of contact with Spinoza, the romantic movement, Plato, and the German idealists. He felt himself closest to the Pietists, of these several groups, because he felt that among them a religion "of the heart" had become real. The religious experience which he himself so strongly felt and valued he thought to be foreign to the other groups, who made it a matter of beliefs and external observances.

One of the main themes of Schleiermacher's theological work was

* In addition to the groups I have mentioned, there was at the time of the publication of The Christian Faith a party of speculative idealists, followers of Hegel, among the theologians. Schleiermacher's book was roundly criticized by its many reviewers, even by those who were closest to him, like Fries. A good summary of the various reviews of The Christian Faith is to be found in Karl Dunkmann's "Die Nachwirkungen der theologischen Prinzipienlehre Schleiermachers" in Beiträge zur Förderung christlicher Theologie, vol. XIX, 1915.

that religion is a unique activity of the human spirit, which consists neither in arguments, proofs, and ideas, nor in being morally upright and worshipping God in specified ways. This point Schleiermacher drove home so thoroughly and emphatically that, even if his
statement was one-sided and exaggerated, the truth in it was not
and cannot now be forgotten.

Schleiermacher did not assert that there is anything mysterious about
this activity of spirit. It is not produced by a mechanical and magical
act of God (a point on which he broke away from most previous theological thought). It is simply the most perfect development of the
affective side of the life of man, which in the Christian tradition is
inspired by contact with the personality of Christ through the community of believers. It is a fact which is open to the scrutiny of science, which ideally should be able to see its continuity with social and
aesthetic experience, and the way in which it is the rounding off of
the human personality.

A second main theme of Schleiermacher's theological thought was
his idea that this spiritual activity is autonomous, immediate, not only
different from but (in his later works) independent of the results of
thought or moral conduct. Religion is an activity grounded in the universal essence of man just as is the manner in which man organizes
sense experience by thought. Religion is an "infinite force." Eduard
Zeller, writing on Schleiermacher's view of the personality of God,[13]
said that his chief historical significance lies in the fact that he
attempted to show that the content of the Christian faith is somehow
the original property of the human mind, evolved from its own
deepest nature and not brought in from outside through a mechanical
transmission of information from God. This statement is essentially
correct. Religion, according to Schleiermacher, is a universal and
essential tendency of mind. It does not need to be induced artificially.
It is natural, and the human spirit is not fully developed until it has
become religious. Religion does not need to be created in a person,
although the tendency to be religious may need to be released (for
example, by Christ). But it is an innate capacity for experience—and
the experience does not depend on the results of other activities of
mind (upon philosophical proofs, for example), but is an independ-

ent activity which has to be taken account of both by the scientific and practical sides of human nature.

It is because religion is an autonomous spiritual activity, it is because the content of faith is brought up from the depths of mind (the feeling of dependence, the spirit of love) that there can be a science of faith which is not simply a collection of speculative arguments and deductions from proof texts—an empirical theology.

On the basis of these assumptions Schleiermacher was prepared to deal with the criticisms coming from the Deists, from the skeptics, and from science. It was not necessary for him to defend the infallibility of Scripture, for as he said, faith does not depend on Scripture but Scripture gets its authority from the fact of faith. So it was possible for Schleiermacher to take a very liberal attitude toward the Bible. He accepted and encouraged the work of the critics of the Bible and he was able to acknowledge errors in the book, since he did not have to assume the orthodox doctrine of inspiration. The Bible he could regard as a natural product of human minds thinking under the influence of the impression of Christ and the spirit of the early church. For similar reasons he did not have to defend the evidential value of miracles, or the fulfillment of prophecies. The mere fact that an event cannot be understood at the present time does not make it of any special significance for the religious consciousness.

The old contrast between reason and revelation took an entirely new turn in his system; it became the contrast between scientific thought and religious experience. Supernaturalism was ruled out, for both science and religion are "natural," when the natures of the world and of man are properly understood.

The result of Schleiermacher's theory was that it was not necessary to defend the actuality of sporadic interruptions of the course of nature by the Deity; his emphasis was on the immanence of God, and he could say that God is present in scientific thought, in moral conduct, and in any religious experience or insight and not merely in certain special events. As we have seen, Schleiermacher's actual view of the activity of God was more pantheistic than most theists would wish to allow, but it was not necessary to read his theological works in that manner.

Schleiermacher's views also enabled him to dispense with a number of other traditional doctrines the defense of which before science and philosophy was a serious difficulty for the church. When he reinterpreted, on the basis of his view that theology is an empirical description of the religious consciousness, such doctrines as creation, original sin, the atoning work of Christ, the presence of the Holy Spirit among men, the church's "power of the keys of heaven and hell," and others, these doctrines were no longer supernatural mysteries but expressions of some fact in the experience of the church which was real and defensible. Schleiermacher hoped that on the basis of his work it would not be possible for science and philosophy to accuse religion of alliance with superstition.

Schleiermacher thus offered a view of religion and theology which apparently made them secure against attack, not by dropping essential parts of it but, as he claimed, by purifying it and striking out alien elements which had entered through misunderstanding. Schleiermacher's theology seemed to answer the challenges of Deism, rationalism, and skepticism, while preserving what was valuable and true in Pietism and orthodoxy.

Schleiermacher did not actually refute orthodoxy. But his work had the effect of superannuating it. He presented an alternative more suited to the modes of thinking, the intellectual currents of a critical and scientific age. He offered a mode of approach to religion more satisfactory to the mind of the nineteenth century, more congruent with its science and philosophy. Therefore largely as a result of his work, the great mass of Protestant theologians of the succeeding generation followed him in his distinction of religion from knowledge and conduct, his break away from dogmas supernaturally transmitted to infallible oracles, his insistence upon the autonomy of religious experience, his view that theology is a description of this experience in some sense. Attention was focused on the nature and value of the religious consciousness itself. This is true even of many theologians who remained predominantly orthodox; it was striking in the case of men like Ritschl, Herrmann, and Troeltsch, who were all heavily indebted to Schleiermacher.

The discoveries of Darwin which were a hard blow for orthodoxy supported Schleiermacher's view of religion. Schleiermacher and

Darwin were probably the two persons most directly responsible for the shaping of modern Protestant religious thought.

The philosophy of Troeltsch offers an interesting example of the remarkably strong influence of Schleiermacher's idea of the autonomy of religion at a very recent date. Troeltsch said that the Kant-Schleiermacher view (which he regarded as the idealist alternative to materialism) is that there is a "possibility of seeing in religion a qualitatively individual and creative power of spiritual life."[14] He believed that there can be a scientific defense of religion, and that it consists in making clear, through an analysis of the psychological and historical facts of religion, the a priori law of the formation of religious ideas or events in the human spirit, and the relation of this law to the other laws of mind. This view is only a development of Schleiermacher's idea, to which Troeltsch expressly attached himself.

Probably the best known contemporary German theologian who acknowledges that his fundamental principles come from Schleiermacher is Professor Georg Wobbermin. Following along the lines laid down by Schleiermacher, Wobbermin argues that the most important desideratum for the philosophy of religion is the determination of the nature of religion, viz., of the moving-spring of religious phenomena in the mind of the religious man. What is needed for the understanding and defense of religion, he says, is appreciation of the "fundamental underlying motive of religious life common to all forms of religious expression."[15] Professor Rudolf Otto is a second well-known German theologian much influenced by Schleiermacher, although his work has been more affected by the writings of deWette and Fries. Professor Karl Heim of Tuebingen is another contemporary writer who has taken a great deal from Schleiermacher.

Almost all German theologians since Schleiermacher's time have been influenced by him to some extent, and therefore to mention those who have followed the main lines of his thought to a greater or less degree is practically to mention the leading figures of German theology since his time. There was naturally considerable variation in the extent to which the details of his view were acceptable to individual theologians. One must say that it is the general tendency of Schleiermacher's work which has been historically influential, rather than the detailed elaboration of his system. Most of his contemporary theologians were sharply critical of him on many important issues, and *The Christian Faith* was roundly criticized by many of its reviewers, although most of them were also aware of its importance. Of the writers prominent in Germany immediately after his death, those who could most appropriately be called disciples of Schleiermacher were Alexander Schweitzer, A. Twesten, C. J. Nitzsch, Richard Rothe, and Johann von Hofmann. Perhaps further away but very sympathetic were R. A. Lipsius, A. E. Biedermann, Dorner, and Julius Müller. Feuerbach and D. F. Strauss were also to some extent obligated to him, as were the more influential theologians I have already mentioned, like Ritschl and Herrmann, who received from him only general ideas. Two Continental writers of wider reputation among philosophers, who have received suggestions from his work, are Harold Höffding and Otto Pfleiderer.*

Schleiermacher's fundamental ideas have had a wide influence in English-speaking countries, both in the past and at the present time. V. F. Storr, writing of the development of British theology from 1800 to 1860,[16] acknowledges the very far-reaching effect which Schleiermacher's writings had in England. Storr says he was the "champion of experimental religion." Referring to the influence of his rejection of infallibility and inspiration, Storr says that it was "Schleiermacher more than anyone else who helped to dispel false opinions as to canonicity and inspiration."[17] In America Schleiermacher has been less directly influential than Ritschl, Herrmann, and Harnack (through whom of course his work has had an indirect effect), but Wieman and Meland point out that Horace Bushnell,[18] L. F. Stearns,[19] and W. N. Clarke[20] formulated his thesis that religious doctrines should be founded upon religious experience, although it is not clear that he had any direct influence on them.

Schleiermacher's main ideas have been widely influential among contemporary writers on theology. Professor E. W. Lyman has remarked that a study of Schleiermacher revealed to him the autonomy of religion.[21] Professor John Baillie praises Schleiermacher because he

* For an account of Schleiermacher's theological influence in Germany, one should consult Karl Dunkmann's, *"Die Nachwirkung der theologischen Prinzipenlehre Schleiermachers,"* in *Beiträge zur Förderung christlicher Theologie*, vol. XIX (1915); Kattenbusch, *Von Schleiermacher zu Ritschl*, 1891; and Ernst Schrecker, *Der Religionsbegriff in Schleiermacher*, 1890.

saw (according to Baillie) that religion has insight of its own which cannot be had in nonreligious cognitive experience.[22] This insight, he says, is obtained through the practice of religion and is superior to what is obtainable from any of the conflicting schools of philosophy. These acknowledgments of indebtedness are indicative of the contribution Schleiermacher has made to those theologians who build theology on the basis of "religious experience," and indeed anyone who thinks there can be an empirical science of theology thereby acknowledges at least indirect dependence upon Schleiermacher. In England, H. R. Mackintosh, C. C. J. Webb, John Oman, and H. H. Farmer are among writers of recent theological books indebted to him in this way. The same situation exists in America, with a somewhat different emphasis, especially among some of the younger theological writers.

There is some resemblance between Schleiermacher's ideas of religious experience and what is now called mysticism. The similarity is not very great and Schleiermacher was strongly opposed to mysticism like that of Boehme, which he thought was empty. He was opposed to intellectualism in religion; he emphasized the value of the higher spiritual life especially in its emotional phases; he thought that religious feeling could be understood only by those who had experienced it;[23] he regarded religious experience as the crown of human life; he was much more interested in religion as a personal experience than as an activity of a community, although he recognized that the latter is indispensable to the former; he thought that God is immanent in the world and that in some sense God is specially present in religious experience, more so than in any other event in the life of man. (Of course, all these phrases are to be understood in terms of Schleiermacher's theory of God and his general system of philosophy.) He came so close and no closer to mysticism. Modern mystics, however, have been able to find theoretical support in Schleiermacher's doctrine, partly in that he insists on the autonomy and self-vindicating character of the religious life, and partly in that he sometimes seems to assert that there is a special nonrational kind of insight in religious experience. Presumably on this account it has been said that most modern mystics like Rufus Jones, Evelyn Underhill, and Dean Inge are indebted to Schleiermacher in one way or another.[24]

A clear implication of Schleiermacher's idea is that there should be a special study of the psychology of religious experience. Schleiermacher himself, however, did not lay down any explicit program for this, and his own psychological analysis is quite defective. There is some controversy about the actual extent of his influence upon the development of this branch of psychology, and in general it appears that his direct influence was slight although his indirect influence must have been considerable.

A result of Schleiermacher's view of theology was that he was able to develop his system of doctrines in a much more systematic way than had previously been possible. The reason for this is that, following the methodological theorems laid down in his introduction, he relates everything in Christian thought to the religious consciousness of absolute dependence upon God, as mediated by Christ. The Christian doctrines of creation, preservation, the original perfection of man, and others, are shown to be an expression of the religious consciousness. Sin is explained in terms of conflict between the religious consciousness and the sensuous consciousness, and the process of redemption by Christ through the church is the process of the development of the religious life through the impression of Christ's personality. Schleiermacher reinterpreted the entire body of Christian doctrines on this basis, and the consequence was that Christian doctrines became an organic intelligible system. This had not been the case before. V. F. Storr writes that prior to Schleiermacher British theologians had evolved artificial systems of dogma, the doctrines of which showed no affiliation for each other, and the eduction of which from fundamental principles was not even attempted. (A similar situation prevailed in Germany.)[25] He says, "Schleiermacher did more than anyone else to effect a change in this matter, and to sketch for theology an evolutionary ideal which profoundly influenced the whole subsequent development of the science."[26]

Thus far I have mentioned only ideas of Schleiermacher's which have met with a generally favorable reception, at least among a large group of theological writers. They represent his large-scale positive contribution to religious thought. (There are of course many points of detail which theologians have been able to use.) But I shall now consider a matter on which there have been both disagreement about the interpretation of Schleiermacher and also a widespread critical reaction.

This disagreement is focused on his decision concerning the essential nature of religious experience, his view that religion is primarily a matter of "feeling," and that feeling is what is expressed in the statements of dogmatic theology. It has been generally agreed since his time that he was right in emphasizing the place of noncognitive or nonintellectual and nonpractical experience in religion, which had previously been neglected by theologians. On the other hand, there is very widespread agreement that if Schleiermacher meant by "feeling" simply affective states or emotional experience, he was mistaken in believing that the essence of religion is feeling and in believing that the affirmations of dogmatic theology can be derived from feeling.

There are two opposite interpretations of Schleiermacher on this point. Some writers hold that Schleiermacher himself saw that there is a special kind of religious insight or cognition (in the feeling of dependence on God, for example, or in the "intuitions" of his earlier thought), and that it is this cognitive experience that he was expressing or formulating in his theology. Baillie, Storr, Otto, Wobbermin, and Mackintosh are among those who believe that Schleiermacher thought there is special nonrational "knowledge" in religious experience. Wobbermin, for example, says that Schleiermacher's "feeling" included objective cognition, and that in particular its content was "precisely the Supreme Reality determining all existence."[27] Mackintosh says that "in the majority of passages, especially in his Dogmatic [The Christian Faith], Schleiermacher seems to mean by 'feeling' a laying hold by the soul of a trans-subjective Reality, supreme over the world. Feeling is an experience . . . in which the self 'apprehends' not itself but God."[28] The writers I have mentioned approve of this view which they attribute to Schleiermacher.

On the other hand, other theological writers deny that Schleiermacher believed anything of the sort. These writers are divided into two groups, those who think Schleiermacher ought to have insisted on this kind of intuition and those who believe he was right in not doing so, but who think that he was mistaken in trying to separate religion from and make it independent of philosophy. Wilhelm Herrmann belongs to the first of these two groups[29] as does Troeltsch, who remarked that Hegel's theological influence has been much stronger than Schleiermacher's at some points, precisely because he more adequately met religion's claim to be in contact with ultimate reality.[30] Of Schleiermacher's critics who believe that he should not have separated theology and religion so sharply from the reflective consciousness, the first to be mentioned is of course Hegel.* English-speaking writers influenced by him, including Baillie,† Lyman, and W. A. Brown, all protest against Schleiermacher's narrow limitation of religion to feeling, his too rigid separation of it from reflective thought, science, and philosophy. Wilhelm Herrmann, without denying that intuition has a place in religious experience, thought that Schleiermacher's segregation of religion from other modes of spiritual activity was adverse to the well-being of religion and a very superficial analysis.[31] Zeller took a slightly different line. Protesting that feeling is an appropriation of what is given in knowledge in the form of meanings and "not a capacity for a self-active production of a definite content," he charged that Schleiermacher's "consciousness of dependence" could not be a feeling at all but is an idea.[32]

Schleiermacher may not have intended to defend the reality of a nonrational intuition in religion, but it is this interpretation of him which has been most influential historically.

One fact is surely clear in the light of this controversy as well as our own analysis, and that is that Schleiermacher's explanation of his own view was not very careful or precise. Historically, this fact may well have been to his advantage. Being vague, his idea was elastic and adaptable. Had he carried through a rigorous analysis of his concepts of "feeling" and religious experience, it is quite possible that the idea would have proved less powerful.

2. SCHLEIERMACHER'S INFLUENCE ON EPISTEMOLOGY AND LOGIC‡

We must now take leave of Schleiermacher's work on theology and religion to consider his influence on logic and epistemology.

* See appendix II.
† Baillie says Schleiermacher believed in a special insight in religion but thinks he was mistaken in identifying religion so closely with feeling.
‡ Ueberweg's research in the history of logic has been freely drawn on in this section.

In philosophy proper, as in theology, Schleiermacher did not found a school, but there was nevertheless a group of philosophers who were influenced by him in varying degrees. Most closely dependent on his work were Heinrich Ritter[33] and Franz Vorländer.[34] Leopold George,[35] the editor of Schleiermacher's manuscript remains on psychology, was also close to him in logic and epistemology and attempted to mediate between him and Hegel. Writers on logic better known in English-speaking countries who have been influenced by him are Ueberweg[36] and Eduard Beneke.[37] There has apparently been contact between Schleiermacher's work and that of Trendelenburg, Lotze, and Sigwart, although in these cases the influence was slighter and the dependence is largely indirect.

Aside from the smaller points on which Schleiermacher made constructive suggestions, that to which the logical writers of last century owed most is expressed in the following remarks of Ueberweg:

Schleiermacher, whose philosophical significance appears to be overlooked only too often in comparison with his theological work, in his lectures on "Dialectic" has attempted to comprehend the forms of thought from knowledge as the purpose of thought, and to establish insight into their parallelism with the forms of real existence. This concept of the forms of thought is midway between the subjective-formal and the metaphysical logics, and is in agreement with the central ideas of Aristotle. The subjective-formal logic, represented chiefly by the Kantian and Herbertian school, asserts that the forms of thought are out of all relation to the forms of being; whereas the metaphysical logic, as Hegel formulated it, identifies the two forms and believes itself to have discovered the self-creation of being in the self-movement of pure thought. Aristotle, equally distant from both extremes, sees in thought a representation [Abbild] of being, which is different from its real correlate without being out of all relation to it, and which corresponds to it, without being identical with it.[38]

Schleiermacher believed that there is a parallelism between the forms of thought and the forms of things. He began with analysis of the meaning of "knowledge," and argued that if there is to be knowledge, there must be correspondence between thought and its objects—not merely between thought and the phenomenal "things," as Kant believed, but independently real objects existing in their own right. Schleiermacher next inferred that if this correspondence is to be possible, the forms of thought must be applicable to the real world, neither meaningless nor misleading when used to refer to the independently real. Coherently with this, he believed that the sense impressions caused by the interaction of external objects with the sense organs have themselves an implicit order responsive to the forms of thought; they are not merely passively receptive to the imposition of an alien form upon them because they are utterly formless in themselves, as Kant sometimes stated. Things can really be known as they are, not fully to be sure but at least to some extent, because of the harmony of the forms of intelligence with the nature of physical existents.

On the other hand, Schleiermacher never considered identifying experience and knowledge with their objects. Experience or thought is one part of the natural world, but there are other parts and it is the unique and further unanalyzable character of thought to reach out and apprehend the other part of reality, to reflect it as in a mirror. Furthermore, Schleiermacher recognized that thought, taken by itself apart from the sense experience which gives it content, is empty and meaningless. Thought can organize and mediate the given of its own strength, but it cannot construct the world dialectically even if granted the initial concept of being. Schleiermacher grasped firmly the two poles of thought, given sense experience and organizing "deductive" logic, and would not permit either to be suppressed in the analysis of expanding scientific knowledge. He was neither an Hegelian nor a sensationalist.

The fundamental theses of Schleiermacher's theory of knowledge were therefore that thought is different from its object, but is capable of reaching out and grasping it intellectually, since things and sense data are intelligible and capable of being ordered by thought. In this process thought is a spontaneous, organizing factor without which sense impressions could not become experience, but the given, with its implicit order, plays a role, providing content and guidance for thought which without the given would be empty and meaningless.

In contrast to many of his contemporaries, Schleiermacher was thus distinguished as a realist and an empiricist (not a sensationalist). It is not surprising that he influenced minds which rebelled at the

Hegelian system. The marks of his work can be seen in Ueberweg's summary of his own position in contrast to Kant and Hegel:

The essence of my objection to Kant [he said] lies in the proof of how scientific insight . . . is achieved not by means of a priori forms of purely subjective origin, which are applicable only to the objects of appearance present in the consciousness of the subject (and also not, as Hegel and others urge, a priori and nevertheless with objective validity) but through the combinations of facts of experience according to logical norms themselves conditioned by the objective order of things, adherence to which secures objective validity. I wish to show how in particular the spatiotemporal and causal order . . . is not brought into a chaotic given stuff by the intuiting and thinking subject, but is copied, through successive experience and thought of the subjective consciousness, in agreement with the reality in which it originally is.

Had Schleiermacher not been so preoccupied both with theology and practical concerns and had his work not appeared in so forbidding a form, he might very well have had a much greater influence here than he actually exercised. For there were in his thought the germs of a moderate empirical realism, and in many matters his theories displayed an accurate description of psychological facts.

I now enumerate a few less important contributions which Schleiermacher has made to the stream of philosophical thought. He was the first to suggest that awareness of the external reality of other persons is prior to the awareness of the impersonal external world and is the basis of the more general distinction between the subjective and the objective—an idea which has been developed by several writers. Second, his theory that judgment is the form for the expression of matter-of-fact relationships, especially causal relations as opposed to the timeless relations of essences, reappeared in practically the same form in the works of Ritter, Trendelenburg, and Lotze. Schleiermacher thought that a complete event included active and passive agents in a certain active relationship and he distinguished primitive, incomplete, and complete judgments according to the comprehensiveness and completeness with which the event is expressed. Thus the primitive judgment, for example, is the action unrelated to agent or patient, expressed in an impersonal verb. Third, he was one of the first to question the operation of conversion in traditional logic. He also doubted the usefulness of syllogistic argument, a matter on which he may have influenced Trendelenburg but where he seems to have gone somewhat too far.

There are other points of direct and indirect influence, but Schleiermacher's significance in the history of philosophy proper rests on his general view of the relation of thought to reality and his analysis of scientific thought.

RELIGIOUS INTUITION AND SCIENTIFIC KNOWLEDGE, 1803-1804

Before 1806, the year in which Schleiermacher brought out the revised edition of the *Discourses*, there was a period of time when his view of the relation of religion to science and philosophy was more than usually obscure. Of course the editions of the *Discourses* were not free from difficulty and confusion on this matter. But during this period he devised some statements which offer specially hard problems, possibly due to the fact that it was at this time that he was trying to work out a system. A more complete picture of his development makes desirable a brief discussion of these intervening years.

The earliest statement for consideration is in his review of Schelling's *Lectures on the Methods of Academic Study*. Here he agreed with Schelling's division of science into physics (the science of the objective side of the world) and ethics or the philosophy of mind (the science of the ideal or subjective side). These two sciences share between them all the possible subject matter for scientific study. Schleiermacher went on, however, to make a suggestion about the function of religion in contrast to these sciences. Religion, he said, must have the same subject matter as they, viz., the whole of the world. But it is distinct from them by virtue of its different method of approach. Science is devoted to ascertaining the necessary forms of reality, but "only in so far as they [the finite objects[8]] are thought of as a whole, and are related to the speculative side of knowledge. But in so far as the series of ideal and real appearances is observed historically [presumably without reference to the whole or speculative system in knowledge], the particular is still regarded as outside the Absolute and separate from it, and is in so far dissimilar to the Whole, the integral part of which it is."[1] This distorting isolation of the particulars from the whole, he said, should be overcome. The particular should also be seen for what it is, a part of the Absolute. This envisagement of the finite objects in the Infinite is the proper achievement of art and religion. Aesthetic creations manifest the Absolute by making the identity of the real and the ideal visible in a work of art. He said of religion: "The particular finite object, be it real or ideal, is immediately intuited in the Infinite, in which, of itself and always, the ideal and the real are viewed as one and the same, which occurs just by virtue of religion." The difference between art and religion is that art promotes the envisagement of the particular as a part of the Infinite by an objective creation, whereas religion accomplishes the same result in subjective intuition.

This suggestion, which at first seems attractively clear and simple, really turns out not to be so when one attempts to fathom the exact meaning of the religious "immediate intuition of the particular in the Infinite," and to distinguish it in some way from the scientific knowledge supposed to be different from it. How is the religious intuition to gets its content except as it appeals to the sciences or proceeds in a fashion similar to their methods? It will be recalled that it was difficult to understand his position on this point in the first edition of the *Discourses,* and there is no indication of a new solution in the review of Schelling. It rather appears that Schleiermacher was still treating religious intuition as a special kind of knowledge, without being willing to admit its dependence on the system of scientific and philosophical thought. Religion is knowledge without being science; but it is not clear what features of religious knowledge distinguish it from science without affecting its right to be called knowledge.

The suggestion that he simply placed religious intuition beside science as a different mode of knowing, without investigating their relations, finds some support in the lecture notes of the same period.[2] These notes discuss religion under the heading of "wisdom," of which Schleiermacher recognized four types: self-intuition, intuition of the world, aesthetic intuition, and philosophical speculation. Religion, he says, belongs primarily to the genus "intuition of the world," which is also the genus to which scientific knowledge belongs in contrast to philosophy, which is more "subjective." He says: "This principle [the intuition of the world] is concerned not only with scientific knowledge, but is the foundation of all intuition, and is in so far really the principle of religion, where all knowledge is posited as an intuition of God or in God. The sphere of its application, therefore, is not only nature in the narrow sense, but history. . . . The higher stage of it is where the consciousness of the identity of the real and the ideal guides the whole work of intuition."[3]

Another comparison explains his view of the relation of science to religion. Speaking of aesthetic intuition, he says: "This principle is not limited to the sphere of what is called art in the narrow sense, but is [applicable] everywhere. There is a general imagination which is related to the aesthetic imagination in the narrow sense, as religious intuition to scientific knowledge."[4]

The most plausible interpretation I can make of this is to say that he thought science and religion are both in some sense "intuitions of the world," and that he believed that religion in some way includes more comprehensive material than does science. Perhaps part of what he means by this is that religion is interested in many things (such as the particular individuality of Henriette Herz) to which science is indifferent.

Schleiermacher then goes on to say that philosophy and religion are alike in that both contain a measure of the subjective and individual, in fact just in so far as either of them is *systematic*. A subjective element gets into religion so soon as any attempt is made to combine its (otherwise objective and universal?) elements into a system. I take it he must mean that in so far as science is a system of this sort, it too is subjective. In other words, he seems to be saying that particular judgments or intuitions (presumably partly perceptual judgments) are objective, but that when a system is made of them the result is primarily the result of the disposition or temperament of the systematizer.

This may mean simply that he believed that some parts of science, philosophy, and religion can be reasonably well established when the system as a whole is still a matter of opinion. If such was his contention, it is worth remarking that he was then not really arguing for the subjectivity of all system as such, because there is some logical system involved in the most empirical parts of science. Where there is none there is not science.

In another passage Schleiermacher contrasts religion and science, saying that "mysticism" is the principle of religion and "idealism" is the principle of science. Since he contrasts mysticism with dialectical argumentation elsewhere,[5] it is possible that he meant that there is dialectical thought in science where there is mysticism (whatever he meant by that, at this time) in religion. This contrast does not seem to be very illuminating.

The result of this examination of some of his discussions of religion cannot be said to be very satisfactory. The main implication of it seems to be simply that Schleiermacher's view was confused, insufficiently considered. Some further points in these lecture notes which exhibit similar confusion might have been mentioned. It is clear that Schleiermacher had not succeeded in discriminating successfully between philosophy, religion, and science—a shortcoming which perhaps ought not to be complained of in the first lectures of a young theologian.

SCHLEIERMACHER AND HEGEL

wwwwwwwwwwwwwwwwwwwwwwwwwwwwwwwwwwwwwwwwwwwwwwwwwwwwwwwwwwwwwwwwwwwwwwwwwwwwwwwwww

Hegel's reaction to Schleiermacher's earliest publications has been described already, and we can therefore limit ourselves here to an account of Hegel's criticism of *The Christian Faith*.

It is a well-known fact that the two men had little sympathy for each other. Schleiermacher, for example, kept Hegel out of the Berlin Academy of which he was the secretary. It is not clear just what the causes of the bad feeling were nor at what date it began. According to one letter there was talk of their mutual antipathy in 1819. The reason for it may have been the clash of personalities or it may have been simply rivalry at the university, possibly between Hegel's lectures and Schleiermacher's courses on *Dialectic*. However, the fact is that there was personal animosity, as a result of which Hegel probably never seriously attempted to appreciate Schleiermacher's later theological work. He had made sarcastic comments about Schleiermacher's capacities before the book was published, and the marginal comments he wrote in his own copy of the book reveal that he approached it in an extremely critical humor.[6] He had ignored all Schleiermacher's work since the *Lucinde* letters, according to Glockner, with the exception of the translation of Plato and his essay on the idea of predestination, which Hegel described as "extremely barren."[7] In 1822, presumably after reading the first volume of *The Christian Faith*, he wrote asking "whether then the dogmatic theology of the United Evangelical Church be what one has had the impudence and shallowness to offer as such."[8]

The most direct assault by Hegel on Schleiermacher's theological views occurred in a preface written (after reading the first volume of *The Christian Faith*) for Hinrich's *Die Religion in innerem Verhältnisse zur Wissenschaft*.[9] Schleiermacher was not explicitly named in this preface, but (although the whole historical movement toward a philosophy of feeling was discussed) there were many extremely caustic remarks which could have been directed only at *The Christian Faith*, whch had just appeared. Schleiermacher and his friends were considerably annoyed by the discussion which scarcely did justice to Schleiermacher's views, but some of the criticism was legitimate.

Hegel began by admitting that there is a perennial conflict between reason and faith, each of which is a legitimate interest of the human mind. It is desirable that there should be some reconciliation of this conflict, but it must be a reconciliation in which the claims of both reason and faith are really satisfied. No satisfactory solution is to be found either in merely becoming indifferent to the higher things of life, or in yielding up the claim about the universe which is the very essence of the religious life, or in dropping the attempt to make experience and beliefs a rational whole. The theology of the Middle Ages, he said, had the great merit of offering a reconciliation which did not require that any essential part of the ideal life be surrendered. It was "a science which has cultivated religion on the side of thought and reason, and has taken pains to grasp by means of thought the deepest doctrines of revealed religion."[10]

Any philosophical or theological theory which neglects some one or more of these essential factors, Hegel thought, falls short of perfection. On the one hand he thought (and here he was in full agreement with Schleiermacher) that the claims of the emotional side of man's being could not be ignored. "Religion will and should," he said, "become a matter of feeling, and turn about into the heart, just as freedom in general sinks itself in feeling, and a feeling of freedom grows in man."[11] Religious knowledge and ideals should penetrate experience; they should enter into the affectional structure of the human mind. But on the other hand—and this was the real point of his criticism, for there was no danger in his day that the emotional side of anything would be neglected—the claims of reason and thought may not be ignored; neither faith nor the rational life can flourish unless in religion (as well as philosophy) there "is a substantial objective content of truth."[12] The whole point of the Christian religion historically, he claimed, is that it has been supposed to offer knowledge of God, given by revelation.

The "philosophy of feeling" (not only of Schleiermacher, presumably, but also of Jacobi and others) was, he thought, a view which in the end frustrated religion by disparaging the rational side of life. This philosophy, however, he admitted, was perfectly intelligible or even necessary as a result of the agnostic outcome of the *Aufklarung*. The Kantian philosophy, in legitimate reaction against the overweening metaphysics of the past, had gone so far as to deny knowledge of God and the independently real in general. All thought, according to Kant, is infected with the blight of finitude by the conditions under which thought in human subjects is alone possible. As a result, although religion has been supposed to be a revelation of God, the Divine Being was thrust out into the unknowable by Kantian epistemology, and as a consequence of Kantian influence "one of the absolute assumptions of the culture of our time is that man knows nothing of the truth."[13] But the natural longing of the soul for the Infinite has avenged itself for this thievery by taking possession of the realm of feeling, and fortifying itself therein against the claims of the finite understanding. The understanding having limited its own proper use to the temporal world given in sense experience, and having emptied the Beyond of all objective content, the soul which seeks unity with and certainty and enjoyment of the Infinite can only retire within the shell of an exclusively emotional religion which is impervious to the dialectical attacks of reason. This was what had happened, Hegel thought, in the philosophy of feeling, as proposed by Schleiermacher and others.

In this emphasis on feeling, Hegel said, these writers claimed that feeling was the only proper form in which religiousness occurred in its purity, and in their consequent disparagement of the importance of rational thought they upset the balance between reason and thought which is necessary to the ideal life. How unsatisfactory this identification of religion with emotional experience to the exclusion of thought must turn out to be is made clear, Hegel thought, simply by an examination of the nature of feeling. For feeling is a form of experience which can be either religious or irreligious, and what transforms (redeems) the feelings of the natural man into spiritual feelings is precisely the ideas of the intellect. Religion is not just being emotional; it is the emotional life of the man whose being has

been imbued with the significance of religious ideas. It is the possibility of rational certification of the ideas which gives to religion its
objective standard; without this standard, religion is likely to be
guided merely by subjective caprice. This subjectivity in religion is
apparently what Hegel thought would be the natural outcome of
Schleiermacher's theology—a judgment that receives a great deal of
support from the historical course of German theology after Schleiermacher's death.

So Hegel struck at the theology of feeling in these words: "There
can be no doubt that feeling is a sphere which, itself undetermined,
includes both the most manifold and the most antithetical. Feeling
for itself is natural subjectivity, equally capable of being good or bad,
pious or godless."[14] "Among the feelings of the natural man is a feeling of the divine; but the natural feeling of the divine is one thing,
the spirit of God another. . . . But that this natural feeling, even, is
a feeling of the divine, is not due simply to its being feeling: the
divine is only in and for spirit. If feeling is to constitute the chief
character of man, he is thereby put at the level of the animal, for it is
characteristic of animals . . . to live according to feeling. And if religion in man is based solely on feeling, it is correct that this has no
further determination than to be a feeling of dependence, and so a
dog would be the best Christian, because it has this feeling most in-
tensely. . . . A dog also has feelings of salvation, if its hunger is
satisfied by a bone."[15]

As a parting shot, perhaps more directly intended for Schleiermacher, Hegel added that the book he was prefacing could expect
only a cool reception in those quarters where "that which calls itself
philosophy and is always carrying Plato on its lips, has no notion of
what is the nature of speculative thought, the contemplation of an
idea—where in philosophy as in theology, the bestial ignorance of
God, and the sophistry of this ignorance which substitutes individual
feeling and subjective opinion for a system of doctrine . . . carries
great weight."[16]

It is clear from this evidence that the later work of Schleiermacher
had little or no positive effect on Hegel, and that Hegel's view of
Schleiermacher's system was an abbreviated and distorted one. Of
course, there was much in Schleiermacher's published work to justify

such an interpretation. But if one emphasizes the other (more consistent) side of Schleiermacher, consisting of those ideas in which the complete independence of the religious life is not insisted upon, one will find that there was much less disagreement between the two men on this subject than has often been supposed to have been the case. There was a distinctly agnostic antirational side to Schleiermacher's later views (perhaps not more so than the traditional theory of negative knowledge of God) but in those passages in which he came closest to defining the relation of God and the world clearly, he seems to identify God with the universe, when viewed as an infinite logical self-organizing system (or at least he came close to this). And while his theories made it possible for him to assert that religion was somehow a natural, necessary, and instinctive aspect of the life of feeling at its highest, there are many passages in which he did not neglect the function of rational thought in the spiritualization of feeling, in the "relating of all feeling to the Infinite." The differences between them here were not clear-cut logical disagreements but more matters of temperament and emphasis—differences which however have been historically decisive, as is clear from the development of German thought after their time.

SELECTED BIBLIOGRAPHY

SCHLEIERMACHER, F. D. E.: *Sämmtliche Werke*, 31 volumes, Berlin, Reimer, 1834. Three parts: I, theological; II, homiletical; and III, philosophical. Cited as *Werke*. For details concerning specific publications, see Chapter I, section 2.

―――― *Schleiermachers Werke: Auswahl in vier Bänden*. Leipzig, Meiner. References to volume II (the *Ethics* edited by Braun) are to the second edition, 1927.

―――― *Aus Schleiermachers Leben in Briefen*, edited by Dilthey, Reimer, Berlin, 1858-1863, 4 volumes. Referred to as *Briefe*. Volumes 1 and 2 translated by F. Rowan, London, 1860; referred to as *Letters*.

―――― *Platons Werke*, translated by Schleiermacher with introductions, Berlin, 1817-1828. Introductions translated into English by W. Dobson, Cambridge, 1836.

―――― *Ueber die Religion: Reden an die gebildeten unter ihren Verächtern*, 1799, 1806, 1821, and 1831 during his lifetime. Critical edition by G. C. B. Pünjer, Jena, 1879. English translation by John Oman, London, 1892, with introduction.

―――― *Monologen*, 1800, 1810, 1821, 1829, during his lifetime. Critical edition by Schiele and Mulert, Leipzig, 1911. English translation with introduction and notes, H. L. Friess, Open Court, Chicago, 1926.

―――― *Grundlinien einer Kritik der bisherigen Sittenlehre*, 1803; reprinted *Werke*, pt. III, vol. I, from which citations are made. Critical edition by Mulert, Leipzig, Meiner, 1908.

―――― *Die Weihnachtsfeier*, 1806, 1827, during his lifetime. English translation by W. Hastie, 1890.

―――― *Kurze Darstellung des theologischen Studiums*, 1811 and 1830 during his lifetime. English translation, William Farrer, Edinburgh, 1850.

―――― *Der christliche Glaube nach den Grundsätzen der evangelischen Kirche im Zusammenhange dargestellt*. First edition, 1821-1822; second edition, 1830. English translation, edited by H. R. Mackintosh and J. S. Stewart, Edinburgh, 1928. Most of it is paraphrased in George Cross, *The Theology of Schleiermacher*, Chicago, 1911.

―――― Manuscripts in *Ethics*, edited by Schweitzer, Berlin, 1835, as *Werke*, pt. III, vol. V. Also by Twesten, Berlin, 1841, and in the Reimer edition above.

SCHLEIERMACHER, F. D. E.: *Briefwechsel mit J. Chr. Gass*, 1852. For further correspondence see *Mitteilungen aus dem Literaturarchiv in Berlin*.

―――― Early manuscripts, diary, and other material in an appendix to vol. I of the first edition of Dilthey, *Leben Schleiermachers*. See below.

―――― *Dialektik*, edited by Jonas, Berlin, 1839, in *Werke*, pt. III, vol. 4, pt. 2; references in the text are made to this book. Critical edition by Halpern, Berlin, 1903.

―――― *Aesthetik*, edited by Lommatzsch, Berlin, 1842, in *Werke*, pt. III, vol. 7. Improved edition (of lectures of 1818) by R. Odebrecht, Berlin, 1931.

―――― *Selected Sermons*, a translation by Mary Wilson, London, 1890.

ADAMSON, ROBERT: *Fichte*, Edinburgh, Blackwood, 1881.

Athenaeum, a journal edited by F. and W. Schlegel, 1799 and 1800.

BARTELHEIMER, W.: *Schleiermacher und die gegenwärtige Schleiermacher Kritik*, Leipzig, 1931.

BENDER, WILHELM: *Schleiermachers Theologie*, Nördlingen, 1876. Cf. *Jahrbuch f. deutsche Theol.*, Bd. XVI, XVII; also *Zeitschr. f. Phil. u. Phil. Kritik*, Bd. 57, nos. 1 and 2.

BETH, KARL: *Die Grundanschauungen Schleiermachers in seinem ersten Entwurf der philos. Sittenlehre*, Berlin, 1898.

BRUNNER, EMIL: *Die Mystik und das Wort*, Tuebingen, 1924.

BUCHHOLZ, PAUL: *Das religiöse Bewusstsein nach Schleiermacher*, Königsberg, 1907.

CAMERER, THEODOR: *Spinoza und Schleiermacher*, Stuttgart and Berlin, 1903.

CLEMEN, C. C.: *Schleiermachers Glaubenslehre in ihrer Bedeutung für Vergangenheit und Zukunft*, Giessen, 1905.

DILTHEY, WILHELM: *Leben Schleiermachers*, Berlin, 1870, vol. I only; with appendix containing early essays by Schleiermacher. Enlarged edition (without the appendix), H. Mulert, Berlin, 1922.

Article in the *Allgemeine Deutsche Biographie*, 1890, vol. 31, pp. 422-457; reprinted in *Gesammelte Schriften*, vol. 4, 1921.

DUNKMANN, D.: *Der Religionsbegriff Schleiermachers in seiner Abhängigkeit von Kant*, Leipzig, 1913.

DUNKMANN, KARL: "Die Nachwirkung der theologischen Prinzipienlehre Schleiermachers," *Beiträge zur Förderung christlicher Theologie*, vol. 19, 1915.

"Die theologische Prinzipienlehre Schleiermachers," same journal, vol. 20, 1916.

EBERHARD, JOH. AUG.: *Allgemeine Theorie des Denkens und Empfindens*, Berlin, 1776.

ESSELBORN, E. W.: *Die philosophischen Voraussetzungen von Schleiermachers Determinismus*, Strassburg, 1897.

FICHTE, JOHANN GOTTLIEB: *Werke, Auswahl in sechs Bänden*, edited by Medicus, Eckardt, Leipzig, 1911; also edition edited by I. H. Fichte.

FORSTHOFF, H.: *Schleiermachers Religionstheorie und die Motive seiner Grundanschauung*, Rostock, 1910.

FUCHS, EMIL: *Schleiermachers Religionsbegriff*, Giessen, 1901. *Vom Werden dreier Denker: Fichte, Schelling, Schleiermacher*, Tuebingen, 1904.

GLOCKNER, HERMANN: "Hegel und Schleiermacher in Kampfe um Religionsphilosophie und Glaubenslehre," *Deutsche Vierteljahrschrift f. Literaturwissenschaft und Geistesgeschichte*, 1930.

HAERING, THEODOR: *Hegel: Sein Wollen und Sein Werk*, Berlin, 1929, vol. I.

HALPERN, ISIDOR: "Der Entwicklungsgang der Schleiermacherschen Dialektik," *Archiv. f. Geschichte der Philosophie*, Bd. XIV.

HARTMANN, NICOLAI: *Die Philosophie des deutschen Idealismus*, 2 vols., Berlin, 1923.

HAYM, RUDOLPH: *Die Romantische Schule*, Berlin, 1870.

HEGEL, G. W. F.: *Werke*, new edition by Lasson; Jubilee edition by Glockner; also an earlier edition. See also Nohl, *Hegels Theologische Jugendschriften*, Tuebingen, 1907; and *Hegel Archiv*, edited by Lasson (especially Bd. I, Heft 2).

HEIM, KARL: *Das Gewissheitsproblem*, Leipzig, 1911.

HOYER, J. i.e. M. J.: *Schleiermachers Erkenntnistheorie in ihrem Verhältnisse zur Erkenntnistheorie Kants*, Leipzig, 1905.

HUBER, EUGEN: *Die Entwicklung des Religionsbegriffs bei Schleiermacher*, Leipzig, 1901.

HUNZINGER, WALTHER: *Der Begriff des Gefühls und seine Wandlungen in Schleiermachers Religionsauffassung*, Hamburg, 1930.

KANT, IMMANUEL: *Werke*, edited by Cassirer, 1922.

KATTENBUSCH, D. F.: *Von Schleiermacher zu Ritschl*, Giessen, 1893.

KIRCHER, ERWIN: *Philosophie der Romantik*, Jena, 1906.

KLUCKHOHN, PAUL: *Die deutsche Romantik*, Leipzig, 1924.

KRONER, RICHARD: *Von Kant bis Hegel*, 2 vols., Tuebingen, 1921-1924.

LASCH, GUSTAV: *Schleiermachers Religionsbegriff in seiner Entwicklung*, Erlangen, 1900.

LOEW, WILHELM: *Das Grundproblem der Ethik Schleiermachers in seiner Beziehung zu Kants Ethik*, Berlin, 1914.

MACKINTOSH, H. R.: *Types of Modern Theology*, London, 1937.

MANN, G.: *Das Verhältnis der Schleiermacherschen Dialektik zu Schellingschen Philosophie*, Stuttgart, 1914.

MEYER, E.: *Schleiermachers und C. G. von Brinkmanns Gang durch die Brüdergemeinde*, Leipzig, 1905.

MULERT, HERMANN: *Schleiermachers geschichtsphilosophische Ansichten in ihrer Bedeutung für seine Theologie*, Giessen, 1907.

MUNRO, ROBERT: *Schleiermacher: Personal and Speculative*, Paisley, 1903.

NAUMANN, FR. (ed.): *Symposium, Schleiermacher, der Philosoph des Glaubens*, Göttingen, 1920.

ODEBRECHT, RUDOLPH: *Schleiermachers System der Aesthetik*, Berlin, 1932.

OSBORN, A. R.: *Schleiermacher and Religious Education*, Oxford, 1934.

OTTO, R.: Introduction to edition of the *Reden*, 1920.

PFLEIDERER, OTTO: *Development of Theology*, London, 1890.
Philosophy of Religion on the Basis of its History, London, 1886.

PIPER, OTTO: *Das religiöse Erlebnis*, Göttingen, 1920.

QUÄBICKER, RICHARD: *Ueber Schleiermachers erkenntnistheoretische Grundansicht*, Breslau, 1871.

RITSCHL, ALBRECHT: *Schleiermachers Reden über die Religion und ihre Nachwirkung auf die evangelische Kirche Deutschlands*, Bonn, 1874.

RITSCHL, OTTO: *Schleiermachers Stellung zum Christentum*, Gotha, 1888.

RUDE, D. M.: *Die Leitsätze der ersten u. zweiten Auflage von Schleiermachers Glaubenslehre nebeneinandergestellt*, Tuebingen, 1904.

SCHELLING, F. W. G.: *Sämmtliche Werke*, 1857 —.

SCHLEGEL, FRIEDRICH VON: *Lucinde, Ein Roman*, 1800. Reprinted Jena, 1907.

SCHOLZ, HEINRICH: *Christentum und Wissenschaft in Schleiermachers Glaubenslehre*, Berlin, 1909.

SCHRECKER, ERNST: *Der Religionsbegriff in Schleiermacher*, 1890.

SCHULTZ, WERNER: *Die Grundprinzipien der Religionsphilosophie Hegels und der Theologie Schleiermachers: Ein Vergleich*, Berlin, 1937.

SELBIE, W. B.: *Schleiermacher*, London, 1913.

SETH (Pringle-Pattison), JAMES: *From Kant to Hegel*, reprinted, Stechert, 1924.

SIEGFRIED, THEODOR: "Kant und Schleiermacher," *Marburger Theologische Studien*, no. 3, 1931.

SIEGMUND-SCHULTZE, F.: *Schleiermachers Psychologie in ihrer Bedeutung für die Glaubenslehre*, Tuebingen, 1913.

SIGWART, C.: "Zum Gedächtnis Schleiermacher," in *Kleine Schriften*, vol. I.

"Schleiermachers Erkenntnistheorie und ihre Bedeutung für die Grund-begriffe der Glaubenslehre," Jahrbuch f. deutsche Theologie, II.

"Schleiermachers psychologische Voraussetzungen," ibid., vol. II.

STOCK, HANS: Fr. *Schlegel und Schleiermacher*, Marburg, 1930.

STORR, V. F.: *The Development of English Theology in the 19th Century*, 1913.

SÜSKIND, HERRMANN: *Der Einfluss Schellings auf die Entwicklung von Schleiermachers System*, Tuebingen, 1909.

Christentum und Geschichte bei Schleiermacher, Tuebingen, 1911.

TALBOT, E. B.: *Fundamental Principles of Fichte's Philosophy*, Macmillan, 1906.

THIMME, G. O. F. A.: *Die religionsphilosophischen Prämissen der Schleiermacherschen Glaubenslehre*, Hanover, 1901.

TODT, BERNHARD: *Ueber Schleiermachers Platonismus*, Wetzlar, 1882.

UNGERN-STERNBERG, ARTHUR VON: *Freiheit und Wirklichkeit.*

VORLÄNDER, FRANZ: *Schleiermachers Sittenlehre ausführlich dargestellt und beurteilt*, Marburg, 1851.

WALZEL, O. F.: *Deutsche Romantik*, Teubner, Leipzig, 1908.

WEHRUNG, GEORG: *Der geschichtsphilosophische Standpunkt Schleiermachers zur Zeit seiner Freundschaft mit den Romantikern*, Strassburg, 1907.

Die philosophisch-theologische Methode Schleiermachers, Göttingen, 1911.

Die Dialektik Schleiermachers, Tuebingen, 1920.

Schleiermacher in der Zeit seines Werdens, Bertelsmann, 1927.

WEISS, BRUNO: *Untersuchungen über Schleiermachers Dialektik*, Breslau, 1878.

WEISSENBORN, GEORG: *Vorlesungen über Schleiermachers Dialektik*, Leipzig, 1847.

WENDLAND, J.: *Die religiöse Entwicklung Schleiermachers*, Tuebingen, 1915.

WILLICH, E. VON: *Aus Schleiermachers Hause*, Berlin, 1909.

WUNDT, MAX: *Fichte*, Stuttgart, 1927.

Fichte Forschungen, Stuttgart, 1929.

ZELLER, EDUARD: *Kleine Schriften*, Berlin, 1911.

REFERENCES

wwwwwwwwwwwwwwwwwwwwwwwwwwwwwwwwwwwwwwwwwwwwwwwwwwwwwwwwwwwwwwwwwwwwwwwww

CHAPTER I

[1] D. F. Strauss said students thought the two men inevitably rivals because "nature did not make one man of them both." Quoted by H. Glockner, *"Hegel und Schleiermacher im Kampfe um Religionsphilosophie und Glaubenslehre," Deutsche Vierteljahrschrift für Literatur- und Geistesgeschichte,* 1930, p. 233.

[2] *Briefe,* vol. III, p. 48. The page references to Schleiermacher's letters occasionally refer, not to the exact page but to the first page of the letter in which the quotation is contained.

[3] *Briefe,* vol. I, p. 169. For more on his view of the status of women, see Dilthey, *Leben Schleiermachers,* Appendix, pp. 83, 84. Throughout this book, references to Dilthey are meant to denote this book, unless otherwise stated.

[4] *Briefe,* vol. II, p. 483.

[5] See new series, nos. 6, 7, 8, 9 and 11.

CHAPTER II

[1] *Briefe,* vol. I, p. 8.

[2] *Briefe,* vol. I, pp. 22-23.

[3] *Briefe,* vol. I, p. 70; *Letters,* vol. I, p. 68.

[4] *Briefe,* vol. I, p. 42; *Letters,* vol. I, p. 44.

[5] *Briefe,* vol. I, p. 44; *Letters,* vol. I, p. 46.

[6] *Briefe,* vol. I, p. 56; *Letters,* vol. I, p. 56.

[7] *Briefe,* vol. IV, p. 88.

[8] *Briefe,* vol. I, p. 308; *Letters,* vol. I, p. 283.

[9] *Briefe,* vol. IV, p. 16.

[10] *Briefe,* vol. I, p. 82; *Letters,* vol. I, p. 78.

[11] *Briefe,* vol. I, p. 70; *Letters,* vol. I, p. 68.

[12] *Briefe,* vol. IV, p. 45.

[13] *Briefe,* vol. IV, p. 24.

[14] *Werke* (Cassirer's ed.), vol. V, p. 120.

[15] Dilthey, *Leben Schleiermachers* (1870), Appendix, p. 14.

[16] *Ibid.,* Appendix, p. 9.

[17] *Ibid.,* Appendix, p. 9. Cf. the *Grundlinien* etc. of 1803, pp. 93 and 231.

[18] Kant's *Werke,* vol. V, p. 147.

[19] *Ibid.,* p. 145.

[20] Dilthey, *op. cit.,* Appendix, p. 12.

[21] *Ibid.,* p. 13.

[22] *Ibid.,* p. 61.

[23] *Ibid.,* p. 25.

[24] *Ibid.,* p. 26.

[25] *Ibid.,* pp. 26, 30, 32, 38.

[26] *Ibid.,* p. 29.

[27] *Ibid.,* pp. 28, 29, 31.

[28] *Ibid.,* p. 32.

[29] *Ibid.*, p. 32.

[30] *Ibid.*, p. 33.

[31] *Ibid.*, p. 34; cf. his father's recommendation of Lessing, *Briefe*, vol. I, p. 87, or *Letters*, vol. I, p. 84. Dilthey feels unable to decide whether Schleiermacher had read Lessing, *op. cit.*, p. 138.

[32] *Ibid.*, p. 35.

[33] Dilthey, *op. cit.*, p. 144 f.; cf. *Briefe*, vol. III, p. 52.

[34] *Werke*, pt. III, vol. IV, pt. 1, Appendix.

[35] Dilthey, *op. cit.*, Appendix, pp. 65-69.

[36] *Werke*, pt. III, vol. IV, pt. 1, p. 293.

[37] *Ibid.*, p. 295.

[38] *Ibid.*, p. 298.

[39] *Ibid.*, pp. 287-291.

[40] *Ibid.*, p. 302.

[41] *Ibid.*, p. 290.

[42] *Ibid.*, pp. 299-300.

[43] *Ibid.*, p. 295.

[44] *Ibid.*, p. 299.

[45] *Ibid.*, pp. 297, 306-308.

[46] Cf. *ibid.*, p. 299.

CHAPTER III

[1] *Briefe bei Gelegenheit der politisch-theologischen Aufgabe und des Sendschreibens jüdischer Hausväter*, and *Versuch einer Theorie des gesellschaftlichen Betragens*.

[2] *Reden*, Pünjer ed., p. x.

[3] *Ibid.*, p. 285, Eng. trans., p. 258.

[4] *Critique of Pure Reason*, 2nd ed., p. XXX.

[5] *Werke* (Medicus ed.), vol. III, pp. 113, 334-335.

[6] *Werke* (*Erste Einleitung*), vol. III, p. 25; I. H. Fichte ed., vol. I, p. 441.

[7] *Werke*, vol. III, pp. 29-30.

[8] *Werke* (*Zweite Einleitung usw.*), vol. III, pp. 82-83; I. H. Fichte ed., vol. I, pp. 498-499.

[9] *Werke*, vol. III, pp. 73-74.

[10] *Sittenlehre*, *Werke*, vol. II, pp. 625-626; I. H. Fichte ed., vol. IV, pp. 231-232.

[11] "*Appelation an das Publikum*," *Werke*, vol. III, 171; I. H. Fichte ed., vol. V, p. 211.

[12] Cf. Wundt, *Fichte Forschungen*, p. 278.

[13] "*Ueber den Grund unseres Glaubens*," *Werke*, vol. III, pp. 131-132.

[14] Edition of Fichte, Intro., p. lxxvii.

[15] *Briefe*, vol. IV, p. 51.

[16] *Werke*, vol. III, pp. 128-129.

[17] Introduction to edition of Fichte, vol. I, p. CXX.

[18] Haym, *Die Romantische Schule*, 5th ed., 1928, p. 564.

[19] *Ibid.*, pp. 578 ff.

[20] *Werke*, vol. II, p. 4, *Ideen zu einer Philosophie der Natur*.

[21] *Werke*, vol. II, p. 70.

[22] *Werke*, vol. II, p. 387.

[23] *Werke*, vol. II, p. 69.

[24] *Werke*, vol. III, pp. 536 ff.

[25] *Briefe*, vol. II, pp. 92-93.

[26] *Lucinde*, (ed. 1907), p. 7.

[27] *Philosophie der Romantik*, p. 5.

[28] *Athenaeum*, vol. I, p. 35.
[29] Schleiermacher had read Hemsterhuis. See *Werke*, pt. III, vol. IV, pt. 1, p. 301.
[30] O. F. Walzel, *Deutsche Romantik*, vol. I, p. 25.
[31] *Ibid.*, p. 10.
[32] *Athenaeum*, vol. II, p. 43.
[33] *Ibid.*, p. 77.
[34] *Ibid.*, p. 56.
[35] Walzel, *op. cit.*, pp. 15-16.
[36] Quoted, Walzel, *op. cit.*, p. 16.
[37] Walzel, *op. cit.*, p. 54. Recent work has shown that Novalis possessed a considerable store of knowledge in the natural sciences. Intuitive speculation of this sort was useful in the science of his day.
[38] Quoted, Walzel, *op. cit.*, p. 21.
[39] Cf. Haym, *op. cit.*, chap. II.
[40] Kircher, *op. cit.*, p. 155.
[41] *Athenaeum*, vol. II, p. 71.
[42] *Ibid.*, p. 69.
[43] Cf. Haym, *op. cit.*, p. 214.
[44] "*Ueber die Philosophie*," *Athenaeum*, vol. I, p. 18.
[45] *Athenaeum*, vol. I, p. 90.
[46] *Athenaeum*, vol. II, p. 101.
[47] *Monologen*, 1st ed., p. 63.
[48] *Briefe*, vol. I, p. 402.
[49] *Briefe*, vol. I, p. 355.
[50] Walzel, *op. cit.*, p. 12.
[51] Republished in Braun's edition of Schleiermacher's *Ethics*, vol. II.
[52] *Briefe*, vol. III, p. 86.
[53] *Briefe*, vol. I, p. 189.
[54] *Werke*, pt. III, vol. I, pp. 430 ff.
[55] Haym, *op. cit.*, p. 514.
[56] *Briefe*, vol. I, p. 320.
[57] *Briefe*, vol. I, p. 178.
[58] *Briefe*, vol. I, p. 274.
[59] *Briefe*, vol. I, p. 363.
[60] *Briefe*, vol. I, p. 289.
[61] *Philosophie des Rechts*, art. 164, Zus., quoted H. Glockner, *Deutsche Vierteljahrschrift für Literatur und Geistesgeschichte*, 1930, p. 235.
[62] Letter of Oct. 5, 1799. Quoted by Haym, *op. cit.*, p. 722.
[63] *Briefe*, vol. III, p. 141.

CHAPTER IV

[1] *Briefe*, vol. IV, p. 74.
[2] *Briefe*, vol. IV, pp. 68 ff.
[3] *Briefe*, vol. IV, p. 55.
[4] *Briefe*, vol. IV, p. 53.
[5] *Reden*, 1st ed., p. 20. All references to this work will be to the first edition, except where specifically stated otherwise.
[6] Schleiermacher's *Soliloquies* relate philosophy and life, as he very possibly thought Fichte should have done it.
[7] *Reden*, p. 171.
[8] *Reden*, p. 129.
[9] *Reden*, p. 75.
[10] *Monologen*, 1st ed., p. 15, Eng. trans., p. 16.

[11] Monologen, 2nd ed., as of Schiele's edition, pp. 15-16. Eng. trans., p. 105. There is a suggestion of a doctrine of innate ideas. Cf. chap. VI, sec. 2.

[12] Monologen, 1st ed., pp. 16-17; Eng. trans., p. 17.

[13] Monologen, 2nd ed., in Schiele's ed., p. 16-17. Eng. trans., pp. 105-106.

[14] Briefe, vol. IV, p. 55.

[15] Reden, pp. 55-56.

[16] Reden, p. 66.

[17] Reden, p. 73.

[18] Reden, pp. 54-55.

[19] Reden, p. 172.

[20] Reden, p. 80.

[21] Reden, p. 83.

[22] Reden, pp. 104-105.

[23] Briefe, vol. IV, p. 90.

[24] Briefe, vol. III, p. 125.

[25] Reden, p. 16.

[26] Briefe, vol. I, p. 328; Letters, vol. I, p. 301.

[27] Reden, p. 128.

[28] Reden, p. 107.

[29] Reden, p. 152.

[30] Reden, p. 17.

[31] Reden, p. 42.

[32] Reden, p. 97.

[33] Reden, pp. 269 ff.

[34] Reden, pp. 83-84.

[35] Reden, p. 92.

[36] Reden, pp. 103-104.

[37] Reden, p. 129.

[38] Reden, pp. 132-133.

[39] Reden, p. 124.

[40] Reden, pp. 43-44.

[41] Reden, p. 133.

[42] Reden, pp. 132-133.

[43] Critique of Pure Reason, 2nd ed., pp. 673 ff.

[44] Reden, pp. 5-6.

[45] Reden, p. 86.

[46] Reden, pp. 6-8.

[47] Glauben und Wissen, Lasson ed., Erste Druckschriften, p. 311.

[48] Reden, p. 42.

[49] Reden, p. 54.

[50] Briefe, vol. I, p. 295.

[51] Briefe, vol. I, p. 270.

[52] Reden, p. 112.

[53] Reden, p. 37.

[54] Reden, p. 52.

[55] Reden, p. 22.

[56] Reden, p. 236.

[57] Reden, p. 144.

[58] Reden, p. 39; cf. pp. 152, 154, 239, 244.

[59] Reden, p. 19.

[60] Reden, p. 144.

[61] Reden, p. 106.

[62] Reden, p. 22.

[63] Reden, p. 40.
[64] Reden, p. 260.
[65] Reden, p. 307.
[66] Reden, p. 248.
[67] Reden, p. 36.
[68] Reden, p. 246.
[69] Werke, vol. VI, p. 302.
[70] Ibid., p. 238.
[71] Reden, p. 42.
[72] Reden, pp. 34-35.
[73] Reden, p. 43.
[74] Reden, p. 44 ff.
[75] A review reprinted in Briefe, vol. IV.
[76] Briefe, vol. I, p. 205.
[77] Reden, p. 66.
[78] Reden, p. 247.
[79] Briefe, vol. I, p. 207.
[80] Reden, p. 15.
[81] Reden, pp. 145-146.
[82] Reden, p. 55. Piper gives a complete list of the words Schleiermacher uses, Das Religiöse Erlebnis, p. 20.
[83] Reden, p. 74.
[84] Reden, p. 56.
[85] Reden, p. 56.
[86] Reden, p. 56.
[87] Reden, p. 57.
[88] Athenaeum, vol. II, p. 95; Dilthey, op. cit., Appendix, p. 81.
[89] Reden, p. 117.
[90] Reden, p. 118.
[91] Reden, p. 118.
[92] Reden, p. 149.
[93] Reden, p. 149.
[94] Reden, pp. 152-153.
[95] Dilthey, op. cit., Appendix, p. 139; cf. also Ethics, p. 81.
[96] Dilthey, op. cit., Appendix, p. 123.
[97] Briefe, vol. I, p. 381; also see p. 295.
[98] Briefe, vol. III, p. 349.
[99] Dilthey, op. cit., Appendix, p. 72.
[100] Briefe, vol. IV, pp. 73, 80.
[101] Briefe, vol. IV, p. 73.
[102] Reden, p. 68.
[103] Reden, p. 72.
[104] Reden, p. 67.
[105] Reden, p. 299.
[106] Reden, p. 111.
[107] Reden, pp. 108-111.
[108] Reden, p. 66.
[109] Reden, p. 75.
[110] Reden, p. 76; Eng. trans., p. 47.
[111] Reden, pp. 73 ff.
[112] Reden, p. 50.
[113] Reden, p. 119.
[114] Reden, p. 66.

[115] *Reden*, p. 67.
[116] *Reden*, p. 72.
[117] *Reden*, p. 73.
[118] Dilthey, *op. cit.*, Appendix, p. 100.
[119] *Reden*, pp. 63 ff.
[120] *Reden*, p. 65.
[121] *Reden*, pp. 90 ff.
[122] *Reden*, pp. 113 ff.
[123] *Reden*, pp. 122 ff.
[124] *Reden*, pp. 264, 271.
[125] *Reden*, p. 52.
[126] *Reden*, p. 198.
[127] *Reden*, p. 140.
[128] *Reden*, p. 116.
[129] *Reden*, p. 59.
[130] *Reden*, pp. 62 ff.
[131] *Reden*, pp. 61-62.
[132] *Reden*, pp. 58-59.
[133] *Reden*, p. 249.
[134] *Reden*, p. 60.
[135] *Reden*, pp. 60-61. My italics.
[136] *Reden*, p. 61.
[137] *Glauben und Wissen* (1802), Lasson ed., pp. 311-313, ed. of 1832, vol. I, pp. 113-114.
[138] *Reden*, pp. 80-81.
[139] *Reden*, p. 83.
[140] *Reden*, p. 86.
[141] *Reden*, p. 85.
[142] *Reden*, p. 119.
[143] *Reden*, p. 162.
[144] *Reden*, p. 149.
[145] *Reden*, p. 89.
[146] *Reden*, p. 107.
[147] *Reden*, p. 263.
[148] *Reden*, p. 158.
[149] *Reden*, p. 289; Eng. trans., p. 240.
[150] *Reden*, p. 291; Eng. trans., p. 241.
[151] *Reden*, p. 126.
[152] *Reden*, p. 148.
[153] *Reden*, pp. 60-61.
[154] *Reden*, pp. 42, 43.
[155] *Reden*, p. 51.
[156] Dilthey, *op. cit.*, Appendix, p. 118.
[157] *Briefe*, vol. I, p. 295.
[158] *Briefe*, vol. III, p. 350.
[159] Dilthey, *op. cit.*, Appendix, p. 72.
[160] *Reden*, p. 53.
[161] *Reden*, p. 54.
[162] *Reden*, p. 172.
[163] Dilthey, *op. cit.*, Appendix, p. 117.
[164] Kroner, *Von Kant bis Hegel*, vol. II, p. 57; cf. Dilthey, *Werke*, vol. VI, p. 297.
[165] *Reden*, p. 247.
[166] *Reden*, p. 242.

[167] Reden, p. 57.
[168] Briefe, vol. I, p. 310.
[169] Reden, p. 82.
[170] Reden, p. 80.
[171] Reden, pp. 80-81.
[172] Briefe, vol. I, p. 208; Letters, vol. I, p. 193.
[173] Reden, p. 86.
[174] Reden, pp. 87-88.
[175] Review of Fichte's Vocation of Man, Werke, pt. III, vol. I.
[176] Werke, pt. III, vol. I, pp. 533-534; cf. Reden, p. 268.
[177] Reden, p. 52.
[178] Reden, p. 143.
[179] Reden, pp. 51-52.
[180] Reden, p. 129.
[181] Monologen, pp. 103-104; Eng. trans., pp. 70-71.
[182] Monologen, p. 40, Eng. trans., p. 31.
[183] Monologen, pp. 40 f.; Eng. trans., p. 31.
[184] Reden, p. 92.
[185] Ibid.
[186] Briefe, vol. IV, p. 51.
[187] Reden, p. 100.
[188] Reden, pp. 103-104; Eng. trans., pp. 81-82.
[189] Hegel: Sein Wollen und Sein Werk, vol. I, p. 560.
[190] Reden, pp. 287-288.
[191] Reden, p. 291.
[192] Briefe, vol. III, p. 285.
[193] Von Schleiermacher zu Ritschl.
[194] Intro. to Eng. trans. of Discourses, pp. xxv and xxxiii.
[195] Von Kant bis Hegel, vol. II, pp. 59 ff.
[196] Reden, pp. 49, 71, 72, 95, 98, 99, 114, 117, 148, 152, 153, 173, 175, 199, 210, 213, 216.
[197] Briefe, vol. II, p. 176; Letters, vol. II, p. 157.
[198] Briefe, vol. I, p. 347; Letters, vol. I, p. 320.
[199] Reden, p. 12.
[200] Briefe, vol. III, p. 107.
[201] Briefe, vol. III, p. 109.
[202] Dilthey, op. cit., Appendix, p. 95; Athenaeum, vol. II, p. 136 ff.

CHAPTER V

[1] Briefe, vol. IV, p. 72.
[2] Briefe, vol. IV, p. 84.
[3] Briefe, vol. IV, p. 107.
[4] Briefe, vol. IV, pp. 145, 175.
[5] Aus Schellings Leben, vol. I, p. 345.
[6] Cf. especially Werke, vol. IV, pp. 339-360.
[7] Werke, vol. IV, p. 84.
[8] Vorlesungen über die Methode usw., ed. of 1803, p. 12.
[9] Darstellung meines Systems usw., Prop. 24.
[10] Werke, vol. IV, p. 128.
[11] Die Philosophie des deutschen Idealismus, pt. I, p. 158.
[12] Werke, vol. IV, p. 49.
[13] Ibid., vol. IV, p. 97.
[14] Ibid., vol. IV, p. 362.

[15] *Ibid.*, vol. IV, p. 390.
[16] *Vorlesungen über die Methode usw.*, chap. XI.
[17] *Ibid.*, chap. II.
[18] *Ibid.*, chap. VII.
[19] *Ibid.*, chap. VIII.
[20] Süskind, *Einfluss Schellings usw.*, pp. 107 ff., 121, 127-128.
[21] *Briefe*, vol. III, p. 378.
[22] Dilthey, *op. cit.*, Appendix, p. 129.
[23] *Ibid.*, p. 131. My italics.
[24] *Ibid.*, p. 129.
[25] *Ibid.*, p. 134.
[26] *Ibid.*, p. 138.
[27] *Briefe*, vol. IV, p. 133.
[28] *Briefe*, vol. IV, p. 94.
[29] *Ethics*, pp. 49-52.
[30] *Briefe*, vol. IV, pp. 580 ff.
[31] Dilthey, *op. cit.*, Appendix, p. 131.
[32] *Ethics*, p. 155.
[33] *Ethics*, p. 176.
[34] *Reden*, Pünjer ed., pp. 53 ff.
[35] For his developed causal theory of perception, see his *Psychologie*, pp. 418-420
[36] *Reden*, Pünjer ed., p. 39.
[37] *Ibid.*, pp. 45-46. Compare this statement with Schelling's assertions.
[38] *Ethics*, p. 50.
[39] *Ibid.*, p. 101.
[40] *Ibid.*, p. 151.
[41] *Ibid.*, p. 160.
[42] *Reden*, Pünjer ed., p. 46.
[43] *Ibid.*, pp. 122-123.
[44] *Ibid.*, p. 122.
[45] *History of Philosophy*, Werke, pt. III, vol. IV, pt. I, pp. 24-25.
[46] *Ethics*, p. 213.
[47] *Grundlinien einer Kritik usw.*, Werke, pt. III, vol. I, p. 18.
[48] *Werke*, pt. III, vol. I, p. 549.
[49] *Ibid.*, p. 561.
[50] *Ethics*, p. 87; cf. Werke, pt. III, vol. I, p. 575.
[51] *Ibid.*, p. 101.
[52] *Briefe*, vol. IV, p. 626.
[53] Cf. Grundlinien, Werke, pt. III, vol. I, pp. 52 ff., 98, 133, 136, 139.
[54] *Ibid.*, pp. 332 f., 270 ff., 294 ff.
[55] *Werke*, pt. III, vol. II, pp. 350 ff.
[56] *Ethics*, Meiner ed., pp. 247 ff.
[57] *Ibid.*, pp. 524 ff.
[58] *Werke*, pt. III, vol. II, p. 474.
[59] *Ibid.*, p. 476.
[60] *Ibid.*, p. 477.
[61] *Ibid.*, p. 477.
[62] *Ibid.*, pp. 358-359.
[63] *Ibid.*, p. 391.
[64] *Werke*, pt. I, vol. XI, p. 624.
[65] Compare this statement with the terminology of Schelling.
[66] *Werke*, pt. I, vol. XI, p. 624.
[67] *Ibid.*, p. 625.

[68] *Briefe*, vol. II, p. 55; *Letters*, vol. II, p. 51.
[69] *Briefe*, vol. IV, p. 125.
[70] *Briefwechsel mit Gass*, p. 44.
[71] *Reden*, Pünjer ed., p. 54 ff.
[72] *Ethics*, pp. 155-156.
[73] *Ibid.*, p. 156; cf. p. 176.
[74] *Werke*, pt. I, vol. XII, Appendix, p. 7.
[75] *Ibid.*, p. 14.
[76] *Reden*, Pünjer ed., p. 72.
[77] *Ibid.*, p. 73; cf. also *Briefe*, vol. II, p. 203.
[78] *Ethics*, pp. 176-177.
[79] *Ibid.*, p. 177.
[80] *Ibid.*, p. 178.
[81] *Ibid.*
[82] *Werke*, pt. I, vol. XII, Appendix, p. 66.
[83] Dilthey, *op. cit.*, Appendix, p. 139.
[84] *Werke*, pt. I, vol. XII, Appendix, p. 14.
[85] *Werke*, pt. I, vol. XI, p. 15.
[86] *Reden*, Pünjer ed., p. 65.
[87] *Ibid.*, p. 283.
[88] *Ibid.*, p. 21.
[89] *Ibid.*, pp. 120-121.
[90] *Ibid.*, p. 130.
[91] *Ibid.*, p. 60.
[92] *Ibid.*, p. 51. My italics.
[93] *Ibid.*, p. 247. My italics.
[94] *Ibid.*, p. 57.
[95] *Ibid.*, pp. 121-122.
[96] *Ibid.*, p. 90.
[97] *Ibid.*, p. 92.
[98] *Ibid.*, p. 103.
[99] *Ibid.*, pp. 125 ff.
[100] *Ibid.*, p. 63.
[101] *Ibid.*, p. 65.
[102] *Werke*, pt. III, vol. I, p. 574.
[103] *Reden*, Pünjer ed., p. 52.
[104] *Ibid.*, p. 114.
[105] *Werke*, pt. III, vol. I, pp. 581-582.
[106] *Ethics*, p. 165.
[107] *Ibid.*, p. 187.
[108] *Briefe*, vol. II, p. 220.
[109] *Ethics*, pp. 178-179.
[110] *Ibid.*, p. 211.
[111] *Reden*, Pünjer ed., p. 55.
[112] *Ibid.*, p. 282.
[113] *Reden*, first ed., pp. 108 ff.
[114] *Reden*, Pünjer ed., pp. 99 ff.
[115] *Ibid.*, pp. 45-46.
[116] *Ibid.*, p. 46.
[117] *Ibid.*, p. 47.
[118] Cf. *ibid.*, pp. 50-52.
[119] *Ibid.*, p. 49.
[120] *Ibid.*, pp. 50-51.

[121] *Ibid.*, p. 79.
[122] *Reden*, first ed., p. 85.
[123] *Reden*, Pünjer ed., p. 92.
[124] *Ibid.*, p. 93.
[125] *Ibid.*, pp. 92-93.
[126] *Ethics*, p. 95.
[127] *Reden*, Pünjer ed., p. 84.
[128] *Ibid.*, p. 86.
[129] *Ibid.*, Eng. trans., p. 66.

CHAPTER VI

[1] *Dialektik*, p. 387; cf. p. 56.
[2] *Ibid.*, pp. 53-54.
[3] *Ibid.*, p. 84.
[4] *Ibid.*, p. 43; cf. p. 43 ff. also for other properties of true judgments.
[5] *Ibid.*, p. 53.
[6] *Ibid.*, pp. 68 ff., 142-143.
[7] *Ibid.*, p. 32.
[8] *Ibid.*, p. 59.
[9] *Ibid.*, pp. 20-21.
[10] *Ibid.*, pp. 24 ff. This statement is probably a criticism of Schelling's idea of intellectual intuition.
[11] *Ibid.*, p. 35, note.
[12] *Ibid.*, p. 95.
[13] *Ibid.*, p. 64.
[14] *Ibid.*, pp. 30-31; cf. *History of Philosophy*, p. 99.
[15] *Ibid.*, p. 103.
[16] *Ibid.*, p. 207.
[17] *Ibid.*, p. 210; cf. *ibid.*, p. 60. His use of the word *schema* is different from Kant's.
[18] *Ibid.*, pp. 63, 85.
[19] Cf. *Ibid.*, p. 502.
[20] Cf. *History of Philosophy*, p. 25.
[21] *Reden*, Pünjer ed., p. 40. For his view of the importance of the "philosophical" deduction of a science, see the *Dialektik*, pp. 2, 3, 4, 6, and 374.
[22] *Dialektik*, p. 112; cf. *Ethics*, p. 525.
[23] *History of Philosophy*, p. 266.
[24] *Dialektik*, pp. 125-126.
[25] Kant, *Critique of Pure Reason*, 2nd ed., p. 679.
[26] *Dialektik*, p. 17.
[27] *History of Philosophy*, p. 75.
[28] *Dialektik*, p. 131.
[29] *History of Philosophy*, p. 267.
[30] *Dialektik*, pp. 89, 280-282, 464.
[31] *Ibid.*, p. 280.
[32] *Ibid.*, p. 512.
[33] *Ibid.*, pp. 95, 411.
[34] *Ibid.*, p. 335.
[35] *Ibid.*, p. 126.
[36] *Ibid.*, p. 301.
[37] *Ibid.*, p. 74.
[38] *Ibid.*, p. 396.
[39] *Ibid.*, p. 121; cf. *History of Philosophy*, pp. 186-187.

[40] *Ibid.*, pp. 456-457.
[41] *Ibid.*, pp. 73-74; cf. p. 495 ff.
[42] Cf. *ibid.*, p. 67.
[43] *Ibid.*, p. 66.
[44] *Ibid.*, pp. 75-77.
[45] Cf. *ibid.*, p. 451.
[46] *Ibid.*, pp. 78-79.
[47] *Ibid.*, p. 104.
[48] *Ibid.*, p. 105.
[49] *Ibid.*, p. 109.
[50] *Ibid.*, p. 413.
[51] History of Philosophy, Werke, pt. III, vol. IV, pt. 1, p. 266.
[52] *Ibid.*, p. 268.
[53] *Dialektik*, p. 397.
[54] *Ibid.*, p. 76.
[55] *Ibid.*, p. 412.
[56] History of Philosophy, p. 166.
[57] *Dialektik*, p. 87.
[58] *Ibid.*, p. 121.
[59] *Ibid.*, p. 412.
[60] *Ibid.*, p. 150; cf. pp. 426-427.
[61] *Werke*, pt. I, vol. II, p. 575 ff.
[62] Cf. Camerer, *Spinoza und Schleiermacher*, p. 162 ff. and Jonas' important notes in Schleiermacher's *Dialektik*, p. 114 ff., and p. 144 ff.
[63] *Ethics*, p. 160.
[64] Reden, Pünjer ed., p. 135.
[65] *Dialektik*, p. 115.
[66] *Ibid.*, p. 352.
[67] *Ibid.*, p. 334.
[68] *Ibid.*, p. 325.
[69] *Ibid.*, p. 136.
[70] *Ibid.*, p. 166.
[71] *Ibid.*, p. 101; cf. p. 465.
[72] *Ibid.*, p. 433.
[73] *Ibid.*, p. 112.
[74] *Ibid.*, p. 319.
[75] *Ibid.*, p. 113; cf. History of Philosophy, p. 250, for his definition of pantheism.
[76] *Ibid.*, p. 135.
[77] *Ibid.*, pp. 416-418; cf. pp. 470-471.
[78] *Ibid.*, p. 164.
[79] *Ibid.*, p. 162.
[80] *Ibid.*, p. 165.
[81] *Ibid.*, pp. 162-166.
[82] *Ibid.*, p. 168.
[83] *Ibid.*, p. 162.
[84] *Ibid.*, p. 433.
[85] *Ibid.*, p. 433.
[86] *Ibid.*, p. 162.
[87] *Ibid.*, p. 167.
[88] *Ibid.*, p. 168.
[89] *Ibid.*, p. 119.
[90] *Ibid.*, p. 167; cf. also p. 432.
[91] *Ibid.*, p. 554.

[92] *Ibid.*, p. 530; cf. pp. 531-533.

[93] *Ethics of 1812*, p. 247.

[94] *Dialektik*, p. 322.

[95] *Ibid.*, p. 328.

[96] *Ibid.*, p. 164.

[97] *Ibid.*, p. 163. In these passages, his theory seems to be quite Kantian.

[98] *Ibid.*, p. 158.

[99] *Ibid.*, p. 432.

[100] *Ibid.*, p. 428.

[101] *The Christian Faith*, 2nd ed., sec. 36.

[102] *Ibid.*, sec. 81. par. 1.

[103] *Ibid.*, sec. 56, par. 1.

[104] *Ibid.*, sec. 96, par. 1.

[105] See also *ibid.*, sec. 109, par. 3.

[106] *Ibid.*, sec. 56, par. 1.

[107] *Ibid.*, sec. 51, par. 1.

[108] *Ibid.*, sec. 52, par. 2.

[109] *Ibid.*, sec. 53.

[110] *Ibid.*, sec. 54.

[111] *Ibid.*, sec. 51, par. 2.

[112] *Ibid.*, sec. 55.

[113] *Ibid.*, sec. 83.

[114] *Ibid.*, sec. 84.

[115] *Ibid.*, sec. 165-167.

[116] *Ibid.*, sec. 165, par. 1.

[117] *Ibid.*, sec. 168, par. 1.

[118] *Ibid.*

[119] *Ibid.*

[120] *Ibid.*, sec. 46, par. 2.

[121] *Briefe*, vol. II, pp. 280 ff.

[122] *Reden*, Pünjer ed., p. 155, 3rd ed. ✔

[123] *Psychologie*, p. 418 ff.

[124] *Ethics*, p. 532; cf. Weissenborn, *Vorlesungen usw.*, p. 283.

[125] *Dialektik*, p. 533.

[126] *Ibid.*, p. 533.

[127] *Ethics*, p. 495.

[128] *Ibid.*, p. 439.

[129] *Dialektik*, p. 138; cf. p. 140.

[130] *Ibid.*, pp. 149-150.

[131] *Ibid.*, p. 149.

[132] *Psychologie*, p. 407.

[133] *Ibid.*, p. 495.

[134] *Werke*, pt. III, vol. III, p. 193.

[135] See *The Christian Faith*, 2nd ed., sec. 13, Postscript. Hereafter I shall refer to this book as Gl. A for the first edition, and Gl. B for the second.

[136] *Kurze Darstellung des theologischen Studiums*, 2nd ed., sec. 23-24; cf. Gl. B, sec. 2 and 7 ff.

[137] *Ibid.*, sec. 97.

[138] Gl. B, sec. 19, Postscript. Also, *Kurze Darstellung*, passim, and Gl. B, sec. 87 and 92.

[139] Gl. A, sec. 28.

[140] Gl. A, sec. 8, par. 2; B (2nd ed.) sec. 3, par. 4.

[141] Gl. B, sec. 3, par. 4.

[142] Gl. A, sec. 9; B, sec. 4.
[143] *Psychologie*, p. 421.
[144] *Dialektik*, p. 429.
[145] *Aesthetik* of 1818, p. 70; cf. Gl. B, sec. 5, par. 4.
[146] Gl. A, sec. 8, Remark.
[147] *Ibid.*, 2nd ed., sec. 3, par. 3; cf. *ibid.*, sec. 3, and *Dialektik*, p. 429.
[148] Odebrecht, *Schleiermachers System der Aesthetik*, p. 61.
[149] Gl. A, sec. 8, par. 2.
[150] *Dialektik*, p. 524.
[151] *Ibid.*, pp. 428-429.
[152] Gl. B, sec. 3, par. 4.
[153] *Ethics*, p. 589.
[154] Gl. B, sec. 3, par. 2, note. The reference is to Steffens, *Falsche Theologie*, etc., pp. 99-100.
[155] Gl. B, sec. 6, par. 1.
[156] Gl. B, sec. 107, par. 1.
[157] *Ibid.*, sec. 88, par. 3; sec. 89, par. 2.
[158] *Ibid.*, sec. 89, par. 1.
[159] *Psychologie*, pp. 454-455.
[160] *Ibid.*
[161] *Ibid.*, pp. 455, 457.
[162] *Ibid.*, pp. 546-547.
[163] *Ibid.*, pp. 460-461.
[164] *Ibid.*, pp. 211-212.
[165] *Ibid.*, p. 190 ff.
[166] *Ibid.*, p. 460.
[167] *History of Philosophy*, Werke, pt. III, vol. IV, pt. 1, p. 260.
[168] Gl. A, sec. 10, par. 2. Italics mine.
[169] Gl. B, sec. 5, par. 1. Italics mine.
[170] *Psychologie*, pp. 546-547.
[171] *Ibid.*, p. 522.
[172] *Dialektik*, p. 430.
[173] Gl. A, sec. 9, par. 3.
[174] *Ibid.*
[175] Gl. B, sec. 4, par. 3.
[176] Gl. B, sec. 33, par. 1. See the previous note.
[177] Gl. B, sec. 64, par. 2.
[178] Werke, pt. I, vol. II, p. 586.
[179] *Psychologie*, p. 461; cf. Gl. B, sec. 13, Postscript.
[180] Gl. B, sec. 4, par. 2; cf. also sec. 16, Postscript.
[181] Gl. A, sec. 18, par. 5; cf. B, sec. 11, par. 5.
[182] Gl. A, sec. 2, par. 1.
[183] *Dialektik*, p. 347.
[184] Gl. A, p. 12.
[185] Gl. A, sec. 2; B, sec. 15.
[186] Gl. A, p. 10.
[187] Gl. A, sec. 3.
[188] Gl. A, sec. 3, par. 2.
[189] Gl. A, sec. 4.
[190] Gl. A, p. 14.
[191] Gl. A, p. 15.
[192] Gl. A, sec. 31, par. 2.
[193] Gl. A, sec. 31, par. 3.

[194] *Werke*, pt. I, vol. II, p. 626.

[195] *Ibid.*, p. 602.

[196] Gl. B, sec. 10, Postscript.

[197] Gl. B, sec. 128 ff.

[198] Compare Gl. B, sec. 13 with sec. 94 ff.

[199] Gl. B, sec. 30, par. 2 and 3.

[200] Gl. B, sec. 36, par. 1; Gl. B, sec. 8, par. 2; Gl. B, sec. 30, par. 1; Gl. B, sec. 79, par. 1.

[201] Gl. A, sec. 44.

[202] *Dialektik*, p. 159.

[203] Sec. 1 and 6.

[204] *Werke*, pt. I, vol. II, p. 602.

[205] Gl. A, sec. 31, par. 1.

[206] Gl. B, sec. 28; cf. A, sec. 31.

[207] There are other cases: *Reden*, Pünjer ed., p. 31; *Psychologie*, p. 464.

[208] Gl. B, sec. 4.

[209] Cf. especially Gl. B, sec. 34.

[210] *Ibid.*, sec. 54, par. 1.

CHAPTER VII

[1] Quoted, Herrmann, *Kultur der Gegenwart*, pt. I, vol. IV, art. "*Christlichprotestantisch Dogmatik*," p. 601.

[2] *Ibid.*, p. 606.

[3] Eduard Zeller, *Vorträge und Abhandlungen*, Leipzig (1875) 2nd ed., p. 195.

[4] For his significance for the theory of education, see Osborne, *Schleiermacher and Religious Education*.

[5] See E. von Hartmann, *Die deutsche Aesthetik seit Kant*, first part, 1886. For a more considered evaluation of his achievement, based on the study of better manuscripts, see R. Odebrecht, *Schleiermachers System der Aesthetik*, Berlin, 1932. Also B. Croce, *Gesammelte Philos. Schriften*, 1st ser., vol. I (1930), pp. 324, 336.

[6] Leon Robin, *Platon*, Paris (1935), p. 34.

[7] Dilthey, *op. cit.*, p. 438 f.

[8] *Ibid.*, p. 434.

[9] Nohl, *Theologische Jugendschriften Hegels*, pp. 345-351.

[10] Theo. Haering, *Hegel: Sein Wollen und Sein Werk*, vol. I, p. 560; cf. Richard Kroner, *Von Kant bis Hegel*, vol. II, p. 63.

[11] *Glauben und Wissen*, Lasson ed., p. 311.

[12] See Appendix, Hegel and Schleiermacher.

[13] *Kleine Schriften*, Berlin (1911), p. 66.

[14] *Die Kultur der Gegenwart*, pt. I, vol. IV, "*Wesen der Religion und der Religionswissenschaft*," p. 464.

[15] *Nature of Religion*, New York (1933), p. 42.

[16] *The Development of English Theology in the Nineteenth Century*, 1913.

[17] *Ibid.*, p. 171.

[18] *God in Christ*, 1849.

[19] *Evidence of Christian Experience; Present Day Theology*, 1893.

[20] *An Outline of Theology*, 1898.

[21] *Contemporary American Theology*, ed. Ferm, New York, 1933, p. 111.

[22] *Ibid.*, pp. 46, 50 ff.

[23] *The Christian Faith*, 2nd ed., sec. 100, par. 3.

[24] *American Philosophies of Religion*, Wieman and Meland, Chicago, 1936.

[25] See Kattenbusch, *op. cit.*

[26] V. F. Storr, op. cit., p. 150.

[27] Wobbermin, The Nature of Religion, p. 79.

[28] H. R. Mackintosh, Types of Modern Theology, p. 65.

[29] Loc. cit., p. 604.

[30] Loc. cit., p. 477.

[31] Loc. cit., p. 593.

[32] Kleine Schriften, pp. 91-92.

[33] Vorlesungen zur Einleitung in die Logik, 1823; Abriss der philosophischen Logik, 1824; System der Logik und Metaphysik, 1856; Encyclopaedie der philosophischen Wissenschaften, 3 vols., 1862-1864.

[34] Wissenschaft der Erkenntnis, 1847.

[35] Die Logik als Wissenschaftslehre, 1868.

[36] System der Logik und Geschichte der logischen Lehren.

[37] Erkenntnislehre in ihren Grundzügen dargelegt, 1820; Lehrbuch der Logik als Kunstlehre des Denkens, 1832; System der Logik als Kunstlehre des Denkens, 1842.

[28] System der Logik, 5th ed., p. v.

APPENDICES

[1] Briefe, vol. IV, p. 584 ff.

[2] The following interpretation should be compared with the results of Süskind, Einfluss Schellings usw., pp. 138 ff.

[3] Ethics, pp. 49-50.

[4] Ibid., pp. 50-51.

[5] Briefe, vol. III, p. 349; vol. IV, p. 73; vol. I, p. 295.

[6] Hegel Archiv, Lasson ed., Bd. I. Heft 2, p. 37 ff.

[7] H. Glockner, "Hegel u. Schleiermacher im Kampfe um Religionsphilosophie u. Glaubenslehre," in Deutsche Vierteljahrschrift für Literatur u. Geistesgeschichte, 1930, p. 235 ff.

[8] Hegel Archiv, Bd. I, Heft 2, p. 42.

[9] Another (but posthumous) publication which contrasts his position with Schleiermacher's is in Lasson's edition of his lectures on the philosophy of religion, Die Beweise vom Dasein Gottes, 1930, p. 32 ff.

[10] Werke, 1st ed., vol. XVII, pt. II, p. 279 ff.; p. 301.

[11] Ibid., p. 297.

[12] Ibid., p. 299.

[13] Ibid., p. 289.

[14] Ibid., p. 294.

[15] Ibid., p. 295; cf. also Lasson's edition of the Die Beweise vom Dasein Gottes, p. 34.

[16] Ibid., p. 303.

INDEX